The General Economic Theory

Wei-Bin Zhang

The General Economic Theory

An Integrative Approach

Springer

Wei-Bin Zhang
Ritsumeikan Asia Pacific University
Beppu, Japan

ISBN 978-3-030-56203-8 ISBN 978-3-030-56204-5 (eBook)
https://doi.org/10.1007/978-3-030-56204-5

This Springer imprint is published by the registered company Springer Nature Switzerland AG
The registered company address is: Gewerbestrasse 11, 6330 Cham, Switzerland

Preface

I seek a unity all-pervading.

Confucius

This book develops a general economic theory, not only integrating various ideas and theories from Adam Smith till Nobel Prize laureates in economics, but also establishing important relations among economic variables unrecognized in the literature of rigorous economic analysis.

I first met with modern economics about 37 years ago. I started to read economics in 1984 when I was sent by China's government to Japan in 1983 as a graduate student in civil engineering at Kyoto University. The library on campus was a dream world for the poor student. There were so many books and academic journals on different subjects freely and easily available. Best of all is that classical works and collected works of some great modern economists like Samuelson and Arrow were always on the shelves for me to pick up, read through, and digest. Samuelson accounted his choice of economics at exactly the right time: "To a person of analytical ability, perceptive enough to realise that mathematical equipment was a powerful sword in economics, the world of economics was his or her oyster in 1935. The terrain was strewn with beautiful theorems begging to be picked up and arranged in unified order." I feel luck to randomly study masters' original works in economics even without any idea to become an economist in Japan. It was an optimal choice for me to have spent the leisure time on economics as reading was the most economical and pleasant consumption among all the affordable activities.

Samuelson arranged the works of classical economists in a unified order with the principles of optimization and comparative statics analysis. Although he did not create a unified economic theory, he first applied many physical theories and concepts to modernize economics with the mathematical kit. When I came to know economics, Samuelson's works had already become classical and each piece of his important works had been mathematically refined and further developed. By the early 1990s after having read Samuelson's and his generation's works in formal economic theories, I began to ask whether it is possible to build a set of equations which unify the basic economic mechanisms of the existing economic theories within a *single* theoretical framework. In the *Foreword* to the Japanese translation of my 1991 book *Synergetic Economics* (Zhang 1994), I outlined my aspiration to build a general economic theory in the following way:

> Indeed, it is only after laborious work in many fields of theoretical economics that I began to be conscious of the fact that it is time to build a logically compact theory which includes the main economic ideas of Smith, Malthus, von Thunen, Ricardo, Marx, Mills, Walras, Marshall, Schumpeter, and Keynes. It should also include, as special cases, the well-established mathematical models, such as the Arrow-Debreu general equilibrium model, the Tobin model, the Solow-Swan-Uzawa growth model, the Oniki-Uzawa trade model, the Kaldo-Pasinetti two-class model, the Ricardian Models by Morishima, Samuelson and Pasinetti, the Keynesian theory, and Alonso location model, to explain certain economic phenomena which cannot be explained by the traditional works. I have concentrated on this single task, since … the spring of 1989.

My *Synergetic Economics* published in 1991, completed in 1989, was perhaps the first comprehensive book on applying modern nonlinear theory and ideas from natural sciences to economics. It is a further development of Samuelson's *Foundation*. This book reports some of my progresses in the mission to build a general economic theory. In this book, by theories by Nobel Prize laureates in economics I refer to formal models proposed by some Nobel laureates in economics. The Nobel Prize is referred to The Sveriges Riksbank Prize in Economic Sciences in Memory of Alfred Nobel.

Over years I received many insightful and constructive comments on my works submitted to academic journals. I am thankful to the comments of many anonymous referees and the journal editors. I am very grateful to Editor Dr. Johannes Glaeser and Editorial Assistant Judith Kripp for effective cooperation. I would like to thank the anonymous referee for the valuable comments and suggestions. I thank for my wife, Gao Xiao, who brings me happiness and is always supportive for my research. I completed this book at the Ritsumeikan Asia Pacific University. I am thankful for and impressed by the timely and professional performances of the research office. The campus, facing the clean ocean illuminated by sun lights through unstable clouds, standing by the fogged-up valley, and relying on the beautiful mountains decorated by colors of leaves and flowers, tranquilizes me with songs of birds in the four seasons. I am grateful to the campus life sustained collectively by the colleagues, students, and staffs from over 100 countries.

Beppu, Japan
Summer 2020

Wei-Bin Zhang

Reference

Zhang WB (1994) The foreword to the Japanese version of Synergetic Economics, translated by Asada T, Aruka Y, Inaba T, Hirosi W. The Chuo University Press, Tyoko

Contents

1 The Time for a Grand Economic Theory 1
1.1 The *Synergetic Economics* Generalizes the *Foundations of Economic Analysis* 1
1.2 Speed and Time Scale in Synergetic Economics 5
1.2.1 Adam Smith (1723–1790) 7
1.2.2 Ricardo (1772–1823) 8
1.2.3 Malthus (1766–1834) 8
1.2.4 Marx (1818–1883) 8
1.2.5 The Walrasian General Equilibrium Theory 9
1.3 The Time to Integrate Economic Theories 10
1.4 The Structure of the Book 11
References 17

2 The Basic Model for the Integration 19
2.1 The Basic Model 19
2.1.1 The Production Sector 20
2.1.2 The Household's Current Income, Disposable Income, and Budget 21
2.1.3 The Utility Function and Optimal Behavior 22
2.2 The Basic Model with the Cobb–Douglas Functions 24
2.3 The Theoretical Foundation of the Utility Function 26
2.4 The Basic Model Generates the Keynesian Consumption Function 28
2.5 The Basic Model Generates the Solow Growth Model with Taste Change 30
2.6 The Basic Model Generates the Ramsey–Cass–Koopmans Model with Preference Change 32
References 38

3 An Integration of Walrasian General Equilibrium, Ricardian Distribution, and Neoclassical Growth Theories 41
3.1 Integrating the Walrasian General Equilibrium, Ricardian Distribution and Neoclassical Growth Theories 43
3.1.1 The Production Functions and Marginal Conditions . . . 44
3.1.2 Household Behavior 45
3.1.3 Demand and Supply of the Three Sectors and Full Employment of Factors 46
3.2 Dynamic Behavior of the Economy 47
3.3 Changes in the Preferences and Human Capital Affect the Dynamics 49
3.3.1 Group 1 Augments the Propensity to Save 49
3.3.2 Group 1 Improves the Human Capital 51
3.3.3 Group 3 Increases Propensity to Consume Agricultural Good 52
3.3.4 Group 3's Population Is Increased 52
3.3.5 Group 1's Population Being Increased 53
3.4 Business Cycles Due to Exogenous Shocks in the General Model 54
3.4.1 Group 1's Propensity to Save Periodically Oscillates 55
3.4.2 Group 1's Human Capital Periodically Oscillates 55
3.4.3 Group 3's Propensity to Consume Agricultural Good Periodically Oscillates 55
3.4.4 Group 3's Population Periodically Oscillates 56
3.5 On Income Gaps and Real Business Cycle Theory 56
Appendix: Dynamics with Multiple Capital and Consumer Goods 58
References 66

4 Education, National Debts, and Development Traps 69
4.1 Growth with Education and Saving 70
4.1.1 The Goods Sector 70
4.1.2 The Household Behavior 71
4.1.3 The Education Sector 71
4.2 The Dynamics and Multiple Equilibrium Points 72
4.3 Unstable Unlimited Growth Versus Poverty Traps 74
4.4 Changes in Policy and Preferences in Stable and Unstable Economies 76
4.4.1 The Education Policy 76
4.4.2 The Impact of the Propensity to Save 78
4.5 Growth by Integrating the Diamond Debt and Uzawa–Lucas Models with Education Subsidies 78
4.5.1 The Labor Force and Factor Input Distribution 79
4.5.2 The Production Sector 79

4.5.3 The Education Sector . . . 79
4.5.4 Accumulation of Human Capital . . . 80
4.5.5 The Disposable Income and Optimal Behavior . . . 81
4.5.6 The Government Expenditure and Tax Income . . . 82
4.5.7 The Dynamics of Government Debt . . . 83
4.5.8 Demand and Supply in Education Market . . . 83
4.6 Short-Run and Long-Run Debts Due to Exogenous Changes . . . 85
4.6.1 A Rise in the Government Subsidy Rate on Education . . . 85
4.6.2 A Rise in the Total Factor Productivity of the Education Sector . . . 86
4.6.3 A Rise in the Total Factor Productivity of the Industrial Sector . . . 86
4.6.4 A Rise in the Propensity to Obtain Education . . . 87
4.6.5 A Rise in the Tax Rate on Consumption . . . 88
4.6.6 Stronger Increasing Returns to Scale in Learning from Education . . . 88
4.7 Some Comments on Poverty . . . 88
References . . . 90

5 Inequalities with Racial Human Capital Externalities . . . 93
5.1 Racial Human Capital Externalities and National Growth . . . 94
5.1.1 The Two Sectors . . . 94
5.1.2 Consumer Behaviors and Wealth Dynamics . . . 95
5.1.3 Demand and Supply of the Two Sectors . . . 95
5.1.4 Human Capital with Racial Human Capital Externalities . . . 96
5.2 Changes in a Race's Preference and Human Capital . . . 97
5.2.1 Race 1's Human Capital Externality is Strengthened . . . 98
5.2.2 Race 1's Population is Increased . . . 99
5.2.3 Race 1's Propensity to Save is Increased . . . 99
5.3 On Inequality of Income and Wealth . . . 100
References . . . 101

6 Growth with Public Knowledge and Private Human Capital . . . 103
6.1 Public Knowledge, Individual Human Capital, and Private Wealth . . . 104
6.1.1 The Total Labor Supply and Behavior of Production Sector . . . 105
6.1.2 The Education Sector . . . 107
6.1.3 Accumulation of Human Capital . . . 107
6.1.4 Knowledge Creation and Government's Research Policy . . . 108
6.1.5 Balance of Demand and Supply and Full Employment of Factors . . . 108

6.2 Growth with Knowledge, Human Capital, and Wealth 109
6.3 The Role of Creativity, Government Policy, and Preference . . . 112
6.3.1 A Rise in the Research Sector's Creativity. 112
6.3.2 Group 3's Population Increases 112
6.3.3 Group 1 Applies Human Capital More Effectively 113
6.3.4 A Rise in the Tax Rate on the Production Sector 113
6.3.5 A Rise in the Tax Rate on Group 1's Consumption of Goods 115
6.3.6 A Rise in Group 1's Propensity to Receive Education 115
6.3.7 Group 1 More Effectively Accumulates Human Capital. 116
6.4 Some Comments on Innovation with Microeconomic Foundation 117
References 118

7 Population Dynamics with Endogenous Birth and Mortality Rates 119
7.1 Haavelmo's Growth Model and Chaos with Population. 120
7.2 Global Population and Economic Growth with Free Trade 124
7.2.1 The Production Sectors and Marginal Conditions 124
7.2.2 Consumer Behaviors. 125
7.2.3 The Birth and Mortality Rates and Population Dynamics 126
7.2.4 Wealth Dynamics 127
7.2.5 Balance Conditions. 127
7.3 Global Population with Changes in National Characters 130
7.3.1 Human Capital of Country 1's Woman Being Improved 131
7.3.2 Country 1's Mother Spending More Time on Per Child Fostering 132
7.3.3 A Rise in Country 1's Total Factor Productivity 133
7.3.4 A Rise in Country 1's Propensity to Have Children . . . 133
7.3.5 Country 1's Income having Stronger Impact on the Mortality Rate 135
7.3.6 A Rise in Woman's Propensity to Pursue Leisure Activities 135
7.3.7 Impact of a Rise in Country 1's Propensity to Save . . . 136
7.4 Population, Human Capital, and Physical Capital 137
7.4.1 The Two Sectors and Marginal Conditions 138
7.4.2 Human Capital Dynamics 138
7.4.3 Consumer Behaviors. 138

7.4.4 The Birth and Mortality Rates and the Population Dynamics 140
7.4.5 Wealth Dynamics 140
7.5 The Population Affected by Preference and Other Conditions 142
7.5.1 A Rise in the Mortality Rate Parameter 142
7.5.2 A Rise in the Propensity to have Children 143
7.5.3 A Rise in the Propensity to Receive Education 143
7.5.4 The Human Capital Utilization Efficiency is Increased 144
7.5.5 The Mortality Rate Elasticity of Human Capital is Enhanced 145
References 145

8 Health, Environment, Resources, and Government 147
8.1 Health, Environment, and Wealth 147
8.1.1 National Labor Supply, Technologies, and Marginal Conditions 148
8.1.2 Modeling of Health Caring 149
8.1.3 Consumer Behaviors 149
8.1.4 Dynamics of Household's Health and Change in Environment 150
8.1.5 Behavior of the Environment Sector 151
8.1.6 Equilibrium Conditions for Outputs and Full Employment of Factors 152
8.2 Taxes and Preferences Changes in Health Caring and Leisure 154
8.2.1 The Household Increases the Propensity to Use Health Caring 154
8.2.2 The Household's Efficiency of Applying Health is Increased 155
8.2.3 The Household's Human Capital is Enhanced 156
8.2.4 A Rise in the Environmental Tax on the Capital Good Sector 156
8.2.5 A Rise in the Tax Rate on the Consumption of Health Service 157
8.2.6 A Rise in the Household's Propensity to Use Leisure Time 158
8.2.7 Pollutants Speed Up Health Deterioration 159
8.3 Renewable Resources, Values, and Economic Structure 159
8.3.1 The Industrial Sector 160
8.3.2 The Agricultural Sector 161
8.3.3 Choice Between Physical Wealth and Land 161
8.3.4 Change of Renewable Resources 161

8.3.5 Consumer Behavior 162
8.3.6 Wealth Accumulation 163
8.3.7 Balances of Demand and Supply for Industrial Goods 164
8.3.8 Balances of Demand and Supply for Agricultural Goods and Renewable Resources 164
8.3.9 All the Land Owned by Households 164
8.3.10 Full Employment of Capital 164
8.3.11 The Value of Physical Wealth and Capital 164
8.3.12 Full Employment of Labor Force 165
8.3.13 The Land Market Clearing Condition 165
8.3.14 Land Use for Renewable Resources 165
8.4 Changes in the Population and the Preference 167
8.4.1 A Rise in the Propensity to Consume Resources 167
8.4.2 A Rise in the Propensity to Consume Housing 168
8.4.3 The Propensity to Consume Industrial Goods Being Enhanced 168
8.4.4 A Rise in the Propensity to Consume Agricultural Goods 170
8.4.5 A Rise in the Propensity to Save 171
8.4.6 The Population Being Augmented 172
8.4.7 A Rise in the Output Elasticity of Capital of the Resource Sector 173
8.5 Comments on Dynamic Environment and Health 173
References 174

9 Preference Change, Social Status, Habits, and Fashion 177
9.1 Social Status and Inequality in Wealth and Income 178
9.1.1 The Production Sectors and Marginal Conditions 178
9.1.2 Disposable Incomes and Utility Functions 179
9.1.3 Social Status and Propensities to Save and to Consume 180
9.1.4 Optimal Household Behavior and Wealth Accumulation 180
9.1.5 Market Equilibrium Conditions and Full Employment 181
9.2 Social Status as Spirit of Capitalism and Other Factor Are Changed 183
9.2.1 Group 1's Spirit of Capitalism Rises 183
9.2.2 The Total Factor Productivity of the Capital Goods Sector Being Enhanced 184
9.2.3 Group 1's Social Status More Strongly Affecting Its Propensity to Save 185

9.2.4 Group 3's Population Being Increased 186
9.2.5 The Depreciation Rate of Physical Capital Rises 186
9.2.6 Group 3's Human Capital Rises 187
9.2.7 A rise in the Output Elasticity of Capital of the Capital Goods Sector 188
9.3 Growth and Fashion with Snobs and Bandwagoners 188
9.3.1 Technologies and Marginal Conditions 189
9.3.2 Disposable Incomes and Budgets 190
9.3.3 Utility Functions and Optimal Decision 190
9.3.4 A Brief Review on Fashion Dynamics and Habit Formation 191
9.3.5 Average Consumption of Fashion and Preference Change 191
9.3.6 Demand and Supply of the Three Sectors and Full Employment of Capital 192
9.4 Fashion and Growth with Different Exogenous Changes 195
9.4.1 The Bandwagoner's Propensity to Consume Fashion is More Strongly Affected by the Average Fashion Consumption 196
9.4.2 The Snob's Propensity to Consume Fashion Is More Negatively Affected by the Average Fashion Consumption 197
9.4.3 The Bandwagoner's Propensity to Consume Fashion is Increased 197
9.4.4 The Bandwagoner's Human Capital is Improved 198
9.4.5 A Rise in the Bandwagoner's Population 199
9.4.6 A Rise in the Snob's Propensity to Save 200
9.5 Modeling Human Behavior by Integrating Psychology 201
References 201

10 Portfolio Choice in General Dynamic Equilibrium 203
10.1 Exchange Values of Gold, Land, Physical Capital, and Human Capital 204
10.1.1 The Industrial Sector 204
10.1.2 The Agricultural Sector 204
10.1.3 The Education Sector and Marginal Conditions 205
10.1.4 Choice Between Physical Wealth, Gold, and Land 205
10.1.5 Disposable Income, Budget, and Decision 205
10.1.6 Dynamics of Human Capital 207
10.1.7 Equilibrium for Demand and Supply and Full Use of Resources 207
10.2 The Dynamics of Exchange Values with Exogenous Conditions Changes 209
10.2.1 The Propensity to Use Gold is Augmented 210

10.2.2 A Rise in the Propensity to Receive Education 210
10.2.3 The Propensity to Consume Housing is Increased 211
10.2.4 A Rise in the Propensity to Save 212
10.2.5 A Rise in the Total Factor Productivity of the Industrial Sector 213
10.2.6 The Population is Increased 214
10.3 A Few Remarks on Asset Prices 215
References 215

11 Money and Unstable Economic Changes 217
11.1 Growth with the Money-in-Utility (MIU) Approach 219
11.1.1 The Real Sector 219
11.1.2 The Money via the "Helicopter Drop" 220
11.1.3 The Disposable Income and Optimal Decision 220
11.2 Equilibrium and Comparative Steady State 222
11.2.1 The Inflationary Policy 224
11.2.2 The Effects of Change in the Propensity to Hold Money 225
11.2.3 Effects of Change in the Propensity to Own Wealth . . . 225
11.3 A Small Open-Country Economy with the Cash-in-Advance Approach 226
11.4 Dynamics and Equilibrium 228
11.5 An Integration of the Taylor Rule and the Solow-Tobin Model 229
11.5.1 The Sector Behavior and Marginal Conditions 230
11.5.2 Household Behavior 230
11.5.3 Monetary and Fiscal Policy 232
11.5.4 The Government's Budget Constraint 232
11.5.5 Capital Change 232
11.6 Comparative Dynamic Analysis 233
11.6.1 The Targeted Inflation Rate Is Enhanced 233
11.6.2 The Total Factor Productivity Is Enhanced 234
11.6.3 The Propensity to Hold Money Is Enhanced 235
11.6.4 An Increase in the Propensity to Save 236
11.6.5 The Tax is Increased 236
11.7 Comments on Further Extensions 237
References 238

12 Growth Theory Enriched with Monopoly, Monopsony, and Game Theories 241
12.1 Monopolies and Perfect Competition in Solow–Uzawa's General Equilibrium Growth Model 241
12.1.1 The Production of Final Product 242
12.1.2 Consumer Behaviors and Wealth Dynamics 242

12.1.3 Wealth Accumulation 243
12.1.4 Equilibrium for Monopoly Product 243
12.1.5 The Behavior of the Monopolies 243
12.1.6 Demand and Supply and Full Employment 245
12.2 Long-Term Growth with Changes in Monopoly Productivity and Preference 246
12.2.1 A Monopoly's Total Factor Productivity Is Enhanced 246
12.2.2 The Share Parameter of a Monopoly Product Is Increased 246
12.2.3 The Share Parameter of Final Goods Is Increased. 247
12.2.4 A Monopoly's Output Elasticity of Labor Is Enhanced 247
12.3 Growth with Monopsony Against Woman in Labor Market . . . 248
12.3.1 Utility, Disposable Income, Budget, and Optimal Behavior 249
12.3.2 Wealth Accumulation 250
12.3.3 Production Sector 250
12.3.4 Demand and Supply Balance 251
12.3.5 Equilibrium and Comparative Statics Analysis 251
12.4 Long-Term Equilibrium with Woman's Characters 252
12.4.1 Woman's Human Capital Is Enhanced. 252
12.4.2 Woman's Propensity to Use Leisure Time Is Increased 252
12.5 Monopsony Against Woman Harms National Economic Performances 253
12.6 Cournot-Nash Family Decision in an Extended Solowian Model 254
12.6.1 The Disposable Income and Optimal Behavior. 255
12.6.2 Utility Functions and Budgets 256
12.6.3 The Production Sector 257
12.6.4 Equilibrium Conditions 257
12.7 Dynamics of Cournot-Nash Family Decision with Exogenous Changes 259
12.7.1 The Husband Derives Less Well-Being from His Wife's Well-Being 259
12.7.2 The Wife's Human Capital Is Enhanced 259
12.7.3 The Wife Increases Her Propensity to Save 260
12.7.4 The Wife Increases Her Propensity to Consume Consumption Goods 261
12.7.5 The Wife Increases Her Propensity to Consume Family Goods 261
12.7.6 The Total Factor Productivity Is Enhanced 262

12.8 On Contract Theory, Agent-Based Economics, and the General Theory 263
References 263

13 Growth with Perfect and Monopolistic Competition 265
13.1 The Dixit–Stiglitz Monopolistic Competition 265
13.2 Integrating the Basic Model and Dixit–Stiglitz Model 268
13.2.1 The Final Good Sector 268
13.2.2 The Middle Good Sector 270
13.2.3 Consumer Behaviors and Wealth Dynamics 271
13.2.4 Demand and Supply of Final Goods and Full Employment 272
13.3 Comparative Dynamic Analysis in the Solow–Dixit–Stiglitz Model 273
13.3.1 A Rise in the Degree of Specialization 273
13.3.2 A Rise in Output Elasticity of Intermediate Inputs 274
13.3.3 The Unit Labor Requirement for the Production of Intermediates Rises 275
13.3.4 The Propensity to Use Leisure Time Rises 275
13.3.5 The Propensity to Save Rises 276
13.3.6 A Rise in Human Capital 277
13.4 An Integration of Neoclassical Growth, Dixit–Stiglitz Monopolistic Competition, and Walrasian General Equilibrium Theories 277
13.4.1 The Total Labor Force 278
13.4.2 The Final Good Sector 278
13.4.3 Disposable Income and Budgets 278
13.4.4 Utility Functions and Optimal Behavior 279
13.4.5 The Middle Good Sector 282
13.4.6 Balances in Final Good Market, Labor Market, and National Wealth 283
13.5 Comparative Dynamic Analysis in Preferences and Market Characters 285
13.5.1 The Elasticity of Substitution Between Two Varieties Rises 286
13.5.2 Fixed Labor Cost of the Middle Goods Firm Is Increased 286
13.5.3 A Rise in Variety of Middle Goods 287
13.5.4 Group 1's Propensity to Consume Middle Goods is Enhanced 287
13.5.5 Group 1's Propensity to Save Is Enhanced 289
13.5.6 Group 3 Enhances Human Capital 289
13.5.7 Group 3's Population Is Increased 290
13.5.8 The Profit Distribution Is Shifted 291

13.6 On Growth with Contracts, Games, and Market Powers 292
References 292

14 Trade Pattern, Tourism, and Global Development 295
14.1 Integrating Heckscher–Ohlin and Oniki–Uzawa Trade Models 296
14.1.1 Production Functions and Marginal Conditions 296
14.1.2 Household Behavior 297
14.1.3 Factor Markets and Demand and Supply 298
14.2 Global Growth and Capital Flows with Various Exogenous Changes 300
14.2.1 A Rise in the Total Factor Productivity of Country 1's Industrial Sector 300
14.2.2 A fall in the Output Elasticity of Country 1's Industrial Sector 301
14.2.3 Country 1's Population is Increased 302
14.2.4 Country 1 Increases Its Propensity to Consume the Domestic Commodity 303
14.2.5 Country 1 Increases Its Propensity to Consume Country 2's Global Commodity 304
14.2.6 Country 1 Increases Its Propensity to Consume Services 304
14.2.7 Country 1 Augments Its Propensity to Save 305
14.3 Habit Formation and Preference Change with Free Trade 306
14.3.1 The Production Sector and Marginal Conditions 306
14.3.2 Households Behavior 306
14.3.3 The Time Preference and Habit Formation 308
14.4 Global Growth and Trade Pattern with Exogenous Changes 310
14.4.1 Country 1's Household Giving Lower Weights to More Distant Values of Consumption 310
14.4.2 Country 1's Wealth Effect on the Propensity to Save Becoming Stronger 311
14.4.3 Country 1's Propensity to Consume Being More Strongly Affected by Habits 312
14.5 Trade in Goods and Tourism with Infrastructure and Externalities 312
14.5.1 Industrial Sector 314
14.5.2 Service Sector 314
14.5.3 Full Employment of Capital and Labor 315
14.5.4 Behavior of Domestic Households 315
14.5.5 Demand Function of Foreign Tourists 316
14.5.6 Full use of Land 317
14.5.7 Demand and Supply for Services 317
14.5.8 Behavior of the Government 317

14.6 Impact of Various Shocks on the Tourist Economy 320
14.6.1 A Rise in the Rate of Interest in the Global Market . . . 320
14.6.2 A Rise in the Total Productivity of the Service Sector 321
14.6.3 Raising Tax Rate on the Service Sector 321
14.6.4 Raising Tax Rate on Consumption of Services 322
14.6.5 An Improvement in Human Capital 323
14.6.6 A Rise in the Household's Propensity to Consume Services 323
14.6.7 Public Services More Strongly Affecting the Productivity of the Industrial Sector 324
14.7 On Nominal Exchange Rates and Capital Flows 325
References 325

15 Alonso Urban and Solow Growth Models Integrated 327
15.1 Land Value, Residential Structure, and Growth 328
15.1.1 The Total Labor Input and Production Sector 329
15.1.2 The Relation Between the Lot Size and Residential Density 329
15.1.3 Choice Between Physical Wealth and Land 329
15.1.4 Travel Time and Cost to the CBD 330
15.1.5 Land Ownership, Disposable Income, and Budget 330
15.1.6 Utility, Amenity, and Optimal Solution 331
15.1.7 Equal Utility Level, Wealth Accumulation and Market Equilibria 332
15.2 Spatial Growth with Land Value Change 333
15.3 Growth and Land Value with Exogenous Changes 333
15.3.1 An Increase in the Interest Rate 334
15.3.2 The Total Factor Productivity Being Enhanced 334
15.3.3 The Propensity to Save Being Increased 336
15.4 A Few Comments on Generalizing the Spatial Model 336
References 337

16 Miscellaneous Issues and Conclusion 339
References 341

Chapter 1
The Time for a Grand Economic Theory

The grand aim of all science is to cover the greatest number of empirical facts by logical deduction from the smallest number of hypotheses or axioms.
Albert Einstein

Mathematics is called the queen of all sciences. Advances in modern economics, especially after World War II, have been associated with applications of different fields of mathematics. The rapid development in nonlinear mathematics and computer in the last few decades has enabled economists to further explore, empirically and theoretically, the complexity of economic systems. The advance of nonlinear economics is a visionary revolution in economic thinking about change, time scale, and speed of changes which are conceptually essential not only for differentiating various schools of economic dynamics, but also for unifying ideas and theories in economics (and other fields in social sciences) within a single analytical framework. Before constructing the general economic theory, I outline a new paradigm of analytical economics in association with applications of nonlinear science and computer.

1.1 The *Synergetic Economics* Generalizes the *Foundations of Economic Analysis*

Funeral by funeral, theory advances.
Paul Samuelson

Economics, especially analytical economics, has experienced revolutionary changes in the last few decades. This revolution is caused by nonlinear science, which is composed of many branches, such as synergetics, theory of complexity, theory of self-organization, and chaos theory. The revolution implies that economics can analytically and effectively treat the economic reality as an organic whole, rather than collections of separate and unconnected parts as in traditional analytical economics.

W.-B. Zhang, *The General Economic Theory*,
https://doi.org/10.1007/978-3-030-56204-5_1

Having been influenced by different branches of nonlinear science, I started to apply nonlinear science to economics about 35 years ago. I call this theory synergetic economics (Zhang 1989 or 1991) as it is based on synergetics created by Haken (1977, 1983). Synergetics deals with collective static or dynamic phenomena in closed or open multi-component systems with cooperative interactions occurring between the units of the system. Synergetics concentrates on the structural self-organizing space–time features of systems on a macroscopic level. It turns out that on this level, there exist close analogies between various systems in physics, chemistry, and biology, though they are composed of different units with completely different elementary interactions. From this new scientific perspective, theories reveal on how order gives way to chaos, order is discovered within chaos, and order is again created out of chaos.

The basic tool in synergetics is nonlinear mathematics. The theory is initiated by Poincaré (1854–1912) who revolutionized the study of nonlinear differential equations by introducing the qualitative techniques of geometry and topology rather than strict analytic methods to discuss the global properties of solutions of these systems. The study of dynamic systems was furthered in the Soviet Union, by mathematicians such as Liapunov, Pontryagin, Andronov, and others. Around 1975, many scientists around the world were suddenly aware that there is a new kind of motion—now called chaos—in dynamic systems. The new motion is erratic, but not simply "quasiperiodic" with many periods. What is surprising is that chaos can occur even in a very simple system. With the recent fast development of computers, scientists have been able to see that complicated behavior of high-dimensional nonlinear dynamic systems.

Before modern nonlinear science was introduced to economics, analytical economics had been dominated by Samuelson's magnum opus *Foundation of Economic Analysis*. Paul Samuelson (1915–2009) made great contributions to development of formal economics. He was awarded the 1970 Nobel Prize in economics: "for the scientific work through which he has developed static and dynamic economic theory and actively contributed to raising the level of analysis in economic science." He had played a great role in bringing rigorous analysis to economics that had previously relied on mostly verbal and graphical analysis. His *Foundation* started a new epoch of economic analysis. The *Foundation* was based on his Harvard Ph.D. dissertation. He attempted to formalize economic problems as maximizing or minimizing subject to constraints. His other influential book *Economics: An Introductory Analysis*, first published in 1948, effectively provided the world a common analytical tool with which microeconomic and macroeconomic phenomena of various parts of the world can be understood, analyzed, interpreted, discussed, and taught. Since its publications, the *Economics* has globally framed textbooks on introduction to modern economics till today. It did not take me long time to generalize the *Foundation* as the generalization was carried out by applying nonlinear science to economics. It has taken me three decades to put many seemingly unconnected ideas and theories in economics into a single analytical framework.

In the *Foundations*, Samuelson broadly classified the development of analytical economics into five steps. First, in Walras one has the final culmination of concept of equilibrium. Pareto and others took a second step which laid the basis of a theory of comparative statics. The third step, which is characterized by maximizing action within an economic unit, was mainly carried out by W. E. Johnson, Slutsky, Hicks, and Allen, and other economists. The fourth advance is due to the discovery of the correspondence principle. There are comparative statics analysis and comparative dynamics analysis according to whether the analysis is completed for a static or a dynamic model. When the system is stable, the comparative dynamics analysis is called the correspondence principle by Samuelson. In his *Foundation*, Samuelson foresaw what should be done in the future:

> A natural fifth step to take after we have investigated the response of a system to change in given parameters is to investigate its behavior as a result of the passage of time.

Inspirited by Haken's synergetics and Prigogine's works (Prigogine 1980; Prigogine and Stengers 1984) on dissipative structures, I generalized Samuelson's *Foundation,* analytically completing the fifth step with nonlinear science and modern computer. After having read the *Foundations* and *The Collected Scientific Papers of Paul A. Samuelson* (the volumes published by 1990) and other classical works in economics, I set myself a task to explore the fifty step of analytical economics unexplored in the *Foundations.* My *Synergetic Economics*, which was finalized and printed in the same day as my Umea Ph.D. dissertation *Economic Development* as research reports of Umea University in 1989, made a progress in analytical economics by examining nonlinear dynamic economic systems. *Synergetic Economics* was late published in Herman Haken's *Synergetics* series in 1991. My dissertation was published in 1990 with title *Economic Dynamics—Growth and Development* by Springer-Verlag.

Synergetic Economics was the first comprehensive book in nonlinear economics, especially in its explicit recognition as completing the fifth step of analytical economics. It contributes the development of the fifth step. Samuelson recognizes the significance of comparative dynamic analysis. But his generation could not create a theory of comparative dynamics in the contemporary standard. Nonlinear science and modern computer were not available then.

In contrast to Samuelson's traditional analytical economics, which is concerned with linearity and stability, synergetic economics emphasizes linearity versus nonlinearity, stability versus instability, continuity versus discontinuity, permanence versus structural change. Synergetic economics treats nonlinearity and instability as sources of the variety and complexity of economic dynamics, rather than nuisance and temporal phenomena as traditional economics does. According to synergetic economics, economic systems may run through a hierarchy of instabilities in which more and more structured patterns evolve. Such instabilities are caused by changes of external parameters and can lead to a new spatiotemporal pattern of the system.

A whole description of economic life needs genuine dynamic model which describes connected movements of every part of the entire whole. A genuine economic theory should be able to describe every individual behavior as an element of the entire economic system. There is no distinction between microeconomics and macroeconomics as individuals live within the whole and the whole consists of individuals. The development of mathematics and computer provides powerful tools to explore complexity of genuine dynamical behavior. Nonlinear science gives a new vision about dynamic evolution. *Synergetic Economics* "completed" the fifth step because of the accumulated knowledge not only in economics, but also in natural sciences and mathematics. Synergetic economics marks the start of a new era of nonlinear dynamic economics. It shows the way in which economic systems far from equilibrium evolve elaborate structures: cycles, aperiodic motion, chaos, and well-organized time-dependent urban pattern formations.

Synergetic economics reveals how such interactions can bring about qualitatively new structures and how the whole is related to and different from its individual components. A modern computer can explore a far wider class of phenomena than it could have been imagined even a few decades ago. The essential ideas about complexity upon which synergetic economics is based have found wide applications among a wide range of scientific disciplines, including physics, biology, ecology, psychology, cognitive science, and sociology. Many complex systems constructed in those scientific areas have been found to share many common properties. The great variety of multiple applied fields manifests a possibly unifying methodological factor in sciences. Nonlinear theory offers scientists a new tool for exploring and modeling the complexity of nature and society. The new techniques and concepts provide powerful methods for modeling and simulating trajectories of sudden and irreversible change in social and natural systems. The range of applications of synergetic economics includes many topics, such as catastrophes, bifurcations, trade cycles, economic chaos, urban pattern formation, sexual division of labor and economic development, economic growth, values and family structure, the role of stochastic noise upon socioeconomic structures, fast and slow socioeconomic processes, and relationship between microscopic and macroscopic structures. All these topics cannot be effectively examined by traditional analytical methods.

The Samuelson generation had refined and developed the classical economic theories, but not in a unified manner. This book aims at unifying the well-developed theories in a comprehensive framework. It tends to do what Samuelson had envisaged long time ago:

> The usefulness of any theoretical structure lies in the light which it throws upon the way economic variables will change when there is a change in some datum or parameter. This commonplace holds as well in the realm of dynamics as in statics. It is a logical next, therefore, to begin to create a theory of comparative dynamics. This will include the theory of comparative statics as a special case, and indeed all of the earlier five subjects, but it will cover a much richer terrain.

This book explores "a much richer terrain."

1.2 Speed and Time Scale in Synergetic Economics

Synergetic economics attempts to provide a new vision of economic dynamics: a vision toward the multiple, the temporal, the unpredictable, and the complex. It tends to replace simplicity with complexity and specialism with generality in economic analysis. The concepts such as totality, nonlinearity, self-organization, structural changes, order, and chaos have found broad and new meanings by the development of this new science. Economic dynamics are considered to resemble a turbulent movement of liquid in which varied and relatively stable forms of current and whirlpools constantly change one another. These changes consist of dynamic processes of self-organization along with the spontaneous formation of increasingly subtle and complicated structures.

Even in basic economic courses, short-run and long-run phenomena are emphasized. An economic theory which tends to explain long-run economic evolution may be meaningless to explain short-run economic phenomena; similarly, the short-run Keynesian theory may be invalid for the long-run Schumpeterian theory of creative destruction. Orphanides and Solow (1990: 258) point out a fundamental problem of economics: "Short-run macroeconomics and long-run growth theory have never been properly integrated. It is only a slight caricature to say that once upon time the long run was treated causally as a forward extension of the short run, whereas nowadays the tendency is to treat the short run causally as a backward extension of the long run."

Before nonlinear science and computer were available, there was no proper tool for building a general nonlinear economic theory in which both short-run and long-run issues in microeconomics and macroeconomics can be analyzed in a single framework. Keynes (1883–1946) emphasizes the significance of studying short-run phenomena as follows: "But this *long-run* is a misleading guide to current affairs. In the long run, we are all dead." It is a common sense that before going to the long-run equilibrium state, death, the human body functions dynamically without going to any unique time-invariant point. The man's organ, health, preference, and human capital are constantly changing. These variables are all interconnected in dynamic ways within the same body. One may die in a few minutes if a subsystem, like heart or blood, disfunctions; a subsystem, like preference structure, has complicated relations with the other subsystems in the long term. No one can naturally avoid the aging process. To live a happy and long life, one take care of short-run as well as long-run health issues. Like human body, a human society is composed of different, such as fast like blood and slow such as bones, processes within closely interconnected whole. Long-run welfare and everyday pleasures are mingled together within an organic whole. Time is at the center of the chief difficulty of almost every economic problem. The role of time in decision makings and action is becoming increasingly complicated as variety of action and social networks are expanding. It is difficult to decide the length of time which affects a special decision making since each kind of human decisions are made with different time scales and two persons may have different time scales with regards to the same kind of decision making. One important issue in synergetic economics is to explore relations between microeconomic and macroeconomic processes within different time scales. As time passes, economic issues with which economists are concerned have shifted. Even since the time of Adam Smith, the economic variables that economists have dealt with appear to have been invariant. But the ways in which these variables are combined and the speeds at which they change have constantly varied and the dominant economic doctrines have shifted over time and space. The complexity of economic reality is constantly increasing in modern time. This is partially because of the expanded capital and knowledge stocks of mankind and fast development of computer. Knowledge, in fields of philosophy, arts, literature, music, technology, and sciences, expands man's imagination and extends possibilities of human action. Knowledge is not only power and sources of money, but also the most durable capital good. Increases in machines, housing, and infrastructures have enriched human environment, increased accessibility to various locations, and enlarged variety of human behavior.

If one examines the complexity of economic evolution from a historical perspective, mankind has experienced three economic structural transformations—from hunting society to agricultural one, agricultural society to industrial one, industrial society to information/knowledge-based one. These transformations are still occurring in different nations in different forms at different speeds. Each of these economic systems has certain corresponding dominant ideologies such as religions, socialism, and capitalism. At each turning point, there tend to be great conflicts among different social classes, though forms of conflicts are affected by geographical conditions, cultural traditions, international environment, and other factors. As an illustration of applying the concept of speeds of changes in analyzing economic structural changes, I choose three variables, the population, capital, and knowledge. These three variables may be roughly considered to be changeable at different speeds in different societies. If one is interested in examining agricultural economies, one may concentrate on population (and power struggle) dynamics. But the analytical conclusions about agricultural economies cannot be applied to explain economic dynamics of industrialized economies, as capital is the dominant variable of industrial economies. Similarly, the analytical conclusions about capital-based societies cannot be applied to explain economic phenomena of knowledge-based societies as knowledge is also created and diffused very rapidly.

Another dimension in analysis is space. Man, action, capital, knowledge, and time can become culturally and socially meaningful only in certain space. Fast technological changes, richness of material living conditions, complicated international interactions, and many other modern phenomena have increased complexity of spatial economies. Without spatial dimension, one can hardly analyze actual processes of, for instance, how Japanese economy affects the world economy. In fact, the choice of spatiotemporal scale is a delicate process and must be made before actual study of any special economic problem. The explicit awareness of this necessity is very important for understanding both economic reality and structure of economics.

In synergetic economics, the key words are space, time, and structure. It is hard to give a precise concept of structure. Here, a structure means a sum of elements and relationships between those elements. In other words, structure stands for the way the elements and constituent parts of a whole are arranged with respect to each other. Structure represents a whole in which each element depends on the others by virtue of its relations with them. According to Thom (1977), structure is defined as a spatiotemporal morphology described by significant spatial discontinuities and by the syntax that determines how these sets of discontinuities form into relatively stable systems. In evolving structures, relations depend on time. The structure includes properties, which are properties of the whole rather than only properties of its component parts. Any change in one element or one relationship will cause a modification in other elements or relationships. By means of the cooperation of the individual parts of different subsystems, new properties may emerge that are not present in the subsystems. Economic evolution involves not only changes in variable levels and functions but also in organizational structures that concern the way elements are connected within subsystems, the way subsystems are embedded in large ones, and the way that organizational structures emerge or disappear.

All these intrinsic difficulties related to economic structures heavily affect the efficiency of modeling economic systems. Multiple levels are described in long-term studies. This requires economic theory to have internal structures to represent the complexity of subsystems and connections of the subsystems. Such structural models will eventually turn out to be very complicated. A study of dynamics of a process on a level can thus be conducted by taking behavior of higher levels as fixed and "enslaving" behavior of the low levels as structurally determined flows. In other words, for the chosen time scale, the behavior of higher levels is so slow that they can be effectively negligible, and the behavior of lower levels is so fast that perturbations generated by the behavior of lower levels can also be effectively neglected. For instance, an economic analysis may be conducted in a time scale short enough to assume changes in ecological processes negligible and long enough to average out noise from processes occurring at individual levels. By the way, according to synergetic economics, in "revolutionary" periods or at such critical points, neither the dynamics of higher levels nor the perturbations generated by the behavior of lower levels are negligible. The model used to describe the dynamic interaction of the chosen subsystem is no longer able to provide reliable information about possible behavior of the subsystem.

As an illustration, a few classical economic theories are mentioned with the concepts of time scale and speed of change.

1.2.1 Adam Smith (1723–1790)

In the *Wealth of Nations*, Adam Smith was concerned with the forces that govern the relative levels of prosperity among countries and that cause differences between countries. He discussed the advantages of the division of labor and its dependence on the scale of activity and the extent of the market. Large-scale activity and extended market permit specification and thus improve skills and labor efficiency. Technological progress, division of labor, and scale of market are interdependent. He emphasized the significance of free institutions under which people freely exploit the advantage of their skill and knowledge and resources. Adam Smith's economic theory with division of labor and competitive equilibrium, irrespective of positive dynamic elements, sets limits on economic growth. His theory of economic equilibrium has been supported by the modern competitive equilibrium approach, while his theory of division of labor is formally modeled in recent years.

1.2.2 Ricardo (1772–1823)

Ricardo's fame relies on his *Principles* published in 1817. Although his interest in economics began with reading Adam Smith, he emphasized manufacturing in studying national economy. He tried to establish laws which regulate what proportion of the whole produce of the society will be allotted to each of three—landowner, capitalist and worker—under the names of rent, profit, and wages, respectively. These laws show how the distribution will change at different stages of society. He was concerned with an economic system consisting of agriculture and industry.

1.2.3 Malthus (1766–1834)

Although Malthus was not the first to examine demographic problems, he developed a theory of population growth. By emphasizing the interdependence of population growth and food supply, his theory lent support to the subsistence theory of wages, which had important influences upon Ricardo, Marx, and Keynes. In the simplest form of the Malthusian growth model, the population grows at a constant rate times the population present, with no limitations on its resources. That is, $\dot{N}(t) = aN(t)$, where $N(t)$ is the population at time t and a is a positive parameter. Such a population growth may be valid for a short time, but it clearly cannot go on forever. Malthus was aware of uncertainty in economic evolution with endogenous population. He believed in the nonlinearity of structural relations, and their complicated multi-connected nature, even though he could not rigorously show consequences of nonlinear interactions.

1.2.4 Marx (1818–1883)

Central to both Ricardo and Marx's economics were issues of the fundamental determinants of relative prices, production and reproduction and the distribution of income among social classes. As Marx created a system that embraced almost all fields of social sciences, his ideas about economic dynamics are quite beyond the scope of this study. According to Schumpeter (1954: 596), "Ricardo, the most unmetaphysical of theorists, introduced the labor-quantity theory of value simply as a hypothesis that was to explain the actual relative prices—or rather the actual long-run normals of relative prices—that we observe in real life. But for Marx, the most metaphysical of theorists, the labor-quantity theory was no mere hypothesis about relative prices." I will model income and wealth distribution between various classes, which is a generalization of Marx's ideas on economic dynamics.

1.2.5 The Walrasian General Equilibrium Theory

The general equilibrium theory is a system in which maximization of households' utilities and producers' profits yields consumption components as functions of prices. The population, capital, natural resources, and technology are fixed in this approach. Price dynamics are specified according to the Tâtonnement. I generally describe the system by

$$s\dot{X}(t) = F_X(X(t), P(t)), \quad \dot{P}(t) = F_P(X(t), P(t)),$$

in which X and P are, respectively, the output and the price of the commodity. I consider that the real variable is "slow." Setting $s = 0$, I get $F_X(X(t), P(t)) = 0$, or $X(t) = X(P(t))$. The functional forms of F_X are determined by the forms of utility and production functions. Substituting $X(t) = X(P(t))$ into the price system yields:

$$\dot{P}(t) = F_P^*(P(t)),$$

where $F_P^*(P(t)) \equiv F_P\{X(P(t)), P(t)\}$.

An important feature of economic structures is that they are intrinsically complicated at each level. Individuals, groups or clubs, regions and nations, even as they develop under similar conditions, are not the same. Detailed studies of their evolution have provided many examples of an intrinsic complexity. For instance, random fluctuations in tastes may affect microeconomic evolutionary processes on a large scale. The economic structure represents the values and principles of the economic organization. The system may be analyzed by dividing the whole system into different levels, each representing a subsystem, which consists of relatively uniform elements that interact with each other either in simple or complicated ways. To find and describe these interactions are the key elements for analyzing order and disorder at any given level.

1.3 The Time to Integrate Economic Theories

> The multitude of books is making us ignorant.
> Voltaire (1694–1778)

In the Foundation, Samuelson predicts what is important for analytical economics (Samuelson 1947): "The further development of analytical economics along the lines of comparative dynamics must rest with the future. It is to be hoped that it will aid in the attack upon diverse problems—from … even to the majestic problems of economic development." My focus in this book is on "the majestic problems of economic development." These problems are analyzed by designing a genuine dynamic economic theory which illustrates actual paths of development with fast and slow processes and long-term and short-term time scales within a single analytical framework. Different economic theories have been proposed to study economic phenomena of different economic systems. The conventional distinction is between micro (household and firm behavior) and macro (nationally or globally aggregated models). There are also intermediate stages such as interactions between the agricultural sector and industrial sector. It is important to build a theory in which micro, intermediate, and macrovariables are treated in an interconnected whole.

The traditional scientific strategy is to decompose the whole into simpler parts until one can deal with simple parts. Economics has tried to find simplicity in a complex reality by this strategy. Economic theories such as Walrasian equilibrium theory, neoclassical growth theory, and new growth theory are developed, independent of each other, even though they deal with the same economic reality. Various fields in economics live in isolation from each other. Students trained in one subfield often have not a shared understanding of the fundamentals of the others. Economists from each subfield do not converge upon a common framework but find themselves in divergent directions. Economists have made various assumptions about the underlying laws of economic systems. The essence of synergetic economics implies that traditional economic theories and ideas which are proved to be valid or insightful for certain speeds of change and certain time scales should be integrated in a greater whole. This book is to construct a general theory with the vision of synergetic economics.

Confronted with limitations of traditional economics, economists have tried to relax assumptions in traditional analytical economics by taking account of, for instance, imperfect competition, imperfect information, institutions, and irrationality into economics. Many theories have been proposed by taking some realistic aspects. One find disequilibrium macroeconomics, family economics, share economy, new growth theory, and so on. Economics has been split between partial and conflicting representations of the same economic world. Diverse economic theories have coexisted but not in a structured relationship with each other. Students majoring in economics are taught severally incompatible theories one by one in the same course. Economic theory has experienced crises, such as in neoclassical growth economics and Keynesian economics. Crises also imply opportunities for improvement. Multiple representations of the same reality itself imply a higher presentation. In order to overcome incoherence among multiple economic theories, economics needs a general theory which accounts for the phenomena explained by different theories in a unified manner. It is important to draw together the disparate branches of economics into a single organized system of knowledge. Causal links between these theories makes one to bridge theoretical gaps that a subtheory may not be able to span. This book makes a theoretical integration of well-established economic theories. The integration is conceptual integration in the sense that I analyze economic phenomena in different subfields with a few common basic concepts and assumptions. The theoretical framework describes dynamic interdependence between capital, knowledge, population, preference, habit, environment, resource, economic structure, family dynamics, different markets, and exchange values. Although it is easy to say that population growth, capital accumulation, creativity, and knowledge utilization, preference changes, resources are the basic determinants of modern economic changes, it is not easy to build a theory which connects them within a single analytical framework under various markets.

In evaluating a new theory, Kuhn (1977) gives a few criteria as summarized by Zhang (1999: 402–403): "(1) accurate within domain; (2) consistent internally and with other currently accepted theories; (3) a broad scope allowing its consequences to extend beyond the particular observations, laws or subtheories it was initially designed to explain; (4) simple but able to bring order to the phenomena that in its absence would be individually isolated and, as a set, confused; and (5) fruitful to disclose new phenomena or previously unnoted relationships among those already known." When claiming that the book proposes a general theory, I pay attention to these five characteristics—accuracy, consistency, scope, simplicity, and fruitfulness. I am also aware of limitations of these principles in evolution of socioeconomic theories as emphasized by Kuhn and other scholars.

1.4 The Structure of the Book

This book develops a general economic theory. It integrates classical theories from Adam Smith to Keynes and formal (mathematical) theories by Nobel Prize laureates in economics. It also establishes important relations among economic variables unrecognized in the literature of rigorous economic analysis. It constructs the theory by proposing a series of models; each of them can be combined to form a more comprehensive model. It is intended to build an economic theory like the *Yi Jing* system. The book is organized as follows.

This chapter shows that it is the time to integrate well-developed economic theories and to build a grand economic theory. Analytical economics has experienced a revolutionary change in the last few decades. This revolution is caused, in association with fast development of computer, by nonlinear science, which is composed of many branches, such as synergetics, theory of complexity, theory of self-organization, and chaos theory. The revolution enables economists to analytically treat an economy as an organic whole, rather than collections of separate and unconnected parts as in traditional analytical economics. Having been influenced by different branches of nonlinear science, I have started to apply nonlinear science to economics about 35 years ago and built a theory in analytical economics, named synergetic economics. The name came from synergetics created by Hermann Haken. My book *Syngenetic Economics* is a further development of Samuelson's magnum opus *Foundation of Economic Analysis*, which was constructed in the time when nonlinear science and computer were not yet well developed. My book does what Samuelson foresaw what should be done after his influential milestone: "A natural fifth step to take after we have investigated the response of a system to change in given parameters is to investigate its behavior as a result of the passage of time." I also show what synergetic economics imply for modern economics. I recognized that it is the time to build a general economic theory in which main economic theories are treated as special cases. I started this process more than 30 years ago and this book reports the main results of the endeavor.

Chapter 2 starts the process of constructing the theory by building a model, called the basic model in this book, similar to the Solow–Swan model with an alternative concept of disposable income and utility function. It defines the basic model and its relations with some core growth models in macroeconomics. The first two sections develop the basic model and examine its behavior. Section 2.3 provides a theoretical foundation for the utility function proposed by the author. Section 2.4 shows that the rational behavior of household in the basic model yields the same economic mechanism as in the Keynesian consumption function. Section 2.5 shows that the basic model generates the same economic phenomena as the Solow growth model if I specify some preference change. Section 2.6 shows that the basic model generates the same economic phenomena as the Ramsey–Cass–Koopmans model with some endogenous preference change.

Chapter 3 generalizes the Walrasian theory. The traditional theory is for a stationary economic system. Walras introduced saving and capital accumulation in his general equilibrium theory. But his treatments of capital accumulation are not proper, especially in the light of modern neoclassical growth theory. Ricardo's *On the Principles of Political Economy and Taxation* of 1817 makes a valuable contribution to economics. Applying the law of diminishing returns in agriculture, he makes important development of the theory of rent. His study shows how wages, interest rate, and rent can be determined within a compact theory. This chapter integrates Walrasian general equilibrium, Ricardian distribution, and neoclassical growth theories as an extension of the basic model proposed in Chap. 2. The chapter also introduces exogenous shocks to the general equilibrium and demonstrates how various business cycles are generated by different exogenous changes. The appendix generalizes the model in cases of multiple capital and consumer goods.

Chapter 4 introduces education and human capital accumulation into the basic model. Adam Smith argues that improvement in the productivity of labor has their origins in the large part of the skill, dexterity, and judgment. Human capital is a consequence of the division of labor. But the opportunities and incentives to which workers respond in their investment in human capital are not fully considered by classical economists such as Smith, Ricardo, and Marx. When they were constructing theories, endogenous human capital accumulation via formal higher education was not very important. This chapter introduces Arrow's learning by doing, Uzawa's an education, my learning through creative leisure and learning through consuming as sources of human capital improvement. The chapter shows possible multiple equilibria when the economic system is composed of increasing returns to and decreasing returns to scale sectors. The chapter then introduces education sector and human capital into the Diamond model with debt. The chapter also provides insights into complexity of poverty traps in a human capital-based economy.

Chapter 5 proposes a general equilibrium growth model with wealth and human capital accumulation in a dynamic multi-race economy. Coexistence of multiple races in same labor and goods markets are common in modern economies. There is no proper theoretical treatment of income and wealth distribution in endogenous growth theories on the issue. Marx's theory on capital accumulation is too simplified to understand processes of complexity of income and wealth distribution between heterogeneous households. In *Capital in the Twenty-First Century*, Piketty examines issues related to wealth accumulation and income and wealth distribution. He collects many interesting data across many countries, but without a profound analytical framework. This chapter focuses on how racial differences in preferences and knowledge accumulation affect the national economic growth and racial income and wealth distributions.

Chapter 6 integrates knowledge as public goods and human capital as private skills with the basic model. Schumpeter admires Walras' general equilibrium theory and considers Keynes and Ricardo the "Ricardian Vice." Schumpeter's "creative destruction" is one of well-known economic ideas. Creative destruction needs conservative construction and conservative construction leads to creative destruction. Through his concept of innovations, Schumpeter argues that the entrepreneur will make innovations which cause the old ideas, technologies, skills, and equipment to become obsolete. Capitalist system contains destructive forces. The creative destruction will lead to social progress and enhance people's living standards. This chapter deals with implications of creativity and innovation for economic growth. In this chapter, knowledge is financially supported by the government, while human capital is accumulated via Arrow's learning by doing, Uzawa–Lucas' formal education, and Zhang's leisure creative activities. It also points out the way and importance of integrating new growth theory of innovations with microeconomic foundation.

Chapter 7 integrates the basic model with some well-accepted ideas in the literature of endogenous birth and mortality rates. Modern economies are characterized of fast capital accumulation, widely spread education and fast accumulated human capital, improved physical health, and unprecedented population dynamics (such as aging and declining fertility rates in developed economies). Malthus (1766–1834) holds that a large proportion of the general population are always poor and miserable. Two obvious trends are occurring in the world: developed countries experience negative population growth (especially minus immigrants), while many developing economies experience positive population growth. In the globalizing world, Malthus is still valid. The chapter first uses the Haavelmo's population model to demonstrate chaos in a simple model. It also shows how to explain dynamic phenomena with the model developed late on. The chapter integrates the basic model, the Haavelmo model, and the Oniki–Uzawa model to show trade, growth and population change in the global economy. Finally, I integrate the model in the previous section and the growth with human capital in Chap. 4 to show how endogenous human capital interacts with wealth accumulation and population growth.

Chapter 8 deals with dynamic interdependence between health, environment, and wealth with government intervention. There are many stock variables, such as physical wealth, resources, human capital, and knowledge, which Walrasian general equilibrium theory fails to properly analyze. The previous chapters introduced some stock variables into the basic model. This chapter introduces two important determinants of growth—health and environment—into the basic model. The chapter shows how to comprehensively explore the complexity of environmental change with economic development.

Chapter 9 introduces endogenous preference change, social status and fashion into the general equilibrium growth model developed in Chap. 3. People have different propensities to save, which affect income and wealth distribution and macroeconomic growth. People brought up in different societies and family conditions have different habits in consumption and decision making. People with different social status behave differently. Preference, habit, social status and fashions and their relations to economic conditions are traditional topics in economics. This chapter is concerned with social status and economic growth in association with income and wealth gaps. It also introduces the growth model with fashion dynamics. The chapter finally comments on how to integrate various ideas about human behavior from psychology with the models in this book.

Chapter 10 introduces issues related to portfolio choice and determination of assets prices into the general equilibrium dynamic model in Chap. 3. Households of contemporary economies are characterized by holding many kinds of assets such as housing, land, stocks, precious metals, cashes in different currencies. The complexity of portfolio is constantly increased in globalizing economies. The mainstreams of formal economic growth theory still pay little attention to the complexity of portfolio choice. The Ramsey approach—the main approach to household behavior in contemporary economics—is not suitable for the problem and the Solow model does not have a microeconomic foundation for rational behavior of households. Traditional dynamic economic theories fail to provide an effective microeconomic foundation for analyzing growth with portfolio choice.

Chapter 11 deals with issues related to money and economic growth. It is generally accepted that the modern monetary theory began from David Hume's essays of 1752, *Of Money and Interest*. Hume holds that the effect of changes in money should depend on the way in which the change is affected. Keynes intensified debates over money after he published *General Theory* in 1936. He holds that a fully competitive economy could get trapped into a disequilibrium situation (with unemployment). Pigou does not agree with Keynes, arguing that Keynes overlooked an important class of regulating mechanisms, namely the real balance, or wealth effects, which are interacting with nominal prices, wages, and interest rates. Different authors emphasize different aspects of money with different modeling frameworks. First, I integrate the basic model with the MIU approach. Then, I integrate the basic model with the CIA approach for a small open economy. Finally, I introduce the Taylor rule into the integrated Solow–Tobin and basic models.

Chapter 12 shows how monopoly theory, monopsony theory, and game theory, respectively, can enrich the theory developed so far on basis of perfect competition and government intervention. Various markets coexist in a modern economy. In modern microeconomic textbooks, students study perfect competition, imperfect competition, oligopoly, monopoly, and various games in the same course in microeconomics. But when students study macroeconomics, heterogeneous markets are seldom introduced in an integrated manner. Most of studies on imperfect competitive markets are not fully integrated with macroeconomics. Partial economic theories are proposed to examine demand and supply equilibrium, efficiencies, issues related to welfare and profit distribution of different market structures under varied rules and institutions. These markets are examined in microeconomics, industrial economics, and organization. This chapter and the next chapter introduce a few of my models to demonstrate how to integrate monopoly, monopsony, monopolistic competition, and games with the basic model.

Chapter 13 integrates neoclassical growth theory of perfect competition and new growth theory of monopolistic competition. Monopolistic competition is an important form of markets in modern economies. Monopolistic competition is characterized by many producers who produce differentiated products. Theory of monopolistic competition is formed initially by Chamberlin in 1933. It has been applied to different issues of economics related to economic structures, growth, economic geography, international trade, and innovation and technological diffusion.

Chapter 14 overcomes some essential problems in the H-O model by extending the basic model to a multi-country and multi-sector economy. Most of the previous chapters neglect the role of trade on national and international economic growth. This chapter deals with interdependence between international trade, global economic growth, and income and wealth distribution between countries. I am now focused on the Heckscher–Ohlin (H-O) model. It is a core model in neoclassical trade theory. The standard H-O model is built for a two-country global economy. Each country has access to the same technology for producing two goods using two fixed factors (labor and capital) under conditions of perfect competition and constant returns to scale. Factors of production are mobile between sectors within a country, but immobile internationally. No international borrowing and lending are allowed. The chapter integrates the basic model, Heckscher–Ohlin trade theory, and Oniki–Uzawa trade model. I also introduce habit formation and preference changes in different countries into the global trade growth model proposed in the previous section. The chapter also comments on the complexity of exchange rates and how to analyze exchange rates within the framework proposed in this book.

Chapter 15 integrates the core model in neoclassical urban economics and the basic model. Genuine dynamic spatial economics is required to understand mechanisms and processes of location as time and space are the elementary variables for spatial location over time. Mainstreams of analytical economics omit space mainly because a genuine spatial analysis results in analytically intractable problems. Only a few research papers in theoretical economics analyze the role of physical capital in spatial growth properly. This chapter provides a rigorous spatial model to show how to integrate urban economics with growth theories. Rigorous spatial economic theory has focused on the role of space on location. Economic theories with endogenous physical capital neglect the role of space. Alonso's residential distribution and Solow's growth models are integrated within a single whole. The land value, residential structure, and growth interact over time and space. The chapter also comments on how to integrate new economic geography and neoclassical growth theory on basis of the models in Chaps. 4, 12, and 13.

Chapter 16 concludes the study by pointing out important issues for future study within the framework proposed in this book. This book applies my concepts of current and disposable incomes and utility function to develop a general economic theory. I deviate from the Ramsey approach to household behavior in theoretical economics. The book has integrated various ideas and theories in economics within an integrated framework. All the models in this book can be integrated in a single model. I provide computational procedures to simulate all the models. An economic theory like the one proposed in this book should appear, even a few decades ago, only conceptual as there was no computer available to visualize movement of complicated dynamic systems. The recent development of mathematics, sciences, and computer and accesses to individuals as well as government data imply that the theory is not only operational and insightful, but also can be tested, extended, and generalized. There are more issues which can be analyzed by my analytical framework. I have focused on the main forces and simplified structures of the traditional theories. Each traditional theory referred in this book has a large amount of the literature. My theory is general with regards to connecting various main economic forces of different theories. From the beginning of constructing the theory, I have had kept in mind that each of my models should be constructed in such a way that it can be integrated with the rest of models without changing its basic assumptions. Moreover, each parameter in any model can be made exogenously or endogenously changeable.

This book involves many key models in different schools of economics. It would be a quite consuming process to follow the modern development of each theory mentioned in the book as, except knowledge about economics, it requires much knowledge in different fields of mathematics. Each theory has a huge amount of the literature equipped with an inextricable maze of symbols and mathematical theories. This book gives an easy to follow framework for examining multiple economic theories within an integrated framework. It is for graduate students and researchers in economics. Applied mathematicians may also find some interesting problems for applying technical skills to solve, for instance, nonlinear dynamic problems, or for building a supermodel, for instance, by integrating two or more models for any two chapters or by integrating other theories or ideas in the literature into some models in the book, not to say to introduce some important variables or relations into the economic theory open to be further developed. Most of the contents are based on my previous publications. I authored some books and peer-reviewed journal articles on the subject pursued in this book. I mention some of these resources when I refer to them in the book. This chapter is mainly based on *Synergetic Economics* and Zhang (1996, 2002). I do not give the proofs of mathematical results if they are available freely on the internet. I provide the paper's journal information when the results in a paper are mentioned. Most of these journal papers are freely available at https://ideas.repec.org/e/pzh151.html. The proofs are available from the author by e-mail: wbz1@apu.ac.jp, if they are not freely available from the website. There are some quotes from the common source: https://www.brainyquote.com, which I don't mention the book. I am grateful to the website.

References

Chamberlin E (1933) The theory of monopolistic competition. Harvard University Press, Cambridge
Haken H (1977) Synergetics: an introduction. Springer, Berlin
Haken H (1983) Advanced synergetics—instability hierarchies of self-organizing systems and devices. Springer, Berlin
Kuhn TS (1977) The essential tension. University of Chicago Press, Chicago
Orphanides A, Solow R (1990) Money, inflation and growth. In: Friedman B, Hahn F (eds) Handbook of monetary economics. North-Holland, Amsterdam
Prigogine I (1980) From being to becoming. W.H. Freeman, San Francisco
Prigogine I, Stengers I (1984) Order out of chaos: man's dialogue with nature. New Science Library, Boulder
Samuelson PA (1947) Foundations of economic analysis. Harvard University Press, Cambridge, MA
Schumpeter JA (1954) History of economic analysis, reprinted in 1994. Oxford University Press, London
Thom R (1977) Structural stability and morphogenesis. Addison Wesley, New York
Zhang WB (1989) Synergetic economics—dynamics, nonlinearity, instability, non-equilibrium, fluctuations and chaos. Working paper of CERUM, University of Umeå, CWP-1989, p 8
Zhang WB (1991) Synergetic economics. Springer, Heidelberg
Zhang WB (1996) Knowledge and value—economic structures with time and space. Umeå Economic Studies, Umeå
Zhang WB (1999) Capital and knowledge—dynamics of economic structures with non-constant returns. Springer, Heidelberg
Zhang WB (2002) Theory of complex systems and economic dynamics. Nonlinear Dyn Psychol Life Sci 6:83–101

Chapter 2
The Basic Model for the Integration

Technical skill is mastery of complexity while creativity is mastery of simplicity.
Chris Zeeman (1977)

I start to construct a general theory from a simple model, deviating from traditional economic theories in modeling human behavior. The model is called the basic model in the rest of the book. I have applied the basic model to integrate growth theory, monetary economics, resource economics, population economics, urban economics, interregional economics, new growth theory, international trade, and some other economic theories within a single framework. After introducing the basic model, in this, chapter 1 shows how the basic model is related to the Keynesian consumption theory, the Solow model, and the Ramsey growth model, which are main approaches to household behavior taught in macroeconomic courses.

2.1 The Basic Model

Simple can be harder than complex: You have to work hard to get your thinking clean to make it simple. But it's worth it in the end because once you get there, you can move mountains.
Steve Jobs

This section introduces the basic model which is the same as the Solow model and the Ramsey growth model with regards to production technology and markets. Its main deviation from the traditional models is how to model behavior of households with alternative concepts of the current and disposable incomes and utility function.

The economy under consideration has one sector and a homogenous population. The sector is composed of any finite number of identical firms. There is only one (durable) good produced and consumed. Households own assets of the economy and distribute their incomes to consume and save. Saving is undertaken only by households (this is assumed in the rest of the book). Firms use labor and capital

W.-B. Zhang, *The General Economic Theory*,
https://doi.org/10.1007/978-3-030-56204-5_2

inputs to produce goods. All markets are perfectly competitive. Factor markets work well and are always fully employed (this is assumed in the rest of the book).

2.1.1 The Production Sector

Let $K(t)$ and $N(t)$ denote capital stock and labor supply at time t. I use the conventional production function to describe a relationship between inputs and output. The production process is described by a neoclassical production function $F(t)$ which satisfies: (1) $F(t) = F(K(t), N(t))$ is non-negative if $K(t)$ and $N(t)$ are non-negative; (2) $F(0, 0) = 0$; (3) marginal products, $F_K(t)$ and $F_N(t)$ are non-negative. A production function $F(t) = F(K(t), N(t))$ is said to be the homogeneity of degree n for capital and labor inputs as follows: $F(\lambda K, \lambda N) = \lambda^n F(K, N)$, where λ is an arbitrary non-negative number. When $n = 1$, the production function is said to exhibit constant returns to scale. It is linearly homogeneous or homogeneous of degree one. A linear homogenous production $F(K, N)$ has the following properties:

(i) The production function can be written in terms of per capita output as a function of per capita capital:

$$\frac{F}{N} = F(k, 1) \equiv f(k), \quad k \equiv \frac{K}{N}.$$

Output per worker depends only on the amount of capital employed by one worker. The function is called the intensive form of production function or the per-worker production function.

(ii) The slope of $f(k)$ represents the marginal product of capital, i.e.,

$$F_K = \frac{\partial F}{\partial K} = \frac{\partial (F/N)}{\partial (K/N)} = f'(k) > 0.$$

(iii) The marginal product of labor can be obtained by:

$$F_N = \frac{\partial F}{\partial N} = \frac{\partial (NF/NK)}{\partial (N/K)} = \frac{\partial (f(k)/k)}{\partial (1/k)} = f(k) - kf'(k) > 0.$$

(iv) The Euler theorem holds:

$$KF_K + NF_N = F.$$

The increment to output per worker declines as capital per worker rises. Although more capital always leads to more output, it does so at a decreasing rate. The current profit of the sector (which is composed of any number of identical firms as in the Solow model) is given by:

$$\pi(t) = p(t)F(t) - (r(t) + \delta_k)p(t)K(t) - w(t)p(t)N(t),$$

where $p(t)$ is the price of product, $r(t)$ is the real interest rate, $w(t)$ is the real wage rate, and δ_k is the fixed depreciation rate of capital. The output good is chosen to be numeraire. I thus set $p(t) = 1$. The interest rate and wage rate are determined by markets. For any firm $r(t)$ and $w(t)$ are given at each point of time. Maximizing $\pi(t)$ with $K(t)$ and $N(t)$ as variables yields:

$$\begin{aligned} r(t) + \delta_k &= F_K(t) = f'(k(t)), w(t) = F_N(t) \\ &= f(k(t)) - k(t)f'(k(t)). \end{aligned} \tag{2.1.1}$$

By (2.1.1), I have:

$$(r(t) + \delta_k)K(t) + w(t)N = F(t). \tag{2.1.2}$$

The revenue is distributed between the payments of the input factors. Free competition and constant returns to scale lead to zero profit.

2.1.2 The Household's Current Income, Disposable Income, and Budget

I now describe behavior of households. I use $\bar{k}(t)$ to stand for the real value of the wealth per household. The representative household's current income $y(t)$ consists of the wage income $w(t)$ and interest of the household's wealth $r(t)\bar{k}(t)$:

$$y(t) = r(t)\bar{k}(t) + w(t). \tag{2.1.3}$$

I have the national wealth $\overline{K}(t) = K(t)$ as follows:

$$\overline{K}(t) = \bar{k}(t)N(t) = K(t) = k(t)N(t), \quad \text{i.e.,} \quad \bar{k}(t) = k(t).$$

The national current income $y(t)N(t)$ is equal to the total output minus the value of capital depreciation. The current income is not necessarily equal to consumption and saving because the household can, for instance, sell wealth to pay for moving to a better place to live. A retired man may live not only on the interest payment (as the Solow model implies) but also spend some of his wealth. It is assumed that selling and buying wealth can be conducted instantaneously without any transaction cost (this strict assumption is assumed in the rest of the book). Without taking account of the possibility of borrowing, the total value of wealth that the household can sell to purchase goods and to save is equal to $p(t)\bar{k}(t)$ (with $p(t) = 1$). The disposable income $\hat{y}(t)$ is defined as the current income and the value of wealth:

$$\hat{y}(t) = y(t) + \bar{k}(t). \tag{2.1.4}$$

In my approach, the value of wealth $\bar{k}(t)$ is a flow variable. The disposable income is used for saving and consumption. The variable $\bar{k}(t)$ might be considered the amount of the income that the household receives at time t by selling all the wealth. Hence, the household has the total amount of income equaling $\hat{y}(t)$ to distribute between saving and consumption. In traditional neoclassical growth theory and most empirical studies, disposable income is defined as the income that a household earns each period after taxes and transfers. It is considered the income available to the household for spending on goods and services and saving. When wealth plays minor role in analyzing behavior of households the traditional concept is not misleading. But when wealth is large and plays an important role in affecting household behavior, the omission in the income available for spending is misleading. Let us consider a case. A rich man with the net value of wealth US$70 billion will save a lot even if he had no current income (no pension and wealth earning a net zero rate of return). According to neoclassical growth theory (such as in the Solow model), the rich man makes neither consumption nor saving as his disposable income is zero. In my model, the man's disposable income is $0+70 = 70$. If his consumption annually is 0.1 billions, his saving is $70-0.1 = 69.9$ US$ billion. His actual saving rate is saving/(disposable income) $= 69.9/70$, rather than 0 as in the national statistical record (i.e., Bill Gate's saving rate may be the same as a beggar on Wall Street in economic papers and books). In my approach, rich people have a high propensity to save than poor people as the rich have too much to spend. Over years, economic students are educated with the propensity to save different from what I mean. The rich have much higher propensity to save than the extreme poor, as Marx knew this.

The household distributes the disposable income between saving $s(t)$ and consumption of good $c(t)$. I have the following budget constraint:

$$c(t) + s(t) = \hat{y}(t). \tag{2.1.5}$$

The household makes decision on how much to consume and to save. I interpret (2.1.5) as that consumption and saving exhaust the consumers' disposable personal income. The slope of the budget line is: -1, i.e., $ds/dc = -1$ due to the assumed homogenous capital goods for consumption and saving.

2.1.3 The Utility Function and Optimal Behavior

The utility level $U(t)$ is related to $c(t)$ and $s(t)$ as follows:

$$U(t) = U(c(t), s(t)).$$

I define the utility maximizing problem as follows:

$$\begin{aligned}&\underset{c(t),s(t)\geq 0}{\text{Max}} \quad U(c(t), s(t))\\&\text{s.t.}: c(t) + s(t) \leq \hat{y}(t).\end{aligned} \tag{2.1.6}$$

Lemma 2.1.1 *Let $U(c, s) : R_+^2 \to R^1$ be a C^1 function that satisfies the monotonicity assumption, which says that $\partial U/\partial c > 0$ and $\partial U/\partial s > 0$ for each (c, s) satisfying the constraint set in problem (2.1.6). Suppose that (c^*, s^*) maximizes U on the constraint set. Then, there is a scalar $\bar{\lambda}^* > 0$ such that*

$$\frac{\partial U(c^*, s^*)}{\partial c} \leq \bar{\lambda}^*, \ \frac{\partial U(c^*, s^*)}{\partial s} \leq \bar{\lambda}^*.$$

I have $\partial U/\partial c = \bar{\lambda}^*$ if $c^* \neq 0$ and $\partial U/\partial s = \bar{\lambda}^*$ if $s^* \neq 0$. If both $c^* > 0$ and $s^* > 0$, then

$$\frac{\partial U(c^*, s^*)}{\partial c} = \bar{\lambda}^*, \ \frac{\partial U(c^*, s^*)}{\partial s} = \bar{\lambda}^*.$$

Conversely, suppose that U is a C^1 function, which satisfies the monotonicity assumption and that $(c^*, s^*) > 0$ and the first-order conditions. If U is C^2 and if

$$\left|\overline{H}\right| = \begin{vmatrix} 0 & 1 & 1 \\ 1 & U_{cc} & U_{cs} \\ 1 & U_{sc} & U_{ss} \end{vmatrix} = 2U_{cs} - U_{cc} - U_{ss} > 0,$$

then (c^*, s^*) is a strict local solution to the utility maximization problem. If U is quasiconcave and $\nabla U(c, s)$ for all $(c, s) \neq (c^*, s^*)$, then (c^*, s^*) is a global solution to the problem.

The proof of this proposition and other general properties of the problem are referred to textbooks of advanced microeconomics or mathematical economics (Chiang 1984; Mas-Colell et al. 1995). It is required that U is a C^2 function and satisfies $U_c > 0$, $U_s > 0$ for any $(c, s) > 0$. It can be shown that $0 < ds/d\hat{y} < 1$ and $0 < dc/d\hat{y} < 1$ in the case of $U_{sc} \geq 0$ under the second-order condition of maximization. Let an optimal solution be represented as function of the disposable income $(c(t), s(t)) = \left(c\left(\hat{y}(t)\right), s\left(\hat{y}(t)\right)\right)$. The vector $\left(c\left(\hat{y}(t)\right), s\left(\hat{y}(t)\right)\right)$ is the Walrasian (or ordinary or market) demand function.

I now consider population as independent of economic conditions, as a first approximation. The population change is exogenously determined in the following way:

$$\dot{N}(t) = nN(t),$$

where n is the fixed growth rate of the population.

The change in the households' wealth follows:

$$\dot{\bar{k}}(t) = s(\hat{y}(t)) - (1+n)\bar{k}(t).$$

In a stationary state, I have:

$$s(\hat{y}(k)) = (1+n)\bar{k}.$$

This equation has a unique solution under certain conditions. The following theorem is proved in Zhang (2005).

Theorem 2.2.1 *Given a neoclassical production function and a utility function that is a C^2 function and satisfies $U_c > 0, U_s > 0$ for any $(c(t), s(t)) > 0$. Let the bordered Hessian be positive for any non-negative $(c(t), s(t))$. Then, the capital–labor ratio converges monotonically to a unique positive steady state. The unique stationary state is stable.*

The stability guaranteed above is local. If $s(\hat{y})$ is concave in $\hat{y}$, the system is globally stable. Because of $d^2c/d\hat{y}^2 = -d^2s/d\hat{y}^2$ from $1 = dc/d\hat{y} + ds/d\hat{y}$, concavity of s implies convexity of c. Asymptotical stability can be proved by applying Lyapunov's theorem.

2.2 The Basic Model with the Cobb–Douglas Functions

This section shows the behavior of the basic model when the production and utility functions are taken on the following Cobb–Douglas functions:

$$F(t) = AK^{\alpha}(t)N^{\beta}(t), \quad \alpha, \beta > 0, \quad \alpha + \beta = 1,$$
$$U(t) = C^{\xi}(t)S^{\lambda}(t), \quad \xi + \lambda = 1, \quad \xi, \lambda > 0, \tag{2.2.1}$$

where A is a number measuring overall productivity, and α, β, ξ, and λ are parameters. I use an aggregated utility function. The marginal conditions for the production sector imply:

$$r(t) = \alpha A k^{-\beta}(t) - \delta_k, \quad w(t) = \beta A k^{\alpha}(t), \quad f(t) = Ak^{\alpha}(t). \tag{2.2.2}$$

It is straightforward to solve the optimal choice of the consumers as:

$$C^*(t) = \xi \widehat{Y}(t), \quad S^*(t) = \lambda \widehat{Y}(t). \tag{2.2.3}$$

As the household's propensity to save becomes higher, out of the same disposable personal income the household saves more. As $\widehat{Y}(t)$ increases, both $C(t)$ and $S(t)$ are increased. An increase in $\widehat{Y}(t)$ may be caused either by increases in the interest rate, or the wage rate, or the wealth. If $r(t)$, $w(t)$, or $K(t)$ is increased, both $C(t)$

and $S(t)$ are increased. By (2.2.3), I have:

$$c(t) = \xi\left(A\bar{k}^{\alpha}(t) + \bar{k}(t)\right), \quad s(t) = \lambda\left(A\bar{k}^{\alpha}(t) + \bar{k}(t)\right).$$

The change in per household wealth follows:

$$\dot{\bar{k}}(t) = \lambda A\bar{k}^{\alpha}(t) - (\xi + n)\bar{k}(t). \tag{2.2.4}$$

Here, the depreciation rate is assumed to be zero. This is a Bernoulli equation in $\bar{k}(t)$. Insert $z(t) = \bar{k}^{\beta}(t)$ in (2.2.4):

$$\dot{z}(t) + (1-\alpha)(\xi + n)z(t) = (1-\alpha)\lambda A,$$

which is a standard first-order linear differential equation. The solution is:

$$z(t) = \left(z(0) - \frac{\lambda A}{\xi + n}\right)e^{-\beta(\xi+n)t} + \frac{\lambda A}{\xi + n}.$$

Insert $z(t) = \bar{k}^{\beta}(t)$ back to the solution:

$$\bar{k}^{\beta}(t) = \left(\bar{k}^{\beta}(0) - \frac{\lambda A}{\xi + n}\right)e^{-\beta(\xi+n)t} + \frac{\lambda A}{\xi + n},$$

where $\bar{k}(0)$ is the initial value of the capital-labor ratio $\bar{k}(t)$, which equals the value of wealth of the household. From the solution, all the variables are known at any point of time. As $t \to +\infty$, the exponential expression will approach zero. The unique steady-state value of $\bar{k}(t)$:

$$\bar{k}^{*} = \left(\frac{\lambda A}{\xi + n}\right)^{1/\beta}. \tag{2.2.5}$$

This steady state varies directly with the propensity to save λ, the total factor productivity A, and inversely with the propensity to consume ξ, and the population growth rate n. The right-hand side of (2.2.4) first increases and then decreases, and eventually becomes and remains negative. These imply the existence of a unique $\bar{k}^{*} > 0$ such that $\bar{k}'(t) > 0$ when $\bar{k}'(t) < \bar{k}^{*}$, $\bar{k}'(t) = 0$ when $\bar{k}'(t) = \bar{k}^{*}$, and $\bar{k}'(t) < 0$ when $\bar{k}'(t) > \bar{k}^{*}$. Thus, $\bar{k}^{*}$ is a globally asymptotically stable equilibrium for $\bar{k}(t)$. To see motion of the growth rate, we divide (1.3.4) by $\bar{k}(t)$. The growth rate $g_k(t)$ of wealth follows:

$$g_k(t) \equiv \frac{\dot{\bar{k}}(t)}{\bar{k}(t)} = \lambda A\bar{k}^{-\beta}(t) - (\xi + n).$$

Here, $g_k(t)$ stands for growth rate of the household's wealth. The above equation says that the growth rate of per capita capital equals the difference between two terms, $\lambda Ak^{-\beta}$ and $\xi + n$. When the economy has reached the stationary capital intensity, capital per capita will remain the same as time passes, but the capital stock $K(t)$ remains growing infinitely at the same predetermined rate as the labor force, n. The sustainable growth rate of the model is exogenously given by n. This can be confirmed by:

$$K(t) = \bar{k}^* N_0 e^{nt}, \quad F(t) = f\left(\bar{k}^*\right) N_0 e^{nt}, \quad C(t) = c\left(\bar{k}^*\right) N_0 e^{nt}.$$

2.3 The Theoretical Foundation of the Utility Function

Everything has beauty, but not everyone sees it.

Confucius

I now provide some insights into utility functions in the basic model. The following discussion on the relationship between the preference structure and utility function is referred to Barten and Böhm (1982).

At any point of time, the consumer has preferences over alternative bundles of commodities, which can be divided into goods, services, and time distribution of the consumer. The behavioral rule consists of maximization of these preferences under budgets restrictions of finance, or time, or human capital, or energy. A commodity is characterized by its location, date at which it is available, and its price. At each point of time, the consumer is faced with a commodity bundle consisting of (finite) real numbers:

$$\left\{x_j(t)\right\}, \quad j = 1, 2, \ldots, m,$$

indicating the quality of each commodity. The commodity space consists of commodity bundles. Here, I omit issues related to spatial location. Let us denote the price of commodity j by $p_j(t)$. For simplicity, I omit time index of x and p except in some circumstances. Both commodity vector x and price vector p can be represented by points in Euclidean space R^m, i.e., $x \in R^m$ and $p \in R^m$. The value of the commodity bundle at any point of time is given by $p(t)x(t) = \sum_j p_j(t)x_j(t)$. The consumption set, denoted by X, consists of all possible consumption bundles. It is required that the consumer's choices are restricted by the fact that the value of his consumption should not exceed his income $w(t)$, at each point of time. The budget set:

$$\beta(p, x, t) \equiv \{x \in X | px \leq w\},$$

is the set of possible consumption bundles whose value does not exceed the income.

The consumer has tastes and desires. Mathematically, the preference structure is represented by the consumer's preference relation, $\succeq_t$, at each point of time which is a binary relation on X. For any two bundles of goods, $x(t)$ and $y(t)$, $x \in X$ and $y \in X$ $x \succeq y$ mean that x is at least as good as y at time t. Before discussing the relation between the preference relation and utility functions, I introduce the following axioms.

Axiom 1 (Reflexibility)
For all $x \in X$, $x \succeq x$, i.e., any bundle is as good as itself.

Axiom 2 (Transitivity)
For any three bundles, x, y, z in X such that $x \succeq y$ and $y \succeq z$, it is true that $x \succeq z$.

Axiom 3 (Completeness)
For any two bundles, x and y in X, $x \succeq y$ or $y \succeq z$.

Axiom 4 (Continuity)
For every $x \in X$, the upper contour set $\{y \in X | y \succeq x\}$ and the lower contour set $\{y \in X | x \succeq y\}$ are closed relative to X.

A preference relation $\succeq$ which satisfies the first three axioms is a complete preordering on X and is called a preference order. A bundle x is strictly preferred to a bundle y, i.e., $x \succ y$ iff $x \succeq y$ and not $y \succeq x$. A bundle x is indifferent to a bundle y, i.e., $x \sim y$ iff $x \succeq y$ and $y \succeq x$. The indifference relation defines an equivalent relation on X, i.e., is reflexible, symmetric, and transitive. It is assumed that X includes at least two bundles x' and x'' such that $x' \succ y''$. In order to solve the problem of the representability of a preference relation by a numerical function, the concept of utility function is defined as follows.

Definition 1.4.1 *Let X denote a set and $\succeq_t$ a binary relation on X at time t. Then, a function u from X into real R is a representation of $\succeq$, i.e., a utility function for the preference relation $\succeq$, if, for any two points x and y, $u_t(x) \geq u_t(y)$ iff $x \succeq_t y$ at point of time t.*

It seems that Pareto was the first to recognize that arbitrary increasing transformation of a given function would result in identical maximization of a consumer. From the above definition I see that for any utility function u_t and any increasing transformation $f : R \to R$, the function $v_t = f \circ u_t$ is also a utility function for the same preference relation $\succeq$. The following theorem is referred to Debreu (1959) or Rader (1963).

Theorem 2.3.1 *Let X denote a topological space with a countable base of open sets and $\succeq$ a continuous preference order defined on X, i.e., a preference relation that satisfies Axioms 1–4. Then, there exists a continuous function u.*

The above theorem shows that under certain conditions, the concepts of utility and of the underlying preferences may be used interchangeably to determine demand at any point of time. When applying to my approach to households, I assume that a consumer is to choose consumption $c(t)$, and saving $s(t)$, with the disposable personal income, $\hat{y}(t)$, at each point of time t. The theorem guarantees the existence of a utility function.

2.4 The Basic Model Generates the Keynesian Consumption Function

The Keynesian theory of consumption is that the current real disposable income is the most important determinant of consumption in the short run. Keynes developed the idea of the consumption function, which consists of autonomous consumption and induced consumption. The autonomous consumption refers to consumption spending done as part of long-term plans for future. The induced consumption refers to increases in consumer spending as disposable income rises. Keynes postulated that current consumption expenditure has a stable relation to current income and that a greater proportion of income is saved as real income rises. According to Keynes (1936: 96): "... men are disposed, as a rule and on the average, to increase their consumption as their income increases, but not by as much as the increase in their income." There are many empirical works on identifying the consumption function. The traditional Keynesian consumption function posits that consumption is determined by current disposable income, i.e.,

$$C(t) = a + bY(t), \quad a > 0, 0 < b,$$

where a and b are constant, $C(t)$ is real consumption at time t, and $Y(t)$ is real disposable income (which is the same as the current income in my model), which equals GNP minus taxes. I swap the real disposable income in the Keynesian model with the disposable personal income, and the Keynesian consumption function with $a = 0$ is identical to the consumption derived from my rational choice assumption. It is called autonomous consumption. If a consumer's income is zero, some of his existing spending could be sustained by using savings. This is known as dissaving. Since Y in the Keynesian consumption function is the current consumption in the basic model, there seems no other relation between the two approaches without further exposition.

The Keynesian consumption is not a proportional relationship between consumption and income. The ratio of consumption to income is termed the average propensity to consume (APC), i.e.,

$$\text{APC} = \frac{C}{Y} = b + \frac{a}{Y}.$$

The average propensity to consume declines as income increases. The average propensity to consume is greater than the marginal propensity to consume, by the amount of a/Y. The ratio of saving to income is termed the average propensity to save (APS), i.e.,

$$\text{APS} \equiv \frac{Y-C}{Y} = 1 - b - \frac{a}{Y}.$$

The following relationship follows:

$$APC + APS = 1.$$

One of the implications of the Keynesian assumption is that the intercept a is independent of any change in wealth and other factors. Consider two persons, A and B, who started to work 5 years ago with the same conditions and the same preference. Their preferences were invariant during the period. Person A inherits a large amount of wealth at the beginning of the period (also assume zero interest income from the inherited wealth). Nevertheless, person B accumulates little from work. At the end of the period, they both lose the job. If the interest rate is almost zero, both persons A and B have no income. According to the Keynesian consumption, at this moment, when they lose job or are retired, persons A and B should have the same level of consumption (which is given by the intercept a). Intuitively, this is invalid as person A is richer than person B. It is reasonable to see that person A consumes more than person B. My theory will solve this problem.

In the rest of this chapter, the basic model is referred to my model with the Cobb–Douglas utility function. As shown before, the relationship between consumption and disposable personal income in the basic model is:

$$C(t) = \xi \hat{Y}(t) = \xi Y(t) + \xi K(t).$$

I now connect the basic model and the Keynesian assumption by treating a in the Keynesian model as a wealth-related variable. If I assume that the intercept a is dependent on wealth and marginal propensity to propensity b is related to the propensity to consume ξ in the following way:

$$a = \xi K(t), \quad b = \xi,$$

then the Keynesian consumption function is identical to the consumption function in the basic model. I call my consumption function as a generalized Keynesian consumption function. I can define the APC and APS, denoted by $\bar{c}(t)$ and $\bar{s}(t)$, respectively, for the basic model in the same way as in the Keynesian consumption function. In the basic model

$$\bar{c}(t) = APC \equiv \frac{C}{Y} = \frac{\xi(Y+K)}{Y} = \xi + \xi \frac{K}{Y},$$

$$\bar{s}(t) = APS \equiv \frac{S - K}{Y} = \frac{\lambda Y - \delta K}{Y} = \lambda - \xi \frac{K}{Y},$$

where I use $\xi + \lambda = 1$. According to the definition of the APS:

$$\bar{s}(t) = APS \equiv \frac{S(t) - K(t)}{Y(t)} = \frac{\dot{K}(t)}{Y(t)}.$$

The APC in the basic model rises as wealth increases or as current income declines; The APS in the basic model rises as wealth falls or as current income rises.

Another popular assumption is the so-called the life cycle hypothesis in analyzing households' behavior. The hypothesis was developed by Fisher (1930) and Harrod (1948). It was extended by Ando and Modigliani (1963); see also Deaton (2005). It assumes that individuals consume a constant percentage of the present value of their life income. This is dictated by preference and income. The hypothesis is to explain the empirical work on consumption function. It has been observed that the relationship between consumption and current income would be non-proportional and the intercept of consumption function is not constant over time. As stated out by Modigliani (1966), "The point of departure of the life cycle model is the hypothesis that consumption and saving decisions of households at each point of time reflect a more or less conscious attempt at achieving the preferred distribution of consumption over the life cycle, subject to the constraint imposed by the resources accruing to the household over its lifetime." Consumption depends not just on the current income but also on long-term expected earnings over their lifetime. Zhang (2005a) shows how the basic model can be related to this hypothesis. As shown in the models on taste change and habit formation in late chapters, my approach can integrate the lifetime cycle theory into the basic model. It should be noted that the life cycle hypothesis is a convenient assumption for empirical research as many kinds of data can be used in the approach, although the complicated conception does not produce some interesting theoretical model on which further theoretical models can be developed.

2.5 The Basic Model Generates the Solow Growth Model with Taste Change

The Solow model is the most well-known economic dynamic model. It is often called the Solow–Swan model because Swan's model is similar to Solow's seminal paper (Solow 1956; Swan 1956). The model is included in courses on introduction to economics. The model is taught to economics major undergraduates and to different major students in natural and social sciences. Its significance and popularity lie at its beauty, simplicity, consistency, and insightfulness. The model is a work horse of economic growth theory. Solow (1924–) received the Nobel Prize in 1987 "for his contribution to the theory of economic growth." In his Nobel Lecture in 1987, Solow

(2000: x) stated what he felt about the traditional growth theory: "Growth theory, like much else in macroeconomics, was a product of the depression of the 1930s and of the war that finally ended it. So was I. Nevertheless, it seemed to me that the story told by these models felt wrong." The Solow model is the main contribution for the prize. It has provided an analytical framework within which the mainstreams of modern macroeconomic theory have been extended, developed, and empirically tested. I was greatly attracted to its logic determination of output, growth rate, wage, interest rate, consumption level, and saving. A major problem for the model is its lack of microeconomic foundation for behavior of household as recognized by many economists. When I decided to generalize economic theories, I was aware of the necessity of overcoming this obstacle. The theory in this book is started from the Solow model, but deviates from it in modeling behavior of households.

The production sector in the basic model is the same as in the Solow model. It assumes that the agents regularly set aside some predictable portion $\hat{s}$ of its output for the purpose of capital accumulation; hence,

$$\dot{k}(t) = \hat{s} f(k(t)) - (n + \delta_k)k(t).$$

The differential equation for per-worker-capital accumulation in the Solow model is mathematically identical to the capital accumulation equation in the basic model:

$$\dot{k}(t) = \lambda f(k(t)) - (\xi + n)k(t).$$

The Solow model and the basic model have the same dynamic properties—the system has a unique stable equilibrium. But the basic model implies that the saving rate defined in the Solow model is time-dependent; the Solow model predetermines the saving rate.

I now show that under certain circumstances the basic model explains what the Solow model implies. For simplicity, let $\delta_k = 0$. The basic's capital accumulation is given

$$\dot{K}(t) = \lambda F(t) - \xi K(t). \tag{2.5.1}$$

In the basic model, the APS is given by

$$\bar{s}(t) = \frac{\lambda F(t) + \lambda K(t) - K(t)}{F(t)}.$$

The question is when $\bar{s}(t)$ is equal to $\hat{s}$, i.e.,

$$\frac{\lambda F(t) + \lambda K(t) - K(t)}{F(t)} = \hat{s}. \tag{2.5.2}$$

If the propensity to save λ is considered as an endogenous variable, the above equation holds if

$$\lambda(t) = \hat{s} + \frac{(1-\hat{s})n}{f(k(t))/k(t) + n} (< 1). \tag{2.5.3}$$

As $\xi(t) + \lambda(t) = 1$, $\xi(t)$ is also a function of $k/f(k)$. It is straightforward to see that under (2.5.3), the evolution of capital in the basic model is identical to that in the Solow model.

Lemma 2.5.1 *Let the production sectors be identical in the basic model and the Solow model. If the saving rate, $\hat{s}$, in the Solow model and the propensity to save $\lambda(t)$ in the basic model satisfy Eq. (2.5.3), then the basic model is identical to the Solow model in terms of the saving rate (out of current income), the consumption rate, the interest rate, the wage rate, output, income, consumption, and saving.*

The propensity to save $\lambda(t)$ is not constant. Take derivatives of (2.5.3) with respect to t:

$$\dot{\lambda} = \frac{(1-\hat{s})w}{(f+k)^2}\dot{k}.$$

The propensity to save out of the disposable income (defined by Zhang) rises (falls) as wealth per capita rises (falls). A fixed saving rate, as assumed in the Solow model, is generally invalid. As shown soon, another well-known growth model also leads to improper description of saving behavior.

2.6 The Basic Model Generates the Ramsey–Cass–Koopmans Model with Preference Change

It is dangerous to be right in manners on which the established authorities are wrong.
Voltaire (1694–1778)

The previous sectors showed why I use the basic model rather than the Solow model in modeling economic growth. The Solow model, simple as it appears, took many years for economics to build a simple mathematical model of economic growth from earlier efforts by, for instance, Cassel (1924), Harrod (1939, 1948), and Domar (1946). Although the Solow model is still a key model in textbooks of macroeconomics, the modeling of household behavior in contemporary literature of growth theory is primarily based on Frank Ramsey's 1928 paper (Ramsey 1928; see also Cass 1965; Koopmans 1965). Ramsey passed away at the age of 26. He made two important contributions to theoretical economics, both published in the Economic Journal.

His 1927 paper, *A Contribution to the Theory of Taxation*, was the seminal work in the formal theory of taxation. The basic idea of the Ramsey paper on taxation was first recently integrated with the growth theory by Zhang (2020a). His 1928 paper, *A Mathematical Theory of Saving*, laid the foundation of modern growth theory as far as broad 'saving' behaviors (such as wealth accumulation, human capital accumulation, and technological change) are concerned. In his obituary remark after Ramsey died, in the Economic Journal (1930, March issue), Keynes describes Ramsey's 1928 paper as:

> one of the most remarkable contributions to mathematical economics ever made, both in respect of the intrinsic importance and difficulty of its subject, the power and elegance of the technical methods employed, and the clear purity of illumination with which the writer's mind is felt by the reader to play about its subject.

I now describe the Ramsey approach. Most aspects of the Ramsey model (which is often referred to as the Ramsey–Cass–Koopmans model) are similar to the basic model, except modeling household behavior. The variables, $F(t)$, $K(t)$, $N(t)$, $k(t)$, $w(t)$, $r(t)$, in the Ramsey model have the same meanings. The difference is the description of household behavior. The Ramsey approach assumes that consumers maximize the discounted value of their flow of utility, using a constant rate of impatience, denoted by ρ. The household's preferences are expressed by an instantaneous utility function, $u(c(t))$, where $c(t)$ is the flow of consumption per person:

$$u(t) = \frac{c^{1-\theta}(t) - 1}{1 - \theta}, \quad \theta > 0, \tag{2.6.1}$$

where θ is a parameter. The household maximizes the following utility U:

$$U = \int_0^\infty u(c(t))e^{-\rho t} dt, \; c(t) \geq 0, \; t \geq 0.$$

The net assets per household are $k(t)$, and the total income at t is $w(t) + r(t)k(t)$. The flow budget constraint for the household is:

$$\begin{aligned} \dot{k}(t) &= w(t) + r(t)k(t) - c(t) - nk(t) \\ &= f(k(t)) - c(t) - nk(t). \end{aligned} \tag{2.6.2}$$

The requirement that the credit market imposes a constraint of borrowing implies that the present value of assets must be asymptotically non-negative:

$$\lim_{t \to \infty} \left[k(t) \exp\left\{ - \int_0^t \rho \, dv \right\} \right] \geq 0.$$

The present-value Hamiltonian is defined:

$$J(t) = u(c(t))e^{-\rho t} + \bar{\lambda}(t)(w(t) + r(t)k(t) - c(t) - nk(t)),$$

where $\bar{\lambda}(t)$ is the present-value shadow price of income. The first-order conditions imply:

$$\frac{\partial J}{\partial c} = 0 \Rightarrow \bar{\lambda}(t) = u'(t)e^{-\rho t},$$
$$\frac{d\lambda}{dt} = -\frac{\partial J}{\partial k(t)} \Rightarrow \frac{d\bar{\lambda}(t)}{dt} = -\rho\bar{\lambda}(t). \tag{2.6.3}$$

By (2.6.3), I derive:

$$r(t) = \rho - \frac{u''(t)c(t)}{u'^{(t)}}\left(\frac{1}{c(t)}\frac{dc(t)}{dt}\right). \tag{2.6.4}$$

Insert (2.6.1) in (2.6.4):

$$\dot{c}(t) = \frac{r(t) - \rho}{\theta}c(t) = \frac{f'(t) - \rho}{\theta}c(t). \tag{2.6.5}$$

The two eigenvalues are given by:

$$\varphi^2 - \rho\varphi + \frac{f''c}{\theta} = 0 \Rightarrow \varphi_{1,2} = \frac{\rho \pm \sqrt{\rho^2 - 4f''c/\theta}}{2}.$$

The system has a unique steady state. Since the two eigenvalues have opposite signs, the equilibrium point is locally saddle-path stable. The saddle point implies that the system will be exploded infinitely if it is not very accurately located on a given path. This is in contrast to what the Solow model (and the basic model) predicts as the Solow model has a unique stable equilibrium. One might imagine a small isolated island in which there is a small of population whose population structure is invariant. There is no technological change, no change in human capital, no monetary system, no taste change, no trade, and no limit on resource. One may rationally expect that people can live peaceful (routinely) over time. Even there is a storm which destroys, for instance, 5% of wealth, the economy will return to its life before the storm after some time. This is what the Solow model predicts. But by the Ramsey model which does not guarantee stability, even for a simplified economy just described, the Ramsey system may be destroyed by a small disturbance.

In summary, the dynamics of the Ramsey model follows:

$$\dot{k}(t) = f(k(t)) - c(t) - nk(t),$$
$$\dot{c}(t) = \frac{r(t) - \rho}{\theta}c(t) = \frac{f'(t) - \rho}{\theta}c(t). \tag{2.6.6}$$

If I find some equation of preference change in the basic model to generate the same behavior as (2.6.6), then the two systems should exhibit the same behavior in terms of consumption, capital accumulation, and incomes, even though they are built on different assumptions.

The basic model also follows the "accounting"—capital accumulation equation in (2.6.6). I now consider consumption of the basic model. The consumption per capita in the basic model is given by:

$$c(t) = (1 - \lambda(t))[f(k(t)) + k(t)].$$

Take derivatives of this equation in time:

$$\frac{\dot{c}(t)}{c(t)} = \frac{f'(t) + n}{f(k(t)) + nk(t)}\dot{k}(t) - \frac{\dot{\lambda}(t)}{1 - \lambda(t)}. \tag{2.6.7}$$

For the two models to have the same consumption change equations, it is sufficient for $\lambda(t)$ to evolve according to:

$$\dot{\lambda}(t) = \frac{f'(t) + 1}{f(t) + k(t)}\xi(t)\dot{k}(t) - \frac{f'(t) - \rho}{\theta}\xi(t). \tag{2.6.8}$$

The propensity to own wealth λ tends to rise (fall) when $\dot{k}$ rises (falls); it tends to rise (fall) when $r < (>)\rho$. I may interpret that the direction of change in λ is influenced by the direction of change in wealth as well as whether the rate of return of wealth is larger or smaller than the rate of time preference. If the wealth is increasing and the rate of time preference is higher than the rate of return, then the propensity to save will rise. If the wealth is falling and the rate of time preference is lower than the rate of return, the propensity tends to fall. In the other cases, the propensity may either increase or decrease.

If the preference change in the basic model follows (2.6.8), the consumption per capita in the basic model evolves in the same way as in the Ramsey model. I now examine the fundamental equation of the basic model, i.e.,

$$\dot{k}(t) = \lambda f(k(t)) - (1 - \lambda + n)k(t).$$

Theorem 2.6.1 *Let the production sectors be identical in the basic model and the Ramsey model. If the propensity to save, $\lambda(t)$, evolves according to Eq. (2.6.8), then the basic model generates the same dynamics of capital–labor ratio $k(t)$, and per capita consumption $c(t)$, as the Ramsey model does.*

This example illustrates how the Ramsey model is related to the basic model. I can similarly examine relationships between the two approaches when utility functions are taken on other forms. I now explain another difference between the Solow and Ramsey approaches. The Solow model determines consumption as follows:

$$c(t) = \left(1 - \hat{s}\right) f(k(t)).$$

Taking the derivatives of this relation with respect to t yields:

$$\dot{c}(t) = \left(1 - \hat{s}\right) f'(k) \dot{k}(t).$$

The change rate of consumption is positively related to the interest rate. The rational household has increasing, stationary, or decreasing consumption according to, respectively, whether the wealth rises, is stationary, or falls. The consumer adapts consumption level not according to the difference between the interest rate and discount rate for utility as the Ramsey model predicts. According to the Solow model theory, a Japanese consumer would consume more, irrespective of low interest, if his wealth increases; he would consume less, irrespective of high interest rate, when his wealth falls. On the other hand, the Ramsey model predicts:

$$\dot{c}(t) = \frac{f'(k(t)) - \rho}{\theta} c(t).$$

This implies that the difference between r and ρ determines whether households choose a pattern of per capita consumption that rises, stays constant, or falls over time. The optimizing household has increasing, stationary, or decreasing consumption according as the current real interest rate exceeds, equals, or falls short of the utility discount rate. According to this result, consumption always falls if the interest rate is low and the utility discount rate is high.

The influences of Ramsey's classical contribution are reflected in the fact that almost all the contemporary dynamic models of national, urban, interregional, or international economic growth with microeconomic foundation for behavior of households are based on the paper and its variations (like the overlapping generations model in discrete version). Since I started to write my thesis as a graduate student in civil engineering in 1984, I had applied the Ramsey model to different issues. But I soon felt uncomfortable about the Ramsey assumption. When deciding to build a general economic theory, I was aware of the necessity to abolish the Ramsey approach. In 1988, I had been aware of the necessity of creating an alternative approach to household behavior as I started to think of creating a general economic theory which should treat many theories within an integrated framework. Mathematically speaking, the Ramsey would not be a proper tool for my goal. Having recognized the limitations of the Ramsey approach, I had thought of some alternative approach for a simplification. I luckily hit on the ideas applied in this book. As many thousands of academic papers and books published in academically highly ranked places are based on this most frequently applied modeling, Keynes' saying: "The difficulty lies not so much in developing new ideas as in escaping from old ones" tells possible difficulties for a new approach to replace the well-accepted approach.

The acceptance of the Ramsey framework has not been based on a profound reason. Samuelson (1937: 161) asked for careful applications of the Ramsey model as follows:

> Any connection between utility as discussed here and any welfare concept is disavowed.
>
> It is completely arbitrary to assume that the individual behaves so as to maximize an integral of the form envisaged in [the discounted utility model].

It is easy to see what Samuelson means by looking at the form of utility formulation in the Ramsey optimal growth theory

$$\int_0^\infty U[C(t)]e^{-\rho t}dt.$$

The specified form means that the household's utility at time 0 is a weighted sum of all future flows of utility. The parameter, $\rho(\geq 0)$, is defined as the rate of time preference. A positive value of ρ means that utilities are valued less the later they are received. There are two assumptions involved in the Ramsey model. The first is that utility is additional over time. Although I may add capital over time, it is unrealistic to add utility over infinite time. Intuitively, it is not reasonable to add happiness over time. The second implication of the above formation is that the parameter ρ is meaningless if utility is not additional over times. It should be noted that Ramsey considered the meanings of this parameter from ethical perspectives. Ramsey interpreted the agent as a social planner, rather than a household. The planner chose consumption and saving for the current and future generations. Ramsey assumed $\rho = 0$ and considered $\rho > 0$ "ethically indefensible." If $\rho = 0$, by equation, consumption per capita always grows if the interest rate is positive irrespective of whether wealth grows or falls. Moreover, no convergence toward an agreed-on rate of impatience is identified. Warner and Pleeter (2001) estimate that individual discount rates vary between 0 and 70% per year. Rader (1981) holds that there is no reason to believe that different consumers have identical time preferences. Becker (1992) argued that if individuals have heterogeneous constant rates of impatience, the representative agent will not in general use a constant rate to discount the future. From their comprehensive survey on the literature on the Ramsey utility function, Frederick et al. (2002: 393–384) observe:

> The [discounted utility] model, which continues to be widely used by economists, has little empirical support. Even its developers—Samuelson, who originally proposed the model, and Koopmans, who provided the first axiomatic derivation—had concerns about its descriptive realism, and it was never empirically validated as the appropriate model for intertemporal choice.
>
> … [D]eveloping descriptively adequate models of intertemporal choice will not be easy.

When Frederick et al. mentioned difficulties of developing adequate models of household behavior over time, I had published my alternative approach one decade ago. As observed by Frederick et al., when the Ramsey approach "eventually became entrenched as the dominant theoretical framework for modeling intertemporal framework for modeling intertemporal choice, it was due largely to its simplicity and its resemblance to the familiar compound interest formula, and not as a result of empirical research demonstrating validity."

Malthus (1766–1834) points out an empirical law of academic games: "Each pursues his own theory, little solicitous to correct or improve it by an attention to what is advanced by his opponents." The Ramsey approach has provided a collectively accepted criterion for evaluating research funds, making professional promotion, providing job securities, determining contents of courses, and accepting academic articles. The main attitude toward the Ramsey approach is described by Turnovsky (2000: 273) as follows:

> Any model as widely employed as the representative agent model begins to take on a life of its own and to be accepted almost as an axiom. It is therefore useful to remind ourselves periodically of its limitations. Despite the criticisms that have been made, I feel that the representative agent model provides a useful framework that offers a good deal of insight, and I shall continue to develop it further.

This attitude has been continued till now and will last for quite some time. This book uses an alternative utility function not only because the validity of the discounted utility concept has been questioned from philosophical, psychological, and empirical aspects, but also because many obviously significant issues, such as growth with heterogeneous households and growth with interregional dynamics, can hardly be properly discussed with the Ramsey approach.

References

Ando A, Modigliani F (1963) The "life cycle" hypothesis of saving: aggregate implications and tests. Am Econ Rev 53:55–84

Barten AP, Böhm V (1982) Consumer theory. In: Arrow KJ, Intriligator MD (eds) Handbook of mathematical economics II. North-Holland Publishing Company, Amsterdam

Becker GS (1992) Habits, addictions and traditions. Kyklos 45:327–345

Cass D (1965) Optimum growth in an aggregative model of capital accumulation. Rev Econ Stud 32:233–240

Cassel G (1967) [1924] Capital and income in the money economy. In: The theory of social economy. Augustus M. Kelley, New York, pp. 51–63

Chiang AC (1984) Fundamental methods of mathematical economics. McGraw-Hill Book Company, London

Deaton A (2005) Franco Modigliani and the life cycle theory of consumption. Banca Nationale del Lavoro Q Rev 58:91–107

Debreu G (1959) Theory of value: an axiomatic analysis of equilibrium. Yale University Press, London

Domar E (1946) Capital expansion, rate of growth, and employment. Econometrica 14:137–147

Fisher I (1930) The theory of interest. Macmillan, New York

Frederick S, Loewenstein G, O'Donoghue T (2002) Time discontinuing and time preference: a critical review. J Econ Lit 40:351–401

Harrod RF (1939) An essay in dynamic theory. Econ J 49:14–33

Harrod RF (1948) Toward a dynamic economics. Macmillan, London

Keynes JM (1936) The general theory of employment, interest rate and money. Harcourt, Brace, New York

Koopmans TC (1965) On the concept of optimal economic growth. In: The econometric approach to development planning. North Holland, Amsterdam

Mas-Colell A, Whinston MD, Green JR (1995) Microeconomic theory. Oxford University Press, Oxford
Modigliani F (1966) The life cycle hypothesis of saving, the demand for wealth and the supply of capital. Soc Res 33:160–217
Rader T (1963) The existence of a utility function to represent preferences. Rev Econ Stud 30:229–232
Ramsey F (1928) A mathematical theory of saving. Econ J 38:543–559
Samuelson PA (1937) A note on measurement of utility. Rev Econ Stud 4:155–161
Solow R (1956) A contribution to the theory of economic growth. Quart J Econ 70:65–94
Solow R (2000) Growth theory–an exposition. Oxford University Press, New York
Swan TW (1956) Economic growth and capital accumulation. Econ Rec 32:334–361
Turnovsky SJ (2000) Fiscal policy, elastic labor supply, and endogenous growth. J Monetary Econ 45:185–210
Warner JT, Pleeter S (2001) The personal discount rate: evidence from military downsizing programs. Am Econ Rev 91:33–53
Zeeman EC (1977) Catastrophe theory: selected papers 1972-1977. Addison-Wesley, Reading
Zhang WB (2005a) Economic growth theory. Ashgate, Hampshire
Zhang WB (2005b) Differential equations, bifurcations, and chaos in economics. World Scientific, Singapore
Zhang WB (2020) Optimal taxation in the Solow-Uzawa growth model with public goods. J Soc Dev Sci 10:1–11

Chapter 3
An Integration of Walrasian General Equilibrium, Ricardian Distribution, and Neoclassical Growth Theories

A good completion takes a long time; a bad completion cannot be changed.
Zhuangzi (369–295 BC)

The most challenging question in history of theoretical economics is how to introduce endogenous wealth accumulation to general equilibrium theory. This question has challenged theoretical economists even since general economic theory was formally established. This chapter gives a solution of this historically challenging question.

In the *History of Economic Analysis*, Schumpeter (1954: 795) evaluated French mathematical economist Walras (1834–1910) as "… greatest of all economists. His system of economic equilibrium, uniting, as it does, the quality of 'revolutionary' creativeness with the quality of classic synthesis, is the only work by an economist that will stand comparison with the achievements of theoretical physics." Walras pioneered mathematically general equilibrium theory, by his 1874 and 1877 publications, *Éléments d'économie politique pure* (Walras 1874). Adam Smith addressed issue-related equilibrium of markets and the efficiency of this equilibrium through his theory of invisible hand. His theory is expressed verbally. He did not formulate his theory in a rigorous matter. Different from Adam Smith, Walras established a system of equations which described individuals' demand for goods and services and their supply of labor and other productive inputs and firms' demand for productive factors and supply of goods and services. In Walras' system, the balance of these demands and supplies is achieved by a set of prices. The equilibrium is mathematically solved by solving the set of equations (Arrow and Debreu 1954; Arrow and Hahn 1971; Arrow 1974; Gale 1955; Nikaido 1956, 1968; Debreu 1959; McKenzie 1959; Mas-Colell et al. 1995). Walrasian general equilibrium theory is a research field that has received a few Nobel Prizes. Maurice Allais (1911–2010) was awarded Nobel Prize in economics in 1988 for his contributions to the theory of markets and efficient utilization of resources. His contribution to general equilibrium theory was made in the 1940s by providing more rigorous mathematical formations of the theory and investigating the efficiency properties of market equilibrium. He also generalized equilibrium theory by taking account of various kinds of returns to scale due to natural monopolies. His works are often compared with (a parallel to) John

W.-B. Zhang, *The General Economic Theory*,
https://doi.org/10.1007/978-3-030-56204-5_3

Hicks' *Value and Capital* and Samuelson's *Foundations*. In 1972, Hicks (1904–1989) and Arrow were jointly awarded the Nobel Prize in economics for their pioneering contributions to general economic equilibrium theory and welfare theory. Allais's mathematical formations were general. His works served a basis for his pupil Gerard Debreu (1921–2004) who was awarded the Nobel Prize in economics in 1982 for his fundamental contribution to general economic equilibrium theory.

The Walrasian theory is for a stationary economic system. Walras introduced saving and capital accumulation in his general equilibrium theory. But his treatments of capital accumulation are not proper, especially in the light of modern neoclassical growth theory (Impicciatore et al. 2012). Over years, many attempts have been made to further develop Walras' capital accumulation theory within Walras' framework (Morishima 1964, 1977; Diewert 1977; Eatwell 1987; Dana et al. 1989; Montesano 2008). These approaches are not successful as they do not build the models on the basis of proper microeconomic foundation of wealth accumulation. To introduce wealth accumulation is challenging as one need microeconomics as behavioral foundation and integrate macroeconomics and microeconomics within a genuine dynamic framework.

As reviewed in the previous chapter, the mainstreams of economic dynamics have been dominated by the Solow and the Ramsey analytical frameworks in the last five decades (Burmeister and Dobell 1970; Barro and Sala-i-Martin 1995; Jensen and Larsen 2005). The two modeling frameworks have coexisted in "harmony" mainly because one cannot effectively replace the other. The Solow analytical framework is empirically friendly and easy to analyze but it lacks behavioral mechanism. The Ramsey analytical framework does seem to be theoretically sound as it is defined with utility maximization and budget constraints, but it lacks empirical support and sound reasoning for the assumed utility. A model based on the Ramsey approach tends to become analytically intractable when economic issue-related heterogeneous households, or multiple sectors, or urban structure, or interregional interactions are introduced. My basic model was developed to overcome the problems associated with the Solow and Ramsey approaches and shows an alternative way to model economic dynamics.

The rest of this book is to enrich Walrasian general economic theory with perfect competition by introducing stock variables such as wealth, human capital, knowledge, preference, environment, resources, money, prices and rents of various assets, portfolio choice, space, monopolistic competition, various games within households, organizations, industries, regions and nations, and many other important issues on the basis of the basic model. This chapter builds an economic growth model with economic structure and heterogeneous households. The model is concerned with not only the basic issues in Walrasian general equilibrium theory and neoclassical growth theory, but also basic economic mechanisms in Ricardian theory of distribution. The Walrasian general equilibrium theory determines economic equilibrium. But it fails to address important issues about interdependent between economic growth, structural change, and wealth and income distribution. Ricardo deals with income distribution. He explains how a shift in this distribution could affect accumulation. His *On the*

Principles of Political Economy and Taxation of 1817 makes a valuable contribution to economics. Applying the law of diminishing returns in agriculture, he makes important development of the theory of rent. His study shows how wages, interest rate, and rent can be determined within a compact theory. Ricardo considers three different production factors, labor, capital, and land. He provides a theory to determine the functional income shares of labor, capital, and land in the total income. Ricardo (1821: preface) states:

> The produce … is divided among three classes of the commodity, namely, the proprietor of land, the owners of the stock or capital necessary for its cultivation, and laborers by whose industry it is cultivated. But in different stages of the society, the proportions of the whole produce of the earth which will be allotted to each of these classes, under the names of rent, profits, and wages, will be essentially different; depending mainly on the actual fertility of the soil, on the accumulation of capital and population, and on the skill, ingenuity, and the instruments in agriculture.

Since the publication of the *principles*, many efforts have been made to generalize and extend the system. The beginning of modeling the Ricardian system perhaps dates back to 1833 with the model of Whewell (see Barkai 1959, 1966). Economists extended and generalized Ricardo's system in different ways (Cochrane 1970; Caravale and Tosato 1980; Negish 1989; Morishima 1989). For instance, Samuelson (1959) studies Ricardo-like models to reveal validity and limitations of the Ricardian propositions in a wider setting than that assumed by Ricardo; Brems (1970) considers fixed capital in the Ricardian problem of machinery; Pasinetti (1960, 1974) deals with the validity of what Ricardo means by making the necessary assumptions for Ricardian conclusions; Casarosa (1985) reforms the Pasinetti model to give a new interpretation of Ricardo with respect to the role of the market wages. What Ricardo (1821: preface) observes long time ago is still proper to state the contemporary situation:

> To determine the laws which regulate this distribution is the principal problem in Political Economy: much as the science has been improved by the writings of Turgot, Stuart, Smith, Say, Sismondi, and others, they afford very little satisfactory information respecting the natural course of rent, profit, and wages.

This chapter will make a further contribution to the literature of Ricardian economics.

3.1 Integrating the Walrasian General Equilibrium, Ricardian Distribution and Neoclassical Growth Theories

This sector studies an economy with three—agricultural, capital good, and consumer goods sectors. As shown in the Appendix in Chap. 2, it is straightforward to generalize the model with any number of capital and consumer goods. This section is based on Zhang (2017b). Let subscript index, *a, i,* and *s* denote agricultural sector, capital goods sector, and consumer goods sector, respectively. The agricultural sector supplies goods, such as vegetables, rice, and corn, for consumption. I follow the Uzawa two-sector model in describing the capital good and consumer goods sectors (Uzawa 1961). The population is classified into multiple groups; each group with fixed population $\overline{N}_j$ $(j = 1, \ldots, J)$. The Walrasian general equilibrium theory assumes $\overline{N}_j = 1$. I measure prices in terms of capital good. The wage rate of household j and interest rate are denoted by $w_j(t)$ and $r(t)$,, respectively. Capital good is selected to serve as numeraire. I use $p_a(t)$ and $p_s(t)$ to stand for, respectively, the prices of agricultural commodity and consumer good. All the markets are perfectly competitive. I denote the fixed land and land rent by L and $R(t)$, respectively. The total capital stock $K(t)$ is allocated among the three sectors. Let $N_m(t)$ and $K_m(t)$ stand for the labor force and capital stocks employed by sector m. The total population $\overline{N}$ and total qualified labor supply N are:

$$\overline{N} = \sum_{j=1}^{J} \overline{N}_j, \quad N = \sum_{j=1}^{J} h_j \overline{N}_j,$$

in which h_j is group j's human capital. Full employment of labor force implies:

$$N_a(t) + N_i(t) + N_s(t) = N.$$

3.1.1 *The Production Functions and Marginal Conditions*

The agricultural sector employs three input factors, land, labor force, and capital. I use $L_a(t)$ to denote the land used by the agricultural sector, $F_m(t)$ to stand for the production function of sector. The agricultural sector's production function is specified as follows:

$$F_a(t) = A_a K_a^{\alpha_a}(t) N_a^{\beta_a}(t) L_a^{\varsigma}(t), \quad \alpha_a, \beta_a, \varsigma > 0, \quad \alpha_a + \beta_a + \varsigma = 1,$$

where A_a, α_a, β_a, and ζ_a are parameters. The marginal conditions imply:

$$r(t) + \delta_k = \frac{\alpha_a p_a(t) F_a(t)}{K_a(t)}, \quad w(t) = \frac{\beta_a p_a(t) F_a(t)}{N_a(t)},$$
$$R(t) = \frac{\varsigma p_a(t) F_a(t)}{L_a(t)}.$$

The production function of the industrial sector and its marginal conditions are:

$$F_i(t) = A_i K_i^{\alpha_i}(t) N_i^{\beta_i}(t), \quad \alpha_i, \beta_i > 0, \quad \alpha_i + \beta_i = 1,$$
$$r(t) + \delta_k = \frac{\alpha_i F_i(t)}{K_i(t)}, \quad w(t) = \frac{\beta_i F_i(t)}{N_i(t)}.$$

The production function of the consumer goods sector and the marginal conditions are:

$$F_s(t) = A_s K_s^{\alpha_s}(t) N_s^{\beta_s}(t), \quad \alpha_s + \beta_s = 1, \quad \alpha_s, \beta_s > 0,$$
$$r(t) + \delta_k = \frac{\alpha_s p_s(t) F_s(t)}{K_s(t)}, \quad w(t) = \frac{\beta_s p_s(t) F_s(t)}{N_s(t)}.$$

3.1.2 Household Behavior

This sector assumes the public land ownership, which means that the revenue of land is distributed among the population equally. I will relax this assumption by assuming that land ownership is determined in free markets in Chap. 15. The total land revenue is given by $R(t)L$. Let $\bar{k}_j(t)$ and $\bar{r}(t)$ stand for household *j*'s wealth and land revenue. I have:

$$\bar{k}_j(t) = \frac{\overline{K}_j(t)}{\overline{N}_j}, \quad \bar{r}(t) = \frac{R(t)L}{\overline{N}},$$

where $\overline{K}_j(t)$ is the total wealth held by group *j*. Household *j*'s disposable income is:

$$\hat{y}_j(t) = (1 + r(t))\bar{k}_j(t) + h_j w(t) + \bar{r}(t).$$

Household *j* distributes the disposable income among savings $s_j(t)$, consumption of agricultural goods $c_{aj}(t)$, housing (measured by lot size $l_j(t)$), and consumption of consumer good $c_{sj}(t)$. The budget constraint implies:

$$R(t) l_j(t) + p_a(t) c_{aj}(t) + p_s(t) c_{sj}(t) + s_j(t) = \hat{y}_j(t). \tag{3.1.1}$$

Household *j*'s utility level $U_j(t)$ is a function of $l_j(t)$, $c_{aj}(t)$, $c_{sj}(t)$, and $s_j(t)$ as follows:

$$U_j(t) = l_j^{\eta_{0j}}(t) c_{aj}^{\mu_{0j}}(t) c_{sj}^{\xi_{0j}}(t) s_j^{\lambda_{0j}}(t), \quad \eta_{0j}, \mu_{0j}, \xi_{0j}, \lambda_{0j} > 0,$$

where η_{0j} is the propensity to consume housing, ξ_{0j} is the propensity to consume agricultural goods, ξ_{0j} is the propensity to consume consumer good, and λ_{0j} the propensity to save. It should be remarked that the heterogeneity in households in the literature of economic growth is due to the differences in the initial endowments of wealth rather than in preferences (Chatterjee 1994; Caselli and Ventura 2000; Maliar and Maliar 2001; Turnovsky and Penalosa 2006; Penalosa and Turnovsky 2006). The households in the traditional approach are essentially homogeneous as all the households are described with the same preference utility function. My approach considers the heterogeneity due to differences in utility function and human capital. Late on, I will model, respectively, social status, discrimination, and racial externalities within the general equilibrium framework.

Maximizing the utility subject to (3.1.1), I get:

$$R(t)l_j(t) = \eta_j \hat{y}_j(t), \quad p_a(t)c_{aj}(t) = \mu_j \hat{y}_j(t),$$

$$p_s(t)c_{sj}(t) = \xi_j \hat{y}_j(t), \quad s_j(t) = \lambda_j \hat{y}_j(t), \tag{3.1.2}$$

where

$$\eta_j \equiv \rho_j \eta_{0j}, \quad \mu_j \equiv \rho_j \mu_{0j}, \quad \xi_j \equiv \rho_j \xi_{0j}, \quad \lambda_j \equiv \rho_j \lambda_{0j},$$
$$\rho_j \equiv \frac{1}{\eta_{0j} + \mu_{0j} + \xi_{0j} + \lambda_{0j}}.$$

Household *j*'s change of wealth follows:

$$\dot{\bar{k}}_j(t) = s_j(t) - \bar{k}_j(t).$$

3.1.3 Demand and Supply of the Three Sectors and Full Employment of Factors

The equilibrium of demand of and supply for the agricultural good is:

$$\sum_{j=1}^{J} c_{aj}(t)\overline{N}_j = F_a(t).$$

The demand and supply equilibrium for the consumer goods sector is:

$$\sum_{j=1}^{J} c_{sj}(t)\overline{N}_j = F_s(t).$$

The output of the capital goods sector equals the net savings and the depreciation of capital stock:

$$S(t) - K(t) + \delta_k K(t) = F_i(t),$$

where

$$S(t) \equiv \sum_{j=1}^{J} s_j(t)\overline{N}_j, \quad K(t) = \sum_{j=1}^{J} \bar{k}_j(t)\overline{N}_j.$$

The total capital stock $K(t)$ is fully used by the three sectors:

$$K_a(t) + K_i(t) + K_s(t) = K(t).$$

The land is fully used:

$$L_a(t) + \sum_{j=1}^{J} l_j(t)\overline{N}_j = L.$$

I completed the model. The model is structurally similar with the Ricardian models formed by Pasinetti and Samuelson. It is structurally similar with the growth models for the dual economy (Todaro 1969; Kaiyama 1973; Marino 1975; Amano 1980).

3.2 Dynamic Behavior of the Economy

Before simulating the model, I introduce a new variable z(t) and expression { } as:

$$z(t) \equiv \frac{r(t) + \delta_k}{w_j(t)/h_j}, \quad \{\bar{k}_j(t)\} \equiv (\bar{k}_2(t), \cdots, \bar{k}_J(t)).$$

In the rest of book, I use { } as defined above. The following lemma holds.

Lemma 3.2.1 *The motion of the economy is given by J differential equations with* $z(t)$ *and* $\{\bar{k}_j(t)\}$ *as variables:*

$$\dot{z}(t) = \Lambda_1\left(z(t), \{\bar{k}_j(t)\}\right),$$
$$\dot{\bar{k}}_j(t) = \Lambda_j\left(z(t), \{\bar{k}_j(t)\}\right), \quad j = 2, \ldots, J,$$

in which $\Lambda_j(t)$ *are unique functions of* $z(t)$ *and* $\{\bar{k}_j(t)\}$ *defined* (Zhang 2017b). *The other variables uniquely as functions of* $z(t)$ *and* $\{\bar{k}_j(t)\}$ *by following a computational procedure.*

In Zhang (2017b), a computational procedure is given for plotting the motion of the economy with any number of types of households. For simulating the model, the parameters are taken on the following values:

$$A_i = 1.3, \quad A_s = 1, \quad A_a = 0.8, \quad L = 10, \quad \alpha_i = 0.34, \quad \alpha_s = 0.3,$$
$$\alpha_a = 0.17, \quad \beta_a = 0.2, \quad \delta_k = 0.05,$$
$$\begin{pmatrix} N_1 \\ N_2 \\ N_3 \end{pmatrix} = \begin{pmatrix} 12 \\ 40 \\ 20 \end{pmatrix}, \quad \begin{pmatrix} h_1 \\ h_2 \\ h_3 \end{pmatrix} = \begin{pmatrix} 3 \\ 1.5 \\ 0.6 \end{pmatrix}, \quad \begin{pmatrix} \lambda_{10} \\ \lambda_{20} \\ \lambda_{30} \end{pmatrix} = \begin{pmatrix} 0.78 \\ 0.75 \\ 0.7 \end{pmatrix}, \tag{3.2.1}$$
$$\begin{pmatrix} \xi_{10} \\ \xi_{20} \\ \xi_{30} \end{pmatrix} = \begin{pmatrix} 0.12 \\ 0.16 \\ 0.18 \end{pmatrix}, \quad \begin{pmatrix} \eta_{10} \\ \eta_{20} \\ \eta_{30} \end{pmatrix} = \begin{pmatrix} 0.2 \\ 0.16 \\ 0.14 \end{pmatrix}, \quad \begin{pmatrix} \mu_{10} \\ \mu_{20} \\ \mu_{30} \end{pmatrix} = \begin{pmatrix} 0.06 \\ 0.08 \\ 0.09 \end{pmatrix}.$$

The population of group 2 is largest, while the population of group 3 is the next. The human capital level of group 1 is highest, while the human capital level of group 3 is lowest. The total factor productivities of the capital good, agricultural, and consumer goods sectors are, respectively, 1.3, 1, and 0.8. I specify the values of the parameters, α_j, in the Cobb–Douglas productions for the capital good and consumer goods sectors approximately equal to 0.3 (for instance, Miles and Scott 2005; Abel et al. 2007). The depreciation rate of physical capital is specified at 0.05. Group 1's propensity to save is 0.78 and group 3's propensity to save is 0.7. The value of group 2's propensity is between the two groups. The initial conditions are specified as in (3.2.2):

$$z(0) = 0.045, \quad \bar{k}_2(0) = 15, \quad \bar{k}_3(0) = 8.5. \tag{3.2.2}$$

The motion of the variables is plotted in Fig. 3.1, in which the national output is defined:

$$Y(t) = F_i(t) + p_s(t)F_s(t) + p_a(t)F_a(t) + (L_0 - L_a(t))R(t).$$

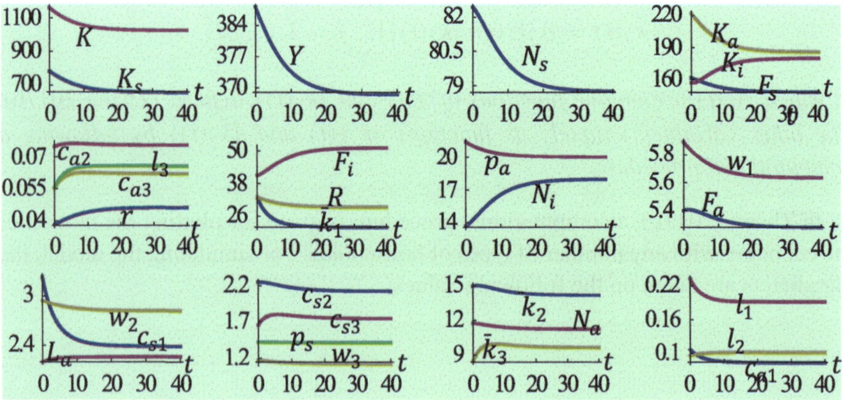

Fig. 3.1 The motion of the economy

The output level of the capital goods sector is enhanced. The output levels of the consumer good and agricultural sectors fall over time. The interest rate rises. The wage rates of the three groups fall. The national capital stocks and output fall. The consumption levels of the three groups also vary over time. The economic structure varies over time.

The simulation shows that the system has a unique equilibrium. The equilibrium values are given as follows:

$$\begin{array}{c} Y = 596.2, \quad K = 1025.6, \quad F_i = 51.28, \quad F_s = 148.9, \quad F_a = 5.28, \\ r = 0.046, \quad R = 29.42, \quad p_a = 20.02, \quad p_s = 1.42, \quad w_1 = 5.64, \\ w_2 = 2.82, \quad w_3 = 1.13, \quad L_a = 2.26, \quad N_a = 11.25, \quad N_i = 18.0, \\ N_s = 78.75, \quad K_a = 186.5, \quad K_i = 180.9, \quad K_s = 658.2, \quad \bar{k}_1 = 22.07, \\ \bar{k}_2 = 14.18, \quad \bar{k}_3 = 9.67, \quad c_{s1} = 2.39, \quad c_{s2} = 2.13, \quad c_{s3} = 1.75, \\ c_{a1} = 0.085, c_{a2} = 0.075, \quad c_{a3} = 0.062, \quad l_1 = 0.192, \quad l_2 = 0.103, \\ l_3 = 0.066. \end{array}$$

It is straightforward to calculate the three eigenvalues as follows:

$$\{-0.335, -0.303, -0.159\}.$$

The real parts of the eigenvalues are negative. The unique equilibrium is locally stable.

3.3 Changes in the Preferences and Human Capital Affect the Dynamics

I now conduct comparative dynamics analysis with regards to different exogenous changes.

3.3.1 Group 1 Augments the Propensity to Save

Preferences of different households are important for understanding economic structures as demonstrate in the Walrasian general equilibrium theory. Nevertheless, economics has not yet an effective analytical framework for analyzing effects of changes in one type of households on national economic growth as well as wealth and income distribution among different households. As my analytical framework integrates the economic mechanism of the Walrasian general equilibrium theory and neoclassical growth theory, in principle I can analyze effects a change in the preference of any people on the dynamic path of the economic growth. First, I examine the case that group 1 increases its propensity to save in the following way:

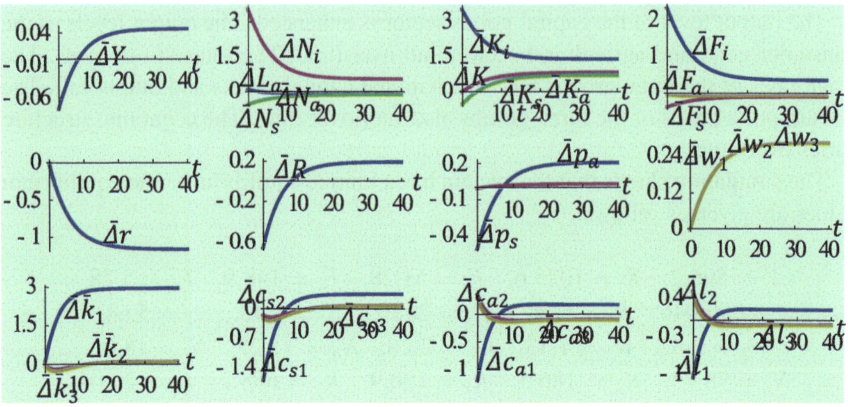

Fig. 3.2 A rise in group 1's propensity to save

λ_{01}: 0.78 ⇒ 0.8. The simulation results are given in Fig. 3.2. Group 1's per capita wealth is increased. The levels of agricultural and service consumption and lot size are lessened initially ad subsequently increased. This occurs as the group saves more from the disposable income, the household consumes less. Nevertheless, as the household has more wealth and the wage rate is also increased, the disposable income is increased in the long term, which leads to the rises in the consumption levels. Hence, group 1 benefits from saving more from the disposable income in the long term. As far as the transitory effects are concerned, the effects on the other two groups are different. The two groups' per capita wealth and service consumption levels are slightly affected, initially being reduced and augmented in the long term. The lot sizes and consumption levels of agricultural goods are initially increased and subsequently lowered. Although the two groups' wage rates are increased, as the land rent and price of agricultural goods fall initially ad rise subsequently, the net effects on the two variables on the two groups are negative. As more capital is accumulated as a consequence of the rise in the propensity to save, the interest rate falls. As more capital good is produced, labor force is shifted from the service and agricultural goods sectors to the capital goods sector. The capital stock employed by the capital goods sector is increased. The capital stocks employed by the other two sectors fall initially but rise subsequently. As group 1 (the rich group) reduces initially the demand for lot size and agricultural good, the land rent and price of consumer goods sector fall; subsequently as the group has more disposable income and its demand for lot size and agricultural good are increased, the land rent and price of consumer goods sector rise. The output level of the capital goods sector is increased, while the output levels of the other two sectors are slightly reduced. The impact on the national output is negative initially and positive in the long term.

3.3.2 Group 1 Improves the Human Capital

The impact of human capital is currently a main topic in economic theory and empirical research. In modern economies, one of the key determinants of economic growth is human capital. There are many studies on estimating the impact of education on earnings since Mincer's seminal work in 1974 (Mincer 1974). Earlier studies Tilak (1989) demonstrate that inequality within countries can be reduced in association with spread education. Could et al. (2001) construct an economic model, concluding that increasing randomness is the primary factor for inequality growth among uneducated workers, but inequality growth within educated workers is mainly due to changes in the composition and return to ability (Tselios 2008; Fleisher et al. 2011). I now re-examine issues related to how differences in human capital affect wealth and income distribution among heterogeneous households during transitory processes and in long-term steady state. I now allow group 1 to improve its human capital as follows: h_1: $3 \Rightarrow 3.1$. I plot the simulation results in Fig. 3.3. The rise in group 1's human capital leads to the rise in the group's wage rate, while the other two groups' wage rates are slightly affected. Hence, the wage gaps between group 1 and the other two groups are enlarged. It should be remarked that the wage gaps due to the change in the propensity to save just analyzed are not so strongly affected like in the case of change in the human capital. As group 1 increases its wage, its lot size, wealth level, and the consumption levels of the two goods are all increased both in the short term and in the long term. The other two groups' lot sizes are reduced. The other two groups reduce their consumption levels of agricultural good. As the households accumulate more wealth, one observes falls in the interest rate. The land rent and the price of agricultural good are increased, while the price of consumer good is almost not affected. The output levels of the three sectors and the national output are increased.

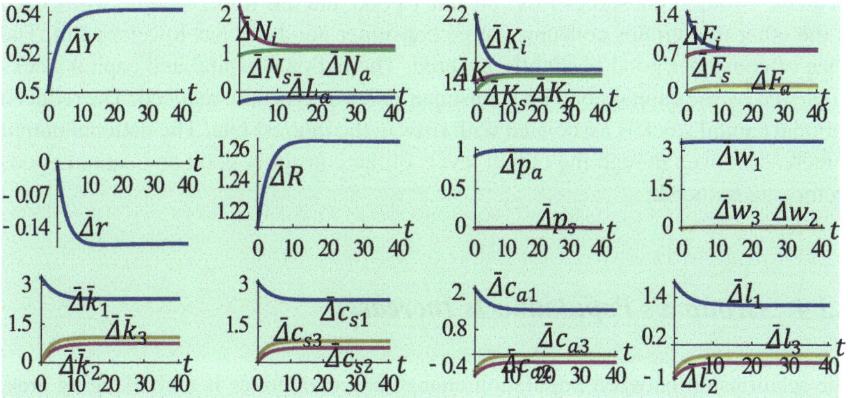

Fig. 3.3 A rise in group 1's human capital

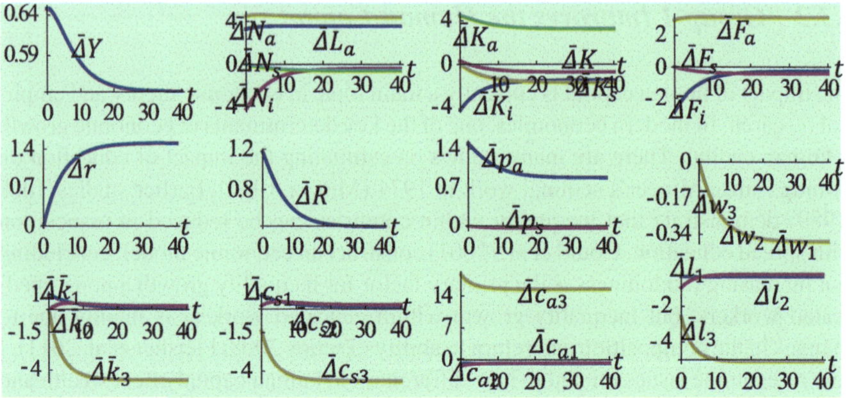

Fig. 3.4 A rise in group 3's propensity to consume agricultural good

3.3.3 Group 3 Increases Propensity to Consume Agricultural Good

I now examine how group 3's preference for agricultural good may affect the economic structure and growth. I allow group 3 to increase its propensity to consume agricultural good as follows: μ_{03}: $0.09 \Rightarrow 0.11$. I plot the simulation results in Fig. 3.4. The preference change leads to more consumption of agricultural good by the group. The increased demand results in the rise of supply in the agricultural sector. The agricultural sector employs more labor, capital, and land. The land rent and the price of agricultural good are thus increased. The increased price of agricultural good makes the other groups consume less agricultural good. As more land is employed by the agricultural sector and the land rent is increased, the other two groups use less lot sizes. Group 3 consumes less consumer good and has lower wealth, while each of the other two groups consumes more consumer good and has lower wealth. The price of consumer good is slightly lowered. The national capital and capital stocks employed by the capital good and consumer goods sectors are reduced. The reduced national capital stock is associated with rises in the interest rate. The national output is increased, even though the output levels of the consumer good and capital goods sectors are reduced.

3.3.4 Group 3's Population Is Increased

The relationship between population change and economics is a challenging area. Although this study assumes the population fixed, it is important to examine effects of changes in the population sizes. As different countries have different levels of knowledge utilization efficiency and creativity, increases in the population sizes may

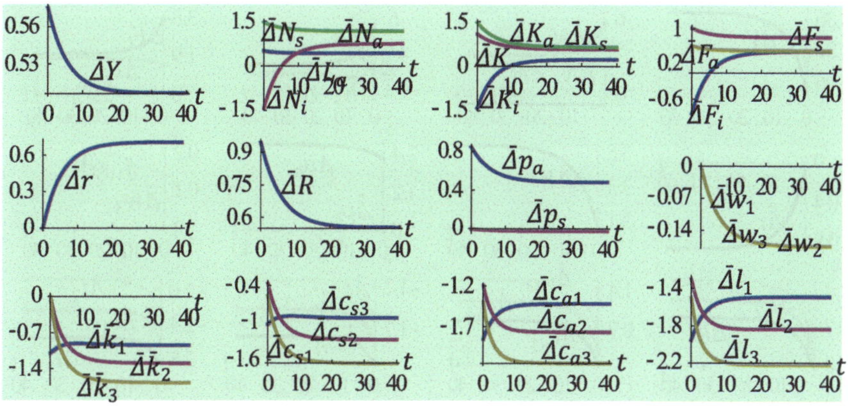

Fig. 3.5 A rise in group 3's population

have different effects upon the global economy. It has been observed that the effect of population growth varies with the level of economic development and can be positive for some developed economies. Theoretical models with human capital predict situation-dependent interdependence of population and economic development. I now allow group 3's population to be increase as follows: N_3: 20 $\Rightarrow$ 22. The results are plotted in Fig. 3.5. I see that as far as the aggregate real variables are concerned, in the long term, the national output, the total capital stock, the capital inputs, the labor inputs and land input, the output levels of the three sectors are all increased. I note that group 3 has the lowest level of human capital. Hence, a rise in the population lowers the average level of human capital of the population. It is expectable to see that the wage rates are reduced as consequences of the fall in group 3's population. The rise in the unskilled population lowers the wealth levels, consumption levels of consumer and agricultural goods, and lot sizes for all the groups. The land rent and the prices of the two goods are enhanced.

3.3.5 Group 1's Population Being Increased

I analyzed the effects of change in group 3's population. It is interesting to compare effects of changes the populations with the highest and lowest levels of human capital. I now allow group 1's population to be increase as follows: N_1: 12 $\Rightarrow$ 13. The results are plotted in Fig. 3.6. I see that as far as the aggregate real variables are concerned, in the long term, the national output, the total capital stock, the capital inputs, the labor inputs and land input, the output levels of the three sectors are all increased. Hence, the aggregated variables are affected similarly by the changes in the two group's population. In contrast to the rise in the rise in group 3's population, a rise in group 1's population enhances the wage rates. The rise in the skilled population lowers the consumption levels of agricultural good and lot sizes for all the groups as

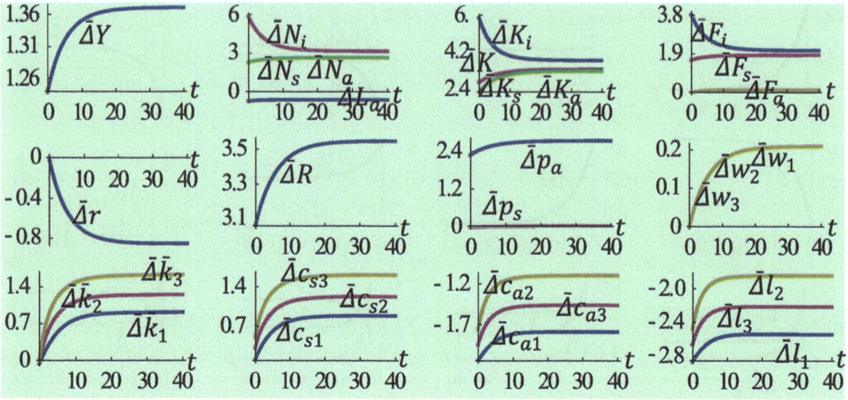

Fig. 3.6 A rise in group 1's population

the rise in the unskilled population; but different from the case of the rise in unskilled population, the rise in the skilled population raises the wealth levels and consumption levels of consumer good for all the groups.

3.4 Business Cycles Due to Exogenous Shocks in the General Model

When I started to construct the general economic theory, I have kept in mind that any partial theory can be related to another other partial theory (theories). Any parameter in the theories can be allowed to be changed either endogenously or exogenously. This section illustrates what I mean by allowing any parameter(s) to be subject to any type of exogenous changes. This section also makes a contribution to the literature of business cycles (Zhang 1991, 2005, 2006; Lorenz 1993; Chiarella and Flaschel 2000; Shone 2002; Gandolfo 2005; Puu 2011; Stachurski et al. 2014). This section is based on Zhang (2018d).

The model in this section is the same as the model in Sect. 3.1, except that any parameter in the system is exogenously dependent on time. It can be shown that the motion of the economic system is given by J differential equations:

$$\dot{z}(t) = \Lambda_1\left(z(t), \left\{\bar{k}_j(t)\right\}, t\right), \quad \dot{\bar{k}}_j(t) = \Lambda_j\left(z(t), \left\{\bar{k}_j(t)\right\}, t\right), \quad j = 2, \ldots, J.$$

If the parameters are taken on the values as in (3.2.1), the system is identical with the dynamics in Sect. 3.1. This section shows oscillations around the paths plotted in Fig. 3.1.

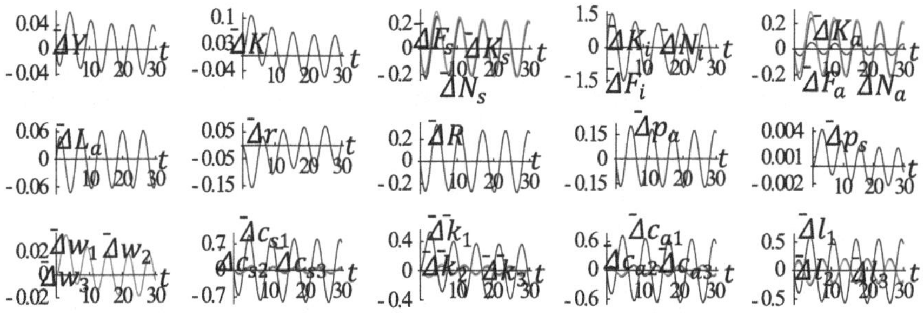

Fig. 3.7 Group 1's propensity to save periodically oscillates

3.4.1 Group 1's Propensity to Save Periodically Oscillates

I now examine a case that group 1's propensity to save periodically oscillates as follows:

$$\lambda_{01}(t) = 0.78 + 0.01 sin(t).$$

Figure 3.7 plots the simulation results. The national economy experiences business cycles. The variables related to group 1's oscillate more greatly than the corresponding variables of the other two groups.

3.4.2 Group 1's Human Capital Periodically Oscillates

Human capital is an important determinant of economic growth. I now examine whether exogenous changes in human capital may result in business cycles. I now allow group 1's human capital to periodically oscillate as follows:

$$h_1(t) = 3 + 0.1 sin(t).$$

I plot the simulation results in Fig. 3.8. Time-dependent perturbations in group 1's human capital result in business cycles in the national economy.

3.4.3 Group 3's Propensity to Consume Agricultural Good Periodically Oscillates

I now examine how group 3's preference for agricultural good may affect the economic structure and growth. I allow group 3 to increase its propensity to consume agricultural good as follows: μ_{03}: 0.09 $\Rightarrow$ 0.11. Figure 3.9 plots the simulation results.

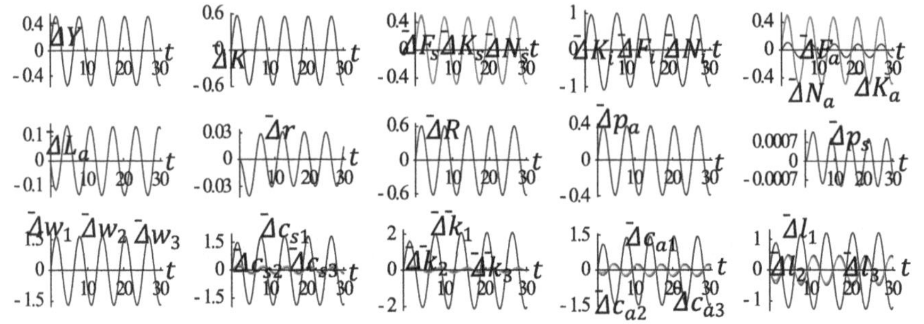

Fig. 3.8 Group 1's human capital periodically oscillates

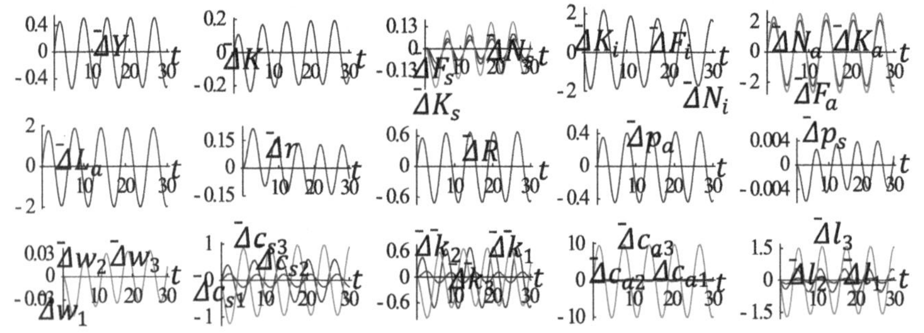

Fig. 3.9 Group 3's propensity to consume agricultural good oscillates

3.4.4 Group 3's Population Periodically Oscillates

There are many theoretical growth models with human capital and population (Galor and Weil 1999; Bretschger 2013). There are mixed conclusions from empirical studies related to issues (Furuoka 2009). Although this section does not analyze endogenous change in population, I show that periodic population change results in business cycles. I consider a case that group 3's population periodically oscillates as follows:

$$N_3(t) = 20 + sin(t).$$

Figure 3.10 plots the simulation results.

3.5 On Income Gaps and Real Business Cycle Theory

The chapter first dealt with relations between inequality and economic growth. Figure 3.2 shows that during the transitory process the rich group's and the other

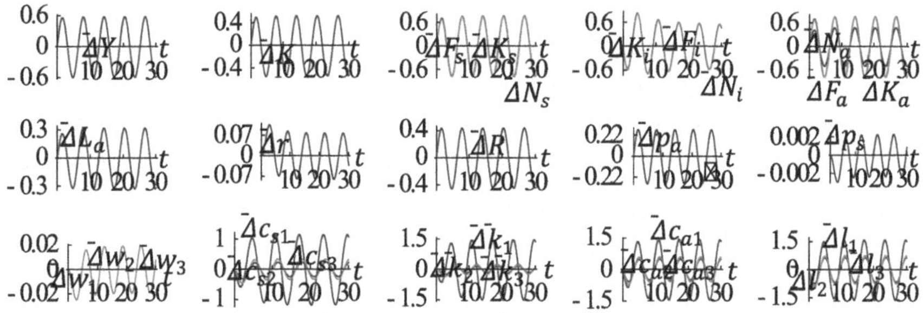

Fig. 3.10 Group 3's population periodically oscillates

two groups' wealth levels are enlarged, the national output experiences negative growth; while in the long term the rich group's and the other two groups' wealth levels continue to be enlarged, the national output experiences positive growth. The comparative analysis shows that to understand growth and development processes, it is important to classify the population into different types according to their preferences and human capital. For instance, if the population of the group with the lowest (highest) level of human capital is increased, the wage rates and the wealth levels and consumption levels of consumer good of all the groups are reduced (enhanced).

Section 3.4 demonstrates how to create business cycles according to exogenous shocks. The real business cycle theory generally believes that large and sudden changes are caused by changes in production technology and that monetary policy is irrelevant for explaining economic fluctuations (Kydland and Prescott 1982; Stadler 1994; Heijdra 2017). The 2004 Nobel Prize was shared by Finn E. Kydland (1943–) and Edward C. Prescott (1940–) for their researches on dynamic macroeconomics. They studied driving forces behind economic fluctuations and the design of economic policy. They are influential in economic theories as well as the practice of monetary and fiscal policy in many countries. They integrated ideas from the theory of business cycles and ideas in the theory of economic growth, only empirically. While earlier economists had emphasized demand side as the cause of business cycles, they chose the supply side as the main determinant. They empirically identified the interdependence between the rate of technological development, GDP, consumption, investment, and hours. The 2006 Nobel Prize was given to Edmund S. Phelps (1933–) for his works on intertemporal trade-offs in macroeconomic policy. He dealt with problems about the relation between short-run and long-run interdependence between economic variables and economic policy. This book, in addition to synergetic economics, provides a more comprehensive theoretical treatment of the subject. The 2011 Nobel Prize was awarded to Thomas J. Sargent (1943–) and Christopher A. Sims (1942–) for their empirical studies on causes and effects in macroeconomics. They applied various econometric methods to examine questions such as how GDP and inflation are affected by an increase in the interest rate or tax? They studied interdependent relations between various variables, such as GDP, inflation, employment, investment, and expectations. They initially applied some essential tools and methods for macroeconomic analysis. The model in Sect. 3.4 shows that both demand and supply sides can cause business cycles. Synergetic economics theoretically demonstrates any factor may be "the cause" of business cycles. That implies that empirical studies cannot, in general, give some convincing causes of business cycles. When a nonlinear dynamic system enters chaos, any small change in some exogenous force may lead to catastrophes in the long term.

Appendix: Dynamics with Multiple Capital and Consumer Goods

The 1973 Nobel Prize was awarded to Wassily Leontief (1905–1999) for the development of the input–output method and its applications to different economic problems (Zhang 1990). The empirically friendly system is widely applied in various parts of the world. It describes interdependence in the production system. The early input–output models are linear and lack a proper mechanism to determine prices mainly because consumption in the system is not determined by rational mechanism. The system describes a technical relationship between inputs and outputs with given consumption functions. This partly explains why it has been applied to different types of economies, such as decentralized market economies and centrally planned economies. The appendix shows how to deal with the input–output system with endogenous consumption and capital investment. The model below may be considered a generalization of the input–output system.

I now show how to introduce multiple capital goods to the general theory (Polterovich 1977, 1983; Bewley 1982; Amir and Evstigneev 1999). The economy consists of $I+J$ distinct production sectors. There are I capital goods sectors, indexed by $i = 1, \cdots, I$, and J consumer goods sectors, indexed by $j = 1, \cdots, J$. Capital good i depreciates at a constant exponential rate $\delta_k \delta_i$. The population is homogeneous with a fixed number denoted by N. Technologies of all the production sectors are characterized of constant returns to scale. All markets are perfectly competitive, and capital and labor are completely mobile between the economy's sectors. I use $p_{1i}(t)$ and $p_{2j}(t)$ to stand for the prices of capital good i and consumer good j, respectively. I assume that capital good 1 serves as a medium of exchange and is taken as numeraire, i.e., $p_{11}(t) = 1$. I denote wage rate and interest rate for capital good i by $w(t)$ and $r_i(t)$,, respectively.

The Capital Goods Sectors

The production functions of the capital goods sectors are taken on the following form

$$F_{1i}(t) = A_{1i} N_{1i}^{\beta_{1i}}(t) \prod_{m=1}^{I} K_{im}^{\alpha_{im}}(t),$$

$$1 > \beta_{1i} > 0, \;\; \alpha_{im} > 0, \;\; \beta_{1i} + \sum_{m=1}^{I} \alpha_{im} = 1, \;\; i = 1, \ldots, I, \tag{3.2.3}$$

where $F_{1i}(t)$ is the output of capital goods sector i, $N_{1i}(t)$ and $K_{im}(t)$ are the labor input and the amount of capital m employed by capital goods sector i, and β_{1i} and α_{im} are parameters. The marginal conditions are given by:

$$r_m(t) + p_{1m}(t)\delta_m = \frac{\alpha_{im} p_{1i}(t) F_{1i}(t)}{K_{im}(t)}, \;\; w(t) = \frac{\beta_{1i} p_{1i}(t) F_{1i}(t)}{N_{1i}(t)}, \quad i = 1, \ldots, I. \tag{3.2.4}$$

The Consumer Goods Sectors

The production functions of the consumer goods sectors are as follows

$$F_{2j}(t) = A_{2j} N_{2j}^{\beta_{2j}}(t) \prod_{m=1}^{I} \widetilde{K}_{jm}^{\widetilde{\alpha}_{jm}}(t),$$
$$1 > \beta_{2j} > 0, \;\; \widetilde{\alpha}_{jm} > 0, \;\; \beta_{2j} + \sum_{m=1}^{I} \widetilde{\alpha}_{jm} = 1, \;\; j = 1, \ldots, J, \tag{3.2.5}$$

where $F_{2j}(t)$ is the output of consumer goods sector j, $N_{2j}(t)$ and $\widetilde{K}_{jm}(t)$ are the labor input and the amount of capital m employed by consumer goods sector j, and β_{2j} and $\widetilde{\alpha}_{jm}$ are parameters. The marginal conditions are given by:

$$r_m(t) + p_{1m}(t)\delta_m = \frac{\widetilde{\alpha}_{jm} p_{2j}(t) F_{2j}(t)}{\widetilde{K}_{jm}(t)}, \;\; w(t) = \frac{\beta_{2j} p_{2j}(t) F_{2j}(t)}{N_{2j}(t)}, \quad j = 1, \ldots, J. \tag{3.2.6}$$

Disposable Income, Utility Function, and Optimal Behavior

Let $a(t)$ stand for the total value asset of the representative household. The assets composition of the household is denoted by $\bar{k}_i(t)$. I have:

$$a(t) = \sum_{i=1}^{I} \bar{k}_i(t). \tag{3.2.7}$$

The household's disposable income:

$$\hat{y}(t) = w(t) + \sum_{i=1}^{I}\left(1 + \frac{r_i(t)}{p_{1i}(t)}\right)\bar{k}_i(t). \tag{3.2.8}$$

The utility function is specified as follows:

$$U(t) = s_q^{\lambda_0}(t)\prod_{q=1}^{I} c_q^{\xi_{q0}}(t)\prod_{h=1}^{J} \tilde{c}_h^{\tilde{\xi}_{h0}}(t), \quad \lambda_0, \xi_{q0}, \tilde{\xi}_{h0} \geq 0,$$

where $s_q(t)$ is the saving made by the household, $c_q(t)$ the level of capital good q used as durable goods by the household, and $\tilde{c}_q(t)$ is the level of consumer good h consumed by the household. I call λ_0, ξ_{q0}, and $\tilde{\xi}_{h0}$ the household's propensities to save, to use durable q, and to consume consumer good h. The budget is given by:

$$s(t) + \sum_{q=1}^{I}\left(r_q(t) + p_{1q}(t)\delta_q\right)c_q(t) + \sum_{h=1}^{J} p_{2h}(t)\tilde{c}_h(t) = \hat{y}(t).$$

Maximizing U subject to the budget yields:

$$\begin{gathered} s(t) = \lambda\hat{y}(t), \left(r_q(t) + p_{1q}(t)\delta_q\right)c_q(t) = \xi_q\hat{y}(t), \\ p_{2h}(t)\tilde{c}_h(t) = \tilde{\xi}_h\hat{y}(t), \end{gathered} \tag{3.2.9}$$

where

$$\lambda \equiv \lambda_0\rho, \quad \xi_q \equiv \xi_{q0}\rho, \quad \tilde{\xi}_h \equiv \tilde{\xi}_{h0}\rho, \quad \rho \equiv \frac{1}{\lambda_0 + \sum_{q=1}^{I}\xi_{q0} + \sum_{h=1}^{J}\tilde{\xi}_{h0}}.$$

The household's wealth changes according to the following differential equation:

$$\dot{a}(t) = s(t) - a(t). \tag{3.2.10}$$

Portfolio Choice

Consider now an investor with one unity of capital good 1. He can either invest in capital good i, thereby earning a profit equal to the net own-rate of return $r_i(t)/p_{1i}(t)$ or invest in capital good h, thereby earning a profit equal to the net own-rate of return $r_h(t)/p_{1h}(t)$. As I assume capital markets to be at competitive equilibrium at any point in time, options must yield equal returns, i.e.,

$$\frac{r_i(t)}{p_{1i}(t)} = \frac{r_1(t)}{p_{11}(t)}, \quad i = 1, \ldots, I, \tag{3.2.11}$$

where $p_{11}(t) = 1$.

The Change in Physical Capital

The change in the stock of capital good i, $K_i(t)$, is equal to its output minus its depreciation. I have:

$$\dot{K}_i(t) = F_{1i}(t) - \delta_i K_i(t). \tag{3.2.12}$$

The Equilibrium Condition for Consumer Goods Sectors

The output of a consumer goods sector is consumed by the households and used by the production sectors. That is

$$\tilde{c}_j(t)\overline{N} = F_{2j}(t), \quad j = 1, \cdots, J. \tag{3.2.13}$$

Full Employment of Input Factors

$$\begin{gathered} \sum_{i=1}^{I} N_{1i}(t) + \sum_{j=1}^{J} N_{2j}(t) = N, \\ c_i(t)N + \sum_{q=1}^{I} K_{qi}(t) + \sum_{j=1}^{J} \widetilde{K}_{ji}(t) = K_i(t), \quad i = 1, \ldots, I. \end{gathered} \tag{3.2.14}$$

The National Wealth Is Owned by the Population

$$\begin{gathered} a(t)N = \sum_{i=1}^{I} p_{1i}(t)K_i(t), \\ \bar{k}_i(t)N = p_{1i}(t)K_i(t), \; i = 1, \ldots, I. \end{gathered} \tag{3.2.15}$$

Find the Differential Equations to Determine the Movement of the Economy

I now find out differential equations which enable us to follow the motion of the dynamic system. From (3.2.4) and (3.2.6) I have:

$$z_m \equiv \frac{r_m + p_m \delta_m}{w} = \frac{\overline{\alpha}_{im} N_{1i}}{K_{im}} = \frac{\widehat{\alpha}_{jm} N_{2j}}{\widetilde{K}_{jm}}, \tag{3.2.16}$$

where I omit time index in expressions and

$$\overline{\alpha}_{im} \equiv \frac{\alpha_{im}}{\beta_{1i}}, \quad \widehat{\alpha}_{jm} \equiv \frac{\widetilde{\alpha}_{jm}}{\beta_{2i}}.$$

From (3.2.3), (3.2.5) and (3.2.16) I get:

$$\begin{aligned} \frac{F_{1i}}{N_{1i}} &= f_{1i}((z_m)) \equiv A_{1i} \prod_{m=1}^{I} \left(\frac{\overline{\alpha}_{im}}{z_m}\right)^{\alpha_{im}}, \\ \frac{F_{2j}}{N_{2j}} &= f_{2j}((z_m)) \equiv A_{2j} \prod_{m=1}^{I} \left(\frac{\widehat{\alpha}_{jm}}{z_m}\right)^{\widetilde{\alpha}_{jm}}. \end{aligned} \tag{3.2.17}$$

From (3.2.4), (3.2.17), (3.2.16) and $p_{11} = 1$, I have:

$$r_1 = \beta_{11} z_1 f_{11} - \delta_1, \quad w = \beta_{11} f_{11}. \tag{3.2.18}$$

By (3.2.4), I have

$$p_{1i} = \frac{w}{\beta_{1i} f_{1i}}, \quad i = 2, \ldots, I. \tag{3.2.19}$$

From (3.2.6) and (3.2.17)

$$p_{2j} = \frac{w}{\beta_{2j} f_{2j}}, \quad j = 1, \ldots, J. \tag{3.2.20}$$

From (3.2.4), I have

$$r_i = \beta_{1i} p_{1i} z_i f_{1i} - p_{1i} \delta_i. \tag{3.2.21}$$

I thus can consider (r_m), w, (p_{1i}), and (p_{2i}) as functions of (z_m). From (3.2.8), I have:

$$\hat{y} = w + a + \sum_{i=1}^{I} \frac{r_i \bar{k}_i}{p_{1i}}. \tag{3.2.22}$$

From (3.2.22) and (3.2.11), I have

$$\hat{y} = w + (1 + r_1)a. \tag{3.2.23}$$

Insert (3.2.9), (3.2.4) and (3.2.6) in (3.2.13)

$$N_{2j} = \frac{\widetilde{\xi}_j \hat{y} N}{p_{2j} f_{2j}}, \quad j = 1, \cdots, J. \tag{3.2.24}$$

From (3.2.14) and (3.2.9)

$$\frac{\xi_i \hat{y} N}{r_i + p_{1i}\delta_i} + \sum_{q=1}^{I} K_{qi} + \sum_{j=1}^{J} \widetilde{K}_{ji} = K_i, \quad i = 1, \ldots, I. \tag{3.2.25}$$

Insert (3.2.16) in (3.2.25)

$$\sum_{q=1}^{I} \overline{\alpha}_{qi} N_{1q} + \sum_{j=1}^{J} \widehat{\alpha}_{ji} N_{2j} = \left(K_i - \frac{\xi_i \hat{y} N}{r_i + p_{1i}\delta_i} \right) z_i, \quad i = 1, \ldots, I. \tag{3.2.26}$$

Insert (3.2.24) in (3.2.26)

$$\sum_{q=1}^{I} \overline{\alpha}_{qi} N_{1q} = Z_i, \quad i = 1, \ldots, I, \tag{3.2.27}$$

where

$$\hat{f}_i \equiv N \sum_{j=1}^{J} \frac{\widehat{\alpha}_{ji} \widetilde{\xi}_j}{p_{2j} f_{2j}} + \frac{z_i \xi_i N}{r_i + p_{1i}\delta_i}, \quad \bar{f}_i \equiv (1 + r_1)\hat{f}_i, \quad Z_i \equiv z_i K_i - \hat{f}_i w - \bar{f}_i a.$$

If I consider (N_{1i}) as variables, equations (A12) have I independent linear equations and I variables. It is straightforward to solve these linear equations. It is also easy to see that in these equations, the variables a and (K_i) appear in the right-hand sides of the linear equations and the right-hand sides are linear in a and (K_i). I can thus express the solution of (3.2.27) as follows:

$$N_{1i} = \sum_{q=1}^{I} \Lambda_{iq}((z_m)) K_q + \Phi_{1i}((z_m)) a + \Phi_{0i}((z_m)), \quad i = 1, \ldots, I. \tag{3.2.28}$$

I see that the labor distribution is expressed as linear functions of a and (K_i). By (3.2.16) and (3.2.28) I solve (K_{im}) and $\left(\widetilde{K}_{jm}\right)$ as linear functions of a and (K_i). Insert (3.2.24) and (3.2.28) in (3.2.14)

$$a = n_{00} - \sum_{q=1}^{I} \Lambda_q K_q, \tag{3.2.29}$$

where

$$\hat{f}_0((z_m)) \equiv N \sum_{j=1}^{J} \frac{\widetilde{\xi}_j}{p_{2j} f_{2j}}, \quad n_{00}((z_m)) \equiv \frac{N - \hat{f}_0 w}{\Phi},$$

$$\Lambda_q((z_m)) \equiv \frac{1}{\Phi} \sum_{j=1}^{J} \Lambda_{jq}, \quad \Phi((z_m)) \equiv (1 + r_1)\hat{f}_0 + \sum_{i=1}^{I} \Phi_{1i}.$$

By (3.2.16), (3.2.24) and (3.2.28). I have:

$$K_{im} = \frac{\overline{\alpha}_{im}}{z_m} \sum_{q=1}^{I} \Lambda_{iq} K_q + \frac{\overline{\alpha}_{im} \Phi_{1i} a}{z_m}, \quad \widetilde{K}_{jm} = \frac{\widehat{\alpha}_{jm} \widetilde{\xi}_j N \hat{y}}{z_m p_{2j} f_{2j}}. \tag{3.2.30}$$

Insert (3.2.30) in (3.2.14)

$$z_i c_i N + \sum_{n=1}^{I} \Lambda_{in} K_n + a\overline{\Phi}_i + \bar{y}_{i0} \hat{y} = z_i K_i, \quad i = 1, \ldots, I, \tag{3.2.31}$$

where

$$\Lambda_{in} \equiv \sum_{q=1}^{I} \overline{\alpha}_{qi} \Lambda_{qn}, \quad \overline{\Phi}_i \equiv \sum_{q=1}^{I} \overline{\alpha}_{qi} \Phi_{1q}, \quad \bar{y}_{i0} \equiv N \sum_{j=1}^{J} \frac{\widehat{\alpha}_{ji} \widetilde{\xi}_j}{p_{2j} f_{2j}}.$$

Insert (3.2.9) in (3.2.31)

$$\frac{N \xi_i \hat{y} z_i}{r_i + p_{1i} \delta_i} + \sum_{n=1}^{I} \Lambda_{in} K_n + a\overline{\Phi}_i + \bar{y}_{i0} \hat{y} = z_i K_i, \quad i = 1, \ldots, I. \tag{3.2.32}$$

Insert (3.2.22) in (3.2.32)

$$\sum_{n=1}^{I} \Lambda_{in} K_n + \left((1 + r_1)\bar{y}_{i1} + \overline{\Phi}_i\right) a = z_i K_i - \bar{y}_{i1} w, \quad i = 1, \ldots, I, \tag{3.2.33}$$

where

$$\bar{y}_{i1} \equiv \frac{N \xi_i z_i}{r_i + p_{1i} \delta_i} + \bar{y}_{i0}.$$

Insert (3.2.29) in (3.2.33)

$$z_i K_i - \sum_{n=1}^{I} \theta_{in} K_n = y_i, \quad i = 1, \ldots, I, \tag{3.2.34}$$

where

$$\theta_{in}((z_m)) \equiv \Lambda_{in} - \left((1 + r_1)\bar{y}_{i1} + \overline{\Phi}_i\right)\Lambda_n,$$
$$y_i \equiv \bar{y}_{i1} w + ((1 + r_1)\bar{y}_{i1} + \Phi_1)\hat{f}_1.$$

Solve linear equations (3.2.34) with (K_m) as the variables

$$K_i = \theta_i((z_m)). \tag{3.2.35}$$

Taking derivatives of (3.2.35) with respect to t yields:

$$\dot{K}_i = \sum_{m=1}^{J} \frac{\partial \theta_i}{\partial z_m} \dot{z}_m. \tag{3.2.36}$$

From (3.2.12) and (3.2.17), I have:

$$\dot{K}_i = N_{1i} f_{1i} - \delta_i \theta_i. \tag{3.2.37}$$

I insert (3.2.30) in (3.2.37):

$$\dot{K}_i = f_{1i} \sum_{q=1}^{I} \Lambda_{iq} \theta_q + \Phi_{1i} f_{1i} a - \delta_i \theta_i, \tag{3.2.38}$$

where I use (3.2.15). Equal (3.2.36) and (3.2.38):

$$\sum_{m=1}^{J} \frac{\partial \theta_i}{\partial z_m} \dot{z}_m = f_{1i} \sum_{q=1}^{I} \Lambda_{iq} \theta_q + \Phi_{1i} f_{1i} a - \delta_i \theta_i. \tag{3.2.39}$$

We have (3.2.39) linear in $(\dot{z}_m)$. I solve (3.2.39) as follows:

$$\dot{z}_i = \Lambda_i((z_m)), i = 1, \ldots, I.$$

It is straightforward to see that once I solve I differential equations, I can get the values of all the variables at any point of time.

References

Abel AB, Bernanke BS, Croushore D (2007) Macroeconomics. Prentice Hall, New Jersey
Amano M (1980) A neoclassical model of the dual economy with capital accumulation in agriculture. Rev Econ Stud 47:933–944
Amir R, Evstigneev IV (1999) Stochastic version of Polterovich's model: exponential turnpike theorems for equilibrium paths. Macroecon Dyn 3:149–166
Arrow KJ (1974) General economic equilibrium: purpose, analytic techniques, collective choice. Am Econ Rev 64:253–272
Arrow KJ, Debreu G (1954) Existence of an equilibrium for a competitive economy. Econometrica 22:265–290
Arrow KJ, Hahn FH (1971) General competitive analysis. Holden-Day Inc., San Francisco
Barkai H (1959) Ricardo on factor prices and income distribution in a growing economy. Economica 26:240–250
Barkai H (1966) Ricardo's second thoughts on rent as a relative share. South Econ J 32:250–285
Barro RJ, Sala-i-Martin X (1995) Economic growth. McGraw-Hill Inc., New York
Bewley T (1982) An integration of equilibrium theory and turnpike theory. J Math Econ 10:233–267
Brems H (1970) Ricardo's long run equilibrium. Hist Polit Econ 2:225–245
Bretschger L (2013) Population growth and natural-resource scarcity: long-run development under seemingly unfavorable conditions. Scand J Econ 115:722–755
Burmeister E, Dobell AR (1970) Mathematical theories of economic growth. Collier Macmillan Publishers, London
Caravale GA, Tosato DA (1980) Ricardo and the theory of value distribution and growth. Routledge & Kegan Paul, London
Casarosa C (1985) The new view of the Ricardian theory of distribution and economic growth. In: Caravale GA (ed) The legacy of Ricardo. Basil Blackwell, London
Caselli F, Ventura J (2000) A representative consumer theory of distribution. Am Econ Rev 90:909–926
Chatterjee S (1994) Transitional dynamics and the distribution of wealth in a neoclassical growth model. J Public Econ 54:97–119
Chiarella C, Flaschel P (2000) The dynamics of Keynesian monetary growth: macro foundations. Cambridge University Press, Cambridge
Cochrane J (1970) The first mathematical Ricardian system. Hist Polit Econ 2:419–431
Could ED, Moav O, Weinberg BA (2001) Precautionary demand for education, inequality, and technological progress. J Econ Growth 6:285–315
Dana RA, Florenzano M, Levy D (1989) Production prices and general equilibrium prices: a long-run property of a Leontief economy. J Math Econ 18:263–280
Debreu G (1959) Theory of value: an axiomatic analysis of equilibrium. Yale University Press, London
Diewert W (1977) Walras' theory of capital formation and the existence of a temporary equilibrium. In: Schwödiauer G (ed) Equilibrium and disequilibrium in economic theory. Reidel, Dordrecht
Eatwell J (1987) Walras' theory of capital. In: Eatwell J, Milgate M, Newmann P (eds) The New Palgrave dictionary of political economy. MacMillan, London
Fleisher B, Hu YF, Li HZ, Kim SH (2011) Economic transition, higher education and worker productivity in China. J Dev Econ 94:86–94
Furuoka F (2009) Population growth and economic development: new empirical evidence from Thailand. Econ Bull 29:1–14
Gale D (1955) The law of supply and demand. Math Scand 3:33–44
Galor O, Weil D (1999) From Malthusian stagnation to modern growth. Am Econ Rev 89:150–154
Gandolfo G (2005) Economic dynamics. Springer, Berlin
Heijdra BJ (2017) Foundations of modern macroeconomics, 3rd edn. Oxford University Press, Cambridge

Impicciatore G, Panaccione L, Ruscitti F (2012) Walras' theory of capital formation: an intertemporal equilibrium reformation. J Econ Theor 106:99–118

Jensen BS, Larsen ME (2005) General equilibrium dynamics of multi-sector growth models. J Econ 10:17–56

Kaiyama M (1973) On the growth model of a dual economy. Econ Stud Q 24:1–15

Kydland FE, Prescott EC (1982) Time to build and aggregate fluctuations. Econometrica 50:1345–1370

Lorenz HW (1993) Nonlinear dynamic economics and chaotic motion. Springer, Berlin

Maliar L, Maliar S (2001) Heterogeneity in capital and skills in a neoclassical stochastic growth model. J Econ Dyn Control 38:635–654

Marino AM (1975) On the neoclassical version of the dual economy. Rev Econ Stud 42:435–443

Mas-Colell A, Whinston MD, Green JR (1995) Microeconomic theory. Oxford University Press, Oxford

McKenzie LW (1959) On the existence of general equilibrium for a competitive market. Econometrica 27:54–71

Miles D, Scott A (2005) Macroeconomics—understanding the wealth of nations. John & Sons Ltd, Chichester

Mincer J (1974) Schooling, experience and earnings. Columbia University Press, New York

Montesano A (2008) A restatement of Walras' theory of capitalization and money. Hist Econ Rev 47:86–109

Morishima M (1964) Equilibrium, stability and growth. Oxford University Press, Oxford

Morishima M (1977) Walras' economics. Cambridge University Press, Cambridge

Morishima M (1989) Ricardo's economics: a general equilibrium theory of distribution and growth. Cambridge University Press, Cambridge

Negishi T (1989) History of economic theory. North-Holland, Amsterdam

Nikaido H (1956) On the classical multilateral exchange problem. Metroeconomica 8:135–145

Nikaido H (1968) Convex structures and economic theory. Academic Press, New York

Pasinetti LL (1960) A mathematical formulation of the Ricardian system. Rev Econ Stud 27:78–98

Pasinetti LL (1974) Growth and income distribution: essays in economic theory. Cambridge University Press, Cambridge

Penalosa CG, Turnovsky SJ (2006) Growth and income inequality: a canonical model. Econ Theor 28:25–49

Polterovich V (1977) Models of equilibrium economic growth. Matecon 13:3–24

Polterovich V (1983) Equilibrium trajectories of economic growth. Econometrica 51:693–730

Puu T (2011) Nonlinear economic dynamics. Springer, Berlin

Ricardo D (1821) The principles of political economy and taxation, 3rd edn, 1965. Everyman's Library, London

Samuelson PA (1959) A modern treatment of the Ricardian economy: I. The pricing of goods and labor and land services. Q J Econ 73:1–35

Schumpeter JA (1954) History of economic analysis, reprinted in 1994. Oxford University Press, London

Shone R (2002) Economic dynamics: phase diagrams and their economic application. Cambridge University Press, Cambridge

Stachurski J, Venditti A, Yano M (2014) Nonlinear dynamics in equilibrium models: chaos, cycles and indeterminacy. Springer, Berlin

Stadler GW (1994) Real business cycles. J Econ Lit 32:1750–1783

Tilak JBC (1989) Education and its relation to economic growth, poverty and income distribution: past evidence and future analysis. World Bank, Washington

Todaro MP (1969) A model of labor migration and urban unemployment in less developed countries. Am Econ Rev 59:138–148

Tselios V (2008) Income and educational inequalities in the regions of the European Union: geographically spillovers under welfare state restrictions. Pap Reg Sci 87:403–430

Turnovsky SJ, Penalosa CG (2006) Distributional dynamics in a neoclassical growth model: the role of elastic labor supply. J Econ Dyn Control 32:1399–1431
Uzawa H (1961) On a two-sector model of economic growth. Rev Econ Stud 29:47–70
Walras L (1874, 1954) Elements of pure economics (trans: Jaffé W). Allen and Unwin, London (in French)
Zhang WB (1990) Economic dynamics: growth and development. Springer, Heidelberg
Zhang WB (1991) Synergetic economics. Springer, Heidelberg
Zhang WB (2005) Economic growth theory. Ashgate, Hampshire
Zhang WB (2006) Growth with income and wealth distribution. Macmillan, London
Zhang WB (2017) Economic growth and structural change—a synthesis of the Walrasian general equilibrium, Ricardian distribution and neoclassical growth theories. Asian Dev Policy Rev 5:17–36
Zhang WB (2018) A general dynamic equilibrium model and business cycles. RAIS J Soc Sci 2:11–24

Chapter 4
Education, National Debts, and Development Traps

The previous chapter integrated the basic economic mechanisms of neoclassical growth and Walrasian general equilibrium theories. It introduced endogenous capital accumulation into general equilibrium theory. Except capital, modern economies show that other variables, such as human capital, preference change, knowledge, environmental change, and resources, play important role even for not very long-term economic development.

Adam Smith argues that improvement in the productivity of labor has their origins in the large part of the skill, dexterity, and judgment. Human capital is a consequence of the division of labor. But the opportunities and incentives to which workers respond in their investment in human capital are not fully considered by classical economists such as Smith, Ricardo, and Marx. When they were constructing theories, endogenous human capital accumulation via formal higher education was not very important. An early formal model of endogenous technical progress was developed by Arrow (1962). He considers learning by doing as the source of human capital accumulation. Uzawa (1965) introduces an education sector specifying in creating human capital into growth theory. The model is late often referred as to the Uzawa–Lucas model since Lucas extends the Uzawa model (Uzawa 1965; Lucas 1988). Human capital is considered as a key determinant of economic growth as in many of studies (Hanushek and Kimko 2000; Barro 2001; Castelló-Climent and Hidalgo-Cabrillana 2012). I introduce learning through creative leisure and learning through consuming into formal growth theory some years ago. The basic idea is that human capital is not necessarily accumulated through taking part in productive activities or formal activities. There are many other sources of learning in life, especially rich people and people in developed economies. Leisure activities, such as playing computer games, sports, driving for fun, grand tours to different parts of the world, communications with educated parents and friends, and spending money on goods or cars, enable people to accumulate human capital. With regards to some human capital, learning

W.-B. Zhang, *The General Economic Theory*,
https://doi.org/10.1007/978-3-030-56204-5_4

through creative leisure may be more effectively than learning through formal education. In my approach to human capital, I take account of the three sources rather than one like Arrow and Uzawa.

Another important variable in explaining modern economies is government debt. Issues related to government debts are complicated as national debts have knotty relations with GDP, taxes, taxation structures, government's social and economic activities, population structure, preferences of the population, and economic growth. The government has a set of control measures including the total expenditures and tax rates on the industrial sector's output, the education sector's output, the wage income, the consumption and the interest income. As most of theoretical growth models are framed with simplified relations among variables (Barro 1990; Lin 2000; Gómez 2008; Park 2009), the complexity of government debt is well addressed but little understood. As the national debt involves the government operations over the entire economy, a proper approach to national debt has to be conducted in a dynamic general equilibrium framework. This chapter applies my approach to examine national debts due to the government's education subsidy.

4.1 Growth with Education and Saving

The model is based on Zhang (2006: Sect. 3.2). The economy is composed of one production sector and one education sector. There is a fixed homogenous labor force N, which is distributed between economic activities, teaching, and studying. The commodity is chosen to serve as numeraire, with all the other prices being measured relative to its price. I introduce:

$F(t)$—output level of the production sector at time t;
$K(t)$—level of capital stocks of the economy;
$H(t)$—level of human capital of the population;
$N_i(t)$ and $K_i(t)$—labor force and capital stocks employed by the production sector;
$N_v(t)$ and N_e—the number of teachers and number of students;
$K_e(t)$—the capital stocks employed by the university;
$w(t)$ and $r(t)$—wage rate and interest rate.

4.1.1 The Goods Sector

The qualified labor force $H^m(t)N_i(t)$ and capital input $K_i(t)$, where m is the efficiency of applying human capital, are combined to produce output as follows:

$$F(t) = AK_i^{\alpha}(t)\big(H^m(t)N_i(t)\big)^{\beta}, \quad A, \alpha, \beta > 0, \quad \alpha + \beta = 1.$$

The marginal conditions imply:

$$r(t) = \tilde{\tau}\,\alpha A k_i^{-\beta}(t), \quad w(t) = \tilde{\tau}\,\beta A H^m(t) k_i^{\alpha}(t), \tag{4.1.1}$$

where $k_i \equiv K_i/H^m N_i$ and $\tilde{\tau} \equiv 1 - \tau$, τ is the tax rate on the product level.

4.1.2 The Household Behavior

The value of household wealth is denoted by $\bar{k}(t)$, where $\bar{k}(t) \equiv K(t)/N$. The disposable income is:

$$\hat{y}(t) = r(t)\bar{k}(t) + w(t) + \bar{k}(t).$$

The budget constraint implies:

$$c(t) + s(t) = \hat{y}(t).$$

The utility function is specified as:

$$U(t) = c^{\xi}(t) s^{\lambda}(t), \quad \xi, \lambda > 0, \quad \xi + \lambda = 1.$$

Maximizing the utility function subject to the budget constraint yields:

$$c(t) = \xi \hat{y}(t), \; s(t) = \lambda \hat{y}(t). \tag{4.1.2}$$

The change in the household's wealth is:

$$\dot{\bar{k}}(t) = s(\hat{y}(t)) - \bar{k}(t) = \lambda \hat{y}(t) - \bar{k}(t). \tag{4.1.3}$$

4.1.3 The Education Sector

I consider two sources of changes in human capital, education, and learning by producing. The change in human capital is given:

$$\dot{H}(t) = \frac{\upsilon_e K_e^{\alpha_e}(t)(H^m(t)N_v)^{\beta_v}(H^m(t)N_e)^{\beta_e}}{N} + \frac{\upsilon_i F(t)}{N H^{\pi}(t)} - \delta_h H(t), \tag{4.1.4}$$

where $\delta_h(>0)$ is the depreciation rate of human capital, υ_e, υ_i, α_e, β_v, and β_e are non-negative parameters. The human capital accumulation equation integrates Arrow's and Uzawa's ideas about human capital accumulation. The term $\upsilon_e K_e^{\alpha_e}(H^m N_v)^{\beta_v}(H^m N_e)^{\beta_e}$ implies that formal education enhances human capital. Human capital rises in the number of students. The term divided by N measures the contribution per student. The effect of learning by doing in human capital accumulation is measured by the term $\upsilon_i F/H^\pi$. Human capital growth is positively related to its production scale F and is dependent on the level of human capital. The term H^π takes account of returns to scale effects in human capital accumulation. The case of $\pi > (<)0$ implies that as human capital is increased it is more difficult (easier) to further improve the level of human capital.

For simplicity of analysis, assume that the students and teachers are paid by government's tax income at the same wage rate as the wage rate of workers. The economy has a fixed ratio of the population who are getting education in the university. The number of students is given by: $N_e = n_e N$. Assume that the total tax income is used for paying the students, teachers and the capital stocks employed by the university. The government spends $w(t)N_e$ on students. The budget for paying teachers and the capital stocks of the university is given by:

$$w(t)N_v(t) + r(t)K_e(t) = \tau F(t) - w(t)N_e. \tag{4.1.5}$$

The university maximizes its output $\upsilon_e K_e^{\alpha_e}(H^m N_v)^{\beta_v}(H^m N_e)^{\beta_e}$ subject (4.1.5). The problem is formed as follows:

$$Max\ \upsilon_e K_e^{\alpha_e}(t)\left(H^m(t)N_v(t)\right)^{\beta_v}\left(H^m(t)N_e\right)^{\beta_e}.$$

The first-order conditions imply:

$$K_e = \frac{\alpha_e(\tau F - wN_e)}{(\alpha_e + \beta_v)r}, \quad N_v = \frac{\beta_v(\tau F - wN_e)}{(\alpha_e + \beta_v)w}. \tag{4.1.6}$$

The full employment of input factors implies:

$$N_i(t) + N_e + N_v(t) = N, \quad K_i(t) + K_e(t) = K(t). \tag{4.1.7}$$

The model is completed.

4.2 The Dynamics and Multiple Equilibrium Points

From (4.1.7), I have $N_i(t) + N_v(t) = N - N_e$. By (4.1.1) and (4.1.6), I obtain:

$$K_e(t) = \frac{\alpha_e k_i(t)N_i(t)H^m(t)(\tau N_i(t) - \bar{\tau}\beta N_e)}{\alpha\tau_0},$$

$$N_v(t) = \frac{\beta_v(\tau N_i(t) - \bar{\tau}\beta N_e)}{\beta\tau_0}, \tag{4.2.1}$$

where $\tau_0 \equiv \bar{\tau}(\alpha_e + \beta_v)$.

From (3.4) and $N_i + N_v = N - N_e$, I have:

$$N_i = \frac{N - N_e + \beta_v N_e/(\alpha_e + \beta_v)}{\tau_0\beta + \tau\beta_v}\tau_0\beta, \quad N_v = \frac{\beta_v(\tau N_i - \bar{\tau}\,\beta N_e)}{\tau_0\beta}. \tag{4.2.2}$$

From (4.2.1), I have:

$$K_e = a\ K_i, \quad a \equiv \frac{\alpha_e(\tau - \bar{\tau}\beta N_e/N_i)}{\alpha\tau_0}. \tag{4.2.3}$$

From (4.2.3) and $K_i + K_e = N\,\bar{k}$, I solve:

$$K_i(t) = \frac{N\,\bar{k}(t)}{1+a}, \quad K_e(t) = \frac{aN\,\bar{k}(t)}{1+a}. \tag{4.2.4}$$

As $k_i = K_i/H^m N_i$, I obtain:

$$k_i(t) = \frac{n_i\bar{k}(t)}{H^m(t)}, \tag{4.2.5}$$

where $n_i \equiv N/N_i(1+a)$. The variable $k_i(t)$ is a function of $k(t)$ and $H(t)$. Summarizing the above discussions, I show that for any given $k(t)$ and $H(t)$, all the other variables in the system are uniquely determined at any point of time. As shown in Zhang (2006: Sect. 3.2), the motion of $\bar{k}(t)$ and $H(t)$ are explicitly given by the following two differential equations:

$$\begin{aligned} \dot{\bar{k}}(t) &= \lambda^*\bar{k}^{\alpha}(t)H^{\beta m}(t) - \xi\,\bar{k}(t), \\ \dot{H}(t) &= \upsilon_e^*\bar{k}^{\alpha_e}(t)H^{\beta_v m+\beta_e m}(t) + \upsilon_i^* H^{m-\pi-\alpha m}(t)\bar{k}^{\alpha}(t) - \delta_h H(t), \end{aligned} \tag{4.2.6}$$

where

$$\lambda^* \equiv \lambda A\,\bar{\tau}\left(\alpha n_i^{-\beta} + \beta n_i^{\alpha}\right), \quad \upsilon_e^* \equiv \left(\frac{aN}{1+a}\right)^{\alpha_e}\frac{\upsilon_e N_v^{\beta_v} N_e^{\beta_e}}{N}, \quad \upsilon_i^* \equiv \frac{\upsilon_i A n_i^{\alpha} N_i}{N}.$$

The system is stationary if:

$$\begin{aligned} &\lambda^*\bar{k}^{\alpha}H^{\beta m} = \xi\bar{k}, \\ &\upsilon_e^*\bar{k}^{\alpha_e}H^{\beta_v m+\beta_e m} + \upsilon_i^* H^{m-\pi-\alpha m}\bar{k}^{\alpha} = \delta_h H. \end{aligned} \tag{4.2.7}$$

From the first equation in (4.2.7), $\bar{k} = (\lambda^*/\xi)^{1/\beta} H^m$ holds. Inserting this equation in the second equation in (4.2.7) yields:

$$\Phi(H) \equiv \Phi_e(H) + \Phi_i(H) - \delta_h = 0, \tag{4.2.8}$$

where

$$\Phi_e(H) \equiv \left(\frac{\lambda^*}{\xi}\right)^{\frac{\alpha_e}{\beta}} \upsilon_e^* H^{x_e}, \quad \Phi_i(H) \equiv \left(\frac{\lambda^*}{\xi}\right)^{\alpha/\beta} \upsilon_i^* H^{x_i},$$
$$x_e \equiv (\alpha_e + \beta_v + \beta_e)m - 1, \quad x_i \equiv m - \pi - 1.$$

The number of economic equilibrium points equals the number of solutions of the equation, $\Phi(H) = 0$ for $0 < H < \infty$. It is straightforward to check: (1) If $x_e < 0$ and $x_i < 0$, the system has a unique stable equilibrium; (2) If $x_e > 0$ and $x_i > 0$, the system has a unique unstable equilibrium; and (3) If $x_e > 0$ and $x_i < 0$ ($x_e < 0$ and $x_i > 0$), the system has either no equilibrium, one equilibrium, or two equilibrium points. When the system has two equilibrium points, the equilibrium with low (high) level of H is stable (unstable). I will demonstrate the case of multiple equilibrium points with simulation. I only interpret the stability condition, $x_e < 0$ and $x_i < 0$. From the definitions of x_e and x_i, I interpret x_e and x_i, respectively, as measurements of returns to scale of the university and the industrial sector in the dynamic system. When $x_e (< (>) 0$, the university is said to display decreasing (increasing) returns to scale in the dynamic economy. If both the university and the production sector display decreasing returns, the dynamic system has a unique stable equilibrium.

If the two sectors exhibit decreasing returns to scale, the system will approach to its equilibrium in the long term. In a traditional society like the one constructed by Adam Smith where increases in human capital mainly come from division of labor and traditional education, the economic system (with stabilized monetary system) is stable. In a newly industrializing economy, education exhibits increasing returns to scale and learning by doing may not be effective in improving human capital. The economy may have multiple equilibrium points. If the society fails to explore increasing returns effects from education, it may not achieve rapid industrialization. I now demonstrate dynamics of the nonlinear system with multiple equilibrium points.

4.3 Unstable Unlimited Growth Versus Poverty Traps

This section examines dynamic behavior when the system has two equilibrium points. The parameters are specified as follows:

$$\alpha = 0.35, \quad N = 1, \quad A = 2, \quad N_e = 0.06, \quad \tau = 0.08, \quad \lambda = 0.7,$$
$$\alpha_e = 0.7, \quad \beta_e = 0.7, \quad \beta_v = 0.7, \quad v_e = 1.8, \quad v_i = 0.02, \tag{4.3.1}$$
$$\delta_h = 0.08, \quad \pi = 0.3, \quad m = 0.8.$$

I have $x_e = 0.4$ and $x_i = -0.5$. The university exhibits increasing return to scale and the production sector is characterized of decreasing return. The system has two equilibrium points:

$$\left(\bar{k}_1, H_1\right) = (17.858, 2.226), \quad \left(\bar{k}_2, H_2\right) = (10.401, 19.509).$$

The one with lower levels of human capital and per capita wealth is stable; the other is unstable, also as analytically proved. I plot the vector field and the steady states in Fig. 4.1. The economy with low level of human capital, even if it was initially rich, tends to converge to the stable equilibrium with low standard of living and low level of human capital. The economy with high level of human capital, even if it was initially poor, tends to experience sustained growth. This nonlinear dynamic system has path-dependent features. This result illustrates the significance of cultural value for education. Japanese, Korean, and Chinese-dominated economies like Singapore and Taiwan could have sustained economic growth irrespective of their initial poor conditions in the 1960s, mainly because of their cultural values on education, rather than due to high saving rates. I systematically studied the modern economic developments of Confucian regions, Japan, Korea, Singapore, Hong Kong, and Mainland China (Zhang 1998, 2002b, 2003a, 2006b). In the 1950s, no one could have foreseen rapid economic development of East Asia, because few economists recognized the significance of education in economic development and fewer knew the validity of rationalism in classical Confucianism for modern economies. Fukuzawa Yukichi (1835–1901) is an exception (Zhang 2010). In the literature of economic growth and development published in the 1960s and 1970s, capital accumulation is the main engine of economic development. Economists failed to properly interpret economic evolution of these regions because they did not properly examine the cultural values of education in this region.

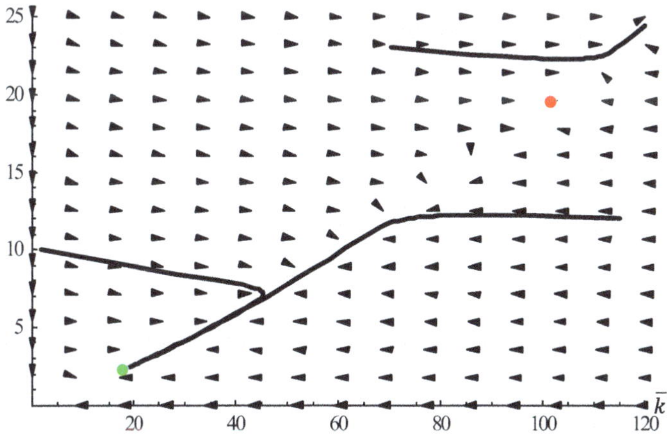

Fig. 4.1 Path-dependent economic evolution

I simulate three paths of the economy with the initial values:

$$\left(\bar{k}_0, H_0\right) = (1.5, 10), \quad \left(\bar{k}_0, H_0\right) = (115, 12), \quad \left(\bar{k}_0, H_0\right) = (70, 23).$$

The paths with $\left(\bar{k}_0, H_0\right) = (1.5, 10)$ and $\left(\bar{k}_0, H_0\right) = (115, 12)$ converge to the low levels of human capital and per capita wealth. The path with $\left(\bar{k}_0, H_0\right) = (115, 12)$ starts with high level of wealth. But its level of human capital is not improved over time. As decreasing returns dominate this path, its prosperity does not last long. The path with $\left(\bar{k}_0, H_0\right) = (70, 23)$ will grow infinitely because increasing return to scale dominates the economic evolution. Surely, this kind of infinite growth will not happen as the model neglects many other significant factors such as endogenous population change, negative externalities such as pollution, and limitations of natural resources which may limit growth.

As far as qualitative features of economic development are concerned, Fig. 4.1 provides some insights into difference in the economic development in Mainland China and Taiwan during the period of 1950–1980. The two areas started the economic development with similar economic conditions but different average educational levels. Before the economic reform in 1978 in Mainland China, the living standards and educational achievements in the two Chinese societies had been enlarging. It is only in recent years that Mainland China has begun to explore the opportunities of economic development. Structurally speaking, Mainland China's political economic system had devaluated modern (Western) education so that no sector in the society could have explored potential benefits of increasing returns offered by the Western civilization. Both cultural values and political systems matter in my approach.

4.4 Changes in Policy and Preferences in Stable and Unstable Economies

The previous section shows that the system experiences different paths if they have different initial conditions. This path-dependent feature is due to the existence of multiple equilibria. I now show how the economic dynamic paths change if some parameters are shifted. In comparative dynamic analysis, I am only interested in the path-dependent case; general cases are fully examined in Zhang (2006: Sect. 3.2).

4.4.1 The Education Policy

The tax income is totally spent on education. I may thus interpret increases in the tax rate as the promotion policy taken by the government. I now examine the impact of the tax rate on the economic structure. Consider the case that the expenditure on

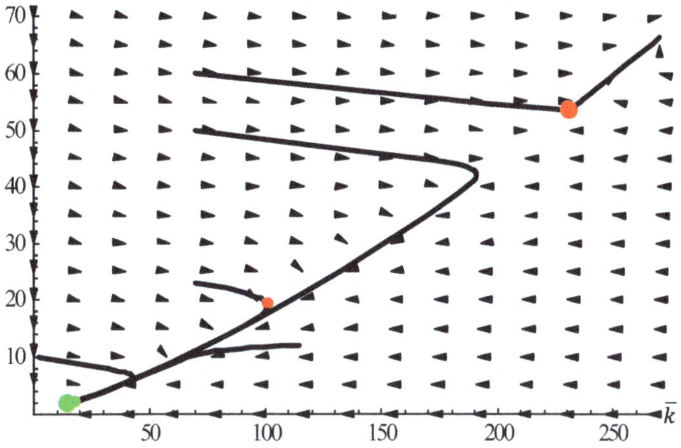

Fig. 4.2 The government discourages education

education is reduced from 8% of the GDP to 7%, that is $\tau : 0.08 \Rightarrow 0.07$. Figure 4.2 shows the simulation results—the points with larger sizes are the new steady states and the other two points with smaller sizes are the old steady states. The two steady states are shifted as follows:

$$\left(\bar{k}_1, H_1\right) : (17.858, 2.226) \Rightarrow (14.758, 1.718),$$
$$\left(\bar{k}_2, H_2\right) : (101.401, 19.509) \Rightarrow (230.783, 53.417).$$

The new stable steady state has lower levels of human capital and per capita wealth; but the new unstable steady states have much higher levels of $\bar{k}$ and H. The new unstable steady state of higher $\bar{k}$ and H is much better than the old unstable one. But the economy with a discouraging policy has more chances to the traditional trap than to the economic miracle. For instance, if I start from the following three points as in the previous example in Fig. 4.2:

$$\left(\bar{k}_0, H_0\right) = (1.5, 10), \quad \left(\bar{k}_0, H_0\right) = (115, 12), \quad \left(\bar{k}_0, H_0\right) = (70, 23).$$

As demonstrated in Fig. 4.2, all the paths with these initial conditions end up in the poverty trap. But in Fig. 4.2, the path with $\left(\bar{k}_0, H_0\right) = (70, 23)$ exhibits the economic miracle. This example shows that the discouraging policy deprives the society from development opportunity. The "chance" for development is loss due to the new policy. For the economy to experience sustained growth, the economy must have a much higher initial level of human capital than in the case of $\tau = 0.08$. Hence, if the society reduces its investment in education, it will have much less opportunities to experience sustained economic growth, even though heavy investment in education will not guarantee sustainable development of the nonlinear system in certainty.

4.4.2 The Impact of the Propensity to Save

Keynes and Adam Smith have the opposite opinions on a change in propensity to save. Keynes holds that a higher propensity to save will reduce the national output, while Adam Smith argues that a higher propensity to save enhances national wealth. I now examine this issue by allowing the propensity to save as follows: $\lambda : 0.7 \Rightarrow 0.73$. Figure 4.3 shows the simulation results. The two steady states are shifted as follows:

$$\left(\bar{k}_1, H_1\right) : (17.858, 2.226) \Rightarrow (14.758, 1.718),$$
$$\left(\bar{k}_2, H_2\right) : (101.401, 19.509) \Rightarrow (230.783, 53.417).$$

The new stable steady state has higher levels of human capital and per capita wealth; but the new unstable steady state has lower levels of $\bar{k}$ and H. Figure 4.3 depicts the impact of change in λ on the dynamics of the system. Both Keynes' and Adam Smith' conclusions on the propensity to save can be valid, depending on the situation. It should be emphasized that the Keynesian conclusion on the issue is derived from different analytical framework. He assumed the existence of unemployment.

4.5 Growth by Integrating the Diamond Debt and Uzawa–Lucas Models with Education Subsidies

This section integrates the economic mechanisms in the four key growth models—Solow's growth model, Arrow's learning by doing model, the Uzawa–Lucas education model (Uzawa 1965; Lucas 1988), and the Diamond growth model with

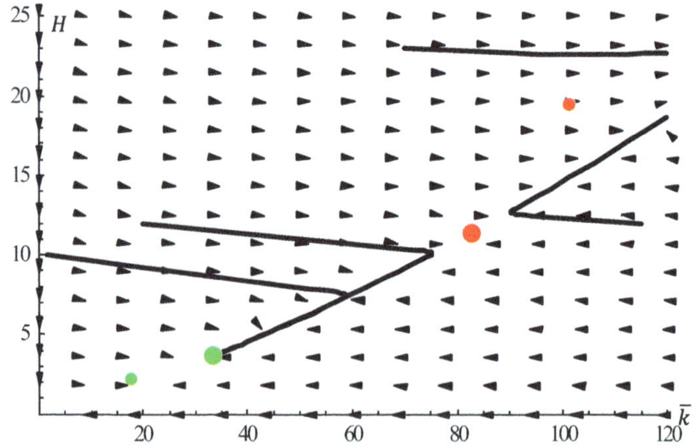

Fig. 4.3 A rise in the propensity to save changes the national output

debts Diamond (1965) see also Alonso-Carrera and Freire-Sere (2004) in a single comprehensive framework. The model is based on Zhang (2017c).

4.5.1 The Labor Force and Factor Input Distribution

The homogenous and fixed population is denoted by $\bar{N}$. I use $T(t)$ and $T_e(t)$ to represent for, respectively, the work time and study time of the representative household. The total labor force $N(t)$ is given by:

$$N(t) = H^m(t)T(t)\bar{N},$$

where $H(t)$ stands for the level of human capital and m is the efficiency of applying human capital. The commodity is selected to be numeraire. The total capital stock of physical capital $K(t)$ is allocated between the two sectors. I use $N_j(t)$ and $K_j(t)$ to stand for the labor force and capital stocks employed by sector $j = e, i$. I represent full employment of labor and capital:

$$K_i(t) + K_e(t) = K(t), \quad N_i(t) + N_e(t) = N(t).$$

4.5.2 The Production Sector

The production function of the sector $F_i(t)$ is taken on the following form:

$$F_i(t) = A_i K_i^{\alpha_i}(t) N_i^{\beta_i}(t), \quad A_i, \alpha_i, \beta_i > 0, \quad \alpha_i + \beta_i = 1.$$

The marginal conditions imply:

$$r(t) + \delta_k = \frac{\alpha_i \, \bar{\tau}_i F_i(t)}{K_i(t)}, \quad w(t) = \frac{\beta \, \bar{\tau}_i F_i(t)}{N_i(t)},$$

where $\bar{\tau}_i \equiv 1 - \tau_i$ and τ_i is the fixed tax rate on the sector.

4.5.3 The Education Sector

Education is subsided by the government through taxing the households as well as the production and education sectors. The government can tax on households and producers in different ways. Education can be public or/and private in different economies. This section assumes that the education sector is characterized of perfect competition and does not receive any government's financial support. The education sector charges students $p(t)$ per unit of time. The production function of the education sector $F_e(t)$ is specified as follows:

$$F_e(t) = A_e K_e^{\alpha_e}(t) N_e^{\alpha_e}(t), \quad \alpha_e, \beta_e > 0, \alpha_e + \beta_e = 1.$$

The education sector pays teachers and capital with the market rates. The cost of the education sector is given by $w(t)N_e(t) + (r(t) + \delta_k)K_e(t)$. The education sector maximizes the following profit:

$$\pi(t) = \bar{\tau}_e p(t) F_e(t) - (r(t) + \delta_k) K_e(t) - w(t) N_e(t),$$

where $\bar{\tau}_e \equiv 1 - \tau_e$, and τ_e is the fixed tax rate on the education service. For given $p(t), H(t), r(t)$, and $w(t)$, the education sector chooses $K_e(t)$ and $N_e(t)$ to maximize the profit. The marginal conditions of the education sector imply:

$$r(t) + \delta_k = \frac{\alpha_e \bar{\tau}_e p(t) F_e(t)}{K_e(t)}, \quad w(t) = \frac{\beta_e \bar{\tau}_e p(t) F_e(t)}{N_e(t)}.$$

4.5.4 Accumulation of Human Capital

I first introduce learning through creative leisure into formal growth theory. Creative leisure has become an important source of learning especially with spread of modern e-products. One learns much through different club activities, traveling different parts of the world, playing computer games, watching TV, and doing sports, not to mention family background and general social environment. I synthesize three sources of improving human capital, "learning through education," "learning by producing," and "learning by creative leisure." Arrow (1962) first introduced learning by doing into growth theory; Uzawa (1965) took account of trade-offs between investment in education and capital accumulation, and Zhang (2016a) introduced impact of consumption on human capital accumulation into growth theory. The change in human capital dynamics is specified as follows:

$$\dot{H}(t) = \frac{\upsilon_e \left(\frac{F_e(t)}{\bar{N}}\right)^{a_e} (H^m(t) T_e(t))^{b_e}}{H^{\pi_e}(t)} + \frac{\upsilon_i \left(\frac{F_i(t)}{\bar{N}}\right)^{a_i}}{H^{\pi_i}(t)} + \frac{\upsilon_h c^{a_h}(t)}{H^{\pi_h}(t)} - \delta_h H(t),$$

where $\delta_h (> 0)$ is the depreciation rate of human capital, υ_e, υ_i, υ_h, a_e, b_e, a_i, and a_h are non-negative parameters. The signs of the parameters, π_e, π_i, and π_h are not specified as they can be either negative or positive. The term $\upsilon_e \left(F_e/\bar{N}\right)^{a_e} (H^m T_e)^{b_e} / H^{\pi_e}$

describes the contribution to human capital improvement through education. Human capital tends to increase with an increase in the level of education service, F_e, and in the (qualified) total study time, $H^m(t)T_e(t)$. I take account of learning by producing effects in human capital accumulation by the term $\upsilon_i\left(F_i/\bar{N}\right)^{a_i}/H^{\pi_i}$. I take account of learning by consuming by the term, $\upsilon_h c^{a_h}/H^{\pi_h}$. I introduce learning by creative leisure due to the observation that people in developed economies have far more human capital than people in developing economies. The differences cannot be explained due to formal education and leaning through producing.

4.5.5 The Disposable Income and Optimal Behavior

Consumers decide the time of education, consumption level of commodity, and amount of saving. The representative household owns wealth $a(t)$. Variable $\bar{k}(t)$ represents the value of physical wealth owned by the household. I have $\bar{k}(t) = K(t)/\bar{N}$. The household owns physical wealth and government debt: $a(t) = \bar{k}(t)+d(t)$, where $d(t)$ is the debt owned by the representative household. Let τ_a, τ_w and τ_c represent for the fixed tax rates on the wealth income, wage income, and consumption. The household's disposable income is the sum of the interest payment $\bar{\tau}_h r(t)\bar{k}(t)$, the wage payment $\bar{\tau}_w H(t)T(t)w(t)$, and the value of wealth:

$$\hat{y}(t) = a(t) + \bar{\tau}_a r(t)a(t) + \bar{\tau}_w H^m(t)T(t)w(t), \tag{4.5.1}$$

where $\bar{\tau}_a \equiv 1 - \tau_a$, and $\bar{\tau}_w \equiv 1 - \tau_w$. Let $\tau(t)$ stand for the subsidy per unit of time people receive from the government for education. The education cost is the price minus the subsidy rate, $p(t) - \tau(t)$. The disposable income is distributed between the total available budget between saving $s(t)$, consumption of goods $c(t)$, and education $T_e(t)$. The budget constraint implies:

$$\bar{\tau}_c c(t) + s(t) + (p(t) - \tau(t))T_e(t) = \hat{y}(t), \tag{4.5.2}$$

where $\bar{\tau}_c \equiv 1 + \tau_c$. The time constraint is $T(t) + T_e(t) = T_0$. Substituting this equation into (4.5.1) yields:

$$\begin{aligned}\hat{y}(t) =& (1 + \bar{\tau}_a r(t))a(t) + \bar{\tau}_w H^m(t)T_0 w(t)\\ &- \bar{\tau}_w H^m(t)T_e(t)w(t).\end{aligned} \tag{4.5.3}$$

Insert (4.5.3) in (4.5.2)

$$\bar{\tau}_c c(t) + s(t) + \bar{p}(t)T_e(t) = \bar{y}(t), \tag{4.5.4}$$

where

$$\bar{p}(t) \equiv p(t) - \tau(t) + \bar{\tau}_w H^m(t) w(t),$$
$$\bar{y}(t) \equiv (1 + \bar{\tau}_a r(t)) a(t) + \bar{\tau}_w H^m(t) T_0 w(t).$$

The right-hand side of (4.5.4) is the "potential" income that the household can obtain. The left-hand side is the total cost of consumption and saving plus opportunity cost of education. The household has the following utility function which is dependent on $c(t)$, $s(t)$, and $T_e(t)$:

$$U(t) = c^{\xi_0}(t) s^{\lambda_0}(t) T_e^{\eta_0}(t),$$

where ξ_0 is the propensity to consume, λ_0 the propensity to own wealth, and η_0 the propensity to receive education. Maximizing $U(t)$ subject to (4.5.4), I have the marginal conditions:

$$c(t) = \xi \bar{y}(t), \quad s(t) = \lambda \bar{y}(t), \quad \bar{p}(t) T_e(t) = \eta \bar{y}(t),$$

where

$$\xi \equiv \frac{\rho \xi_0}{\bar{\tau}_c}, \quad \lambda \equiv \rho \lambda_0, \quad \eta \equiv \rho \eta_0, \quad \rho = \frac{1}{\xi_0 + \lambda_0 + \eta_0}.$$

The change in the household's wealth is:

$$\dot{a}(t) = s(t) - a(t).$$

4.5.6 The Government Expenditure and Tax Income

Each student is assumed to receive education subsidy $\tau(t)$ in proportion to the education price as follows:

$$\tau(t) = \tilde{\tau} p(t),$$

where $\tilde{\tau}(<1)$ is a non-negative parameter. The government subsidy is endogenously determined in such a way that the price that each student pays for per unit of time is $(1 - \tilde{\tau}) p(t)$. The government finances its current spending by collecting taxes and issuing interest-bearing debt. Let $T_p(t)$ stand for the government's tax income. The income comes from taxing the two sectors, the ownership of wealth, and consumption:

$$T_p(t) = \tau_i F_i(t) + \tau_e p(t) F_e(t) + \tau_a r(t) a(t) \bar{N} + \tau_c c(t) \bar{N} + \tau_w H^m(t) T(t) w(t) \bar{N}.$$

4.5.7 The Dynamics of Government Debt

The government debt is $D(t) : D(t) = d(t)\bar{N}$. I have the change equation for the government debt as follows:

$$\dot{D}(t) = r(t)D(t) + \tau(t)\bar{N} - T_p(t).$$

4.5.8 Demand and Supply in Education Market

The total demand for education is $T_e(t)\bar{N}$. I express the equilibrium of the demand and supply at any point in time:

$$T_e(t)N_0 = F_e(t).$$

The model is completed. To show the dynamics, I introduce a variable $z(t)$:

$$z(t) \equiv \frac{r(t) + \delta_k}{w(t)}.$$

Lemma 4.5.1 *The dynamics of the economic system is given by three differential equations with $z(t)$, $H(t)$ and $D(t)$ as the variables:*

$$\dot{z}(t) = \Omega_z(z(t), H(t), D(t)),$$
$$\dot{H}(t) = \Omega_H(z(t), H(t), D(t)),$$
$$\dot{D}(t) = \Omega_D(z(t), H(t), D(t)),$$

where Ω_z, Ω_H and Ω_D are functions of $z(t)$, $H(t)$ and $D(t)$ defined in Zhang (2017c). *All the other variables are given as functions of $z(t)$, $H(t)$ and $D(t)$.*

The parameters are taken on the following values:

$$\alpha_i = 0.45, \quad \alpha_e = 0.3, \quad \lambda_0 = 0.6, \quad \xi_0 = 0.1, \quad \eta_0 = 0.006, \quad \bar{N} = 10,$$
$$T_0 = 1, \quad A_i = 0.8, \quad A_e = 1, \quad m = 0.6, \quad \tilde{\tau} = 0.2, \quad v_e = 0.8, \quad v_i = 2.5,$$
$$v_h = 0.7, \quad a_e = 0.3, \quad b_e = 0.5, \quad a_i = 0.4, \quad a_h = 0.1, \quad \pi_e = 0.1,$$
$$\pi_i = 0.7, \quad \pi_h = 0.3, \quad \tau_i = \tau_c = 0.05, \quad \tau_w = \tau_a = \tau_e = 0.01,$$
$$\delta_k = 0.03, \quad \delta_h = 0.06.$$

The propensity to save is 0.6 and the propensity to consume education is 0.006. The propensity to consume goods is 0.1. The technological parameters of the two sectors are specified at $A_i = 0.8$ and $A_e = 1$. The conditions $\pi_e = 0.1$, $\pi_i = 0.7$, and $\pi_h = 0.3$ mean that the learning by education exhibits decreasing effects in human capital; the learning by producing exhibits decreasing effects in human capital; and the learning by consuming exhibits decreasing effects in human capital. The values of the equilibrium point are listed as follows:

$$K = 3549, \quad N = 68.4, \quad H = 27.1, \quad Y = 341.4, \quad r = 0.009, \quad w = 62.2,$$
$$p = 33.3, \quad D = 23031, \quad F_i = 322.7, \quad F_e = 0.56, \quad N_i = 68.2, \quad N_e = 0.2,$$
$$K_i = 3543.6, \quad K_e = 5.68, \quad a = 2658, \quad c = 421.9, \quad T_e = 0.056.$$

The consumer spends about 5.6% of the total available time for education. It is straightforward to calculate the three eigenvalues: {0.9, −0.09, −0.02}. As the two eigenvalues are negative and one is positive, the unique equilibrium is unstable. Hence, the system tends to be away from its equilibrium. The instability implies that I cannot effectively conduct comparative dynamic analysis as the system will not approach to an equilibrium point in the long term. Nevertheless, I can follow short-run movement of the system when some parameters are changed. I am now concerned with short-run motion of the system. I specify initial conditions as follows:

$$z(0) = 0.03, \quad H(0) = 14, \quad D(0) = 8000.$$

The simulation result is plotted in Fig. 4.4. The level of the human capital, total labor input, and total physical capital increase from the initial variable values. The education time and output level of the education sector rise initially and then fall during the study period. The changes in the other variables are provided in Fig. 4.4.

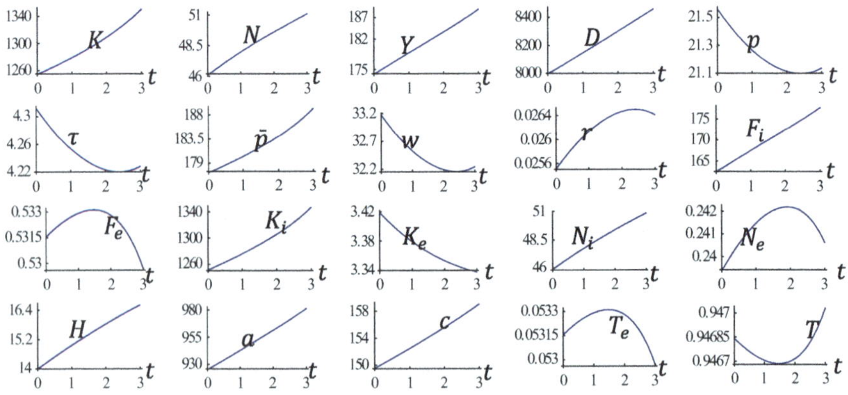

Fig. 4.4 The motion of the economy with national debt

4.6 Short-Run and Long-Run Debts Due to Exogenous Changes

This section studies how the economic system is affected by changes in some parameters.

4.6.1 A Rise in the Government Subsidy Rate on Education

The government subsidy rate on education is assumed to be increased as follows: $\tilde{\tau} : 0.2 \Rightarrow 0.25$. The simulation result is plotted in Fig. 4.5. As the system is unstable, the simulation period is short run. The subsidy amount τ rises. The price of education falls. The opportunity cost of education $\tilde{p}$ becomes lower. The household receives more education subsidy. The household spends more time on education time. The economy produces more. It has less capital and labor supply. The government debt is augmented. The education sector produces more and employs more the two input factors. The industrial sector produces less and employs less the two input factors. The household owns less wealth and consumes less good. Although the household spends more time on education, the human capital is reduced. As there are three resources of accumulating human capital, the education enhances human capital and the other two sources reduce the human capital. The net result reduces human capital as the resource is shifted to education and the education activities have relative weak contribution to human capital accumulation.

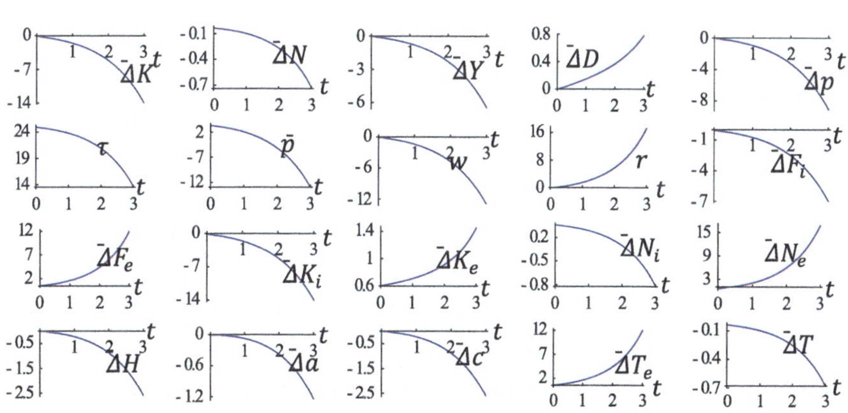

Fig. 4.5 A rise in the government subsidy rate on education

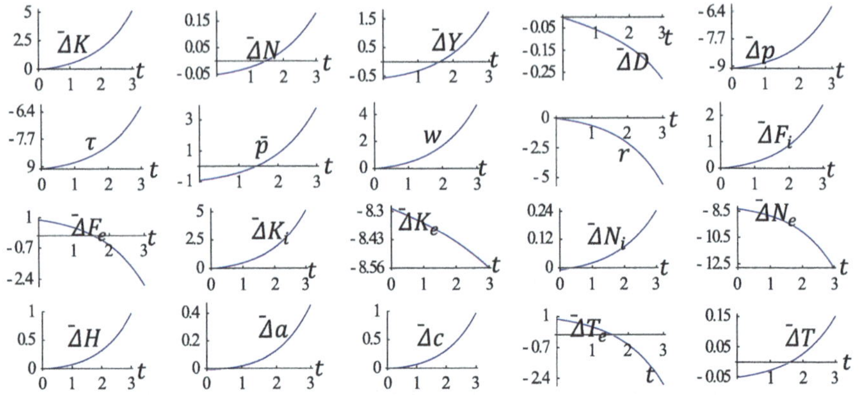

Fig. 4.6 A rise in the total factor productivity of the education sector

4.6.2 A Rise in the Total Factor Productivity of the Education Sector

The total factor productivity of the education sector is increased as follows: A_e : $1 \Rightarrow 1.1$. The simulation result is plotted in Fig. 4.6. When A_e is increased, according to the demand and supply equation, $T_e \bar{N} = F_e$, the education time will be increased. The education fee and education subsidy fall. The opportunity cost of education become lower initially but higher late on. The human capital rises. The wage rate rises. The interest rate becomes lower. The government debt falls. The economy accumulates more capital. The economy has more labor force. It produces less initially, and more in the long term. The education sector produces more initially and less late on. The sector employs less the two input factors.

4.6.3 A Rise in the Total Factor Productivity of the Industrial Sector

The total factor productivity of the industrial sector is assumed to rise as follows: A_i: $0.8 \Rightarrow 0.85$. The simulation result is plotted in Fig. 4.7. The economy has more labor force and produces more. The education sector produces less. The industrial sector produces more and employs more input factors. The price, education subsidy, and opportunity cost become higher. The wage rate and interest rate rise. The education time is decreased. The human capital, wealth per household, and consumption are increased.

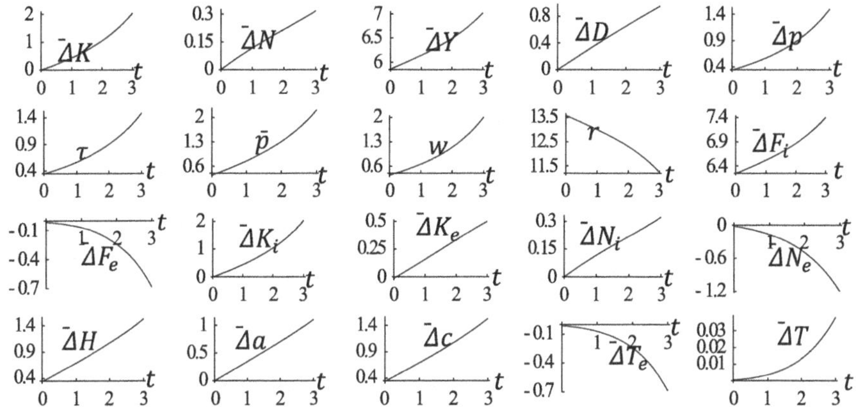

Fig. 4.7 A rise in the total factor productivity of the industrial sector

4.6.4 A Rise in the Propensity to Obtain Education

The propensity to receive education is assumed to increase in the following way: $\eta_0 : 0.006 \Rightarrow 0.007$. The simulation result is demonstrated in Fig. 4.8. The household spends more time on education. The education fee becomes higher. The education sector employs more capital and labor force. The education sector's output rises. Human capital falls. The government debt is increased.

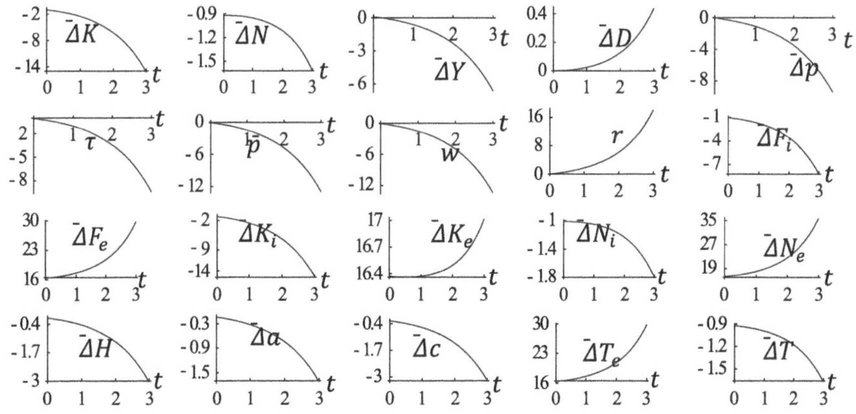

Fig. 4.8 A rise in the propensity to obtain education

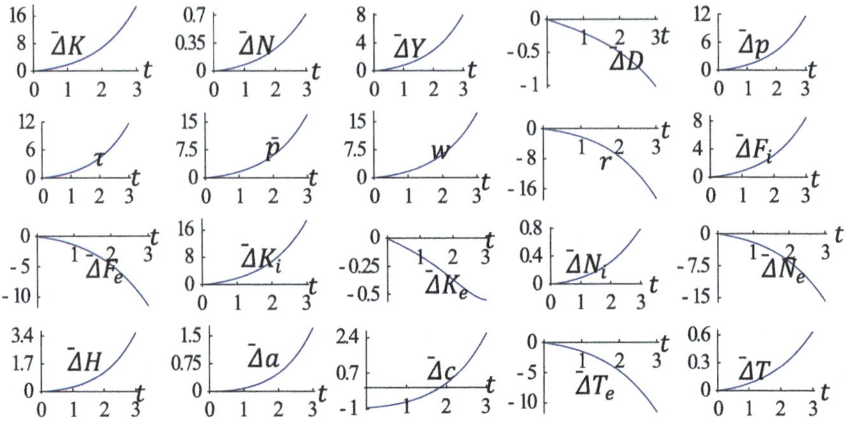

Fig. 4.9 A rise in the tax rate on consumption

4.6.5 *A Rise in the Tax Rate on Consumption*

The tax rate on the consumption of the industrial good is assumed to rise in the following way: $\tau_c\ :\ 0.05\ \Rightarrow\ 0.06$. The simulation result is plotted in Fig. 4.9. The government debt falls. The education price and education subsidy rise. The opportunity cost rises. The wealth per household is increased. The consumption falls initially and rises late on. The physical capital, labor force, and total output are augmented. The industrial sector expands, and the education sector shrinks.

4.6.6 *Stronger Increasing Returns to Scale in Learning from Education*

The returns to scale in learning from education is assumed to become stronger in the following way: $\pi_e : 0.1 \Rightarrow -0.1$. The simulation result is plotted in Fig. 4.10. The government debt is increased. The education price and education subsidy are decreased. The opportunity cost becomes higher. The wealth per household and consumption are increased. The physical capital, labor force, and total output are increased.

4.7 Some Comments on Poverty

Mr. Deng Xiaoping, whose formal education was up to elementary school, made contributions to alleviating China's poverty by reforming its economic system, enabling some hundreds of millions of Chinese people to escape from poverty traps

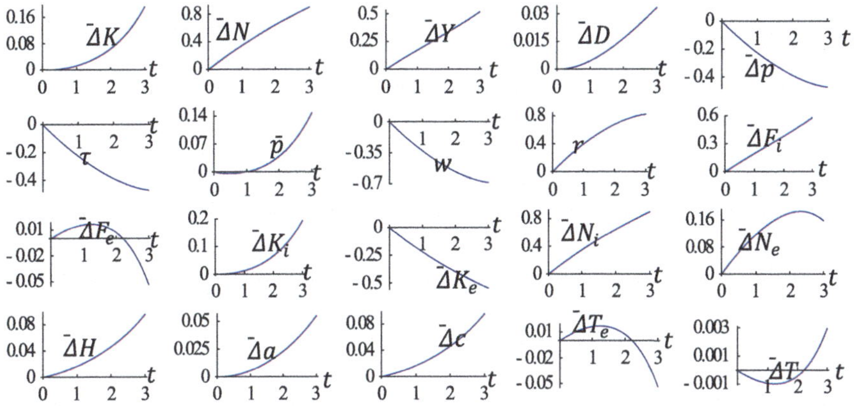

Fig. 4.10 Stronger increasing return to scale in learning from education

within a short period of time. To explain such a dramatic change in human history, one needs a dynamic economic theory which connects education, population change, saving, and policy as a connected organic whole. Suggestion-based partial economic theories might speed up poverty rather than, as shown in economic history, alleviate it. Many partial theories in development economics have not yet had much positive effects on poverty reduction in the political economic environments in which they are perceived.

Quite a few economists were awarded the Nobel Prize for their works on economics of poverty. Theodore W Schultz (1902–1998) and Sir Arthur Lewis (1915–1991) shared the 1979 Nobel Prize for making contributions to economic development research especially concerned with developing countries. Schultz made a lot of studies on agriculture in many countries in perspectives of economic structures. He also systematically studied education and economic development. He emphasized higher returns from human capital. Lewis is a pioneer in developing economy research. His model on duel economy is influential in the literature of economics of development. The 1998 Nobel Prize was awarded to Amartya Sen for his works in welfare economics. His works on welfare economics, poverty indexes, and empirical studies of famine are influential. His theoretical works are mostly static and have much to do with distribution (how to share given national wealth) without much attention paid to how fairly to increase national wealth. Sen's insights into welfare, poverty, and famine can be applied to enrich the framework proposed in this study. Especially, his insights into how various social and economic factors influence different people in the economy. Our heterogeneous-households dynamic approach makes formal analysis possible in short-term as well as long-term aspects. The 2015 Nobel Prize was awarded to Angus Deaton for his contributions to analysis of consumption, poverty, and welfare. He analyzes consumption behavior and economic policy that promotes welfare and poverty. He made efforts to connect individual choices and aggregate outcomes, like this book, integrating microeconomics and macroeconomics with poverty in mind. One of his important insights is that the prevailing consumption theory could not explain individual variables and macroeconomic variables as the aggregate income and consumption. This seems trivial with the theory developed in this book. But when he was creating his ideas, dynamic macroeconomic theory has no proper analytical framework to analyze behavior of heterogeneous households with national economic development. The 2019 Nobel Prize was awarded jointly to Abhijit Banerjee, Esther Duflo, and Michael Kremer because they applied experimental approach to alleviating global poverty. Their research results provide insights into behavior patterns of people living in poverty, insightful especially for academic economists brought up in developed economies. It is beyond the scope of this book to make judgment on experimental approaches. It should be remarked that one should be careful in interpreting results from experimental approaches to poverty partly because relevant and unbiased data collected from poor and uneducated environment are difficult to get. Equipped with relevant data but without any profound theory, some researchers on poverty tend to give misleading solutions to issues related to long-term poverty. The 1989 Nobel Prize winner Haavelmo (1954:5) valued economic theory and empirical research in the following way: "Experience from many fields of human activity suggests that it may be efficient not only to plan well for practical operations to be carried out but also to approach the practical problems in a more round-about way, by seeking first to clarify basic principles. And the desire for theoretical groundwork world seem to be the more justified the larger the magnitude of operations to be carried out." As my approach can treat micro and macroworlds as a connected whole, it is possible to examine issues related to poverty in broader and long-term perspectives on basis of important insights from the previous literature.

References

Alonso-Carrera J, Freire-Sere MJ (2004) Multiple equilibria, fiscal policy and human capital accumulation. J Econ Dyn Control 28:841–856

Arrow KJ (1962) The economic implications of learning by doing. Rev Econ Stud 29:155–173

Barro RJ (1990) Government spending in a simple model of endogenous growth. J Polit Econ 98:S103–S125

Barro RJ (2001) Human capital and growth. Am Econ Rev 91:12–17

Castelló-Climent A, Hidalgo-Cabrillana A (2012) The role of education quality and quantity in the process of economic development. Econ Educ Rev 31:391–409

Diamond PA (1965) National debt in a neoclassical growth model. Am Econ Rev 55:1126–1150

Gómez MA (2008) Convergence speed in the AK endogenous growth model with habit formation. Econ Lett 100:16–21

Haavelmo T (1954) A study in the theory of economic evolution. North-Holland, Amsterdam

Hanushek E, Kimko D (2000) Schooling, labor-force quality and the growth of nations. Am Econ Rev 90:1194–1204

Lin SL (2000) Government debt and economic growth in an overlapping generations model. South Econ J 66:754–763

Lucas RE (1988) On the mechanics of economic development. J Monet Econ 22:3–42

Park H (2009) Ramsey fiscal policy and endogenous growth. Econ Theor 39:377–398

Uzawa H (1965) Optimal technical change in an aggregative model of economic growth. Int Econ Rev 6:18–31
Zhang WB (1998) Japan versus China in the industrial race. Macmillan, London
Zhang WB (2002) Singapore's modernization: westernization and modernizing confucian manifestations. Nova Science, New York
Zhang WB (2003) Taiwan's modernization. World Scientific, Singapore
Zhang WB (2006a) Growth with income and wealth distribution. Macmillan, London
Zhang WB (2006b) Hong Kong: the pearl made of the British mastery and the Chinese docile-diligence. Nova Science, New York
Zhang WB (2010) Fukuzawa Yukichi: the pioneer of East Asia's westernization with ancient confucianism. Publish America, Frederick, MD
Zhang WB (2016) Exchange values of gold, land, physical capital, and human capital in a neoclassical growth model. Econ Altern 3:265–286
Zhang WB (2017) Government debt and education subsidies by synthesizing the Uzawa-Lucas two-sector model and diamond growth-debt model. J Interdisc Econ Res 2017:22–33

Chapter 5
Inequalities with Racial Human Capital Externalities

The rich, by unfair combinations, contribute frequently to prolong a season of distress among the poor.
Thomas Malthus (1766–1834)

Marx's theory on capital accumulation is too simplified to understand processes of complexity of income and wealth distribution between heterogeneous households. In *Capital in the Twenty-First Century*, (Piketty 2014) examines issues related to wealth accumulation and income and wealth distribution. He collected many interesting data across many countries. Following Marx's visions, he holds that the main driver of inequality is due to capital. As the returns on capital tend to exceed, the rate of economic growth, inequality between the rich and the other tend to be enlarged. As he does not use a general equilibrium framework and has no proper microeconomic foundation, his arranged data are practically interesting, even though his arguments are theoretically misleading. This book shows various sources of inequalities, such as cultural attitudes toward saving and learning, knowledge creation and utilization, social status, market power such as monopoly and monopsony, with the basic model and Walrasian general equilibrium theory as the starting point. This chapter shows racial inequalities in income and wealth in association with economic growth.

Issues related to differences in income and wealth among countries are formally modeled in modern growth theory. But theoretical economists have seldom modeled dynamics of income and wealth distributions between ethnic groups. Ethnic differences should be an important determinant for understanding economic growth and development of different peoples within countries or cross-countries. For instance, there are great differences in living conditions and income among different ethnic groups in the USA. There are many studies that emphasize the role of ethnic elements on human capital, cooperativeness, and trust. In *The End of History and the Last Man*, the American–Japanese Fukuyama (1992) studies the role of culture on economic performance. He characterizes China, Italy, Korea, and France as low-trust societies, while German and Japan are high-trust ones. According to him, high-trust societies are capable of building innovative organizations and holding down the cost of doing business. Other studies on the topic also identify externalities associated with social relations and interactions within a group on economic performance.

W.-B. Zhang, *The General Economic Theory*,
https://doi.org/10.1007/978-3-030-56204-5_5

Most studies in economics on racial issues are empirical. There are a few rigorous dynamic models with endogenous wealth in the literature of economic growth theory. This chapter introduces a model with racial externalities (Zhang 2014). The model is concerned with interactions of racial human capital externalities, income and wealth distribution among races, and economic growth in a national economy. The model is an integration of Walrasian general equilibrium, neoclassical growth theories, and Arrow's learning by doing with racial human capital externalities.

5.1 Racial Human Capital Externalities and National Growth

The economy has capital goods and consumer good sectors. Its population is classified into multiple races without cross-marriages. All markets are perfectly competitive. One may easily integrate models of games, monopoly and monopoly in late chapters with the model in this chapter to examine the effects of racial discrimination. Each race's population $\bar{N}_j (j = 1, \ldots, J)$ is fixed and homogenous within each race. Prices are measured in terms of capital good. Variables $w_j(t)$ and $r(t)$ stand for wage rate of race j and interest rate, respectively. Let $p(t)$ stand for price of consumer good. National capital stock $K(t)$ is fully employed by the two sectors. I use subscript index i and s to stand for capital goods and consumer goods sectors, respectively. I use $N_m(t)$ and $K_m(t)$ to stand for the labor force and capital stocks employed by sector m. The total population $\bar{N}$ and total qualified labor supply $N(t)$ are

$$\bar{N} = \sum_{j=1}^{J} \bar{N}_j, \quad N(t) = \sum_{j=1}^{J} h_j(t) \bar{N}_j, \tag{5.1.1}$$

where $h_j(t)$ is the human capital of race j.

5.1.1 The Two Sectors

The two sectors' production functions are specified as follows:

$$F_m(t) = A_m K_m^{\alpha_m}(t) N_m^{\beta_m}(t), \quad \alpha_m, \beta_m > 0, \quad \alpha_m + \beta_m = 1. \tag{5.1.2}$$

The full employment of labor and capital and marginal conditions are

$$N_i(t) + N_s(t) = N(t), \quad K_i(t) + K_s(t) = K(t),$$
$$r(t) + \delta_k = \frac{\alpha_i F_i(t)}{K_i(t)} = \frac{\alpha_s p(t) F_s(t)}{K_s(t)},$$

$$w(t) = \frac{\beta_i F_i(t)}{N_i(t)} = \frac{\beta_s p(t) F_s(t)}{N_s(t)}. \tag{5.1.3}$$

5.1.2 Consumer Behaviors and Wealth Dynamics

I use $\bar{k}_j(t)$ to stand for the value of wealth of race j's representative household. I have $\bar{k}_j(t) = \bar{K}_j(t)/\bar{N}_j$, where $\bar{K}_j(t)$ is the total wealth held by race j. The disposable income of household j is

$$\hat{y}_j(t) = r(t)\bar{k}_j(t) + h_j(t)w(t) + \bar{k}_j(t). \tag{5.1.4}$$

Household j distributes the disposable income between savings $s_j(t)$ and consumer goods $c_j(t)$:

$$p(t)c_j(t) + s_j(t) = \hat{y}_j(t). \tag{5.1.5}$$

Household j's utility level $U_j(t)$ is dependent on $c_j(t)$ and $s_j(t)$ as follows:

$$U_j(t) = c_j^{\xi_{0j}}(t) s_j^{\lambda_{0j}}(t), \quad \xi_{0j}, \lambda_{0j} > 0.$$

Maximizing the utility subject to (5.1.5), I have the marginal conditions

$$p(t)c_j(t) = \xi_j \hat{y}_j(t), \quad s_j(t) = \lambda_j \hat{y}_j(t), \tag{5.1.6}$$

where

$$\xi_j \equiv \rho_j \xi_{0j}, \quad \lambda_j \equiv \rho_j \lambda_{0j}, \quad \rho_j \equiv \frac{1}{\xi_{0j} + \lambda_{0j}}.$$

The change in the household j's wealth is

$$\dot{\bar{k}}_j(t) = s_j(t) - \bar{k}_j(t) = \lambda_j \hat{y}_j(t) - \bar{k}_j(t). \tag{5.1.7}$$

5.1.3 Demand and Supply of the Two Sectors

$$\sum_{j=1}^{J} c_j(t)\bar{N}_j = F_s(t), \quad S(t) - K(t) + \delta_k K(t) = F_i(t), \tag{5.1.8}$$

where

$$S(t) \equiv \sum_{j=1}^{J} s_j(t)\bar{N}_j, \quad K(t) = \sum_{j=1}^{J} \bar{k}_j(t)\bar{N}_j.$$

5.1.4 Human Capital with Racial Human Capital Externalities

I take a simplified form of the human capital accumulation in Chap. 4. The changes in human capital $h_j(t)$ follow the following differential equations:

$$\dot{h}_j(t) = \frac{\upsilon_j c_j^{a_j}(t)\bar{K}_j^{\bar{\theta}_j}(t)}{h_j^{\pi_j}(t)}\left(\frac{\bar{K}_j(t)}{K(t)}\right)^{\theta_j} - \delta_{hj}h_j(t). \tag{5.1.9}$$

The term $\bar{K}_j^{\bar{\theta}_j}$ implies that race j experiences positive (negative) human capital externalities if $\bar{\theta}_j > (<)0$. For instance, if race j becomes richer, the people within the same culture may make more efforts to educate their children and adults might be encouraged from each other within the race due to internal competition, as a result, learn more effectively. The term $\left(\bar{K}_j/K\right)^{\theta_j}$ measures possible effects on the relative share of wealth (or relative economic conditions) of the race in the whole economy. It also may be considered as an index of the social status of the race. If $\theta_j > (<)0$, I may interpret that as the relative social status has a positive (negative) impact on the human capital accumulation. The following lemma is proved in (Zhang 2014).

Lemma 5.1 *The motion of the economic system is determined by 2 J differential equations with $z(t)$ and $\{\bar{k}_j(t)\}$, and $(h_j(t))$ as follows:*

$$\begin{aligned}
\dot{z}(t) &= \Lambda_1\left(z(t), \{\bar{k}_j(t)\}, (h_j(t))\right), \\
\dot{\bar{k}}_j(t) &= \Lambda_j\left(z(t), \{\bar{k}_j(t)\}, (h_j(t))\right), \quad j = 2, \ldots, J, \\
\dot{h}_j(t) &= \Omega_j\left(z(t), \{\bar{k}_j(t)\}, (h_j(t))\right),
\end{aligned} \tag{5.1.10}$$

in which

$$\{\bar{k}_j(t)\} \equiv \left(\bar{k}_2(t), \ldots, \bar{k}_J(t)\right), \quad (h_j(t)) \equiv \left(h_1(t), \ldots, \bar{k}_J(t)\right),$$
$$z(t) \equiv \frac{(r(t) + \delta_k)h_j(t)}{w_j(t)},$$

and $\Lambda_j(t)$ are unique functions of $z(t)$, $\{\bar{k}_j(t)\}$, and $(h_j(t))$ defined in (Zhang 2014). At any point of time, the other variables are unique functions of $z(t)$, $\{\bar{k}_j(t)\}$, and $(h_j(t))$ are calculated by the procedure given by Zhang.

The parameter values are taken on the following values:

$$A_i = 1.3, \quad A_s = 1, \quad \alpha_i = 0.34, \quad \alpha_s = 0.3, \quad \delta_k = 0.05,$$

$$\begin{pmatrix} \bar{N}_1 \\ \bar{N}_2 \\ \bar{N}_3 \end{pmatrix} = \begin{pmatrix} 10 \\ 30 \\ 60 \end{pmatrix}, \quad \begin{pmatrix} \lambda_{10} \\ \lambda_{20} \\ \lambda_{30} \end{pmatrix} = \begin{pmatrix} 0.8 \\ 0.75 \\ 0.7 \end{pmatrix}, \quad \begin{pmatrix} \xi_{10} \\ \xi_{20} \\ \xi_{30} \end{pmatrix} = \begin{pmatrix} 0.12 \\ 0.18 \\ 0.2 \end{pmatrix},$$
$$\begin{pmatrix} \delta_{h1} \\ \delta_{h1} \\ \delta_{h1} \end{pmatrix} = \begin{pmatrix} 0.04 \\ 0.05 \\ 0.06 \end{pmatrix}, \quad \begin{pmatrix} \upsilon_1 \\ \upsilon_2 \\ \upsilon_3 \end{pmatrix} = \begin{pmatrix} 0.8 \\ 0.6 \\ 0.5 \end{pmatrix}, \quad \begin{pmatrix} a_1 \\ a_2 \\ a_3 \end{pmatrix} = \begin{pmatrix} 0.1 \\ 0.15 \\ 0.2 \end{pmatrix},$$
$$\begin{pmatrix} \pi_1 \\ \pi_2 \\ \pi_3 \end{pmatrix} = \begin{pmatrix} 0.1 \\ 0.2 \\ 0.3 \end{pmatrix}, \quad \begin{pmatrix} \theta_1 \\ \theta_2 \\ \theta_3 \end{pmatrix} = \begin{pmatrix} 0.2 \\ 0.1 \\ 0.01 \end{pmatrix}, \quad \begin{pmatrix} \bar{\theta}_1 \\ \bar{\theta}_2 \\ \bar{\theta}_3 \end{pmatrix} = \begin{pmatrix} 0.2 \\ 0.1 \\ 0.01 \end{pmatrix}. \tag{5.1.11}$$

Race 1's propensity to save is 0.8, race 2's is 0.75, and race 3's is 0.7. The depreciation rates of human capital of races 1, 2, and 3 are, respectively, 0.04, 0.05, and 0.06. The decreasing returns to scale effects in human capital of races 1, 2, and 3 are, respectively, 0.01, 0.02, and 0.03. Race 1 (3) has the lowest (highest) depreciation rate and lowest (highest) decreasing return to scale in human capital. I consider race 1 to learn lest effectively from consuming, while race 3 to do it most effectively. Race 1's human capital externality is the strongest, while race 3's is the weakest. The relative social status has the strongest impact on race 1's human capital accumulation, while it has negligible impact on group 3's human capital accumulation. I specify the initial conditions as follows:

$$z(0) = 0.03, \quad \bar{k}_2(0) = 225, \quad \bar{k}_3(0) = 64, \quad h_1(0) = 150, \quad h_2(0) = 22, \quad h_3(0) = 8.$$

The motion of the variables is plotted in Fig. 5.1, where the national income is

$$Y(t) = F_i(t) + p(t)F_s(t).$$

The equilibrium point can be approximately seen in Fig. 5.1. The accurate values are given in Zhang (2014). It is straightforward to confirm that the six eigenvalues are negative.

5.2 Changes in a Race's Preference and Human Capital

I can calibrate the effects of changes in all the parameters on transitory processes as well as stationary states of all variables. I change a few characters of race 1 to illustrate how the race can affect not only its own economic conditions, but also the other races and national economic performance.

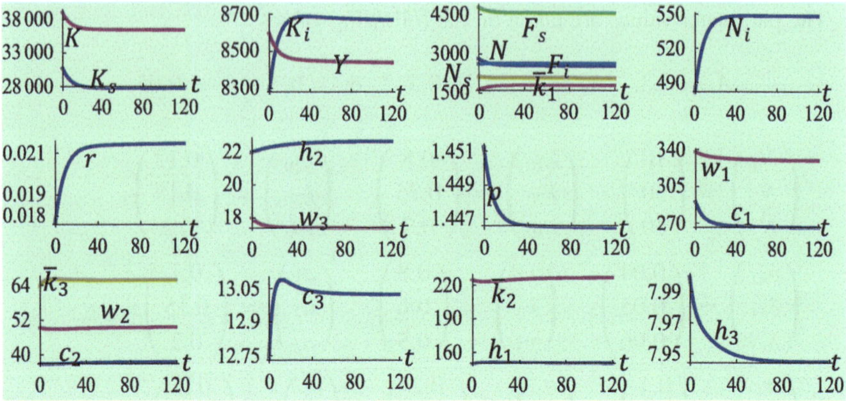

Fig. 5.1 Motion of the economic system

5.2.1 Race 1's Human Capital Externality is Strengthened

Race 1 is assumed to strengthen its human capital externalities as follows: $\bar{\theta}_1 : 0.2 \Rightarrow 0.21$. The simulation result is plotted in Fig. 5.2. The race's human capital is augmented. The race's wage rate becomes higher. Race 1's per capita levels of wealth and consumption become higher. Race 2's human capital, wage rate, and per capita levels of wealth and consumption become slightly lower, while race 3's human capital, wage rate, and per capita levels of wealth and consumption become slightly higher. The change has positive effects on the macroeconomic variables. The GDP, the two sectors' output levels, the total labor and capital, and labor and capital inputs are all increased. The price of consumer good is slightly changed, while the interest rate becomes higher initially and lowers in the long term. The strengthened

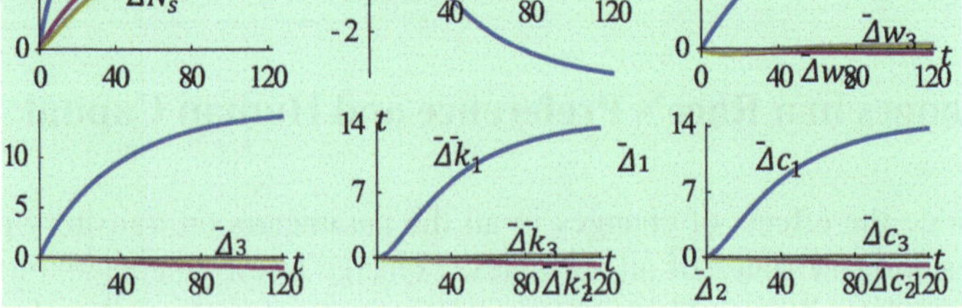

Fig. 5.2 Race 1's human capital externality is strengthened

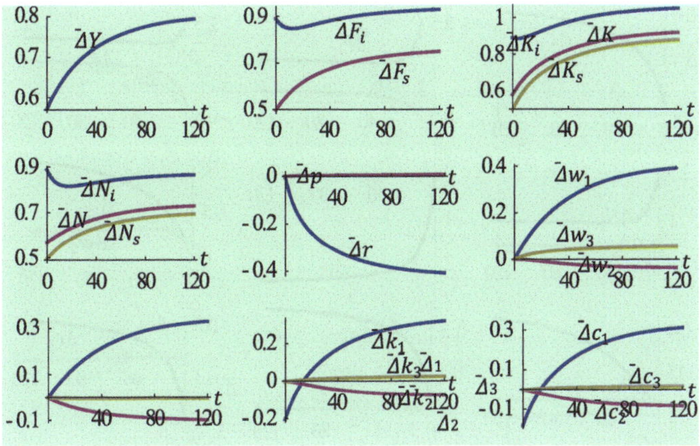

Fig. 5.3 Rise in race 1's population

racial human capital extensity benefits the race itself and national economy, while one race suffers and another race benefits. The inequalities of income and wealth between race 1 and the other races are enlarged.

5.2.2 *Race 1's Population is Increased*

The relationship between population change and economic development is empirically ambiguous and theoretically difficult. Race 1's population is assumed to be increased as follows: $\bar{N}_1 : 10 \Rightarrow 10.1$. The simulation result is plotted in Fig. 5.3. As far as the aggregated real variables are concerned, the national output, the total capital stock, the total labor supply, the capital inputs, the labor inputs, and the output levels of the two sectors are increased during the transitory process as well as in the long term. Race 1's per household's wealth and consumption level become lower initially, but higher in the long term. The rise in the population enlarges the wealth stocks and tends to increase the relative social status. The race's wage rate becomes higher. The effects on the other two races are opposite. Race 2's human capital, wage rate, and per capita levels of wealth and consumption are all reduced, while race 3's human capital is slightly reduced but wage rate and per capita levels of wealth and consumption are increased.

5.2.3 *Race 1's Propensity to Save is Increased*

Race 1 is assumed to increase its propensity to save as follows: $\lambda_{01} : 0.8 \Rightarrow 0.81$. The simulation result is plotted in Fig. 5.4. As race 1 increases its patience for future

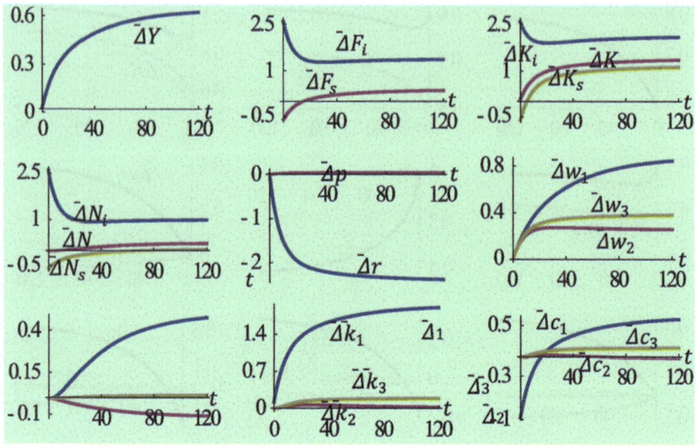

Fig. 5.4 Race 1 increases its propensity to save

consumption, its wealth is augmented. The consumption level of consumer good becomes lower initially and subsequently higher. As race 1 initially saves more, it consumes less. As race 1 has more wealth and the wage rate becomes higher, the disposable income is enhanced in the long term. The consumption level becomes higher. Race 1 benefits from saving greater part of the disposable income in the long term. Race 3's human capital, wage rate, and consumption and wealth levels are increased. Race 2's wage rate is increased, while its human capital is reduced. Race 2's wealth and consumption levels are slightly affected. The total capital stock, total labor supply, capital inputs, labor inputs, output levels of the two sectors, and GDP are all increased in the long term. The interest rate is reduced. The price of consumer good changes slightly.

5.3 On Inequality of Income and Wealth

This chapter described dynamics of income and wealth inequality between races (without intermarriages). An interesting case which I omit here is when some races exhibit increasing returns to scale, while some others exhibit decreasing returns to scale. Some races may lead the country to infinite growth or poverty trap due to their characters, as shown in Chap. 3. There are many studies on relations between wealth and income distribution and development. Kaldor (1956) holds that as the income gap is larger, growth is faster because of more savings. The positive relation between income inequality and growth is tested by, for instance, (Bourguignon 1981; Forbes 2000; Frank 2009). There are other studies which find negative relations between income distribution and growth. There are some formal models which show negative relations (Galor and Zeira 1993; Galor and Moav 2004; Benabou 2002). The model in this chapter and Chap. 3 shows how to explain income and wealth gaps between different groups due to various factors by my approach.

This chapter is concerned with Arrow's learning by doing with racial human capital externalities. Racial differences in education and learning through leisure activities might also play an important role in determining racial differences in income and wealth. Another key determinant is differences in attitudes to children. Different races have various propensities to have children and to make investment in bringing up children. A proper analysis of the endogenous population will make analysis more complicated, even though it can be done as shown in Chap. 7. It is also important to examine the implications of various public goods, such as infrastructures and general knowledge, for different races.

References

Benabou R (2002) Tax and education policy in a heterogeneous-agent economy: What levels of redistribution maximize growth and efficiency? Econometrica 70:481–517

Bourguignon F (1981) Pareto-superiority of unegalitarian equilibria in Stiglitz's model of wealth distribution with convex saving function. Econometrica 49:1469–1475

Forbes K (2000) A reassessment of the relationship between inequality and growth. Am Econ Rev 90:869–870

Frank MW (2009) Inequality and growth in the United States: evidence from a new state-level panel of income inequality measures. Econ Inq 47:55–68

Fukuyama F (1992) The end of history and the last man. Free Press, New York

Galor O, Moav O (2004) From physical to human capital accumulation: inequality in the process of development. Rev Econ Stud 71:1001–1026

Galor O, Zeira J (1993) Income distribution and macroeconomics. Rev Econ Stud 60:35–52

Kaldor N (1956) Alternative theories of distribution. Rev Econ Stud 23:83–100

Piketty T (2014) Capital in the twenty-first century. Belknap Press, New York

Zhang WB (2014) Ethnic human capital externalities and inequality in a general equilibrium growth model. J New Econ Assoc 21:33–54

Chapter 6
Growth with Public Knowledge and Private Human Capital

The year 1883 is special for the history of the world economy and the history of economic analysis. It saw the death of Karl Marx (1918–1883), the birth of John Maynard Keynes (1883–1946), and the birth of Josephy Alois Schumpeter in the now Czech Republic (1883–1950). As mentioned in Chap. 3, Schumpeter admires Walras' general equilibrium theory. He considers Keynes and Ricardo the "Ricardian Vice", a term after Ricardo who plays a great role in bringing mathematical formality to economics. It refers to the tendency for economists to build mathematical theories without properly taking account of complexities of real world. According to Schumpeter, Keynes explains economic reality with a few variables in abstract models, with all other possibly important variables frozen. In the vision of synergetic economics, although they were concerned with the same economy, Keynes focuses on short-term issues, and Schumpeter is concerned with long-term issues.

Schumpeter's "creative destruction", proposed in his *Capitalism, Socialism and Democracy,* is one of well-known economic ideas. The idea is applicable not only to economic fields, but also to cultures and institutions. Creative destruction needs conservative construction, and conservative construction leads to creative destruction. In terms of synergetic economics, economic growth is not a smooth progress, but characterized by (positive or negative) catastrophes, different bifurcations, chaos, endogenous as well as exogenous oscillations, and possibly but rare a long-run unique equilibrium point. This dynamic view is verbally reflected in Schumpeter's *Theory of Economic Development* published in 1911. Through his concept of the entrepreneur and innovations, Schumpeter argues that the entrepreneur will make innovations which cause the old ideas, technologies, skills, and equipment to become obsolete. Capitalist system contains destructive forces. The creative destruction will lead to social progress and enhance people's living standards. This chapter deals with implications of creativity and innovation for economic growth.

Much of basic knowledge is public good. There are many channels of knowledge accumulation. This chapter considers that knowledge production is solely conducted by research institutions which are financially supported by the government. An early

W.-B. Zhang, *The General Economic Theory*,
https://doi.org/10.1007/978-3-030-56204-5_6

rigorous approach to knowledge creation is taken by, for instance, Kennedy (1964), Samuelson (1965) and Weisäcker (1966), who take account of the assumption of "inducement through the factor prices." There are other studies on endogenous technical progresses (Sato and Tsutsui 1984; Nelson and Winter 1982). But theoretical economists had been relatively silent on the topic from the end of the 70s until the publication of Romer's 1986 paper (Romer 1986). Since then there has been an increasing number of publications on the literature (Grossman and Helpman 1991; Aghion and Howitt 1992, 1998). In Romer's approach, knowledge is taken as an input in the production function, and competitive equilibrium is rendered consistent with increasing aggregate returns owing to externalities. It is assumed that knowledge displays increasing marginal productivity, but new knowledge is produced by investment in research technology, which exhibits diminishing returns. Various other issues related to innovation, diffusion of technology, and behavior of economic agents under various institutions have been discussed in the recent literature. There are also many other models emphasizing different aspects, such as education, trade, R&D policies, entrepreneurship, division of labor, learning through trading, brain drain, economic geography, of dynamic interactions among economic structure, development, and knowledge. This chapter deals with interactions between wealth accumulation, knowledge, and human capital in an economy with heterogeneous households.

This chapter includes not only endogenous knowledge, but also endogenous human capital. Endogenous human capital is modeled in Chaps. 3 and 5. Knowledge growth is through research, while human capital accumulation is private and through education and other sources. An economy which may create not much scientific knowledge but make great efforts in accumulating human capital by formal education can experience economic miracles. Western economies dominate the world economy and innovation through pure as well as applied research. Japan made great contributions to natural (applied) sciences which are strongly related to wealth creation and individuals' income. China's economic growth is much due to emphasis on education. There are various channels to enhance national productivities. The following model shows how various factors of growth interact together to sustain economic development.

6.1 Public Knowledge, Individual Human Capital, and Private Wealth

The model is based on Zhang (2018c). There are three determinants of growth—human capital (qualified labor force), machines, and knowledge. Human capital is the basic factor for high labor productivity. Machines enable economy to produce things and supply services. Knowledge is a public good which enhances productivities of human capital growth, knowledge accumulation, and production. There are J types of households, indexed by $j = 1, \ldots, J$. The economy is composed of one production/industrial sector, one education sector, and one research sector. All prices are measured in terms of the commodity. The production sector employs physical capital, labor, and knowledge to produce goods and services. Knowledge accumulation is through research. The research sector is financially supported by the government through taxing households and production sector. I introduce

i, e, and r—subscript index for production, education, and research sectors, respectively;
$\overline{N}_j$—fixed population of group j;
τ and $\bar{\tau}$—fixed tax rate on production sector and $\bar{\tau} \equiv 1 - \tau$;
τ_{jc} and $\tilde{\tau}_{jc}$—fixed tax rate on group j's consumption and $\tilde{\tau}_{jc} \equiv 1 + \tau_{jc}$;
τ_{jw} and $\bar{\tau}_{jw}$—fixed tax rate on wage income and $\bar{\tau}_{jw} \equiv 1 - \tau_{jw}$;
τ_{jk} and $\bar{\tau}_{jk}$—fixed tax rate on interest income and $\bar{\tau}_{jw} \equiv 1 - \tau_{jw}$;
$r(t)$ and $w_j(t)$—interest rate and wage rate per unit time of one qualified labor service;
$p(t)$—price of education service per unit of time;
$T_j(t)$ and $T_{je}(t)$—work time and study time of household j;
$s_j(t)$ and $\bar{k}_j(t)$—saving made by and wealth owned by household j;
$c_j(t)$—consumption of good by household j;
$Z(t)$ and $H_j(t)$—knowledge stock and level of human capital of household j;
$K(t)$ and $\overline{K}_j(t)$—capital stocks of the economy and wealth owned by group j; and
$K_m(t)$ and $N_m(t)$—capital stock and labor force employed by sector m, $m = i, e, r$.

6.1.1 The Total Labor Supply and Behavior of Production Sector

The labor supply of the economy is

$$N(t) = \sum_{j=1}^{J} N_j(t) = \sum_{j=1}^{J} H_j^{m_j}(t) T_j(t) \overline{N}_j, \tag{6.1.1}$$

where m_j is household j's efficiency of applying human capital. The production function of the production sector is

$$F(t) = A_i Z^{m_i}(t) K_i^{\alpha_i}(t) N_i^{\beta_i}(t), \quad A_i, \alpha_i, \beta_i > 0, \quad \alpha_i + \beta_i = 1,$$

where m_i is the production sector's efficiency of knowledge utilization. The marginal conditions imply

$$r(t)+\delta_k=\frac{\alpha_i \bar{\tau} F_i(t)}{K_i(t)}, \quad w(t)=\frac{\beta_i \bar{\tau} F_i(t)}{N_i(t)}.$$

The household's disposable income $\hat{y}_j(t)$ is the value of $\bar{k}_j(t)$, the interest payment $\bar{\tau}_{jk} r(t) \bar{k}_j(t)$, and the wage payment $\bar{\tau}_{jw} H^{m_j}(t) T_j(t) w(t)$:

$$\hat{y}_j(t)=\bar{k}_j(t)+\bar{\tau}_{jk} r(t) \bar{k}_j(t)+\bar{\tau}_{jw} H_j^{m_j}(t) T_j(t) w(t). \tag{6.1.2}$$

Household j chooses the saving $s_j(t)$, the hours of education $T_{je}(t)$, and consumption $c_j(t)$, subject to the budget constraint:

$$\tilde{\tau}_{jc} c_j(t)+s_j(t)+p_j(t) T_{je}(t)=\hat{y}_j(t). \tag{6.1.3}$$

Insert time constraint $T_j(t)+T_{je}(t)=T_0$ in (6.1.2):

$$\hat{y}_j(t)=\bar{y}_j(t)-\bar{\tau}_{jw} H^{m_j}(t) T_{je}(t) w(t), \tag{6.1.4}$$

where

$$\bar{y}_j(t) \equiv \left(1+\bar{\tau}_{jk} r(t)\right) \bar{k}_j(t)+\bar{\tau}_{jw} H^{m_j}(t) T_0 w(t).$$

The variable $\bar{y}_j(t)$ is the "potential" disposable income. Insert (6.1.4) in (6.1.3):

$$\tilde{\tau}_{jc} c_j(t)+s_j(t)+\bar{p}(t) T_{je}(t)=\bar{y}_j(t), \tag{6.1.5}$$

where

$$\bar{p}(t) \equiv p(t)+\bar{\tau}_{jw} H_j^{m_j}(t) w(t).$$

I specify the utility function:

$$U_j(t)=c_j^{\xi_{0j}}(t) s_j^{\lambda_{0j}}(t) T_e^{\eta_{0j}}(t),$$

where η_{0j} the propensity to receive education. Household j maximizes $U_j(t)$ subject to (6.1.5). I get the first-order conditions:

$$c_j(t)=\xi_j \bar{y}_j(t), \quad s_j(t)=\lambda_j \bar{y}_j(t), \quad \bar{p}_j(t) T_{je}(t)=\eta_j \bar{y}_j(t),$$

where

$$\xi_j \equiv \frac{\rho_j \xi_{j0}}{\tilde{\tau}_{jc}}, \quad \lambda_j \equiv \rho_j \lambda_{j0}, \quad \eta_j \equiv \rho_j \eta_{j0}, \quad \rho_j=\frac{1}{\xi_{j0}+\lambda_{j0}+\eta_{j0}}.$$

The change in wealth follows

$$\dot{\bar{k}}_j(t) = s_j(t) - \bar{k}_j(t).$$

6.1.2 The Education Sector

The student pays the education fee $p(t)$ per unit of time. The education sector uses capital input, labor input, and knowledge to supply education service. The education sector has the following production function:

$$F_e(t) = A_e Z^{m_e}(t) K_e^{\alpha_e}(t) N_e^{\beta_e}(t),$$
$$m_e \geq 0, \quad \alpha_e, \beta_e > 0, \quad \alpha_e + \beta_e = 1,$$

where A_e, α_e, and β_e are positive parameters. The parameter m_e is the education sector's efficiency of knowledge utilization. The marginal conditions imply

$$r(t) + \delta_k = \frac{\alpha_e p(t) F_e(t)}{K_e(t)}, \quad w(t) = \frac{\beta_e p(t) F_e(t)}{N_e(t)}.$$

6.1.3 Accumulation of Human Capital

I apply a generalized Uzawa's human capital accumulation as follows:

$$\dot{H}_j(t) = \frac{\upsilon_{je} Z^{m_{jh}}(t) \left(H^{m_j}(t) T_{je}(t)\right)^{b_{je}}}{H^{\pi_{je}}(t)} - \delta_{jh} H_j(t),$$

where $\delta_{jh} (> 0)$ is the depreciation rate of group j's human capital, υ_{je}, m_{jh}, a_{je}, and b_{je} are nonnegative parameters. The sign of π_{je} may be negative or positive. Human capital rises in education service per unit time and in the (qualified) total study time, $\left(H^{m_j}(t) T_{je}(t)\right)^{b_{je}}$. The term $1/H^{\pi_{je}}$ implies that learning through education may exhibit increasing returns to scale in the case of $\pi_{je} < 0$ or decreasing returns to scale in the case of $\pi_{je} > 0$.

6.1.4 Knowledge Creation and Government's Research Policy

Knowledge growth is through research. Knowledge growth is positively related to the knowledge sector's inputs as follows:

$$\dot{Z}(t) = \upsilon_r Z^{m_r}(t) K_r^{\alpha_{0r}}(t) N_r^{\beta_{0r}}(t) - \delta_Z Z(t),$$

in which $\delta_Z(\geq 0)$ is the depreciation rate of knowledge, and υ_r, m_r, α_{0r}, and β_{0r} are positive parameters. The governments collect taxes to support research sector. The government's tax income $Y_p(t)$ is

$$Y_p(t) = \tau F_i(t) + \sum_{j=1}^{J} \left[\tau_{jc} c_j(t) \overline{N}_j + \tau_{jk} r(t) \bar{k}_j(t) \overline{N}_j \right.$$
$$\left. + \tau_{jw} H_j^{m_j}(t) T_j(t) \overline{N}_j w(t) \right].$$

The budget constraint for the research sector is

$$(r(t) + \delta_k) K_r(t) + w(t) N_r(t) = Y_p(t).$$

The total capital cost for the research sector is $(r(t) + \delta_k) K_r(t)$, and the total labor cost is $w(t) N_r(t)$. The government spends the total budget to maximize research output $\upsilon_r Z^{m_r}(t) K_r^{\alpha_{0r}}(t) N_r^{\beta_{0r}}(t)$ as follows:

$$\text{Max } \upsilon_r Z^{m_r}(t) K_r^{\alpha_{0r}}(t) N_r^{\beta_{0r}}(t)$$

The marginal conditions of the research sector are

$$(r(t) + \delta_k) K_r(t) = \alpha_r Y_p(t), \quad w(t) N_r(t) = \beta_r Y_p(t),$$

where

$$\alpha_r \equiv \frac{\alpha_{0r}}{\alpha_{0r} + \beta_{0r}}, \quad \beta_r \equiv \frac{\beta_{0r}}{\alpha_{0r} + \beta_{0r}}.$$

6.1.5 Balance of Demand and Supply and Full Employment of Factors

The total demand for education service in group j is $T_{je}(t) N_0$. The demand and supply for education balance

$$\sum_{j=1}^{J} T_{je}(t)\overline{N}_j = F_e(t).$$

The labor force and capital stock are fully employed:

$$K_i(t) + K_e(t) + K_r(t) = K(t), \quad N_i(t) + N_e(t) + N_r(t) = N(t).$$

Wealth is owned by households:

$$\sum_{j=1}^{J} \bar{k}_j(t)\overline{N}_j = K(t).$$

I constructed a dynamic general equilibrium model with endogenous wealth, human capital, and knowledge.

6.2 Growth with Knowledge, Human Capital, and Wealth

The dynamics of the economy is expressed by 2 J + 1 dimensional differential equations. I introduce

$$z(t) \equiv \frac{r(t) + \delta_k}{w(t)}, \quad \{\bar{k}_j(t)\} \equiv (\bar{k}_2(t), \ldots, \bar{k}_J(t)), \cdots$$
$$(H_j(t)) \equiv (H_1(t), \ldots, H_J(t)).$$

Lemma 6.2.1 *The dynamics of J—type household economy is governed by the following 2 J + 1 differential equations with* $z(t)$, $Z(t)$, $\{\bar{k}_j(t)\}$, *and* $(H_j(t))$, *as the variables:*

$$\dot{z}(t) = \Omega_z\big(z(t), Z(t), (H_j(t)), \{\bar{k}_j(t)\}\big),$$
$$\dot{Z}(t) = \Omega_Z\big(z(t), Z(t), (H_j(t)), \{\bar{k}_j(t)\}\big),$$
$$\dot{\bar{k}}_j(t) = \Omega_{jk}\big(z(t), Z(t), (H_j(t)), \{\bar{k}_j(t)\}\big), \quad j = 2, \ldots, J,$$
$$\dot{H}_j(t) = \Omega_{jH}\big(z(t), Z(t), (H_j(t)), \{\bar{k}_j(t)\}\big), \quad j = 1, \ldots, J,$$

in which functions $\Omega(t)$ *are uniquely determined by variables* $z(t)$, $Z(t)$, $\{\bar{k}_j(t)\}$, *and* $(H_j(t))$, *and as shown in Zhang* (2018c). *For any given solution* $z(t)$, $Z(t)$, $\{\bar{k}_j(t)\}$, *and* $(H_j(t))$, *I can determine all the variables of the economy at any point of time.*

I choose the parameters as follows:

$$T_0 = 1, \quad \tau = 0.01, \quad \alpha_i = 0.35, \quad \alpha_e = 0.31, \quad \alpha_{0r} = 0.5,$$
$$\beta_{0r} = 0.5, \quad \delta_k = 0.04, \quad \delta_Z = 0.03$$

$$\begin{pmatrix} \overline{N}_1 \\ \overline{N}_2 \\ \overline{N}_3 \end{pmatrix} = \begin{pmatrix} 10 \\ 5 \\ 100 \end{pmatrix}, \quad \begin{pmatrix} A_i \\ A_e \\ \upsilon_r \end{pmatrix} = \begin{pmatrix} 1 \\ 1 \\ 0.7 \end{pmatrix}, \quad \begin{pmatrix} m_1 \\ m_2 \\ m_3 \end{pmatrix} = \begin{pmatrix} 0.5 \\ 0.3 \\ 0.1 \end{pmatrix}, \quad \begin{pmatrix} m_i \\ m_e \\ m_r \end{pmatrix} = \begin{pmatrix} 0.3 \\ 0.2 \\ 0.2 \end{pmatrix},$$

$$\begin{pmatrix} \xi_{10} \\ \xi_{20} \\ \xi_{30} \end{pmatrix} = \begin{pmatrix} 0.1 \\ 0.1 \\ 0.1 \end{pmatrix}, \quad \begin{pmatrix} \lambda_{10} \\ \lambda_{20} \\ \lambda_{30} \end{pmatrix} = \begin{pmatrix} 0.8 \\ 0.75 \\ 0.65 \end{pmatrix}, \quad \begin{pmatrix} \eta_{10} \\ \eta_{20} \\ \eta_{30} \end{pmatrix} = \begin{pmatrix} 0.03 \\ 0.025 \\ 0.02 \end{pmatrix},$$

$$\begin{pmatrix} \tau_1 \\ \tau_2 \\ \tau_3 \end{pmatrix} = \begin{pmatrix} 0.01 \\ 0.01 \\ 0.01 \end{pmatrix}, \quad \begin{pmatrix} \tau_{1k} \\ \tau_{2k} \\ \tau_{3k} \end{pmatrix} = \begin{pmatrix} 0.01 \\ 0.01 \\ 0.01 \end{pmatrix}, \quad \begin{pmatrix} \tau_{1w} \\ \tau_{2w} \\ \tau_{3w} \end{pmatrix} = \begin{pmatrix} 0.02 \\ 0.01 \\ 0.01 \end{pmatrix},$$

$$\begin{pmatrix} \tau_{1c} \\ \tau_{2c} \\ \tau_{3c} \end{pmatrix} = \begin{pmatrix} 0.02 \\ 0.01 \\ 0.01 \end{pmatrix}, \quad \begin{pmatrix} m_{1e} \\ m_{2e} \\ m_{3e} \end{pmatrix} = \begin{pmatrix} 0.4 \\ 0.4 \\ 0.2 \end{pmatrix}, \quad \begin{pmatrix} \upsilon_{1e} \\ \upsilon_{2e} \\ \upsilon_{3e} \end{pmatrix} = \begin{pmatrix} 1 \\ 0.7 \\ 0.5 \end{pmatrix},$$

$$\begin{pmatrix} b_{1e} \\ b_{2e} \\ b_{3e} \end{pmatrix} = \begin{pmatrix} 0.1 \\ 0.1 \\ 0.1 \end{pmatrix}, \quad \begin{pmatrix} \pi_{1e} \\ \pi_{2e} \\ \pi_{3e} \end{pmatrix} = \begin{pmatrix} 0.4 \\ 0.6 \\ 0.6 \end{pmatrix}, \quad \begin{pmatrix} \delta_{1h} \\ \delta_{2h} \\ \delta_{3h} \end{pmatrix} = \begin{pmatrix} 0.03 \\ 0.04 \\ 0.05 \end{pmatrix}.$$

Group 1, 2, and 3'*s* populations are, respectively, 10, 50, and 100. Group 1 has the smallest population, and group 3 has the largest population. Group 1, 2, and 3'*s* human capital utilization efficiencies rank from high to low. The representative household of group 1 applies human capital mostly effectively. The representative household of group 3 applies lest effectively. The tax rates are fixed lowly. The depreciation rate of physical capital is fixed at 4%. The depreciation rates of human capital vary between 3 and 5%. The returns to scale parameters in human capital accumulation are all positive. The motion of the system starts with the initial conditions:

$$z(0) = 0.0001, \quad H_1(0) = 480, \quad H_2(0) = 150, \quad H_3(0) = 20,$$
$$\bar{k}_2(0) = 15500, \quad \bar{k}_3(0) = 4100, \quad Z(0) = 264700.$$

The simulation result is plotted in Fig. 6.1. The system has an equilibrium point in the long term. Three variables $Y(t)$, $Y(t)$, and $F_r(t)$ are defined as follows:

$$Y(t) = F_i(t) + p(t)F_i(t), \quad y(t) = \frac{Y(t)}{N(t)},$$
$$F_r(t) = \upsilon_r Z^{m_r}(t) K_r^{\alpha_{0r}}(t) N_r^{\beta_{0r}}(t).$$

The variable $Y(t)$ measures the total national output, excluding knowledge creation. The variable $y(t)$ is the total output per unit of national labor force. The variable $F_r(t)$ is knowledge output by the research sector. Before the system approaches its equilibrium point, the knowledge stock rises and then falls. The national income

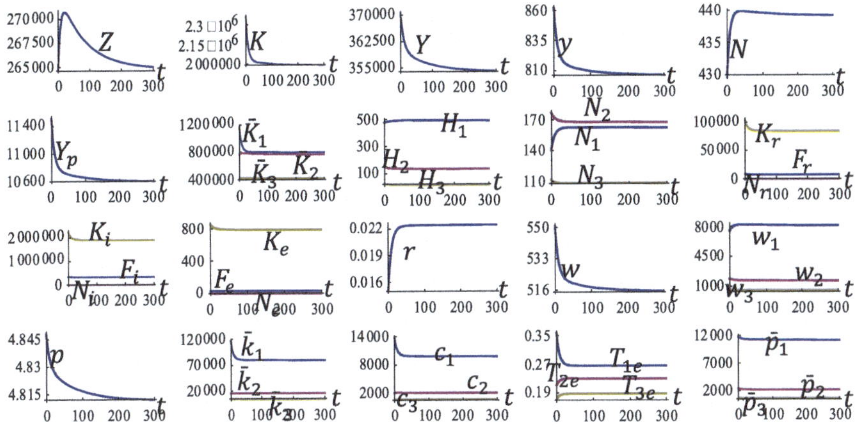

Fig. 6.1 Motion of the economy

falls over time. As the system starts not far from the equilibrium point, most the variables change slightly over time.

The equilibrium point is listed as follows:

$$\begin{pmatrix} Z \\ K \\ N \end{pmatrix} = \begin{pmatrix} 264780 \\ 1.99x10^6 \\ 439.2 \end{pmatrix}, \quad \begin{pmatrix} Y \\ y \\ Y_P \end{pmatrix} = \begin{pmatrix} 343467 \\ 782.1 \\ 10597.6 \end{pmatrix}, \quad \begin{pmatrix} r \\ w \\ p \end{pmatrix} = \begin{pmatrix} 0.023 \\ 515.3 \\ 4.81 \end{pmatrix},$$

$$\begin{pmatrix} H_1 \\ H_2 \\ H_3 \end{pmatrix} = \begin{pmatrix} 492.5 \\ 135.8 \\ 18.4 \end{pmatrix}, \quad \begin{pmatrix} N_1 \\ N_2 \\ N_3 \end{pmatrix} = \begin{pmatrix} 162.6 \\ 167.9 \\ 108.7 \end{pmatrix}, \quad \begin{pmatrix} \bar{K}_1 \\ \bar{K}_2 \\ \bar{K}_3 \end{pmatrix} = \begin{pmatrix} 799024 \\ 770651 \\ 420469 \end{pmatrix},$$

$$\begin{pmatrix} F_i \\ F_e \\ F_r \end{pmatrix} = \begin{pmatrix} 343309 \\ 33 \\ 7943.4 \end{pmatrix}, \quad \begin{pmatrix} N_i \\ N_e \\ N_r \end{pmatrix} = \begin{pmatrix} 428.7 \\ 0.21 \\ 10.28 \end{pmatrix}, \quad \begin{pmatrix} K_i \\ K_e \\ K_r \end{pmatrix} = \begin{pmatrix} 1.91x10^6 \\ 788.1 \\ 84834.9 \end{pmatrix},$$

$$\begin{pmatrix} w_1 \\ w_2 \\ w_3 \end{pmatrix} = \begin{pmatrix} 8380 \\ 1730.8 \\ 559.9 \end{pmatrix}, \quad \begin{pmatrix} \bar{p}_1 \\ \bar{p}_2 \\ \bar{p}_3 \end{pmatrix} = \begin{pmatrix} 11212.3 \\ 2230.9 \\ 687.6 \end{pmatrix}, \quad \begin{pmatrix} \bar{k}_1 \\ \bar{k}_2 \\ \bar{k}_3 \end{pmatrix} = \begin{pmatrix} 79902.4 \\ 15413 \\ 4204.7 \end{pmatrix},$$

$$\begin{pmatrix} c_1 \\ c_2 \\ c_3 \end{pmatrix} = \begin{pmatrix} 9792 \\ 2034.7 \\ 640.5 \end{pmatrix}, \quad \begin{pmatrix} T_{1e} \\ T_{2e} \\ T_{3e} \end{pmatrix} = \begin{pmatrix} 0.267 \\ 0.23 \\ 0.188 \end{pmatrix}.$$

The eigenvalues are calculated as follows:

$$-0.136, \quad -0.125, \quad -0.122, \quad -0.08, \quad -0.064, \quad -0.043, \quad -0.012.$$

The equilibrium point is locally stable.

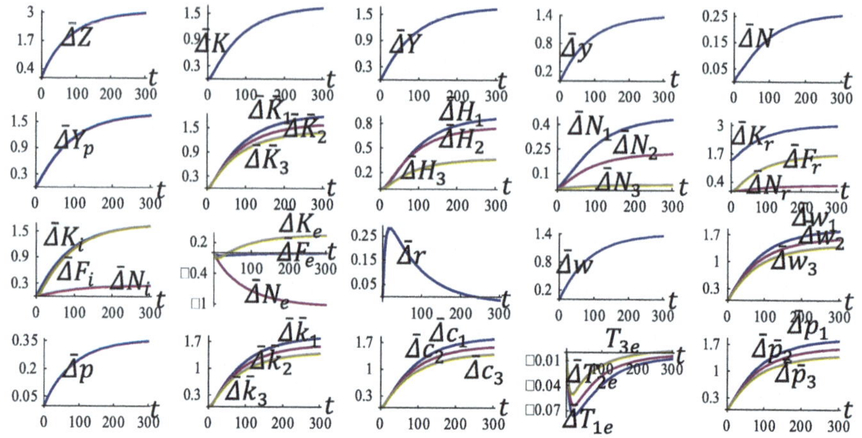

Fig. 6.2 Research sector's creativity rises

6.3 The Role of Creativity, Government Policy, and Preference

I now carry out comparative dynamic analysis with regards a few parameters.

6.3.1 A Rise in the Research Sector's Creativity

The research sector's creativity is assumed to be increased in the following way: $\upsilon_r : 0.7 \Rightarrow 0.71$. The simulation result is plotted in Fig. 6.2. The knowledge stock and national wealth are enhanced. The national output is increased. The economy has more labor supply, and each group supplies more labor. The households' education time is slightly reduced. The price of education becomes higher. The opportunity costs of education for all groups are increased. Three groups all augment their human capital. They receive higher wage incomes. Household 1's wage income and wealth are increased more in percentage than the other two groups. The gaps in income and wealth distributions are enlarged. The production and research sectors are expanded. The education sector's output remains almost invariant. The educator sector's capital input is increased. The sector's labor input becomes lower.

6.3.2 Group 3's Population Increases

Group 3's population is assumed to be increased as follows: $\overline{N}_3 : 100 \Rightarrow 105$. The simulation result is plotted in Fig. 6.3. The knowledge stock and national wealth are

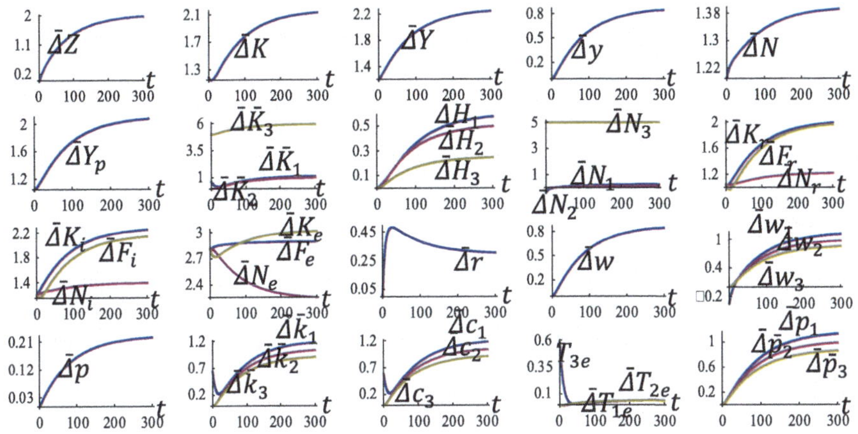

Fig. 6.3 Group 3's population increases

enhanced. The economy produces more. The total labor supply and each group's labor supply are augmented. All the households increase education hours. The price of education becomes higher. The opportunity costs of education for all the groups are increased. All the groups have higher human capital and higher wage incomes. The three sectors all produce more. Each group's per household wealth and consumption levels are augmented. A rise in the population will benefit everyone in the knowledge-based economy.

6.3.3 Group 1 Applies Human Capital More Effectively

Group 1's human capital utilization efficiency is assumed to be enhanced as follows: $m_1 : 0.5 \Rightarrow 0.51$. The simulation result is plotted in Fig. 6.4. The economy has more knowledge stock and wealth. The economy produces more. The total labor supply and each group's labor supply are augmented. The households spend fewer hours on education. The opportunity costs of education fall for all groups. Three groups have higher human capital and wage incomes. The production and research sectors expand. The education sector produces slightly more. The sector employs more capital input but less labor input.

6.3.4 A Rise in the Tax Rate on the Production Sector

The government's tax rate on the production sector is assumed to be increased as follows: $\tau : 0.01 \Rightarrow 0.012$. The simulation result is plotted in Fig. 6.5. The government gets more tax income. The research sector is expanded. The economy has more

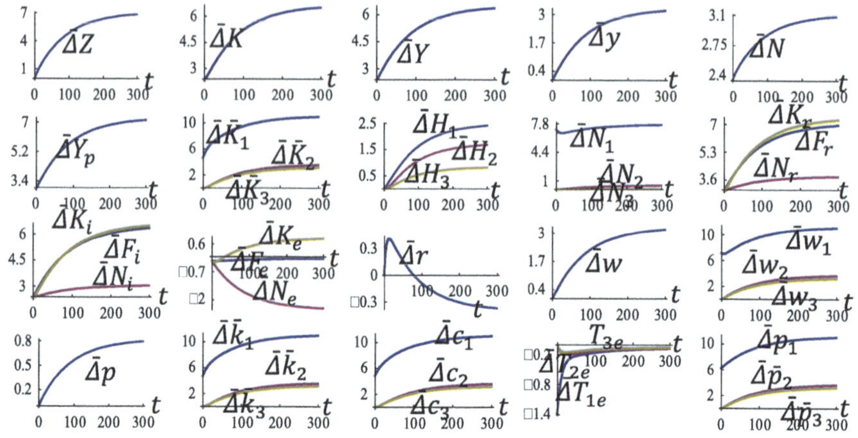

Fig. 6.4 Group 1 applies human capital more effectively

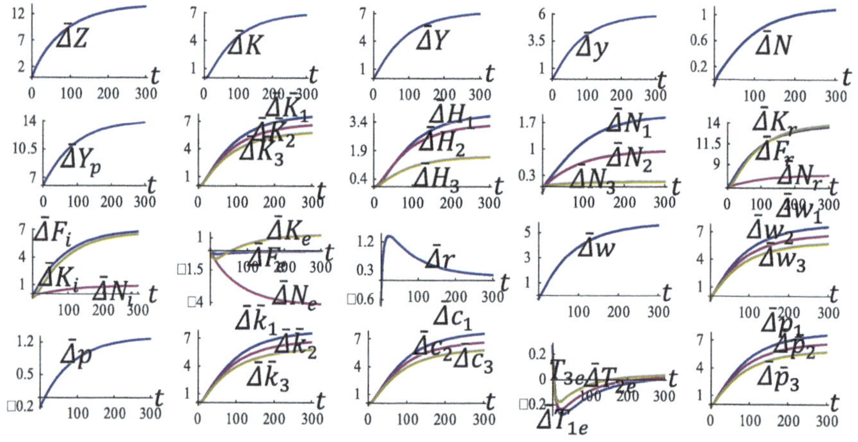

Fig. 6.5 Rise in the tax rate on the production sector

knowledge stock and wealth. The national output is increased. The economy has more labor supply. Each household supplies more labor. All the households initially increase education hours, then reduce education hours, and change little in the long term. The price of education becomes higher. Each household spends more on the opportunity costs of education. Each household has higher human capital and more wage income. The three sectors expand. Each group's per household wealth and consumption levels are enhanced.

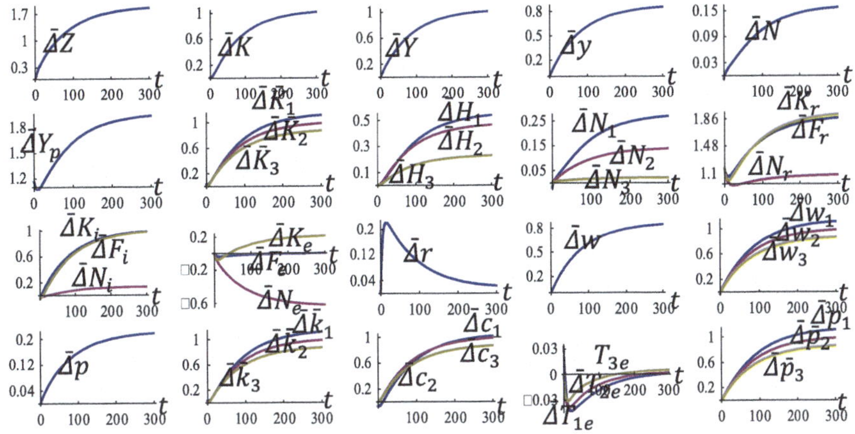

Fig. 6.6 Rise in the tax rate on group 1's consumption of goods

6.3.5 A Rise in the Tax Rate on Group 1's Consumption of Goods

The government's tax rate on group 1's consumption of goods is assumed to be increased as follows: $\tau_{1c}: 0.02 \Rightarrow 0.021$. The simulation result is plotted in Fig. 6.6. The government gets more tax income. The research sector is expanded. The economy has more knowledge stock and more wealth. The national output is increased. The economy has more labor supply. Each household supplies more labor. All the households initially increase education hours, then reduce education hours, and change little in the long term. The price of education becomes higher. Each household pays more the opportunity costs of education. Each household has more human capital and more wage income. The three sectors expand. Each household has more wealth and consumption.

6.3.6 A Rise in Group 1's Propensity to Receive Education

The propensity to receive education is assumed to be increased as follows: $\eta_{01}: 0.03 \Rightarrow 0.031$. The simulation result is plotted in Fig. 6.7. Household 1 spends more time on education. The economy has less knowledge stock, wealth, and output. Household 1's human capital rises initially and falls in the long term. Household 1's labor supply falls. The other two groups' labor supplies are reduced slightly. Each household has less wage income. The price of education is reduced. The opportunity costs of education for all the groups become lower. Each household has lower human capital. The three sectors shrink.

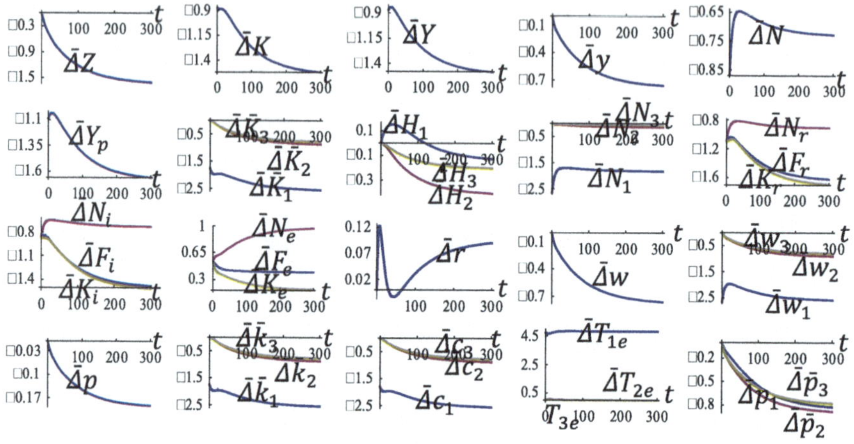

Fig. 6.7 Rise in group 1's propensity to receive education

6.3.7 *Group 1 More Effectively Accumulates Human Capital*

Group 1 is assumed to enhance the propensity to receive education as follows: b_{1e}: $0.1 \Rightarrow 0.11$. The simulation result is plotted in Fig. 6.8. Household 1 reduces education time. The other two groups' education hours are slightly decreased. The knowledge stock, national wealth, and national output are augmented. Household 1's human capital and labor supply are enhanced. The other two groups' human capital and labor supply are slightly augmented. The economy has more labor supply. Each household has more wage income. The price of education becomes higher. The opportunity costs of education for all the groups become higher. The production and

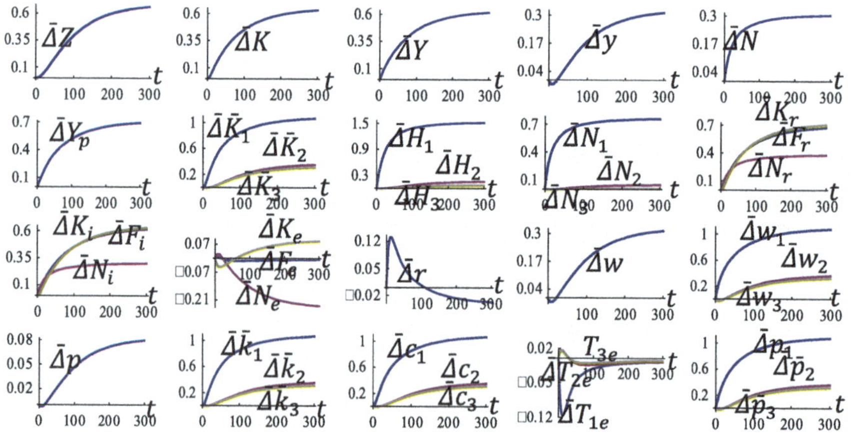

Fig. 6.8 Group 1 more effectively accumulates human capital with education time

research sectors are expanded. The education sector's output is slightly affected. It employs more capital and less labor force.

6.4 Some Comments on Innovation with Microeconomic Foundation

The 2018 Nobel Prize in economics was awarded to Paul M. Romer (1955–) for integrating technological innovations into long-run macroeconomic analysis. The prize was shared with Nordhaus whose contribution is related to environmental change. The basic analytical framework for Romer's approach is related to the Dixit–Stiglitz 1977 model. His model also provides a formal analysis of Schumpeter's ideas on economic development. In the *Theory of Economic Development* published in 1911, Schumpeter argues that development should be understood as only such changes in economic life as are not forced upon it from without but arise by its own initiative, from within. Schumpeter holds that successful carrying out of new combinations of productive services is the essence of this process. It is spontaneous and discontinuous changes in the channels of the flow, disturbance of equilibrium, which alters and displaces the equilibrium state previously existing. The carrying out of new combinations is innovation, which consists of the following five cases: (i) introduction of a new good or a new quality of an old good; (ii) introduction of a new method of production; (iii) the opening of a new market for a product; (iv) the conquest of a new source of raw materials or half-manufactured articles; and (v) the carrying out of a new organization of an industry like the creation of a monopoly position or the breaking up of a monopoly position. Profits are temporary in the sense that they emerge at one point in the economy and accrue to the innovator, then start dwindling as they are shared by an increasing number of innovators on one hand and eaten up by rising costs and falling prices on the other, till they finally disappear. By this time, the development achieved in the form of the newly introduced method has been generalized, completely replacing the old inferior methods. Profits are thus both the child and the victim of economic development. Once again the competitive process establishes cost-price equality all round. Factorial rewards equal marginal productivities. Wages and rents are now higher and prices of consumer good lower. But the circular flow once again comes into its own. A dynamic flow is again disturbed by some new innovations. Creative destruction is continued by competition over profits. The competitive process will strike not at the margins of the profits of existing firms but at their very existence. The fear for survival encourages operating efficiency. The dynamic competition among the entrepreneurs creates innovations and destroys old equilibria by establishing new combinations. The process of such "creative destruction" brings about progress in productivity. I had integrated the basic ideas in Romer's approach with Walrasian general equilibrium and neoclassical growth theories. How the integration can be carried out is referred to Chaps. 13

and 14. A much more profound analysis of Schumpeter's theory can be carried by further applying synergetic economics.

References

Aghion P, Howitt P (1992) A model of growth through creative destruction. Econometrica 60:323–351

Aghion P, Howitt P (1998) Endogenous growth theory. The MIT Press, Mass, Cambridge

Grossman GM, Helpman E (1991) Innovation and growth in the global economy. The MIT Press, Mass, Cambridge

Kennedy C (1964) Induced bias in innovation and the theory of distribution. Econ J 74:541–547

Nelson RR, Winter SG (1982) An evolutionary theory of economic change. Harvard University Press, Mass, Cambridge

Romer D (1986) A simple general equilibrium version of the Baumol-Tobin model. Quart J Econ 101:663–686

Samuelson PA (1965) A theory of induced innovation along Kennedy-Weizsäcker lines. Rev Econ Stat 47:343–356

Sato R, Tsutsui S (1984) Technical progress, the Schumpeterian hypothesis and market structure. J Econ S4:1–37

Weizsäcker CC (1966) Tentative notes on a two-sector model with induced technical progress. Rev Econ Stud 33:245–251

Zhang WB (2018) Public knowledge, individual human capital, and private wealth in a generalized dynamic Walrasian general equilibrium theory. Soc Econ Debates 7:74–99

Chapter 7
Population Dynamics with Endogenous Birth and Mortality Rates

Modern economies are characterized by fast capital accumulation, widely spread education and fast accumulated human capital, improved physical health, and unprecedented population dynamics (such as aging and declining fertility rates in developed economies). In many parts of the world, life expectancy has increased dramatically. Two obvious trends are occurring in the world: developed countries experience negative population growth (especially minus immigrants), while many developing economies experience positive population growth.

In the eighteenth and early nineteenth centuries, many intellectuals believed in linear positive economic growth. Malthus (1766–1834) argues for the opposite, by pointing that a large proportion of the general population are always poor and miserable. The checking force of economic progress is due to population dynamics. Malthus argues: "Population, when unchecked, goes on doubling itself every 25 years or increases in a geometrical ratio." As farmland is limited and a main input factor of the economy is land, fast increasing world population implies that growth cannot be always positive. The Malthusian trap results from his belief that people tend to use their incomes for more babies, rather than for maintaining a lifestyle with high standard of material conditions, child-free leisure activities, and investment in human capital of their own as well as their children. As history shows, people's preference for number of children has been changed in some parts of the world. Modern economic growth in association with technological changes, increased power over nature, migration, and newly cultivated lands makes the dynamics between population and economic growth far more complicated than Malthus' time. Contemporary developed economies have perhaps the problem opposite to what Malthus points out due to reduced birth rates. If one thinks the world as an organic whole, Malthus is valid as a much great portion of the world population are still living in poor conditions and the world population growth not only causes continuation of poverty but also even threatens survival of humanity by causing global problems related to, for instance, environment and resources.

W.-B. Zhang, *The General Economic Theory*,
https://doi.org/10.1007/978-3-030-56204-5_7

Chapter 4 modeled economic growth when physical capital and human capital are determinants of growth. This chapter introduces population change into growth theory with wealth and human capital. If migration is neglected, population change consists of net changes in birth and death. Many factors may interact with changes in fertility. In the literature of population and economic growth, these factors include, for instance, changes in gender gap in wages (Barro and Becker 1989; Galor and Weil 1996), labor market frictions (Adsera 2005), age structure (Hock and Weil 2012), and endogenous fertility and human capital accumulation (Chu et al. 2013). In the studies by Galor and Weil (1999) and Doepke (2004), the quality–quantity trade-off on children has been treated as a factor which affects the transition of economies from a stage of stagnation to perpetual growth. Schultz (1993, 1998) demonstrates that children's life expectancy increases with parent's human capital and education. This chapter models impact of various factors on birth and death rates on microeconomic foundation.

7.1 Haavelmo's Growth Model and Chaos with Population

Trygve Haavelmo (1911–1999) was awarded Nobel Prize in economics in 1989 for his contribution to the foundation of econometrics. His works involve many fields in economics. His contributions to formal growth theory are reflected in *A Study in the Theory of Economic Evolution* (Haavelmo 1954). His broad views on economic evolution are advanced in the time when the book was published. He emphasized formal models for empirical studies. This section introduces his growth model with endogenous population.

The model in this section is based on Sect. 6.2 in Zhang (1991). The model is constructed by Haavelmo (1954) in continuous form. Its discrete form was examined by Stutzer (1980) by applying modern mathematics for one-dimensional mappings. The Haavelmo model is given as follows:

$$\dot{N}(t) = N(t)\left(a - \frac{\beta N(t)}{Y(t)}\right), \quad a, \beta > 0,$$

$$Y(t) = AN^{\alpha}(t), \quad A > 0, \quad 0 < \alpha < 1,$$

where $N(t)$ is the population, $Y(t)$ is real output, and a, β, α, and A are parameters. Substituting $Y(t) = AN^{\alpha}(t)$ into the differential equation yields

$$\frac{\dot{N}(t)}{N(t)} = a - \frac{\beta}{f(t)} = a - \frac{\beta N^{1-\alpha}(t)}{A},$$

where $f(t) \equiv Y(t)/N(t)$ is per capita output. The growth law is a generalization of the familiar logistic form widely used in biological population and economic analysis. If the initial condition satisfies $N(0) > (<)(aA/\beta)^{1/(2-\alpha)}$, then both N and Y will decrease (increase) monotonically until approaching their unique equilibrium points, respectively. As the change rate in the population is the birth rate minus the mortality rate, I interpret that in the Haavelmo model the birth rate (=a) is constant and the mortality rate ($= \beta/f(t)$) is negatively related to per capita income.

Stutzer (1980) reforms Haavelmo's model in continuous form into discrete form:

$$N(t+1) = N(t)\left[(1+a) - \frac{\beta N(t)^{1-\alpha}}{A}\right],$$

which can be further simplified as:

$$x(t+1) = (1+a)x(t)\left(1 - x^{1/2}(t)\right) = F(x(t); a, 0.5), \qquad (7.1.1)$$

in which the new variable $x(t)$ is defined by the transformation:

$$N(t) = \left[\frac{A(1+a)}{\beta}\right]^{1/(1-\alpha)} x(t),$$

with $\alpha = 1/2$. None of the qualitative properties of the system are affected by a particular choice of $0 < \alpha < 1$. This model is an early formal economic growth model which demonstrates chaotic behavior. For each value of a, equilibrium points are given by the intersection of the graph of $F(x(t); a)$ with the 45° line. For each value of a, there are two equilibria $x_0 = 0$ and $x_0 = \{a/(1+a)\}^2$. The point $x_0 = 0$ is unstable and repels nearby points. The local stability of the other can be determined by linearization at the equilibrium. I have:

$$F'(x_0; a) = 1 - \frac{a}{2} = \theta(a). \qquad (7.1.2)$$

The eigenvalue $\theta(a)$ determines the local stability of x_0. When $0 < \theta < 1$, x_0 attracts nearby points in an exponential, monotonic fashion. When $0 > \theta > -1$, x_0 attracts nearby points in a damped oscillatory manner. When $\theta = 1$, x_0 is neither stable nor unstable. Finally, if $|\theta| > 1$, x_0 is unstable. These behaviors occur when $0 < a < 2, 2 < a < 4$, $a = 4$, and $4 < a < 5.57$, respectively. When the equilibrium is stable, i.e., $a < 4$, the trajectory starting at any point always approaches it. In this region, a traditional comparative statics analysis shows that an increase in the parameter a will increase x_t for sufficiently large t. If $4 < a < 5.57$, trajectories do not approach the equilibrium, but bounded by 0 and 1. In fact, as the parameter a exceeds 4, the unstable equilibrium point bifurcates into two stable points of period two, i.e., into a stable periodic orbit of length 2. The 2-period cycle becomes unstable

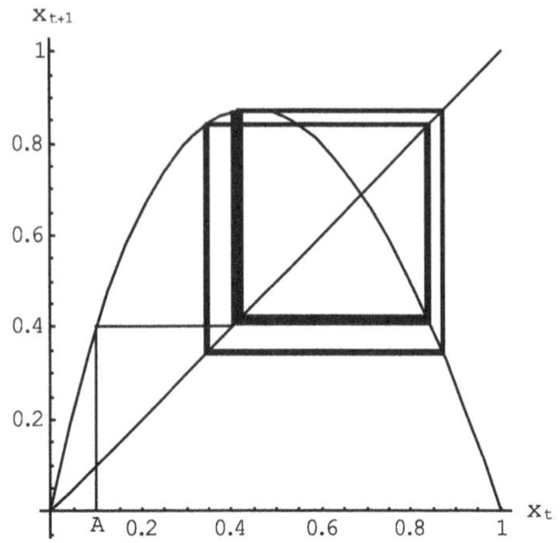

Fig. 7.1 4-period orbit for $a = 4.9$

for values of a in excess of about 4.8, and each 2-period point bifurcates into two 4-period points, producing an stable cycle of length four denoted by $\left\{x_{01}^4, x_{02}^4, x_{03}^4, x_{04}^4\right\}$. Figure 7.1 illustrates the phenomenon.

This pitchfork bifurcation process continues as the parameter a increases, producing non-degenerate orbits of length $2k(k = 2, \ldots)$. These orbits are called harmonics of the 2-period orbit. It can be shown that all the harmonics occur prior to the parameter a reaching 5.54, although how much prior to this value is not known. Thus, the range of a, within which a stable orbit of length k first appears and later becomes unstable and bifurcates to a $2k$-period orbit, decreases in length as the parameter a increases to a limiting value $a_c < 5.54$. The range of $a_c < a \leq 5.75$ is termed the chaotic region. As the parameter a enters this region, even stranger behavior can occur. For example, a 3-period orbit exists at values of a near 5.540. This then gives rise to orbits of periods $3k(k = 2, \ldots)$ via the pitchfork process just described. In fact, if I can locate the 3-period orbit, a remarkable theorem of Li and Yorke (1975) demonstrates that for any $F(x(t); a)$ in which a non-degenerate 3-period orbit arises, there must also exist non-degenerate points of all periods, as well as an uncountable set of periodic (not asymptotically periodic) points whose trajectories wander "randomly" throughout the domain of F. Our dynamic economic system satisfies the requirements in the Li–Yorke theorem for some values of a. This guarantees the existence of chaotic behavior as illustrated in Fig. 7.2.

The existence of chaos implies that no one can precisely know what will happen in society in the future, except that it will be changing. To illustrate why no one precisely foresees the consequences of the intervention policy, one finds out what happen to the chaotic system when it starts from two different but very near states, $x_0 = 0.400$ and $x_0 = 0.405$ over 100 years.

The difference $x[t, 0.400]-x[t, 0.405]$ between the path started at $x_0 = 0.400$ and the one at $x_0 = 0.405$ over 100 years is illustrated in Fig. 7.3.

In summary, as the autonomous growth rate a exceeds a certain value, the steady state ceases being approached monotonically, and an oscillatory approach occurs. If

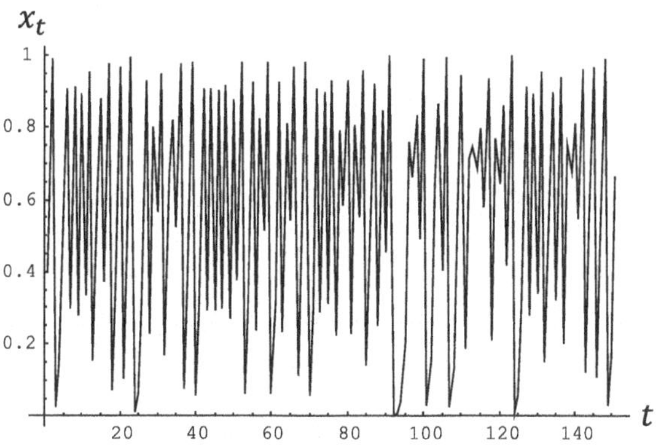

Fig. 7.2 Existence of chaos for $a = 5.75$ with $x_0 = 0.4$

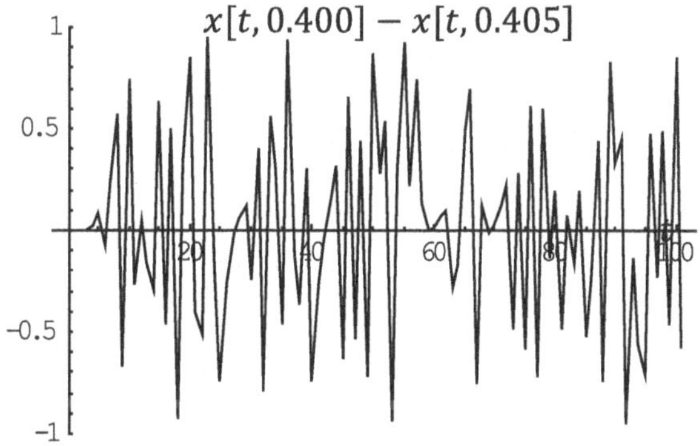

Fig. 7.3 Small differences at the beginning signify much

a is increased further, the steady state becomes unstable and repels nearby points. As a increases, one can find a value of a where the system possesses a cycle of period k for arbitrary k (see Fig. 7.4). Also, there exists an uncountable number of initial conditions from which emanate trajectories that fluctuate in a bounded and

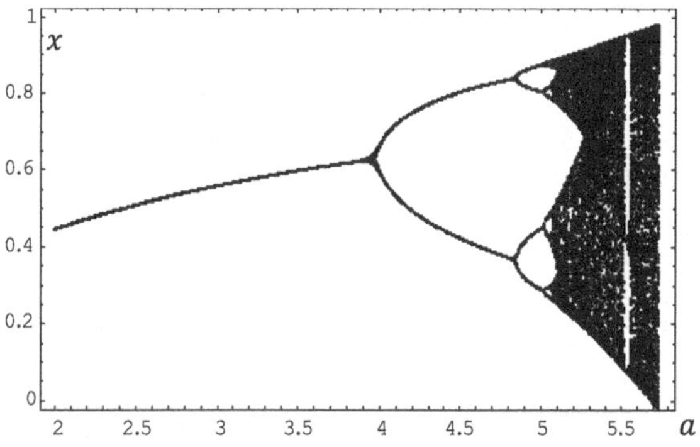

Fig. 7.4 Map of bifurcations for $a \in [2, 5.75]$

aperiodic fashion and are indistinguishable from a realization of some stochastic (chaotic) process.

7.2 Global Population and Economic Growth with Free Trade

This section deals with global dynamic interdependence between economic growth, population growth, and inequalities in income and wealth in a multi-country model with free markets and free trade. It builds a trade model with endogenous wealth, endogenous birth and mortality rates, population dynamics, time distributions between leisure, work, and children caring under perfectly competitive markets and free trade. The model is by Zhang (2016). The world consists of J countries, indexed by j, $j = 1, \dots J$. All the countries produce the internationally homogenous capital good. Country j's depreciation rate is δ_{kj}. Let prices be measured in terms of the capital good and the price of the capital good be unit. I denote wage and interest rates by $w_j(t)$ and $r(t)$, respectively, in the jth country. I assume that each family consists of husband, wife, and children. All the families are identical. I use subscripts $q = 1$ and $q = 2$ to stand for man and woman, respectively. I use $\overline{N}_j(t)$ to stand for the population of each gender in country j. Country j has the population, $2\overline{N}_j(t)$. I use (j, q) to index a person of gender q in country j. Let $T_{jq}(t)$ and $\overline{T}_{jq}(t)$ stand for work time and time spent on taking care of children of (j, q) and $N_j(t)$ for country j's labor force used in time t for production. I have $N_j(t)$ as follows:

$$N_j(t) = \sum_{j=1}^{J} \left[h_{j1}T_{j1}(t) + h_{j2}T_{j2}(t)\right]\overline{N}_j(t), \quad j = 1, \dots, J,$$

where h_{jq} is the level of human capital of person (j, q).

7.2.1 The Production Sectors and Marginal Conditions

Let $K_j(t)$ stand for the capital stock employed by country j. The production functions are taken on the following forms:

$$F_j(t) = A_j K_j^{\alpha_j}(t) N^{\beta_j}(t), \quad \alpha_j, \beta_j > 0, \quad \alpha_j + \beta_j = 1,$$

The marginal conditions are:

$$r(t) + \delta_{kj} = \frac{\alpha_j F_j(t)}{K_j(t)}, \quad w_j(t) = \frac{\beta_j F_j(t)}{N_j(t)}, \quad w_{jq}(t) = h_{jq} w_j(t). \qquad (7.2.1)$$

7.2.2 Consumer Behaviors

Family j's disposable income is given by:

$$\hat{y}_j(t) = (1 + r(t))\bar{k}_j(t) + \left[h_{j1}T_{j1}(t) + h_{j2}T_{j2}(t)\right]w_j(t). \tag{7.2.2}$$

Let $n_j(t)$ and $p_{bj}(t)$ stand for the birth rate and the cost of birth. In addition to the time spent on children, the cost of the parent is given by $p_{bj}(t) = n_j(t)\bar{k}_j(t)$. The fertility rate and the parent's time on raising children are assumed to have the following relation:

$$\overline{T}_{jq}(t) = \theta_{jq}n_j(t), \quad \theta_{jq} \geq 0. \tag{7.2.3}$$

The specified function form implies that if the parents want more children, they spend more time on childcaring. This linear formation is a strict requirement as childcaring tends to exhibit increasing return to scale. For instance, the time per child tends to fall as the family has more children. Clothes and housing are shared among family members. In this stage of modeling, I assume constant return to scale because this assumption makes the analysis mathematically tractable. The household distributes the total available budget between saving, $s_j(t)$, consumption of goods $c_j(t)$, and bearing children $p_{bj}(t)$. The budget constraint is:

$$p_j(t)c_j(t) + s_j(t) + \bar{k}_j(t)n_j(t) = \hat{y}_j(t). \tag{7.2.4}$$

Except work and childcaring, parents have their leisure. The leisure time of person (j, q) is denoted by $\widetilde{T}_{jq}(t)$. Each person is faced with the following time constraint:

$$T_{jq}(t) + \overline{T}_{jq}(t) + \widetilde{T}_{jq}(t) = T_0. \tag{7.2.5}$$

Substituting (7.2.5) and (7.2.5) into (7.2.4) yields:

$$\begin{aligned} &p(t)c_j(t) + s_j(t) + \bar{k}_j(t)n_j(t) + \overline{T}_{j1}(t)w_{j1}(t) + \overline{T}_{j2}(t)w_{j2}(t) \\ &\quad + \widetilde{T}_{j1}(t)w_{j1}(t) + \widetilde{T}_{j2}(t)w_{j2}(t) = \bar{y}_j(t), \end{aligned} \tag{7.2.6}$$

where

$$\bar{y}_j(t) \equiv (1 + r(t))\bar{k}_j(t) + \left(w_{j1}(t) + w_{j2}(t)\right)T_0.$$

The right-hand side is the "potential" income that the family obtains by spending all the available time on work. The left-hand side is the sum of the consumption cost, the saving, the opportunity cost of bearing children, and opportunity cost of leisure. Insert (7.2.3) in (7.2.6):

$$c_j(t) + s_j(t) + \tilde{w}_j(t)n_j(t) + \widetilde{T}_{j1}(t)w_{j1}(t) + \widetilde{T}_{j2}(t)w_{j2}(t)$$
$$= \overline{y}_j(t), \tag{7.2.7}$$

where

$$\widetilde{w}_j(t) \equiv \overline{k}_j(t) + h_j w_j(t), \quad h_j \equiv \theta_{j1}h_{j1} + \theta_{j2}h_{j2}.$$

The variable $\widetilde{w}_j(t)$ is the opportunity cost of children fostering. The utility function is dependent on $c_j(t)$, $s_j(t)$, $\widetilde{T}_{jq}(t)$, and $n_j(t)$ as follows:

$$U_j(t) = c_j^{\xi_{j0}}(t)s_j^{\lambda_{j0}}(t)\widetilde{T}_{j1}^{\sigma_{j01}}(t)\widetilde{T}_{j2}^{\sigma_{j02}}(t)n_j^{\upsilon_{j0}}(t),$$

where ξ_{j0} is called the propensity to consume, λ_{j0} the propensity to own wealth, σ_{j0q} the gender q's propensity to use leisure time, and υ_{j0} the propensity to have children. Maximizing $U_j(t)$ subject to (7.2.6) yields:

$$c_j(t) = \xi_j \overline{y}_j(t), \quad s_j(t) = \lambda_j \overline{y}_j(t), \quad \widetilde{T}_{jq}(t) = \frac{\sigma_{jq}\overline{y}_j(t)}{w_{jq}(t)},$$
$$n_j(t) = \frac{\upsilon_j \overline{y}_j(t)}{\tilde{w}_j(t)}, \tag{7.2.8}$$

where

$$\xi_j \equiv \rho_j \xi_{j0}, \quad \lambda_j \equiv \rho_j \lambda_{j0}, \quad \sigma_{jq} \equiv \rho_j \sigma_{jq0}, \quad \upsilon_j \equiv \rho_j \upsilon_{j0},$$
$$\rho_j \equiv \frac{1}{\xi_{j0} + \lambda_{j0} + \sigma_{j10} + \sigma_{j20} + \upsilon_{j0}}.$$

7.2.3 *The Birth and Mortality Rates and Population Dynamics*

The population change of each country follows:

$$\dot{\overline{N}}_j(t) = \left(n_j(t) - d_j(t)\right)\overline{N}_j(t), \tag{7.2.9}$$

where $d_j(t)$ is the mortality rate. The mortality rate is negatively related to the disposable income in the following way:

$$d_j(t) = \frac{\overline{\upsilon}_j \overline{N}_j^{b_j}(t)}{\overline{y}_j^{a_j}(t)}, \tag{7.2.10}$$

where $\overline{\upsilon}_j \geq 0$, $a_j \geq 0$. I call $\overline{\upsilon}_j$ the mortality rate parameter. The sign of b_j is generally ambiguous in the sense that the population may have positive or positive impact on mortality. Insert (7.2.7) and (7.2.9) in (7.2.8):

$$\dot{\overline{N}}_j(t) = \left(\frac{\upsilon_j \overline{y}_j(t)}{\tilde{w}_j(t)} - \frac{\overline{\upsilon}_j \overline{N}_j^{b_j}(t)}{\overline{y}_j^{a_j}(t)} \right) \overline{N}_j(t).$$

7.2.4 *Wealth Dynamics*

The change in the household's wealth is given by:

$$\dot{\overline{k}}_j(t) = s_j(t) - \overline{k}_j(t).$$

7.2.5 *Balance Conditions*

The value of global physical capital is equal to the value of global wealth:

$$\sum_{j=1}^{J} \overline{k}_j(t) \overline{N}_j(t) = K(t).$$

The assumption that the global capital is fully employed implies:

$$\sum_{j=1}^{J} K_j(t) = K(t).$$

As the global output is the sum of the net savings and the depreciations of capital, I have:

$$S(t) - K(t) + \sum_{j=1}^{J} \delta_{kj} K_j(t) = \sum_{j=1}^{J} F_j(t),$$

where

$$S(t) = \sum_{j=1}^{J} s_j(t) \overline{N}_j(t), \; C(t) = \sum_{j=1}^{J} c_j(t) \overline{N}_j(t).$$

The trade balances of the economies are given by:

$$B_j(t) = \left(\overline{K}_j(t) - K_j(t)\right) r(t).$$

I built the model. I show that the dynamics can be expressed by differential equations with $z_1(t)$, $\{\overline{k}_j(t)\}$ and $(N_j(t))$ where

$$\{\overline{k}_j(t)\} \equiv \left(\overline{k}_2(t), \ldots, \overline{k}_J(t)\right), \quad z_1(t) \equiv \frac{r(t) + \delta_{k1}}{w_1(t)}.$$

Lemma 7.2.1 *The dynamics of the economic system is governed by:*

$$\begin{aligned}
\dot{z}_1(t) &= \Omega_1\left(z_1(t), \{\overline{k}_j(t)\}, \left(\overline{N}_j(t)\right)\right), \\
\dot{\overline{k}}_j(t) &= \Omega_j\left(z_1(t), \{\overline{k}_j(t)\}, \left(\overline{N}_j(t)\right)\right), \quad j = 2, \ldots, J, \\
\dot{\overline{N}}_j(t) &= \Lambda_j\left(z_1(t), \{\overline{k}_j(t)\}, \left(\overline{N}_j(t)\right)\right), \quad j = 1, \ldots, J.
\end{aligned}$$

where $\Omega_j(t)$ and $\Lambda_j(t)$ are functions of $z_1(t)$, $\left(\overline{k}_j(t)\right)$, and $\left(\overline{N}_j(t)\right)$ defined Zhang (2016). *All the other variables are determined as functions of $z_1(t)$, $\left(\overline{k}_j(t)\right)$, and $\left(N_j(t)\right)$ and can be calculated by a given computational procedure for computer.*

I choose $T_0 = 24$. I specify the other parameters as follows:

$$\alpha_j = 0.25, \quad b_j = 0.5, \quad a_j = 0.4, \quad \delta_{k1} = \delta_{k2} = 0.05, \quad \delta_{k3} = 0.06,$$

$$\begin{pmatrix} A_1 \\ A_2 \\ A_3 \end{pmatrix} = \begin{pmatrix} 1.2 \\ 1 \\ 0.8 \end{pmatrix}, \quad \begin{pmatrix} h_{11} \\ h_{21} \\ h_{31} \end{pmatrix} = \begin{pmatrix} 2 \\ 1.5 \\ 1 \end{pmatrix}, \quad \begin{pmatrix} h_{12} \\ h_{22} \\ h_{32} \end{pmatrix} = \begin{pmatrix} 1.5 \\ 1 \\ 0.5 \end{pmatrix},$$

$$\begin{pmatrix} \xi_{10} \\ \xi_{20} \\ \xi_{30} \end{pmatrix} = \begin{pmatrix} 0.2 \\ 0.2 \\ 0.2 \end{pmatrix}, \quad \begin{pmatrix} \lambda_{10} \\ \lambda_{20} \\ \lambda_{30} \end{pmatrix} = \begin{pmatrix} 0.6 \\ 0.55 \\ 0.5 \end{pmatrix}, \quad \begin{pmatrix} v_{10} \\ v_{20} \\ v_{30} \end{pmatrix} = \begin{pmatrix} 0.5 \\ 0.6 \\ 0.7 \end{pmatrix},$$

$$\begin{pmatrix} \sigma_{110} \\ \sigma_{210} \\ \sigma_{310} \end{pmatrix} = \begin{pmatrix} 0.1 \\ 0.12 \\ 0.16 \end{pmatrix}, \quad \begin{pmatrix} \sigma_{120} \\ \sigma_{220} \\ \sigma_{320} \end{pmatrix} = \begin{pmatrix} 0.13 \\ 0.14 \\ 0.18 \end{pmatrix}, \quad \begin{pmatrix} \overline{v}_1 \\ \overline{v}_2 \\ \overline{v}_3 \end{pmatrix} = \begin{pmatrix} 0.02 \\ 0.03 \\ 0.035 \end{pmatrix},$$

$$\begin{pmatrix} \theta_{11} \\ \theta_{21} \\ \theta_{31} \end{pmatrix} = \begin{pmatrix} 0.1 \\ 0.2 \\ 0.1 \end{pmatrix}, \quad \begin{pmatrix} \theta_{12} \\ \theta_{22} \\ \theta_{32} \end{pmatrix} = \begin{pmatrix} 0.5 \\ 0.3 \\ 0.2 \end{pmatrix}.$$

For the same gender, country 1's human capital is higher than country 2's and country 2's human capital is higher than country 3's. The total productivity factors vary between countries. The relative propensities are listed as follows:

$$\begin{pmatrix} \nu_1 \\ \lambda_1 \\ \xi_1 \\ \sigma_{11} \\ \sigma_{12} \end{pmatrix} = \begin{pmatrix} 0.327 \\ 0.392 \\ 0.131 \\ 0.065 \\ 0.085 \end{pmatrix}, \begin{pmatrix} \nu_2 \\ \lambda_2 \\ \xi_2 \\ \sigma_{21} \\ \sigma_{22} \end{pmatrix} = \begin{pmatrix} 0.373 \\ 0.342 \\ 0.124 \\ 0.075 \\ 0.087 \end{pmatrix}, \begin{pmatrix} \nu_3 \\ \lambda_3 \\ \xi_3 \\ \sigma_{31} \\ \sigma_{31} \end{pmatrix} = \begin{pmatrix} 0.402 \\ 0.287 \\ 0.115 \\ 0.092 \\ 0.103 \end{pmatrix}.$$

Country 1's propensity to have children is lower than country 2's and country 2's propensity to have children is lower than country 3's. Both man and woman of country 3 have the highest propensities to stay at home. Country 1 has the highest propensity to save. The father has lower propensity to pursue leisure than the mother. The initial conditions are specified as:

$$z_1(0) = 0.38, \quad \bar{k}_2(0) = 34, \quad \bar{k}_3(0) = 10, \quad N_1(0) = 91{,}200,$$
$$N_2(0) = 39{,}900, \quad N_3(0) = 22{,}900.$$

The simulation result is plotted in Fig. 7.5. The population grows from its low initial condition. As the population rate rises, the mortality rate is also increasing. The labor force is increased, and the wage rates are reduced. The falling wage rates reduce the opportunity cost of children fostering, resulting in the rise of birth rate. The rising in birth rate is associated with rising in both man's and woman's time of children fostering. As the income falls, both men and women work longer hours. Their leisure hours are reduced. The national wealth and output are increased in association with rising labor force. Nevertheless, both consumption level and wealth

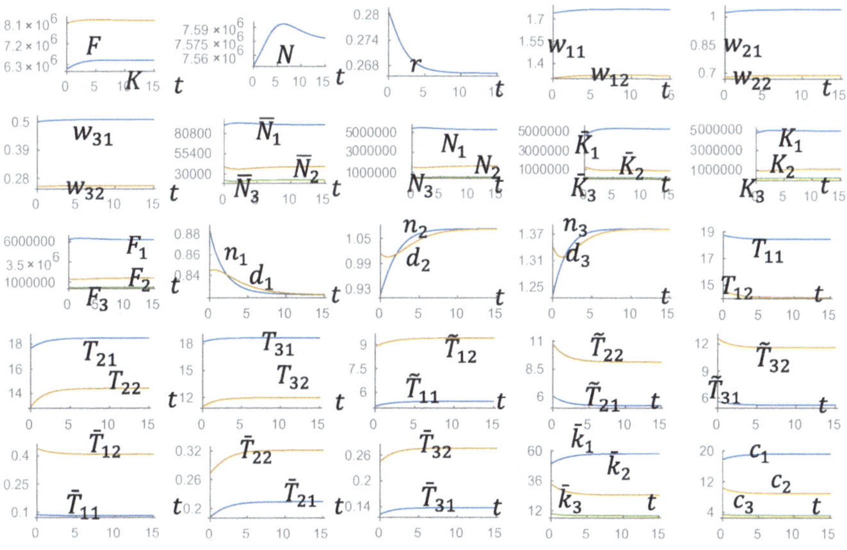

Fig. 7.5 Motion of the economic system

per household are reduced. Some studies confirm that there is a decline of the fertility rate alone the process of economic development (Kirk 1996; Ehrlich and Lui 1997; Galor 2012). Figure 7.5 shows that the relations between consumption and birth rates vary for different groups in different stages of economic growth.

The simulation confirms the existence of the following equilibrium point:

$$\begin{aligned}
&K = 6.49 \times 10^6, \quad N = 5.33 \times 10^6, \quad F = 8.22 \times 10^6, \quad r = 0.266, \\
&\overline{N}_1 = 91667, \quad \overline{N}_2 = 39741, \quad \overline{N}_3 = 22991, \quad N_1 = 5.33 \times 10^6, \\
&N_2 = 1.68 \times 10^6, \quad N_3 = 567067, \quad K_1 = 4.97 \times 10^6, \quad K_2 = 1.23 \times 10^6, \\
&K_3 = 295285, \quad F_1 = 6.28 \times 10^6, \quad F_2 = 1.55 \times 10^6, \\
&F_3 = 385368, \quad n_1 = d_1 = 0.82, \quad n_2 = d_2 = 1.07, \\
&n_3 = d_3 = 1.38, \quad w_{11} = 1.77, \quad w_{12} = 1.33, \quad w_{21} = 1.04, \\
&w_{22} = 0.69, \quad w_{31} = 0.51, \quad w_{32} = 0.26, \quad T_{11} = 18.47, \quad T_{21} = 18.53, \\
&T_{31} = 18.66, \quad T_{12} = 14.14, \quad T_{22} = 14.48, \quad T_{32} = 12.02, \quad \widetilde{T}_{11} = 5.45, \\
&\widetilde{T}_{21} = 5.25, \quad \widetilde{T}_{31} = 5.20, \quad \widetilde{T}_{12} = 9.45, \quad \widetilde{T}_{22} = 9.19, \quad \widetilde{T}_{32} = 11.71, \\
&\overline{T}_{11} = 0.08, \quad \overline{T}_{21} = 0.22, \quad \overline{T}_{31} = 0.14, \quad \overline{T}_{12} = 0.41, \quad \overline{T}_{22} = 0.32, \\
&\overline{T}_{32} = 0.28, \quad \bar{k}_1 = 57.86, \quad \bar{k}_2 = 25.05, \quad \bar{k}_3 = 8.29, \quad c_1 = 19.29, \\
&c_2 = 9.11, \quad c_3 = 3.32.
\end{aligned}$$

The countries have different populations. These differences are due to the differences in human capital, the propensities to have children, and other factors. The dynamic comparative statics will demonstrate how changes in these determining factors will affect the population dynamics. Before effectively conducting dynamic comparative analysis, I guarantee stability of the equilibrium point by calculating the following six eigenvalues:

$$-2.97, \quad -2.13, \quad -1.63, \quad -0.68, \quad -0.6, \quad -0.54.$$

7.3 Global Population with Changes in National Characters

The previous section defines the model and shows that the system has a locally stable equilibrium. I now show how the global population is affected when nations change their preferences or enhance their productivities.

7.3.1 Human Capital of Country 1's Woman Being Improved

Stotsky (2006: 18) argues that "the neoclassical approach examines the simultaneous interaction of economic development and the reduction of gender inequalities. It sees the process of economic development leading to the reduction of these inequalities and also inequalities hindering economic development." There are many other studies about gender inequalities (Beneria and Feldman 1992; Forsythe et al. 2000). I now examine how the following rise in the human capital of country 1's woman affects the global economic and population dynamics: $h_{12} : 1.5 \Rightarrow 1.7$. The result is plotted in Fig. 7.6. The global labor force, global output, and global capital are enhanced. The interest rate is reduced. The wage rate of country 1's woman is increased, and the wage rates of other groups are slightly increased. Country 1's population and labor force are increased, and the other two countries' labor force and population are slightly affected. For country 1, the opportunity cost of child fostering is increased in association with the mother's wage rising. At the same time, the wage rate increased. The net result on the country's birth rate is that it falls. Country's mortality rate falls more than the birth rate till the two rates converge. All the countries produce more and employ more capital. Country 1's level of national wealth is increased, and the other two countries' levels of national wealth are slightly affected. Country 1's representative household has more wealth and consumes more. The consumption and wealth levels of the other two countries' households are slightly affected. Country 1's man works fewer hours and woman more hours. The time distributions that country 1's parents spend change correspondingly. The mother from country 1 works more hours and the father works fewer hours. The father has more leisure time and the

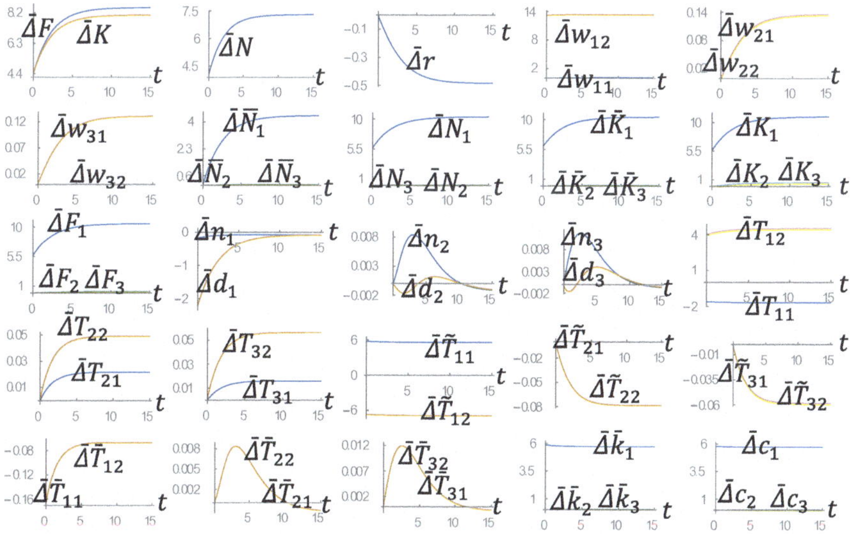

Fig. 7.6 Country 1's woman has higher human capital

mother has less. The parents reduce the hours on children fostering. With regards to the effects on the other two countries' time distributions, each one works longer hours and has less leisure time. The long-term effects reduce slightly the two countries' birth and mortality rates.

7.3.2 Country 1's Mother Spending More Time on Per Child Fostering

I consider what happen to the global economic growth and population dynamics when country 1's mother spends more time on per child fostering in the following way: θ_{12}: $0.5 \Rightarrow 0.7$. The result is plotted in Fig. 7.7. Country 1's mother spends more time on children caring and the father slightly changes his time on children caring. Both the father and the mother spend less time on leisure. The mother works fewer hours and the father works more hours. The other two countries' parents slightly increase work hours and reduce leisure time. The global wealth, capital, and output are reduced. The interest rate falls, and all the wage rates rise. Country 1's population is reduced, and other two countries' populations are slightly increased.

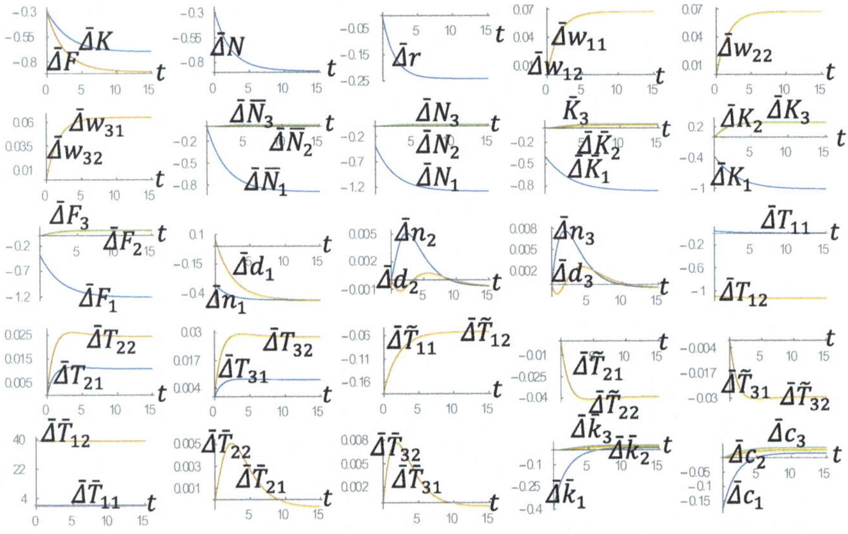

Fig. 7.7 Country 1's mother spends more time on per child fostering

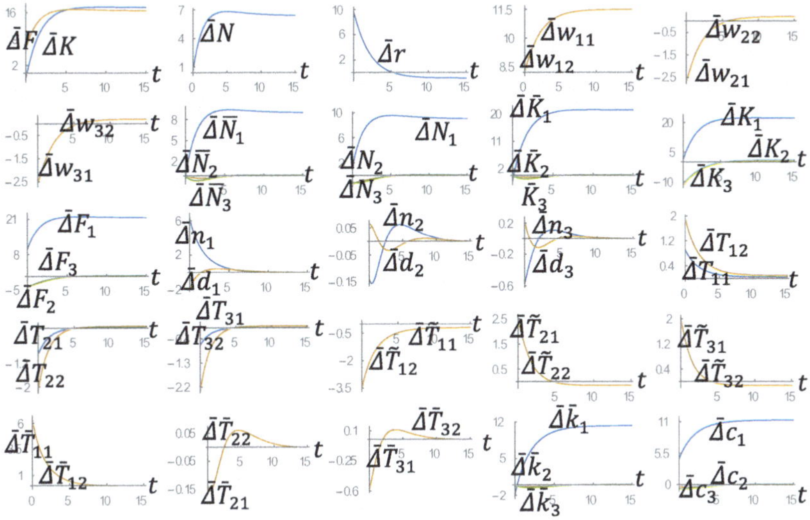

Fig. 7.8 A rise in country 1's total factor productivity

7.3.3 A Rise in Country 1's Total Factor Productivity

I am now concerned with how country 1's total factor productivity affects economic growth and population change. Technological change in the traditional Solow model has positive effects on the long-term economic growth. I now increase country 1's total factor productivity as follows: $A_1: 1.2 \Rightarrow 1.3$. The simulation results are plotted in Fig. 7.8. As the productivity is enhanced, the global output, wealth, and labor force are increased. In the long term, all the wage rates are increased. The interest rate rises initially and falls in the long term. Country 1's population rises. The other two countries' populations are reduced slightly and are affected slightly in the long term. Country 1's birth rate is increased. Mortality rate is reduced initially. They are slightly affected in the long term. The other two countries' birth and mortality rates vary initially and are slightly affected in the long term. As shown in Fig. 7.8, country 1's representative household consumes more and holds more wealth.

7.3.4 A Rise in Country 1's Propensity to Have Children

Tournemaine and Luangaram (2012: 925) observe: "depending on the country, population growth may contribute, deter, or even have no impact on economic development. This ambiguous result is explained by the fact that the effects of population growth change over time. For example, a higher fertility rate can have a short-term negative effect caused by the cost of expenditures on children whereas it has a long-run positive effect through the larger labor force it generates." As interactions between

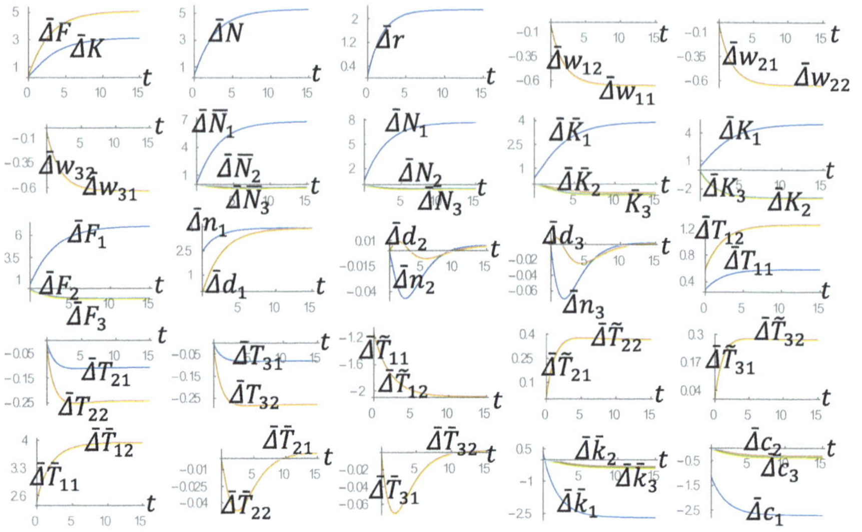

Fig. 7.9 A rise in country 1's propensity to have children

population change and economic growth are complicated, it is expected that there may be positive, negative or even neutral interdependence between economic growth and population change. I now examine the effects of the following rise in country 1's propensity to have children: $\upsilon_{10}: 0.5 \Rightarrow 0.52$. The simulation results are plotted in Fig. 7.9. As country 1 has more interest in having more children, the country's birth and mortality rates rise. The rise in the mortality rate is due to the reduction in consumption level, and the rise in the birth rate is due to the strengthened preference for more children. The net consequence results in the population expansion. I see that the other two countries' mortality and birth rates vary. In the long term, the birth and mortality rates in the two countries are increased slightly. The global output, capital and labor force are increased. The interest rate rises, and the wage rates of all the groups fall. Country 1's population is increased, and the other two countries' populations are reduced slightly. Country 1 produces more and employs more capital. The other two countries produce less and employ less capital. Country 1 has more wealth and the other two countries have less wealth. Country 1's man and woman work more hours, spend fewer hours on leisure, and spend more hours on children caring. Country 2's (3's) man and woman work fewer hours, spend more hours on leisure, and spend fewer hours on children caring initially and more hours in the long term. The per household consumption and wealth levels are reduced for all the households in the in the global economy.

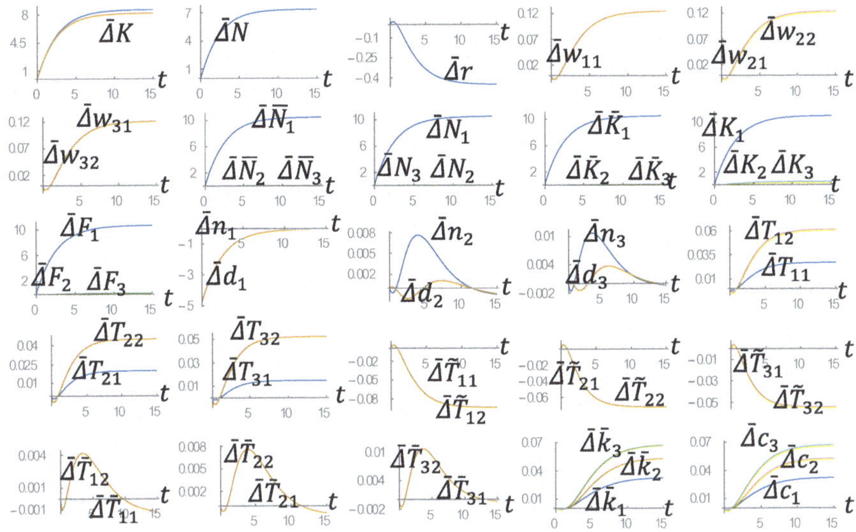

Fig. 7.10 Country 1's income having stronger impact on the mortality rate

7.3.5 *Country 1's Income having Stronger Impact on the Mortality Rate*

I now examine what will happen to the economy when country 1's mortality rate is more negatively related to the disposable income in the following way: $a_1 : 0.4 \Rightarrow 0.41$. The result is plotted in Fig. 7.10. Country 1's population and labor force are increased. The other two countries' populations and labor forces are slightly affected. The global labor force, capital and output are increased. The interest rate falls and the wage rates of all the groups rise. Country 1's output and capital input are increased, and the other two countries' output levels and capital inputs are slightly increased. Country 1's mortality rate is reduced. Its birth rate is slightly affected. The other two countries' birth and mortality rates slightly vary over time. There are also slight changes in the time distributions. The consumption and wealth levels of all the groups are increased.

7.3.6 *A Rise in Woman's Propensity to Pursue Leisure Activities*

It is important to examine the economic consequences when woman strengthens her preference for pursuing leisure activities. I now deal with the effects when country 1's woman increases her propensity to pursue leisure as follows: $\sigma_{120}: 0.13 \Rightarrow 0.15$. The result is plotted in Fig. 7.11. An immediate consequence of the preference change

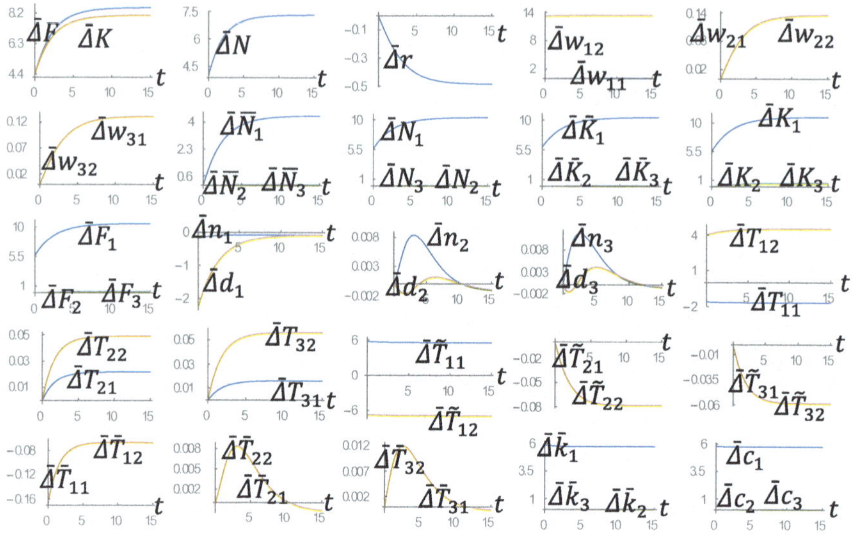

Fig. 7.11 A rise in woman's propensity to pursue leisure activities

is that the wife from country 1 spends more time on leisure and the husband has less leisure hours. Country 1's birth and mortality rates are reduced. The husband works more, and the wife works less. Both the husband and wife reduce their time of children fostering. The other two countries' households slightly vary their time distributions.

7.3.7 *Impact of a Rise in Country 1's Propensity to Save*

According to the Solow model, a rise in the propensity to save will increase per capita wealth but reduce per capita consumption level. I will show that the impact in my model is different from the result in the Solow model in the long term. I now allow country 1' propensity to save to be enhanced as follows: $\lambda_{10}: 0.6 \Rightarrow 0.62$. The result is plotted in Fig. 7.12. Country 1's per household consumption level falls initially and rises in the long term. The per household wealth in all the countries is augmented. The households in countries 2 and 3 increase their consumption levels. Both man and woman from country 1 work more hours initially and slightly change their work hours in the long term. In the long term, the global output, global capital, and global labor force are reduced. The interest rate falls. The wage rates rise. Country 1's population and labor force are reduced. The other two countries' populations and labor forces are increased.

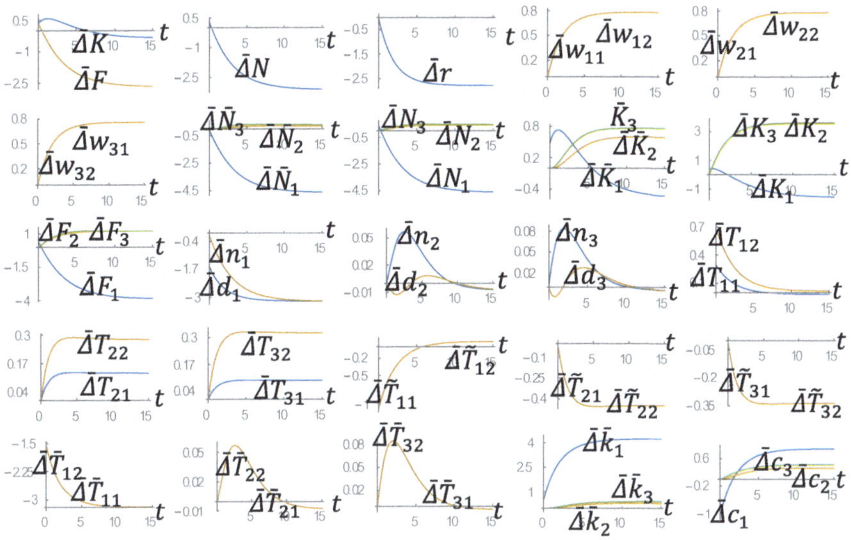

Fig. 7.12 Impact of a rise in country 1's propensity to save

7.4 Population, Human Capital, and Physical Capital

The previous section examines the role of trade on global and national populations. This section introduces endogenous human capital to population change theory. It is based on Zhang (2014). The economy has one production sector and one education sector. I assume a homogenous population $\overline{N}(t)$ at time. Let $T(t)$ and $T_e(t)$ represent for, respectively, the work time and study time of the household. The total work time is $T(t)\overline{N}(t)$. I use $H(t)$ to stand for the level of human capital of the population. The total labor force is:

$$N(t) = T(t)H^m(t)\overline{N}(t),$$

where the parameter m describes how effectively the population uses human capital. I select the commodity to serve as numeraire. Let $K(t)$ stand for the total capital stock of physical capital. I use $N_j(t)$ and $K_j(t)$ to stand for the labor force and capital stocks employed by sector j, $j = i, e$. Full employment of input factors implies:

$$K_i(t) + K_e(t) = K(t), \quad N_i(t) + N_e(t) = N(t).$$

The above equations are rewritten:

$$n_i(t)k_i(t) + n_e(t)k_e(t) = k(t), \quad n_i(t) + n_e(t) = 1,$$

in which

$$k_j(t) \equiv \frac{K_j(t)}{N_j(t)}, \quad n_j(t) \equiv \frac{N_j(t)}{N(t)}, \quad k(t) \equiv \frac{K(t)}{N(t)}, \quad j = i, e.$$

7.4.1 The Two Sectors and Marginal Conditions

The production functions are:

$$F_j(t) = A_j K_j^{\alpha_j}(t) N_j^{\beta_j}(t), \quad A_j, \alpha_j, \beta_i > 0, \quad \alpha_j + \beta_j = 1.$$

The interest rate $r(t)$ and wage rate $w(t)$ are determined in free markets. The marginal conditions are:

$$r(t) + \delta_k = \frac{\alpha_i F_i(t)}{K_i(t)} = \frac{\alpha_e p(t) F_e(t)}{K_e(t)}, \quad w(t) = \frac{\beta_i F_i(t)}{N_i(t)} = \frac{\beta_e p(t) F_e(t)}{N_e(t)}.$$

The demand for and supply of education balances at any point in time:

$$T_e(t)\overline{N}(t) = F_e(t).$$

7.4.2 Human Capital Dynamics

Following the Uzawa–Lucas model (Uzawa 1965; Lucas 1988), human capital is accumulated through education as follows:

$$\dot{H}(t) = \frac{\upsilon_e F_e^{a_e}(t)\left(H^m(t) T_e(t)\overline{N}(t)\right)^{b_e}}{H^{\pi_e}(t)\overline{N}(t)} - \delta_h H(t),$$

where $\delta_h (>0)$ is the depreciation rate of human capital, υ_e, a_e, and b_e, are non-negative parameters. The sign of π_e is not specified as it may be either negative or positive.

7.4.3 Consumer Behaviors

Per household's wealth $\bar{k}(t)$ is $\bar{k}(t) = K(t)/\overline{N}(t)$. The disposable income is:

$$\hat{y}(t) = (1 + r(t))\bar{k}(t) + T(t)w(t).$$

Let $n(t)$ and $p_n(t)$ stand for the birth rate and the cost of birth at time. It is assumed that children will have the same level of wealth as that of the parent. The cost of the parent is thus given by $p_n(t) = n(t)\bar{k}(t)$. It should be noted that in the fertility choice model by Barro and Becker (1989), the cost also includes consumption of goods. Becker (1981) emphasizes costs of the mother's time on rearing children to adulthood. Wang et al. (1994) introduce time spent on child-bearing into their fertility choice model. The household distributes the total available budget among saving $s(t)$, consumption of goods $c(t)$, education $T_e(t)$, and bearing children $n(t)$. The budget constraint is:

$$c(t) + s(t) + p(t)T_e(t) + \bar{k}(t)n(t) = (1 + r(t))\bar{k}(t) + T(t)w(t).$$

Insert the time constraint $T(t) + T_e(t) = T_0$ in the above equation:

$$c(t) + s(t) + \bar{p}(t)T_e(t) + \bar{k}(t)n(t) = \bar{y}(t) \equiv (1 + r(t))\bar{k}(t) + T_0 w(t),$$

where $\bar{p}(t) \equiv p(t) + w(t)$ (the opportunity cost of education). As in Barro and Becker (1989), I assume that the parents' utility is dependent on the number of children. The utility level is a function of $c(t)$, $s(t)$, $T_e(t)$, and $n(t)$ as follows:

$$U(t) = c^{\xi_0}(t)s^{\lambda_0}(t)T_e^{\eta_0}(t)n^{\upsilon_0}(t),$$

where ξ_0 is called the propensity to consume, λ_0 the propensity to own wealth, η_0 the propensity to obtain education, and υ_0 the propensity to have children. Maximizing $U(t)$ subject to the budget constraint yields:

$$c(t) = \xi\bar{y}(t), \quad s(t) = \lambda\bar{y}(t), \quad \bar{p}(t)T_e(t) = \eta\bar{y}(t),$$
$$\bar{k}(t)n(t) = \upsilon\bar{y}(t), \tag{7.4.1}$$

where

$$\xi \equiv \rho\xi_0, \lambda \equiv \rho\lambda_0, \quad \eta \equiv \rho\eta_0, \quad \upsilon \equiv \rho\upsilon_0,$$
$$\rho = \frac{1}{\xi_0 + \lambda_0 + \eta_0 + \upsilon_0}.$$

The demand for education is given by $T_e = \eta\bar{y}/\bar{p}$. The demand for education falls in the price of education but rises in the wealth income. A rise in the propensity to receive education increases the education time when the other variables are fixed. The demand for children is given by $n = \upsilon\bar{y}/\bar{k}$. Demand for children is positively related to the propensity to have children and the wage rate but is negatively related to the wealth level.

7.4.4 The Birth and Mortality Rates and the Population Dynamics

The population dynamics follows:

$$\dot{\overline{N}}(t) = (n(t) - d(t))\overline{N}(t), \tag{7.4.2}$$

where $d(t)$ is the mortality rate. It should be noted that Tournemaine and Luangaram (2012) use the following technology of production of children: $n(t) = bT_b^{\theta}(t)$, where $T_b(t)$ is the time of rearing children and b and θ are parameters. From (7.4.1), the birth rate is given by:

$$n(t) = \frac{\upsilon\overline{y}(t)}{\overline{k}(t)}. \tag{7.4.3}$$

As mentioned before, in the Haavelmo model, the mortality rate is negatively related to per capita income. The mortality rate is negatively related to the disposable income and the level of human capital in the following way:

$$d(t) = \frac{\overline{\upsilon}}{\overline{y}^{a}(t)H^{b}(t)}, \tag{7.4.4}$$

where $\overline{\upsilon} \geq 0$, $a \geq 0$, and $b \geq 0$. The parameter $\overline{\upsilon}$ is called the mortality rate parameter. As in the Haavelmo model, an improvement in living conditions implies that people live longer. Human capital negatively affects the mortality rate. Insert (7.4.3) and (7.4.4) in (7.4.2):

$$\dot{\overline{N}}(t) = \left(\frac{\upsilon\overline{y}(t)}{\overline{k}(t)} - \frac{\overline{\upsilon}}{\overline{y}^{a}(t)H^{b}(t)}\right)\overline{N}(t). \tag{7.4.5}$$

In the literature of mathematical biology, it is essential to describe dynamics of age structure. In economics, there are also some studies on the issue (Fanti et al. 2013).

7.4.5 Wealth Dynamics

The change in the household's wealth follows:

$$\dot{\overline{k}}(t) = s(t) - \overline{k}(t).$$

I built the dynamic model. I introduce $z(t) \equiv (r(t) + \delta_k)/w(t)$. The dynamics can be expressed by three-dimensional differential equations system with $z(t)$, $N(t)$, and $H(t)$ as the variables.

Lemma 7.4.1 *The dynamics is governed by three-dimensional differential equations as follows*:

$$\dot{z}(t) = \widetilde{\Omega}_z\big(z(t), \overline{N}(t), H(t)\big),$$
$$\dot{\overline{N}}(t) = \widetilde{\Omega}_N\big(z(t), \overline{N}(t), H(t)\big),$$
$$\dot{H}(t) = \widetilde{\Omega}_H\big(z(t), \overline{N}(t), H(t)\big),$$

where $\widetilde{\Omega}_z$, $\widetilde{\Omega}_N$, *and* $\widetilde{\Omega}_H$ *are functions of* $z(t)$, $\dot{\overline{N}}(t)$ *and* $H(t)$ *defined in* Zhang (2014). *The other variables are determined as functions of* $z(t)$, $N(t)$, *and* $H(t)$.

The parameters and initial conditions are taken on the following values:

$$T_0 = 1, \quad \alpha_i = 0.35, \quad \alpha_e = 0.45, \quad \lambda_0 = 0.7, \quad \xi_0 = 0.08, \quad \eta_0 = 0.01,$$
$$\upsilon_0 = 0.2, \quad A_i = 1.2, \quad A_e = 1.2, \quad m = 0.8, \quad v_e = 1.3, \quad a_e = 0.2,$$
$$b_e = 0.1, \quad \pi_e = -0.1, \quad a = 0.3, \quad b = 0.1, \quad \overline{\upsilon} = 0.6, \quad \delta_k = 0.05,$$
$$\delta_h = 0.05, \quad z(0) = 0.3, \quad N(0) = 2.7, \quad H(0) = 4.$$

The simulation result is plotted in Fig. 7.13. The population and human capital rise initially and then fall. The birth rate falls. The mortality rate falls initially and then rises. Most of the labor force is employed by the industrial sector. The motion of the rest variables is plotted in Fig. 7.13.

The system has a unique equilibrium point. The equilibrium values of the variables are:

$$\overline{N} = 3.04, \quad H = 4.34, \quad K = 15.65, \quad N = 9.47, \quad N_i = 9.40,$$
$$N_e = 0.067, \quad K_i = 15.48, \quad K_e = 0.17, \quad F_i = 13.43, \quad F_e = 0.12,$$
$$n = d = 0.286, \quad r = 0.234, \quad p = 1.02, \quad w = 0.93,$$
$$\overline{k} = 5.14, \quad T = 0.96, \quad c = 0.59.$$

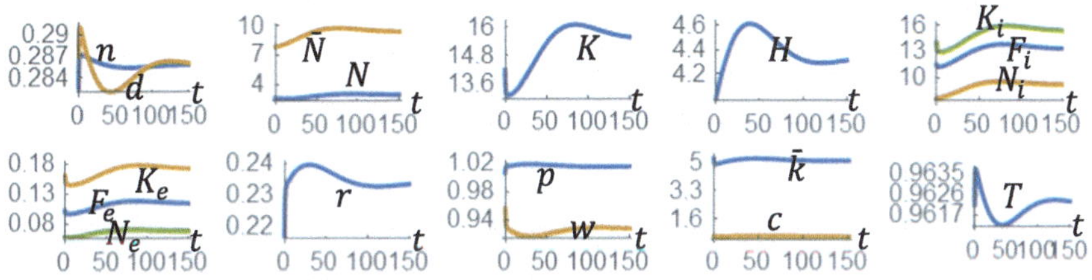

Fig. 7.13 Motion of the economy

The three eigenvalues are: −0.21, −0.08, and −0.04. As the three eigenvalues are real and negative, the unique equilibrium is locally stable.

7.5 The Population Affected by Preference and Other Conditions

This section examines effects of changes in various parameters on the population dynamics over time.

7.5.1 A Rise in the Mortality Rate Parameter

I now examine the case that the mortality rate parameter is increased as follows: $\overline{\upsilon}$: 0.6 ⇒ 0.62. The simulation results are plotted in Fig. 7.14. To examine how each variable is affected over time, I should follow the motion of the entire system as each variable is related to all the others in the dynamic system. When $\overline{\upsilon}$ is increased, the mortality rate is increased, and the population is reduced. As the population falls, the total labor force is reduced. The total capital stocks, labor and capital inputs, and output levels of the two sectors are reduced. The human capital, education time, and consumption level and wealth per person are increased. The education fee and the interest rate are increased, while the wage rate is reduced. The birth rate is increased initially but not affected in the long term. The mortality rate rises initially, then falls, but is not affected in the long term. Although the birth and mortality rates are not almost affected by the change in the mortality rate parameter in the long terms, the other micro- and macrovariables are strongly affected.

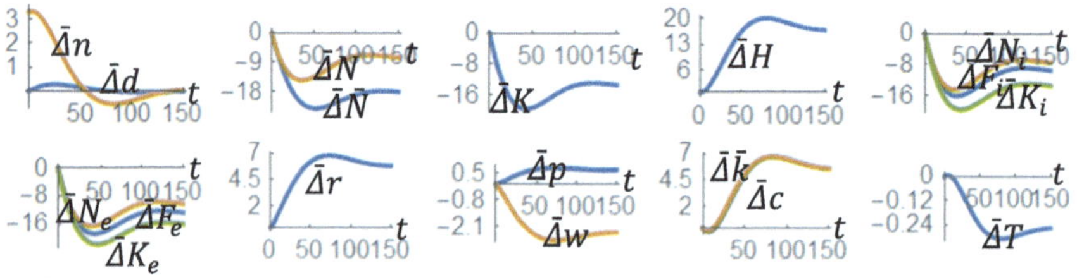

Fig. 7.14 A rise in the mortality rate parameter

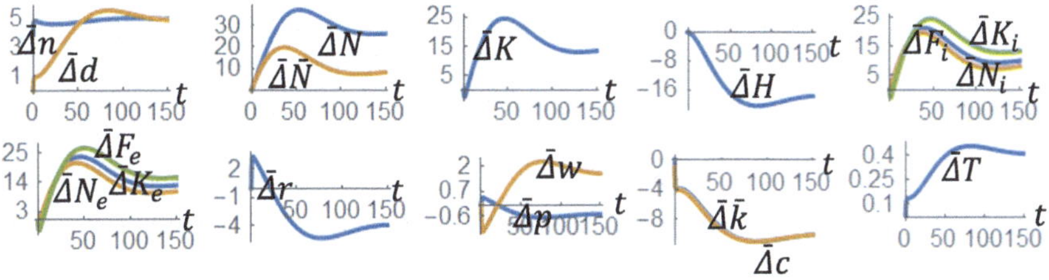

Fig. 7.15 A rise in the propensity to have children

7.5.2 A Rise in the Propensity to have Children

I allow the propensity to have children to be increased as follows: $\upsilon_0 : 0.2 \Rightarrow 0.21$. The simulation results are plotted in Fig. 7.15. When the propensity to have children is increased, the birth rate is increased. The population is increased, while human capital is reduced. The net result of the rise in the population and the reduction in human capital leads to the rise in the total labor supply. The total capital is increased in association with the rise in the population and labor supply. The wage rate falls initially in association with the fall of the capital intensities of the two sectors. As the capital intensities of the two sectors are increased in the long term, the wage rate is increased in the long term. The labor and capital inputs, and output levels of the two sectors are increased. The education time is slightly reduced as the work time is increased. The interest rate and the education price fall. The mortality rate is increased as human capital and the wealth level per person are reduced.

7.5.3 A Rise in the Propensity to Receive Education

I consider the propensity to receive education be increased in the following way: $\eta_0 : 0.01 \Rightarrow 0.013$. The simulation results are plotted in Fig. 7.16. As people are more interested in receiving education, they increase education time. As they spend more time and money on education, the education fee is increased. The education sector employs more capital and people, and the education sector's output is increased. As

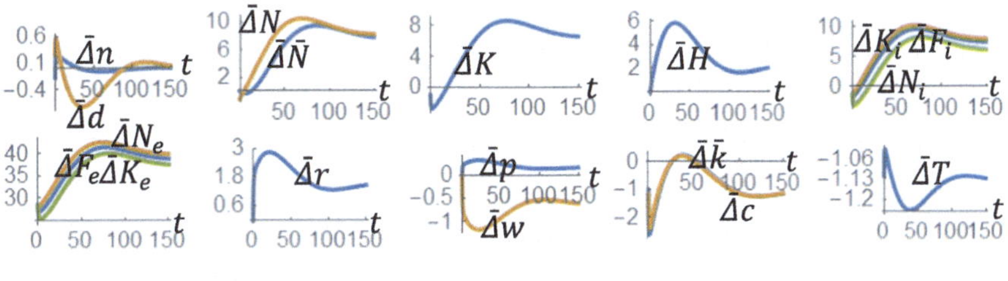

Fig. 7.16 A rise in the propensity to receive education

people spend more time on formal education, their human capital is increased. The birth and mortality rates rise initially and then fall. The population is increased, while the human capital is reduced. The net result leads to the fall in the capital intensities of the two sectors. The wage rate falls, and the interest rate rises. The labor and capital inputs and output level of the industrial sector are reduced initially but increased in the long term. The labor and capital inputs and output level of the education sector are increased. As the household's propensity to receive education increases, the per person level of consumption and wealth are reduced in the long term. It should be noted that according to Arrow (1973), a stronger interest in education may not lead to human capital and economic growth. The conclusion results from the assumption that students choose education also for the purpose of signaling. In the literature of education and economics, the signaling view of education was initially formally presented by Spence (1973), Arrow (1973), and Stiglitz (1975). This implies that direct productivity gains are not necessary to explain the choice of quantity and quantity of education. My result shows that even if I consider that people increase their propensity to receive education and they increase formal education for learning, the long-run consumption and wealth levels per person are reduced. This occurs because I take account of endogenous population growth.

7.5.4 The Human Capital Utilization Efficiency is Increased

Students may spend much time on different subjects on history and Japanese literature. But these learning activities may not become useful for economic activities. Education and economic efficiency are closely related, but not necessarily positively. This kind of issues may be examined, for instance, by detailing human capital into different components and modeling accumulation of each component. This approach will greatly complicate the analysis. This study considers how changes in human capital may affect productivity is through the parameter of human capital utilization efficiency. I now change this parameter by: $m: 0.8 \Rightarrow 0.82$. The simulation results are plotted in Fig. 7.17. A rise in the efficiency increases the total labor supply. The mortality rate initially falls. The birth rate is slightly changed. The population is enlarged initially. In the long term, the population is reduced as the mortality rate is enhanced and the birth rate is almost not changed. The household wealth is reduced.

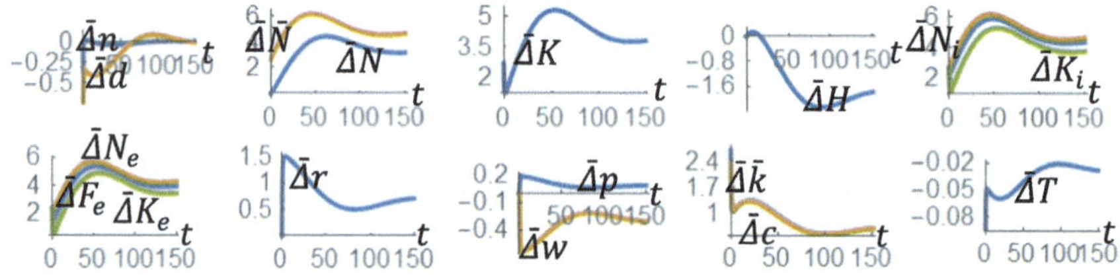

Fig. 7.17 A rise in the human capital utilization efficiency

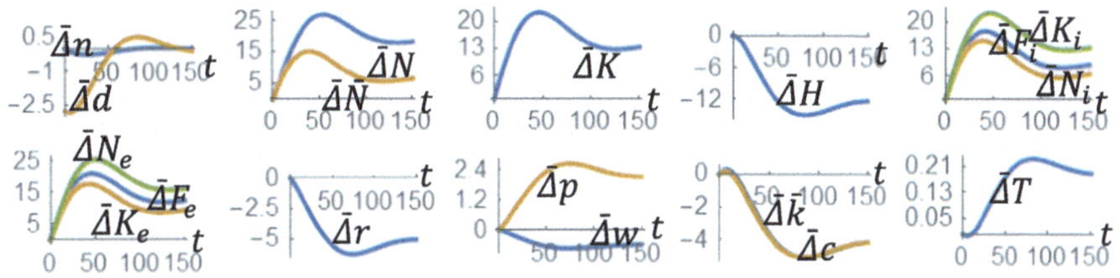

Fig. 7.18 A rise in the mortality rate elasticity of human capital

The total capital stock is enhanced. The two sectors employ less the labor and capital inputs. The output levels of the two sectors fall. In association of fall in the capital intensities of the two sectors, the economy has lower wage rate but higher interest rate.

7.5.5 The Mortality Rate Elasticity of Human Capital is Enhanced

Education and human capital are generally believed to have strong effects in population dynamics. There are other factors, such as medical conditions and cultural environment which may affect the dynamics. A change in the mortality rate elasticity of human capital rate is made as follows $b: 0.1 \Rightarrow 0.12$. The simulation results are plotted in Fig. 7.18. A higher b initially reduces the mortality rate and enlarges the population. The rise in population increases the total labor supply and total capital. Higher total capital and labor force lead to more labor and capital inputs and higher output levels of the two sectors. The capital sock grows faster than the labor supply. This implies that the capital intensities of the two sectors become higher. These change result in lower interest rate and higher wage rate. The demand for education is reduced due to the fall in the mortality rate. The net result of less education time and higher output of the education sector implies a lower level of human capital. In association with the fall in the level of human capital, the mortality rate becomes higher before it becomes lower. In the long term neither the birth rate nor mortality rate is affected by a higher mortality rate elasticity of human capital rate. As the population is increased and human capital is reduced, the consumption and wealth levels per household become lower. I also analyze the impact of the following change: $a: 0.3 \Rightarrow 0.32$. The effects are quantitatively similar with those in Fig. 7.18.

References

Adsera A (2005) Vanishing children: from high unemployment to low fertility in developed countries. Am Econ Rev 95:189–193

Arrow KJ (1973) Higher education as a filter. J Public Econ 2:193–216
Barro RJ, Becker GS (1989) Fertility choice in a model of economic growth. Econometrica 57:481–501
Becker GS (1981) A treatise on the family. Harvard University Press, Cambridge, MA
Beneria L, Feldman S (eds) (1992) Unequal burden: economic crises, persistent poverty, and women's work. Westview, Boulder
Chu AC, Cozzi G, Liao CH (2013) Endogenous fertility and human capital in a Schumpeterian growth model. J Population Econ 26:181–202
Doepke M (2004) Accounting for fertility decline during the transition to growth. J Econ Growth 9:347–383
Ehrlich I, Lui F (1997) The problem of population and growth: A review of the literature from Malthus to contemporary models of endogenous population and endogenous growth. J Econ Dyn Control 21:205–242
Fanti L, Iannelli M, Manfredi P (2013) Neoclassical growth with endogenous age distribution: poverty vs low-fertility traps as steady states of demographic transitions. J Popul Econ 26:1457–1484
Forsythe N, Korzeniewicz RP, Durrant V (2000) Gender inequalities and economic growth: a longitudinal evaluation. Econ Dev Cult Change 48:573–617
Galor O (2012) The demographic transition: cause and consequences. Cliometrica 6:1–28
Galor O, Weil DN (1996) The gender gap, fertility, and growth. Am Econ Rev 86:374–387
Galor O, Weil D (1999) From Malthusian stagnation to modern growth. Am Econ Rev 89:150–154
Haavelmo T (1954) A study in the theory of economic evolution. North-Holland, Amsterdam
Hock H, Weil DN (2012) On the dynamics of the age structure, dependency, and consumption. J Popul Econ 25:1019–1043
Kirk D (1996) Demographic transition theory. Popul Stud 50:361–387
Li TY, Yorke JA (1975) Period three implies chaos. Am Math Mon 8:481–485
Lucas RE (1988) On the mechanics of economic development. J Monetary Econ 22:3–42
Schultz PT (1993) Mortality decline in the low-income world: causes and consequences. Am Econ Rev 83:337–342
Schultz PT (1998) Health and schooling investments in Africa. J Econ Perspect 13:67–88
Spence M (1973) Job market signaling. Q J Econ 87:355–374
Stiglitz JE (1975) The theory of screening, education, and the distribution of income. Am Econ Rev 65:283–300
Stotsky JG (2006) Gender and its relevance to macroeconomic policy: a survey. IMF working paper, WP/06/233
Stutzer M (1980) Chaotic dynamics and bifurcation in a macro economics. J Econ Dyn Control 2:253–273
Tournemaine F, Luangaram P (2012) R&D, human capital, fertility, and growth. J Popul Econ 25:923–953
Uzawa H (1965) Optimal technical change in an aggregative model of economic growth. Int Econ Rev 6:18–31
Wang P, Yip CK, Scotese CA (1994) Fertility choice and economic growth: theory and evidence. Rev Econ Stat 71:255–266
Zhang WB (1991) Synergetic economics. Springer, Heidelberg
Zhang WB (2014) Endogenous population with human and physical capital accumulation. Int Rev Econ 61:231–252
Zhang WB (2016) Endogenous population dynamics and economic growth with free trade between countries. Soc Sci Educ Res Rev 3:3–30

Chapter 8
Health, Environment, Resources, and Government

There are many stock variables, such as physical wealth, resources, human capital, and knowledge, which Walrasian general equilibrium theory fails to properly analyze. The previous chapters introduced some stock variables into the basic model. This chapter introduces two important determinants of growth—health and environment—into the basic model.

Health is important in economic development. Health caring consumes national resources and individual incomes. On the other hand, healthier workers tend to have higher productivity and happier life. Healthier workers tend to get higher wage income. Much effort has been made to theoretically or empirically examine possible interactions between health and economic systems (Grossman 1972; van Zon and Muysken 2001; Kelly 2017).

Environment and growth are causing public debates and academic attention. There are many studies on dynamic interdependence between production, consumption, and pollution (Ploude 1972; Forster 1973; Grossman 1995; Dinda 2004; Managi 2007; Kijima et al. 2010; Mesagan 2015; Kasztelan 2017; Halkos and Managi 2017; Gupta and Dutta 2018). The unique feature of this chapter is to connect the environment, health, and wealth on microeconomic foundation within a comprehensive framework.

8.1 Health, Environment, and Wealth

The model in this chapter is based on Zhang (2018). The economy has four sectors—health caring sector, environment sector, plus the two sectors in the Uzawa two-sector growth model. The health caring sector produces health service. The environment sector protects environment. The government uses taxes to financially support the environment sector. All markets are perfectly competitive. The government taxes the

W.-B. Zhang, *The General Economic Theory*,
https://doi.org/10.1007/978-3-030-56204-5_8

production sectors and households' incomes and consumption. It is assumed that environment affects productivities. For all the sectors, there are capital and labor factors. I introduce

$\bar{N}$ and $N(t)$	fixed population and total labor supply;
$\ell(t)$ and $E(t)$	level of health stock of the population and level of pollution;
i, s, h, and e	subscript index standing for capital good sector, consumer good sector, health sector, and environment sector;
$N_q(t)$ and $K_q(t)$	labor force and capital stocks employed by sector $q, q = i, s, h, e$;
$F_q(t)$ and $p_q(t)$	output level of sector q and price of good q, $q = i, s, h$, $p_i(t) = 1$;
$T(t)$, $\bar{T}(t)$, and $\hat{T}(t)$	representative household's work time, leisure time, and time spent on health caring;
$c(t)$, $c_s(t)$ and $c_h(t)$	household's consumption levels of capital good, consumer good, and health service;
$\bar{k}(t)$	household's wealth;
$r(t)$ and $w(t)$	interest rate and wage rate;
τ_q and $\bar{\tau}_q$	tax rate on sector $q's$ output and $\bar{\tau}_q \equiv 1 - \tau_q, q = i, s, h$;
τ_j and $\bar{\tau}_j$	tax rate on the household's wealth interest income ($j = k$) and wage income ($j = w$), and $\bar{\tau}_j \equiv 1 - \tau_j$, $j = k, w$;
$\tilde{\tau}_j$ and $\hat{\tau}_j$	tax rates on the household's consumption of capital good ($j = i$), consumption of consumer good ($j = s$), and consumption of health service ($j = h$), and $\hat{\tau}_j \equiv 1 + \tilde{\tau};_j$ and
δ_k and δ_ℓ	depreciation rates of physical capital and health.

8.1.1 National Labor Supply, Technologies, and Marginal Conditions

The total labor supply is related to human capital, health condition, and work hours as follows:

$$N(t) = hT(t)\ell^m(t)\bar{N}, \tag{8.1.1}$$

in which h and m are positive parameters. I interpret h as level of human capital and m as a parameter of labor's productivity due to worker's health (Weil 2007; Tobing 2011). The three sectors' production technologies are described with the following Cobb–Douglas functions:

$$F_q(t) = A_q \Gamma_q(E(t)) K_q^{\alpha_q}(t) N_q^{\beta_q}(t), \quad A_q, \alpha_q, \beta_q > 0, \ \alpha_q + \beta_q = 1, \ q = i, s, h,$$

where A_q, α_q and β_q are positive parameters and $\Gamma_q(E)$ is a function of environment. The parameters α_q and β_q are the output elasticities of capital and labor, respectively.

The marginal conditions for the three sectors are

$$r(t) + \delta_k = \frac{\alpha_q \bar{\tau}_q p_q(t) F_q(t)}{K_q(t)}, \; w(t) = \frac{\beta_q \bar{\tau}_q p_q(t) F_q(t)}{N_q(t)}, \quad q = i, s, h, \qquad (8.1.2)$$

8.1.2 Modeling of Health Caring

Health caring is a joint production of different inputs for health caring. Let $\bar{c}(t)$ represent for level of health caring. I consider health caring to be dependent on health service $c_h(t)$ and the representative household's time for health caring. Health caring function is taken on the following Cobb–Douglas function:

$$\bar{c}(t) = \tilde{A} c_h^{\tilde{\alpha}}(t) \hat{T}^{\tilde{\beta}}(t), \quad \tilde{A}, \tilde{\alpha}, \tilde{\beta} > 0, \qquad (8.1.3)$$

where $\tilde{A}$, $\tilde{\alpha}$, and $\tilde{\beta}$ are parameters.

8.1.3 Consumer Behaviors

The disposable income is

$$\hat{y}(t) = R(t)\bar{k}(t) + W(t),$$

where

$$W(t) \equiv \bar{\tau}_w h \ell^m(t) T(t) w(t), \, R(t) \equiv 1 + \tau_k r(t).$$

The disposable income is distributed between consumption and saving. The budget constraint implies

$$\hat{\tau}_i c_i(t) + \hat{\tau}_s p_s(t) c_s(t) + \hat{\tau}_h p_h(t) c_h(t) + s(t) = \hat{y}(t).$$

Time constraint for the household is

$$T(t) + \bar{T}(t) + \hat{\tau}(t) = T_0.$$

Insert the time constraint in the budget

$$\begin{aligned} &\bar{p}(t)\bar{T}(t) + \bar{p}(t)\hat{T}(t) + \hat{\tau}_i c_i(t) + \hat{\tau}_s p_s(t) c_s(t) + \hat{\tau}_h p_h(t) c_h(t) \\ &\quad + s(t) = \bar{y}(t), \end{aligned} \qquad (8.1.4)$$

where

$$\bar{p}(t) \equiv \bar{\tau}_w h \ell^{m_h}(t) w(t), \ \bar{y}(t) \equiv R(t)\bar{k}(t) + \bar{\tau}_w h \ell^{m}(t) T_0 w(t).$$

The variable $\bar{p}(t)$ is the opportunity cost of health caring and opportunity cost of leisure time. The variable $\bar{y}(t)$ is called potential disposable income which is the disposable income that the household obtains by spending the available time on working. The potential disposable income is distributed between opportunity costs of health caring and leisure, costs for consumption of goods and services, and saving. The utility function is taken on the following form:

$$U(t) = \Gamma_c(E(t))\bar{T}^{\sigma_0}(t) c_i^{\xi_0}(t) c_s^{\gamma_0}(t) \bar{c}_h^{\psi_0}(t) s^{\lambda_0}(t), \quad \sigma_0, \xi_0, \gamma_0, \psi_0, \lambda_0 > 0,$$

where ψ_0 is the propensity to use health caring, σ_0 the propensity to use leisure time, γ_0 the propensity to consume consumer good, ξ_0 the propensity to consume capital good, and λ_0 the propensity to own wealth. I have the first-order conditions as follows:

$$\begin{aligned} &\bar{p}(t)\bar{T}(t) = \sigma \bar{y}(t), \ \bar{p}(t)\hat{T}(t) = \hat{\psi}\bar{y}(t), \ c(t) = \xi \bar{y}(t), \\ &p_s(t) c_s(t) = \gamma \bar{y}(t), \ p_h(t) c_h(t) = \psi \bar{y}(t), \ s(t) = \lambda \bar{y}(t), \end{aligned} \tag{8.15}$$

where

$$\begin{aligned} &\sigma \equiv \sigma_0 \rho, \ \xi \equiv \frac{\xi_0 \rho}{\hat{\tau}_i}, \ \gamma \equiv \frac{\gamma_0 \rho}{\hat{\tau}_s}, \ \psi \equiv \frac{\psi_0 \tilde{\alpha} \rho}{\hat{\tau}_h}, \ \hat{\psi} \equiv \psi_0 \tilde{\beta} \rho, \ \lambda \equiv \lambda_0 \rho, \\ &\rho = \frac{1}{\sigma_0 + \xi_0 + \gamma_0 + \psi_0 \tilde{\alpha} + \psi_0 \tilde{\beta} + \lambda_0}. \end{aligned}$$

The change in wealth equals saving $s(t)$ minus dissaving $\bar{k}(t)$:

$$\dot{\bar{k}}(t) = s(t) - \bar{k}(t).$$

8.1.4 Dynamics of Household's Health and Change in Environment

Changes in health stock are affected by health caring, nutrition, environment, and lifestyle. Health is also subject to natural depreciation of health. The change in health stock is described by a differential equation

$$\dot{\ell}(t) = \frac{\bar{\upsilon}_h \bar{c}^{a_h}(t)}{\ell^{\pi_h}(t)} + \frac{\bar{\upsilon}_c c^{a_c}(t) c_s^{a_s}(t) \bar{T}^{a_T}(t)}{\ell^{\pi_c}(t)} - \Gamma_\ell(E(t), \ell(t)) - \delta_h \ell(t),$$

where $\bar{\upsilon}_h$, $\bar{\upsilon}_c$, $\bar{a}_h$, $\bar{a}_c$, and $\bar{a}_T$ are non-negative parameters. I consider signs of returns-to-scale parameters $\bar{\pi}_h$ and $\bar{\pi}_c$ ambiguous as they may be either negative (when there are increasing returns to scale) or positive (when there are decreasing returns to scale). It is possible to treat rate of depreciation as endogenous variable (Grossman 1972; Johansson and Löfgren 1995). Function $\Gamma_\ell(E(t), \ell(t))$ implies how environmental quality affects health.

Changes in pollutants are related to production activities, consumption activities, environmental protection, and natural purification as follows:

$$\dot{E}(t) = \theta_i F_i(t) + \theta_s F_s(t) + \tilde{\theta}_i C_i(t) + \tilde{\theta}_s C_s(t) - Q_e(t) - \theta_0 E(t),$$

in which θ_i, θ_s, $\tilde{\theta}_i$, $\tilde{\theta}_s$, and θ_0 are positive parameters and

$$Q_e(t) = A_e \Gamma_e(E(t)) K_e^{\alpha_{0e}}(t) N_e^{\beta_{0e}}(t), \quad A_e, \alpha_e, \beta_e > 0,$$

where A_e, α_{0e}, and β_{0e} are positive parameters. The term $\theta_i F_i$ (or $\theta_s F_s$) implies the emission of pollutants in production of capital (consumer) good sector (Gutiérrez, 2008). The parameter, $\tilde{\theta}_i$ (or $\tilde{\theta}_s$) is the emission that the household makes when consuming one unit of capital (consumer) good. The term $\theta_0 E(t)$ describes the rate that the nature purifies environment. Variable Q_e implies the effect that the environment sector purifies environment.

8.1.5 Behavior of the Environment Sector

The government chooses labor capital inputs to maximize purification output with limited budget. Capital and labor inputs are paid according to their market values. The government's tax incomes are spent on environment. The government collects taxes from the production sectors, consumption, wage income, and income of interest from wealth. The government's income is

$$Y_e(t) = \tau_i F_i(t) + \tau_s p_s(t) F_s(t) + \tau_h p_h(t) F_h(t) + I_c(t) \bar{N},$$

in which

$$I_c(t) \equiv \tilde{\tau}_i c_i(t) + \tilde{\tau}_s p_s(t) c_s(t) + \tilde{\tau}_h p_h(t) c_h(t) + \tau_k r(t) \bar{k}(t) + \tau_w h \ell^m(t) T(t) w(t).$$

The government budget is

$$(r(t) + \delta_k) K_e(t) + w(t) N_e(t) = Y_e(t).$$

The government maximizes the level of environment protection subject to its budget. I get the first-order conditions

$$(r(t) + \delta_k)K_e(t) = \alpha_e Y_e(t), \; w(t)N_e(t) = \beta_e Y_e(t),$$

where

$$\alpha_e \equiv \frac{\alpha_{0e}}{\alpha_{0e} + \beta_{0e}}, \; \beta_e \equiv \frac{\beta_{0e}}{\alpha_{0e} + \beta_{0e}}.$$

8.1.6 *Equilibrium Conditions for Outputs and Full Employment of Factors*

Equilibrium for consumer good, health services, and capital good implies:

$$c_s(t)\bar{N} = F_s(t), \; c_h(t)\bar{N} = F_h(t),$$
$$c(t)\bar{N} + s(t)\bar{N} - \bar{k}(t)\bar{N} + \delta_k K(t) = F_i(t).$$

Full employment of capital stock and labor force implies

$$K_i(t) + K_s(t) + K_h(t) + K_e(t) = K(t),$$
$$N_i(t) + N_s(t) + N_h(t) + N_e(t) = N(t).$$

The households own wealth

$$\bar{k}(t)\bar{N} = K(t).$$

I completed building the model. I introduce a variable

$$z(t) \equiv \frac{r(t) + \delta_k}{w(t)}.$$

As shown in Zhang (2019), the following Lemma holds.

Lemma 8.1.1 The movement of the economic dynamic system follows three differential equations with three variables $z(t)$, $\ell(t)$, and $E(t)$:

$$\dot{z}(t) = \Lambda_z(z(t), \ell(t), E(t)),$$
$$\dot{\ell}(t) = \Lambda_\ell(z(t), \ell(t), E(t)),$$
$$\dot{E}(t) = \Lambda_E(z(t), \ell(t), E(t)),$$

where functions Λ_j are defined in Zhang (2019). All the other variables are given as functions of the three variables.

The environment-related functions are taken on the following forms:

$$\Gamma_j(t) = E^{-b_j}(t),\ j = i, s, h,\ \Gamma_e(t) = E^{b_e}(t),\ \Gamma_\ell(t) = E^{b_\ell}(t)\ell^{a_\ell}(t),$$
$$b_i = b_h = b_\ell = a_\ell = 0.1,\ b_s = 0.05,\ b_e = 0.2.$$

Productivities are negatively related to the level of pollutants. Health falls in the level of pollutants. The other parameter values are specified as follows:

$$T_0 = 24,\ \bar{N} = 100,\ h = 2,\ m = 0.6,\ A_i = 1.2,\ A_s = 1.3,$$
$$A_h = 1.1,\ \alpha_i = 0.33,\ \alpha_s = 0.32,\ \alpha_h = 0.31,\ \alpha_{0e} = 0.4,$$
$$\beta_{0e} = 0.4,\ \tau_j = \tilde{\tau}_j = 0.01,\ j = i, s, h, k, w,\ \theta_i = 0.04, \tilde{\theta}_i = 0.02,$$
$$\theta_s = 0.1,\ \tilde{\theta}_s = 0.05,\ \theta_0 = 0.05,\ \delta_k = 0.05,\ \delta_h = 0.03, \tilde{A} = 1,$$
$$\tilde{\alpha} = 0.35,\ \tilde{\beta} = 0.35,\ \lambda_0 = 0.7,\ \xi_0 = 0.1,\ \gamma_0 = 0.03,\ \psi_0 = 0.01,$$
$$\sigma_0 = 0.25,\ \pi_h = 0.3,\ \pi_c = 0.4,\ a_c = 0.2,\ a_s = 0.2,$$
$$a_T = 0.2,\ \bar{v}_h = 0.7,\ a_h = 0.4,\ \bar{v}_c = 0.3.$$

I require $\tilde{\alpha} + \tilde{\beta} < 1$ which means decreasing returns to scale in health caring. The conditions $\pi_c > 0$ and $\pi_h > 0$ indicate decreasing returns to scale in change of health stock. The initial conditions are

$$z(0) = 0.065,\ \ell(0) = 8.6,\ E(0) = 7.8.$$

Figure 8.1 provides the simulation result. The system moves away from the initial state and approaches the equilibrium point in the long term.

The equilibrium values are given as follows:

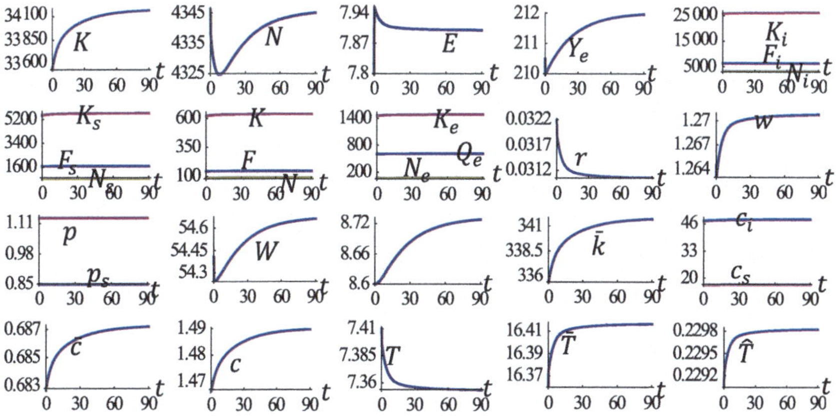

Fig. 8.1 Motion of the economic system

$$K = 34181,\ N = 4346,\ E = 7.9,\ Y_e = 212,\ K_i = 26376,$$
$$K_s = 5669,\ K_h = 640.7,\ K_e = 1495,\ N_i = 3415,\ N_s = 768,$$
$$N_h = 91,\ K_e = 71.5,\ F_i = 6543.6,\ F_s = 1707.5,\ F_h = 149,$$
$$Q_e = 614.2,\ r = 0.031,\ w = 1.27,\ W = 54.7,\ p_s = 0.85,$$
$$p_h = 1.14,\ \ell = 8.73,\ \bar{k} = 341.8,\ c_i = 48.3,\ c_s = 17.1,$$
$$\bar{c}_h = 0.69,\ c_h = 1.49,\ T = 7.35,\ \bar{T} = 16.4,\ \hat{T} = 0.23.$$

It is straightforward to calculate the three eigenvalues as follows:

$$\{-20.85, -0.24, -0.04\}.$$

The three eigenvalues are real and negative. The stability of the equilibrium point is guaranteed.

8.2 Taxes and Preferences Changes in Health Caring and Leisure

This section examines the effects of changes in some parameters on the dynamics of the economic system.

8.2.1 The Household Increases the Propensity to Use Health Caring

I first increase the propensity to use health caring as follows: ψ_0: $0.01 \Rightarrow 0.012$. The result is plotted in Fig. 8.2. The household spends more time on health caring and consumes more health service. The household has better health. There is a rise in the total labor supply. The wage rate falls. The interest rate rises. The price of consumer good rises. The price of health service falls. The household's wealth is enhanced. The household consumes more capital good, consumer good, and health service. Health caring is enhanced. National wealth becomes higher. Environment becomes better. The government has more tax income. The four sectors are expanded.

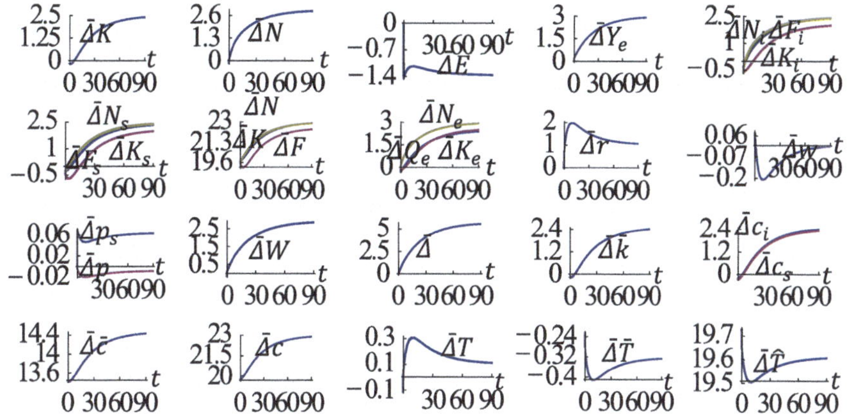

Fig. 8.2 Household increases the propensity to use health caring

8.2.2 *The Household's Efficiency of Applying Health is Increased*

The household's efficiency of applying health is assumed to become higher as follows: $m: 0.5 \Rightarrow 0.51$. The result is plotted in Fig. 8.3. The household initially spends more hours on working and fewer hours on leisure and health caring but does not change the time distribution in the long term. Health caring is improved. The total labor supply is augmented. The economy has more capital. The environmental quality becomes lower. The four sectors are expanded. The government has tax income. The prices of capital good and consumer good are reduced slightly. The

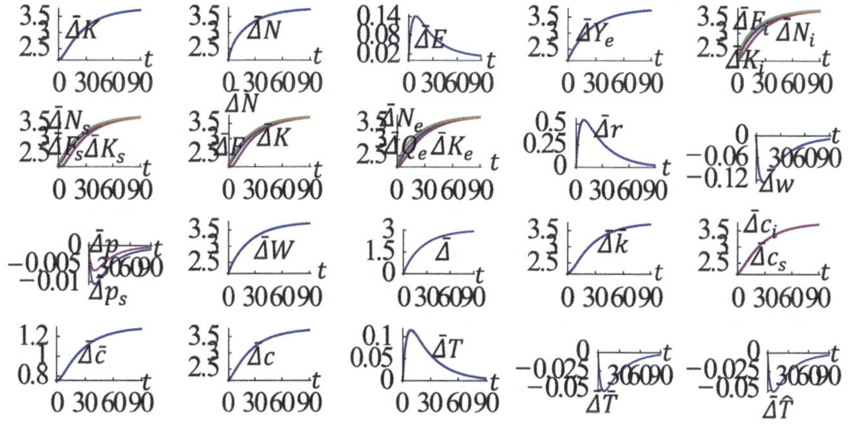

Fig. 8.3 Household's efficiency of applying health is enhanced

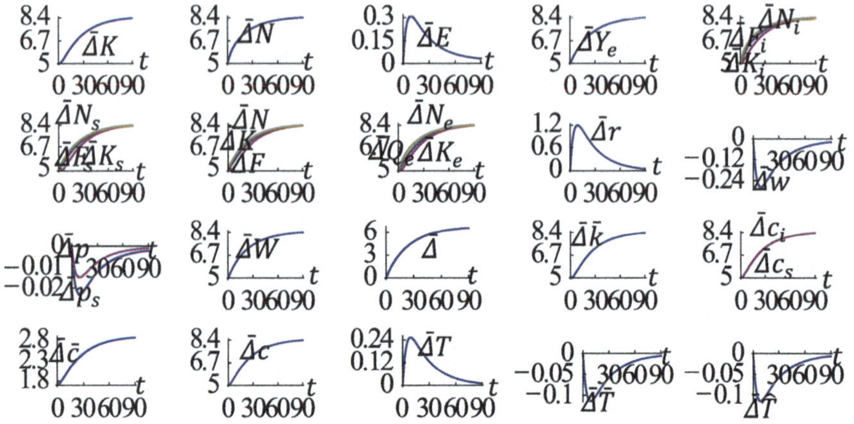

Fig. 8.4 Household's human capital is enhanced

wage income becomes higher. The household's wealth is increased. The household consumes more capital good, consumer good, and health service.

8.2.3 The Household's Human Capital is Enhanced

The household's efficiency of applying health is assumed to be enhanced as follows: $h: 2 \Rightarrow 2.1$. The result is plotted in Fig. 8.4. The household initially spends more hours on working and fewer hours on leisure and health caring but does not change the time distribution in the long term. The prices of capital good and consumer good become slightly lower. The wage income is increased. The household's wealth is augmented. The household consumes more capital good, consumer good, and health service. Health caring is improved. There is more labor supply. The nation has more capital. Environment is deteriorated. The four sectors are expanded. The government's tax income is increased.

8.2.4 A Rise in the Environmental Tax on the Capital Good Sector

I deal with a situation that the government enhances environmental tax rate on the capital good sector in the following way: $\tau_i: 0.01 \Rightarrow 0.011$. The result is plotted in Fig. 8.5. The government collects more taxes. The environment sector's scale is expanded. More capital and labor inputs are employed. Environment becomes better, and health is improved. The national capital and labor supply are increased. The scales of the capital good, consumer, and health caring sectors are expanded in

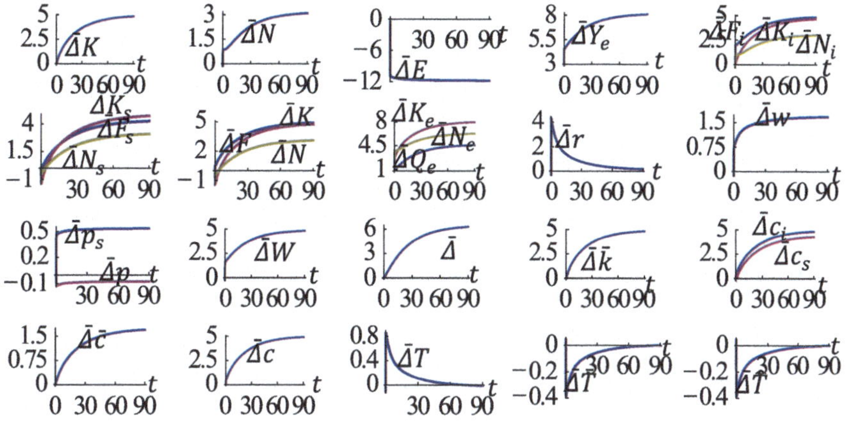

Fig. 8.5 Rise in the environmental tax on the capital good sector

the long term. The price of capital good becomes higher. The price of health service becomes lower. The time distribution is invariant in the long term. The wage income is enhanced. The household accumulates more wealth. The household consumes more capital good, more consumer good, and more health service. Health caring is improved.

8.2.5 *A Rise in the Tax Rate on the Consumption of Health Service*

The government's tax rate on the household's consumption of health service is augmented in the following way: $\tilde{\tau}_h: 0.01 \Rightarrow 0.014$. The result is plotted in Fig. 8.6. The government gets more tax income. The environment sector's output becomes higher. The sector employs more capital and labor inputs. Environmental quality becomes lower. Health becomes better. The nation has more capital and more labor supply. The scales of the capital good and consumer sectors are expanded. The health caring sector has less labor force employed. The sector initially produces less and employs less capital input, but in the long term produces more and employs more capital input. The prices of capital good and health service become higher. The time distribution remains invariant in the long term. The wage income becomes higher. The household owns more wealth. The household consumes more capital good and consumer good. The consumption levels of health service and health caring become lower initially and higher in the long term.

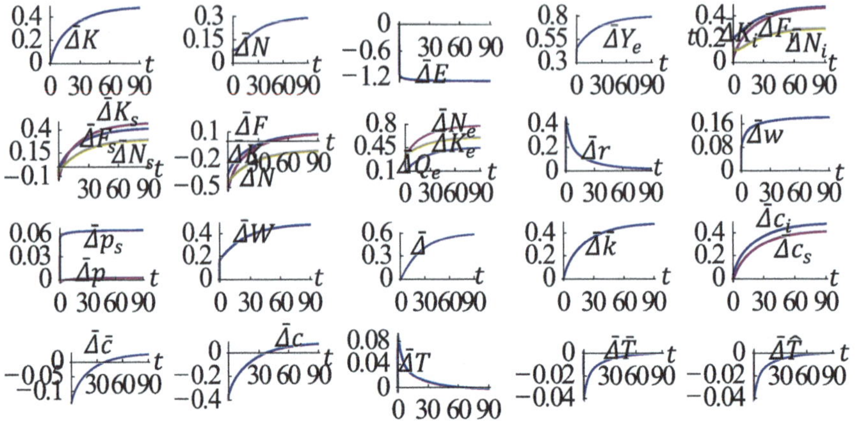

Fig. 8.6 Rise in the tax rate on the consumption of health service

8.2.6 A Rise in the Household's Propensity to Use Leisure Time

The household is assumed to increase the propensity to use leisure time in the following way: $\sigma_0 : 0.25 \Rightarrow 0.26$. The result is plotted in Fig. 8.7. The household has more leisure time and fewer hours on health caring and working. The total labor supply is reduced. The environmental quality becomes slightly higher. The production scales of the four sectors are reduced. The government has less tax income. Health is deteriorated. The wage income becomes lower. The prices of consumer good and

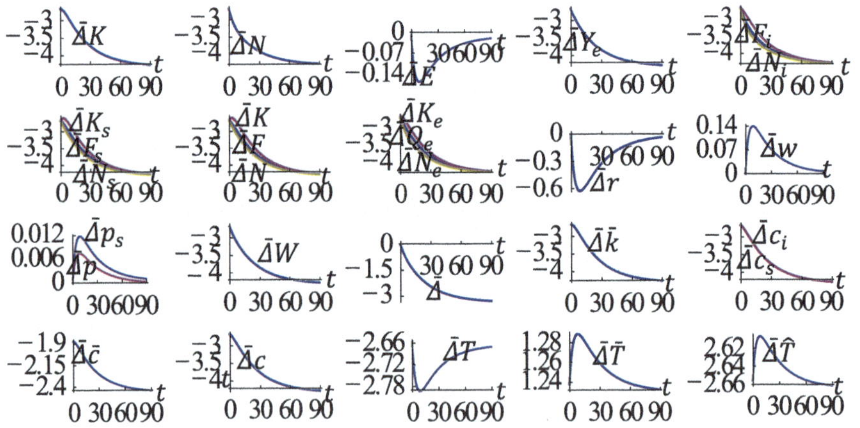

Fig. 8.7 Rise in the household's propensity to use leisure time

health service become slightly higher. The household's wealth is reduced. The household consumes less capital good, consumer good, and health service. Health caring is improved.

8.2.7 *Pollutants Speed Up Health Deterioration*

Pollutants stock is assumed to speed up health deterioration in the following way: $b_{\ell}: 0.1 \Rightarrow 0.11$. The result is plotted in Fig. 8.8. The change in the parameter has slight impact on the long-term time distribution. The total labor supply is reduced. The environmental quality becomes slightly improved in association with shrinking of production scales of the four sectors. The government has less tax income. Health is deteriorated. The wage income falls. The prices of consumer good and health service are slightly increased. The household's wealth is reduced. The household consumes less capital good, consumer good, and health service. Health caring is improved.

8.3 Renewable Resources, Values, and Economic Structure

This section introduces renewable resource and agricultural sector into the basic model. The model is referred to Zhang (2015). The economy includes the households, and industrial, agricultural, and resource sectors. The economy has labor, renewable resources, capital accumulation, and land. Stock of renewable resources is changeable according to how fast agents utilize resources and how fast renewable resources grow. Natural resources are incorporated into the neoclassical growth

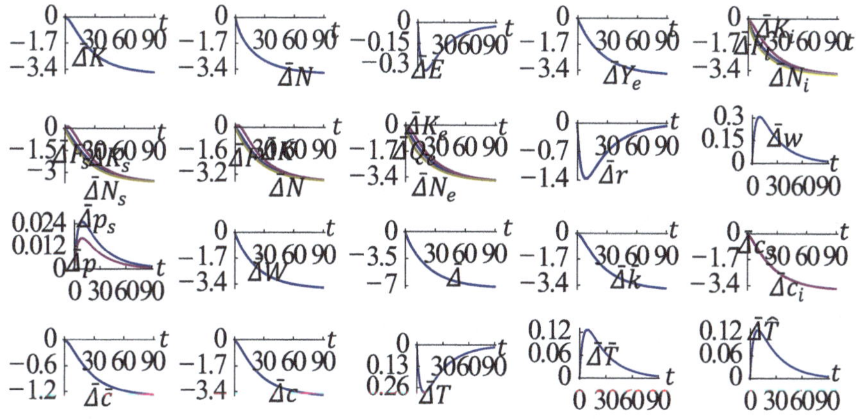

Fig. 8.8 Pollutants speed up health deterioration

theory in the 1970s (e.g., Plourde 1970, 1971; Stiglitz 1974; Clark 1976; Dasgupta and Heal 1979). Economists were aware of the necessity of modeling resources with dynamic theory long before. As early as in 1956, Gordon (1956) emphasized the need for a dynamic approach to fisheries economics: "The conservation problem is essentially one which requires a dynamic formulation… The economic justification of conservation is the same as that of any capital investment—by postponing utilization we hope to increase the quantity available for use at a future date. In the fishing industry we may allow our fish to grow and to reproduce so that the stock at a future date will be greater than it would be if we attempted to catch as much as possible at the present time. … [I]t is necessary to arrive at an optimum which is a catch per unit of time, and one must reach this objective through consideration of the interaction between the rate of catch, the dynamics of fish population, and the economic time-preference schedule of the community or the interest rate on invested capital. This is a very complicated problem and I suspect that we will have to look to the mathematical economists for assistance in clarifying it." As pointed out by Gaffney (2008: 119), "Most economists today live in a two-factor world: There is just labor and capital. Land, so central to classical political economy, has been swallowed into capital and "disappeared."" Common households may accumulate wealth by owning land and other kinds of wealth. The determination of land values involves taking account of nonlinear dynamic interactions between many variables. This section applies the basic model to provide insights into issues. The economy has industrial, agricultural, and renewable resource sectors. The population $\bar{N}$ and the total land L are homogenous and constant.

8.3.1 The Industrial Sector

I use the conventional production function to describe a relationship between inputs and output. The production function $F_i(t)$ is specified as follows:

$$F_i(t) = A_i K_i^{\alpha_i}(t) N_i^{\beta_i}(t), \quad A_i, \alpha_i, \beta_i > 0, \ \alpha_i + \beta_i = 1, \tag{8.3.1}$$

where $N_i(t)$ and $K_i(t)$ are, respectively, the labor force and physical capital, and A_i, α_i and β_i are parameters. The rate of interest $r(t)$ and wage rate $w(t)$ are determined by markets. The marginal conditions are

$$r(t) + \delta_k = \frac{\alpha_i F_i(t)}{K_i(t)}, \ w(t) = \frac{\beta_i F_i(t)}{N_i(t)}, \tag{8.3.2}$$

where δ_k is the fixed depreciation rate of physical capital.

8.3.2 The Agricultural Sector

The agricultural production with capital $K_a(t)$, labor force $N_a(t)$, and land $L_a(t)$ is described as follows:

$$F_a(t) = A_a K_a^{\alpha_a}(t) N_a^{\beta_a}(t) L_a^{\varsigma}(t),$$
$$A_a, \alpha_a, \beta_a, \varsigma > 0, \ \alpha_a + \beta_a + \varsigma = 1. \tag{8.3.3}$$

The marginal conditions are

$$r(t) + \delta_k = \frac{\alpha_a p_a(t) F_a(t)}{K_a(t)}, \ w(t) = \frac{\beta_a p_a(t) F_a(t)}{N_a(t)},$$
$$R(t) = \frac{\varsigma p_a(t) F_a(t)}{L_a(t)}, \tag{8.3.4}$$

where $p_a(t)$ is the price of agricultural goods and $R(t)$ is the land rent.

8.3.3 Choice Between Physical Wealth and Land

The land is privately owned by households. Let $p_L(t)$ denote the price of land. Consider now an investor with one unity of money. He can either invest in capital good thereby earning a profit equal to the net own-rate of return $r(t)$ or invest in land thereby earning a profit equal to the net own-rate of return $R(t)/p_L(t)$ As I assume capital and land markets to be at competitive equilibrium at any point in time, two options must yield equal returns, $r(t) = R(t)/p_L(t)$. This equation enables us to determine choice between owning land and wealth. Issues related to transaction costs, time delay, expectations, and information are omitted here.

8.3.4 Change of Renewable Resources

Let $X(t)$ stand for the stock of the resource. I am concerned with a single kind of resource. The natural growth rate of the resource is taken on the following logistic function:

$$\varphi_0 X(t) \left(1 - \frac{X(t)}{\varphi(L_x)} \right),$$

where the variable $\varphi(L_x)$ is the maximum possible size for the resource stock, called the carrying capacity of the resource, and the variable φ_0 is "uncongested" or "intrinsic" growth rate of the renewable resource. If the stock is equal to φ, then the growth rate should equal zero. If the carrying capacity is much larger than the current stock, then the growth rate per unit of the stock is approximately equal to the intrinsic growth rate. That is, the congestion effect is negligible. Let $F_x(t)$ stand for the harvest rate of the resource. The change rate in the stock is then equal to the natural growth rate minus the harvest rate:

$$\dot{X}(t) = \varphi_0 X(t)\left(1 - \frac{X(t)}{\varphi(L_x)}\right) - F_x(t). \tag{8.3.5}$$

This study accepts the assumption that assumed an open-access renewable resource [which was initially examined by Gordon (1954)]. With open access, harvesting occurs up to the point at which the current return to a representative entrant equals the entrant's cost. I use $N_x(t)$ and $K_x(t)$ to stand for the labor force and capital stocks employed by the resource sector. I assume that harvesting of the resource is carried out according to the following harvesting production function:

$$F_x(t) = A_x X^b(t) L_x^{b_x}(t) K_x^{\alpha_x}(t) N_x^{\beta_x}(t),$$
$$A_x, b, b_x, \alpha_x, \beta_x > 0, \ \alpha_x + \beta_x = 1, \tag{8.3.6}$$

where A_x, b, b_x, α_x and β_x are parameters. The specified form implies that if the capital (like machine) and labor inputs are simultaneously doubled, then harvest is also doubled for given levels of technology and resource at any time. Let $p_x(t)$ denote the price of the resource. The marginal conditions are given as follows:

$$r(t) + \delta_k = \frac{\alpha_x p_x(t) F_x(t)}{K_x(t)}, \ w(t) = \frac{\beta_x p_x(t) F_x(t)}{N_x(t)}. \tag{8.3.7}$$

8.3.5 Consumer Behavior

We denote, respectively, physical wealth by $\bar{k}(t)$ and land $\bar{l}(t)$ owned by the representative household. The total value of wealth owned by the household $a(t)$ is the sum of the two assets

$$a(t) = \bar{k}(t) + p_L(t)\bar{l}(t).$$

The current income from the interest payment $r(t)\bar{k}(t)$, the wage payment $w(t)$, and the land revenue $R(t)\bar{l}(t)$ is

$$y(t) = r(t)\bar{k}(t) + w(t) + R(t) - \bar{l}(t).$$

The disposable income is

$$\hat{y}(t) = y(t) + a(t).$$

The household distributes the disposable income between saving $s(t)$, the consumption of commodity $c_i(t)$, consumption of the resource good $c_x(t)$, the consumption of agricultural good, $c_a(t)$, and housing, $l_h(t)$. The budget constraint is given by

$$c_i(t) + s(t) + p_a(t)c_a(t) + p_x(t)c_x(t) + R(t)l_h(t) = \hat{y}(t).$$

The household decides five variables, $s(t)$, $c_i(t)$, $c_x(t)$, $c_a(t)$, and $l_h(t)$. The consumer's utility function is specified as follows:

$$U(t) = c_i^{\xi_0}(t)c_a^{\mu_0}(t)c_x^{\chi_0}(t)l_h^{\eta_0}(t)s^{\lambda_0}(t), \quad \xi_0, \mu_0, \chi_0, \eta_0, \lambda_0 > 0,$$

in which ξ_0, μ_0, χ_0, η_0, and λ_0 are propensities to consume the commodity, the agricultural goods, the resource, and housing, and to hold wealth, respectively. Maximizing $U(t)$ subject to the budget constraint yields

$$c_i(t) = \xi\hat{y}(t), \; p_a(t)c_a(t) = \mu\hat{y}(t), \; p_x(t)c_x(t) = \chi\hat{y}(t),$$
$$R(t)l_h(t) = \eta\hat{y}(t), \; s(t) = \lambda\hat{y}(t),$$

where

$$\xi \equiv \rho\xi_0, \; \mu \equiv \rho\mu_0, \; \chi \equiv \rho\chi_0, \; \eta \equiv \rho\eta_0, \; \lambda \equiv \rho\lambda_0,$$
$$\rho \equiv \frac{1}{\xi_0 + \mu_0 + \chi_0 + \eta_0 + \lambda_0}.$$

8.3.6 Wealth Accumulation

The change in the household's wealth follows

$$\dot{a}(t) = s(t) - a(t).$$

8.3.7 Balances of Demand and Supply for Industrial Goods

Demand and supply for the industrial sector's output balance at any point of time

$$c(t)\bar{N} + s(t)\bar{N} + \delta_k K(t) = F_i(t) + K(t).$$

8.3.8 Balances of Demand and Supply for Agricultural Goods and Renewable Resources

$$C_a(t) = c_a(t)\bar{N} = F_a(t).$$
$$c_x(t)\bar{N} = F_x(t).$$

8.3.9 All the Land Owned by Households

The land owned by the population is equal to the national available land

$$\bar{l}(t)\bar{N} = L.$$

8.3.10 Full Employment of Capital

We use $K(t)$ to stand for the total capital stock. I have

$$K_i(t) + K_a(t) + K_x(t) = K(t).$$

8.3.11 The Value of Physical Wealth and Capital

The value of physical capital is equal to the value of physical wealth

$$\bar{k}(t)\bar{N} = K(t).$$

8.3.12 Full Employment of Labor Force

$$N_i(t) + N_a(t) + N_x(t) = \bar{N}.$$

8.3.13 The Land Market Clearing Condition

The land is fully used

$$l_h(t)\bar{N} + L_a(t) + L_x(t) = L.$$

8.3.14 Land Use for Renewable Resources

I now introduce a mechanism to decide the amount of land used for renewable resource. The land of renewable resource is assumed to be

$$L_x(t) = \varphi L_a(t),$$

where φ is a parameter. I thus built the model. Introduce a variable $z(t)$:

$$z(t) \equiv \frac{r(t) + \delta_k}{w(t)}.$$

Lemma The motion of the system is determined by the following two differential equations

$$\dot{z}(t) = \Lambda(z(t)),$$

$$\dot{X}(t) = \Omega(z(t), X(t)),$$

where functions of $\Lambda(z(t))$ and $\Omega(z(t), X(t))$ are given in Zhang (2005). Moreover, all the other variables are determined as functions of $z(t)$ and $X(t)$.

We specify the parameters as follows:

$$\bar{N} = 5,\ L = 10,\ \alpha_i = 0.3,\ \alpha_a = 0.1,\ \beta_a = 0.2,\ \alpha_x = 0.34,$$
$$A_i = 1,\ A_a = 0.5,\ A_x = 0.5,\ \lambda_0 = 0.5,\ \xi_0 = 0.07,\ \chi_0 = 0.02,$$
$$\eta_0 = 0.01,\ \mu_0 = 0.02,\ \phi = 1.6,\ \varphi = 4,\ \varphi_0 = 5,\ b = 0.7,$$

$$b_x = 0.01,\ \delta_k = 0.05.$$

The population is fixed at 5, and the land is 10. The propensity to save is much higher than the propensity to consume industrial goods, resources, and agricultural goods. It can be shown that the following variables are invariant in time:

$$l_h = 0.43,\ L_a = 3.02,\ L_x = 4.83,\ \bar{l} = 2.$$

The initial conditions are specified as follows:

$$X(0) = 3.4,\ z(0) = 0.18.$$

I plot the motion of the variables in Fig. 8.9, in which the national gross product (GDP) is defined as follows:

$$Y(t) \equiv F_i(t) + p_a(t)F_a(t) + p_x(t)F_x(t) + l_h\bar{N}R(t).$$

The GDP and national capital stock fall over time till they become stationary. The stock of resources rises. The wage rate, price of land, price of resource, price of agricultural goods, and land rent are reduced, and the rate of interest is enhanced. The output level of the agricultural sector is increased, and the output level of the industrial sector is reduced. Some of the force is shifted from the industrial sector to the agricultural sector. The capital inputs of the two sectors are increased. The physical wealth, total wealth, and consumption levels of the two goods are increased. It should be noted that the dynamic relationship between the GDP and the land price

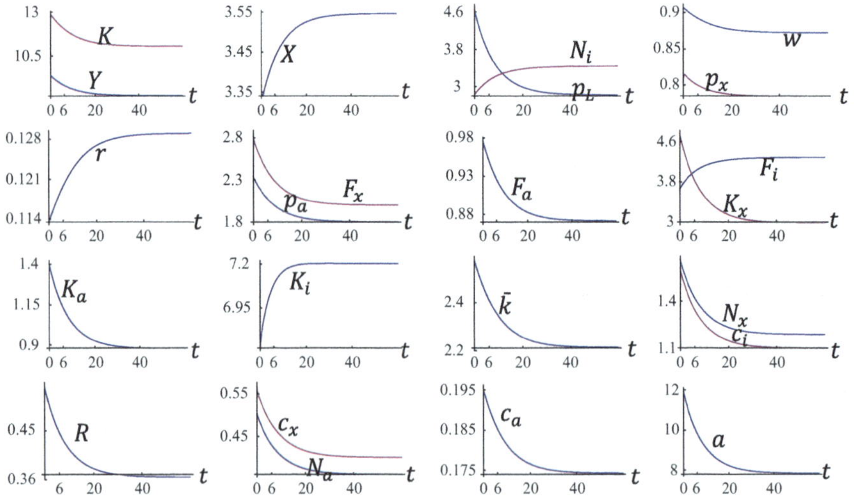

Fig. 8.9 Motion of the economic system

plotted in Fig. 8.9 is similar to the phenomenon described by Liu et al. (2011: 1): "The recent financial crisis caused by a collapse of the housing market propelled the U.S. economy into the Great Recession. A notable development during the crisis period was a slump in business investment in tandem with a sharp decline in land prices." The conclusions made by Liu et al. are based on the data for the Great Recession period as well as for the entire sample period from 1975 to 2010. Our comparative dynamic analysis in the rest of the chapter also shows similar conclusions.

The existence of a unique equilibrium point is listed as follows:

$$Y = 8.24,\ K = 11.07,\ X = 3.55,\ w = 0.87,\ p_L = 2.83,\ R = 0.37,$$
$$r = 0.13,\ p_a = 1.81,\ p_x = 0.79,\ F_a = 0.87,\ F_i = 4.3,$$
$$F_x = 2.01,\ K_a = 0.88,\ K_i = 7.21,\ K_x = 2.99,\ N_a = 0.36,$$
$$l_h = 0.43,\ \bar{k} = 2.22,\ c_a = 0.17,\ c_x = 0.4,\ c_i = 1.1,\ a = 7.88.$$

The eigenvalues at the equilibrium point are −4.265 and −0.116. This guarantees the stability of the steady state.

8.4 Changes in the Population and the Preference

We now examine the effects of changes in some parameters on the motion of the economic system.

8.4.1 A Rise in the Propensity to Consume Resources

We first examine the effects of the following change in the propensity to consume resources: χ_0: 0.02 ⇒ 0.03. The land use pattern is not affected by the change in the preference. The effects on the other variables are plotted in Fig. 8.10. The household consumes more resources, and the stock of resources is reduced. The price of resources is enhanced. The household reduces the consumption levels of agricultural and industrial goods. The household's physical wealth and national physical capital rise initially and fall in the long term. The GDP is reduced. The land rent and land value are lowered. The price of agricultural goods is reduced. The wage rate falls in tandem with rising in the rate of interest. The output level and two inputs of the industrial and agricultural sectors are lowered. The output level and two inputs of the resource sector are augmented. Debates about whether natural resources are a blessing or a curse for human development are still a hot topic in the literature of economic development.

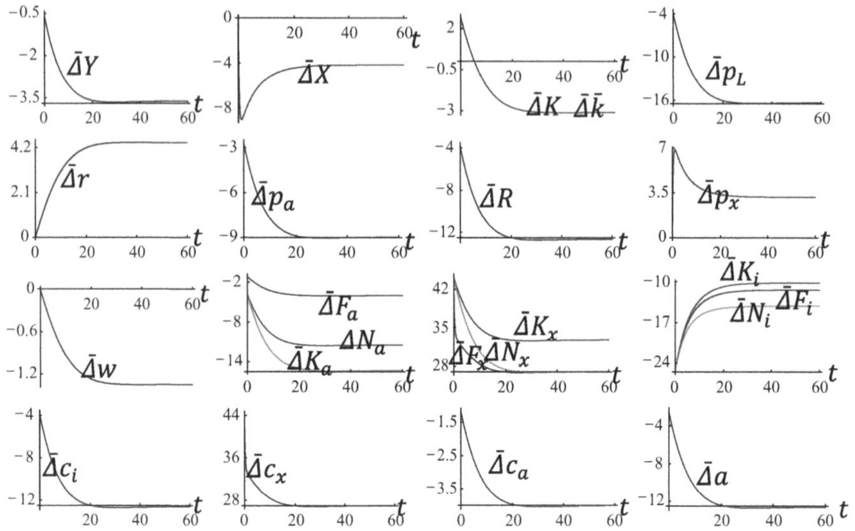

Fig. 8.10 Rise in the propensity to consume resources

8.4.2 A Rise in the Propensity to Consume Housing

The propensity to consume housing is shifted as follows: η_0: 0.01 $\Rightarrow$ 0.015. The land use is redistribution as follows:

$$\bar{\Delta} L_a = \bar{\Delta} L_x = -1.07, \ \bar{\Delta} l_h = 3.88, \ \bar{\Delta} \bar{l} = 0.$$

The household has larger house size. The resource and agricultural sectors use less land. The effects on the other variables are plotted in Fig. 8.11. The land rent and land value are augmented. The price of agricultural goods and price of resources are increased. The wage rate is lowered in tandem with rising in the rate of interest. The household's physical wealth and national total capital stocks are augmented initially and reduced in the long term. The household consumes more agricultural goods, resources, and goods. The household also owns more wealth. The national output rises. The output level and two inputs of the industrial sector are lowered. The output level and two inputs of the resource and agricultural sectors are augmented.

8.4.3 The Propensity to Consume Industrial Goods Being Enhanced

We now study the effects that the following changes in the propensity to consume industrial goods: ξ_0: 0.07 $\Rightarrow$ 0.075. The land use pattern is not affected. The effects

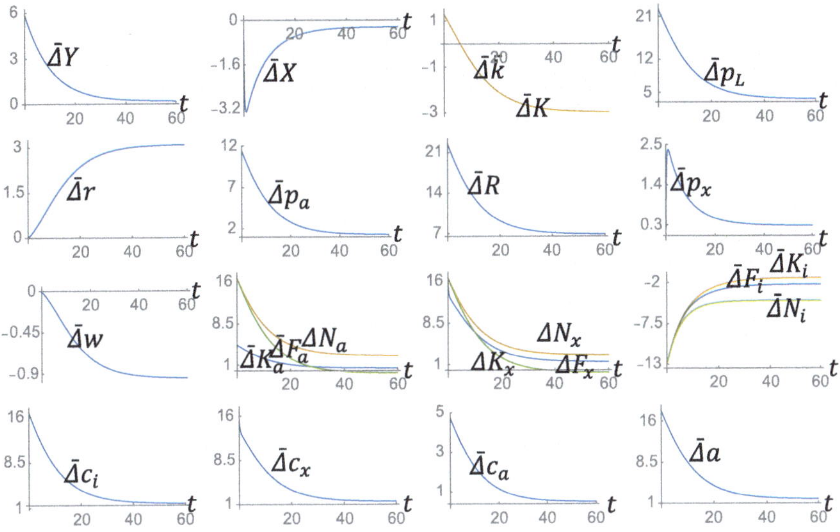

Fig. 8.11 Rise in the propensity to consume housing

on the other variables are plotted in Fig. 8.12. As the household spends more out of the disposable income on consuming industrial goods, the total capital stock and the GDP are lowered. The household owns less physical wealth and wealth. The households consume more industrial goods and less resources and agricultural goods. The stock

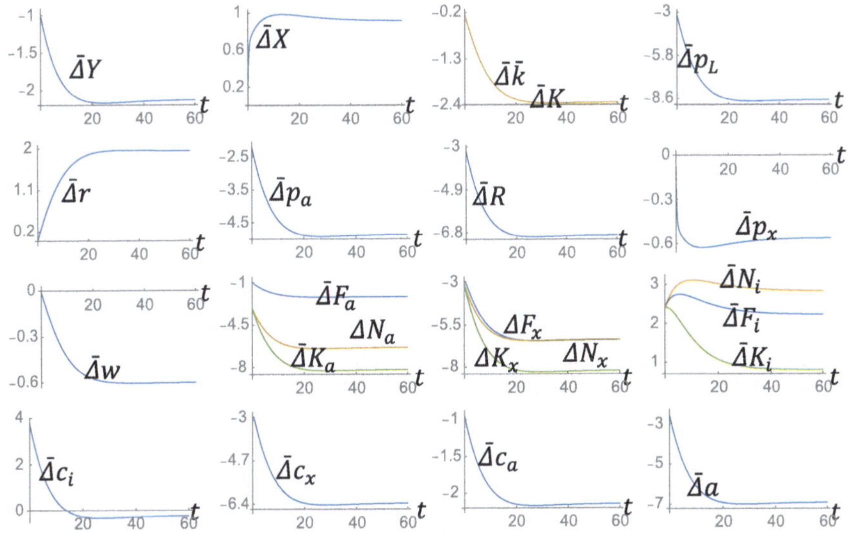

Fig. 8.12 Rise in the propensity to consume industrial goods

of resource is increased in association with falling price of the resource. The wage rate is reduced, and the rate of interest is enhanced. Both the land value and the land rent are reduced. The price of agricultural goods falls. The output levels and two inputs of the agricultural and resource sectors reduced. In the long term, the increase in the output of the industrial sector is due to the reallocation of labor force from the agricultural sector to the industrial sector. The capital inputs of the two sectors are reduced in the long term.

8.4.4 A Rise in the Propensity to Consume Agricultural Goods

We now study the effects that the propensity to consume agricultural goods is increased as follows: μ_0: $0.02 \Rightarrow 0.025$. The impact on land use pattern is as follows:

$$\bar{\Delta} L_a = \bar{\Delta} L_x = 4.51, \ \bar{\Delta} l_h = -16.4, \ \bar{\Delta} \bar{l} = 0.$$

More land is devoted to agricultural and resource supplies and less to housing. The effects on the system over time are plotted in Fig. 8.13. As the household spends more out of the disposable income on consuming agricultural goods, the total capital stock is reduced. The GDP is augmented. The wage rate is reduced, and the rate of interest is enhanced. The land rent and the value of land are lowered. The household holds less wealth and physical wealth. The household's consumption level of agricultural

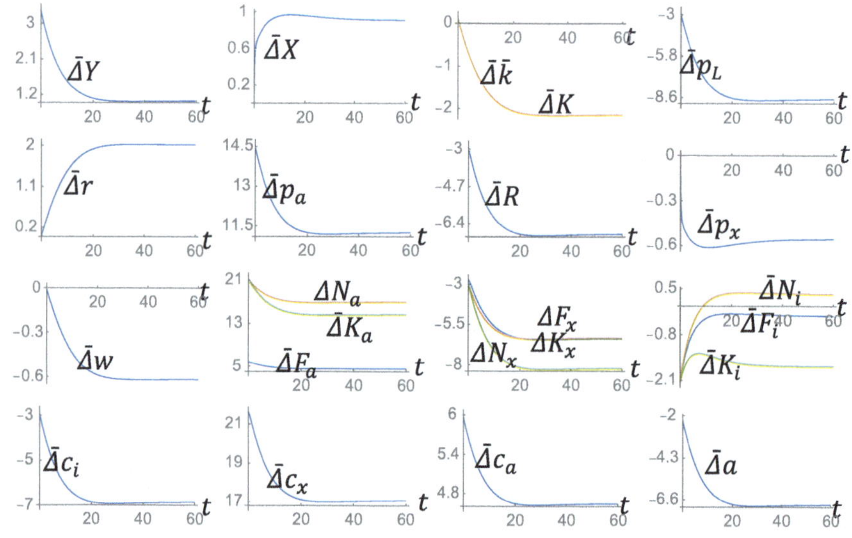

Fig. 8.13 Propensity to consume agricultural goods being enhanced

goods rises. The household's consumption level of industrial goods falls. The price of agricultural goods rises. The output level and two input factors of the agricultural sector are augmented. The output level and capital input of the industrial sector are reduced. The stock of resources is increased in association with falling in the resource price. The output level and the two inputs of the resource sector are reduced.

8.4.5 A Rise in the Propensity to Save

We now change the propensity to save as follows: λ_0: 0.5 $\Rightarrow$ 0.52. The land use pattern is not affected. The effects on the variables over time are plotted in Fig. 8.14. As the household tends to save more out of the disposable income, the physical wealth falls initially and rises in the long term. The GDP falls initially and rises in the long term. The household consumes industrial goods, agricultural goods, and resource less initially and more in the long term. The household owns wealth less initially and more in the long term. The land value falls initially and rises in the long term. The land rent and the price of agricultural goods are reduced initially and increased in the long term. The wage rate rises, and the rate of interest falls. The output and two input factors of the industrial sectors are expanded. The output and two capital input of the agricultural sectors are reduced initially and expanded in the long term. The stock of resources is augmented initially and reduced in the long term. The price of resources falls.

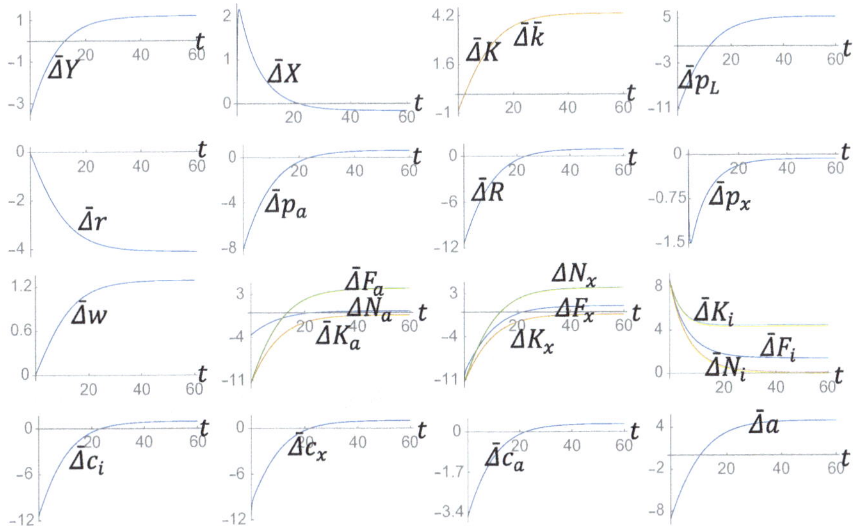

Fig. 8.14 Propensity to save being enhanced

8.4.6 The Population Being Augmented

We now study the effects that the population is expanded as follows: $\bar{N}: 5 \Rightarrow 5.2$. The impact on land use pattern is as follows:

$$\bar{\Delta} L_a = \bar{\Delta} L_x = 0, \; \bar{\Delta} l_h = \bar{\Delta} \bar{l} = -3.85.$$

The land inputs of the agricultural and resource sectors are not affected. The lot size is increased. The household owns less land. The effects on the system over time are plotted in Fig. 8.15. As the nation has more people, the total capital stock and GDP are increased initially and reduced in the long term. The wage rate is reduced, and the rate of interest is enhanced. The land rent and the value of land are lowered. The household holds less wealth and physical wealth. The household's consumption levels of agricultural goods, industrial goods, and resource all fall. The price of agricultural goods is lowered. The output levels and two inputs of the agricultural and resource sectors are reduced. The output level and two inputs of the industrial sector are augmented. The stock of resources is increased in association with falling in the resource price.

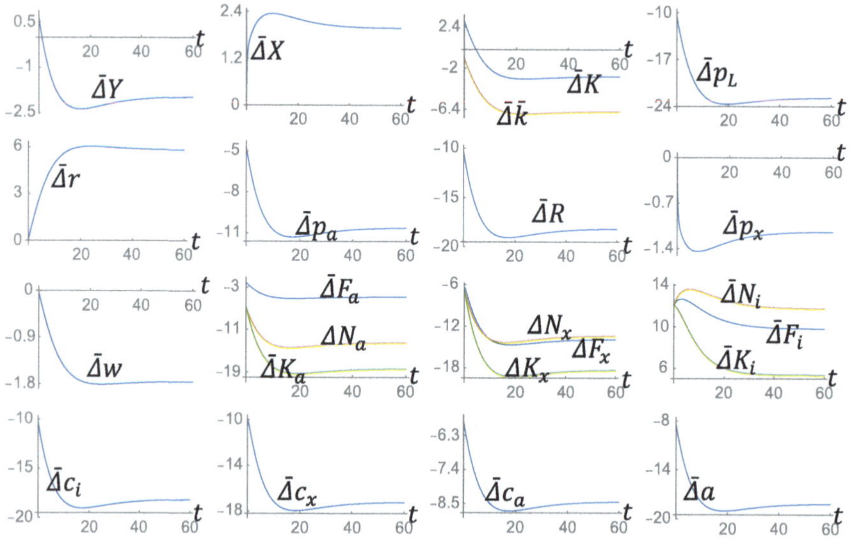

Fig. 8.15 Population being augmented

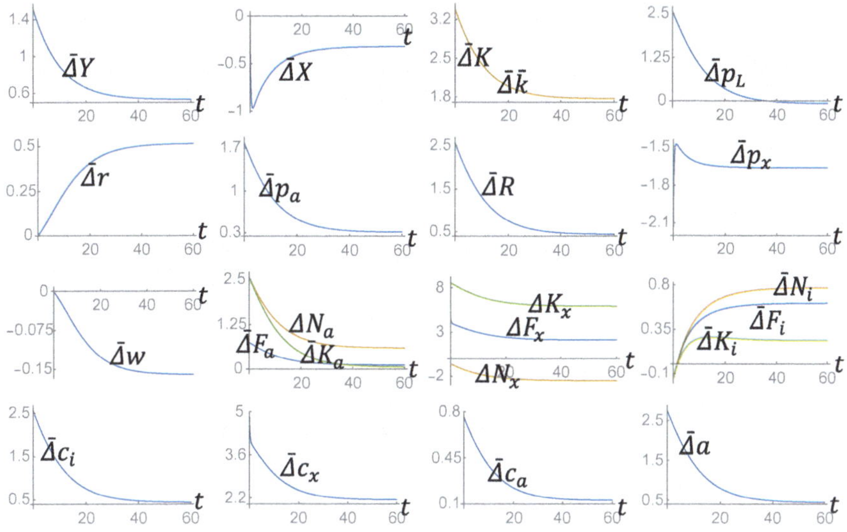

Fig. 8.16 Rise in the output elasticity of capital of the resource sector

8.4.7 A Rise in the Output Elasticity of Capital of the Resource Sector

We now examine the effects of the following rise in the output elasticity of capital of the resource sector: $\alpha_x: 0.34 \Rightarrow 0.36$. The land use pattern is not affected. The effects on the other variables are plotted in Fig. 8.16. A rise in this parameter implies that the capital share of the total factor cost is increased in the optimal decision. The total capital and the GDP are increased. The rate of interest, the price of agricultural goods, the land rent, and land value are all increased. The wage rate and price of resources are reduced.

8.5 Comments on Dynamic Environment and Health

The 2018 Nobel Prize in economics was awarded to William D. Nordhaus (1941–) "for integrating climate change into long-run macroeconomic analysis." The prize was shared with Romer whose contribution is about technological innovations. Nordhaus' models deal with many interactions with different approaches. It is not difficult to see that my unified approach to economic dynamics with institutions, society, environment, resource, knowledge, and education integrates his relevant ideas to a larger whole. This chapter is concentrated on the interdependence between health, environment, and growth. The previous chapters show how to introduce other important variables, such as population, human capital, and knowledge into the model in this chapter.

References

Clark CW (1976) Mathematical bioeconomics: the optimal management of renewable resources. Wiley, New York

Dasgupta PS, Heal GE (1979) The economics of exhaustible resources. Cambridge University Press, Cambridge

Dinda S (2004) Environmental Kuznets curve hypothesis: a survey. Ecol Econ 49:431–455

Forster BA (1973) Optimal consumption planning in a polluted environment. Econ Rec 49:534–545

Gaffney M (2008) Keeping land in capital theory: Ricardo, Faustmann, Wicksell, and George. Am J Econ Sociol 67:119–142

Gordon HS (1954) The economic theory of a common property resources: the fishery. J Polit Econ 62:124–142

Gordon HS (1956) Obstacles to agreement on control in the fishing industry. In: Turvey R, Wiseman J (eds) The economics of fisheries, 65-72. Food and Agricultural Organization of the United Nations, Rome

Grossman M (1972) On the concept of health capital and the demand of health. J Polit Econ 80:223–255

Grossman GM (1995) Pollution and growth: what do we know? In: Goldin I, Winters LA (eds) The economics of sustainable development. Cambridge University Press, Cambridge

Gupta MR, Dutta PB (2018) Tourism development, environmental pollution and economic growth: a theoretical analysis. J Int Trade Econ Dev 27:125–144

Gutiérrez M (2008) Dynamic inefficiency in an overlapping generation economy with pollution and health costs. J Pub Econ Theor 10:563–594

Halkos G, Managi S (2017) Recent advances in empirical analysis on growth and environment: Introduction. Environ Dev 22:649–657

Johansson PO, Löfgren KG (1995) Wealth from optimal health. J Health Econ 14:65–79

Kasztelan A (2017) Green growth, green economy and sustainable development: theoretical and relational discourse. Prague Econ Papers 26:487–499

Kelly M (2017) Health capital accumulation, health insurance, and aggregate outcomes: a neoclassical approach. J Macroecon 52:1–22

Kijima M, Nishide K, Ohyama A (2010) Economic models for the environmental Kuznets curve: a survey. J Econ Dyn Control 34:1187–1201

Liu Z, Wang PF, Zha T (2011) Land-price dynamics and macroeconomic fluctuations. Working Paper, Federal Reserve Bank of Atlanta, No. 2011-11

Managi S (2007) Technological change and environmental policy: a study of depletion in the oil and gas industry. Edward Elgar, Cheltenham

Mesagan E (2015) Economic growth and environment nexus: the role of foreign direct investment. Res J Contemp Issues Dev 4:44–52

Plouder GC (1972) A model of waste accumulation and disposal. Can J Econ 5:119–125

Plourde GC (1970) A simple model of replenishable resource exploitation. Am Econ Rev 60:518–522

Plourde GC (1971) Exploitation of common-property replenishable resources. W Econ J 9:256–266

Stiglitz JE (1974) Growth with exhaustible natural resources: efficient and optimal growth paths. In: Review of economic studies, symposium on the economics of exhaustible resources, pp 123–138

Tobing E (2011) Public health spending, tax reform, and long-run growth. Econ Lett 112:119–121

van Zon A, Muysken J (2001) Health and endogenous growth. J Health Econ 20:169–185

Weil DN (2007) Accounting for the effective of health on education growth. Q J Econ 122:1265–1306

Zhang WB (2005) Differential equations, bifurcations, and chaos in economics. World Scientific, Singapore

Zhang WB (2015) Values of land and renewable resources in a three-sector economic growth model. Stud Bus Econ 10:156–186

Zhang WB (2018) Health, environment, and wealth. Econ Sci Ser 7:109–123

Zhang WB (2019) A simple growth model based on neoclassical growth, monopolistic competition, and Walrasian general equilibrium theories. Int J Acad Res Bus Soc Sci 9:1005–1027

Chapter 9
Preference Change, Social Status, Habits, and Fashion

Viewed as a geometric figure, the ant's path is irregular, complex, and hard to describe.
Herbert A. Simon (1916–2001).

People have different propensities to save, which affects income and wealth distribution and macroeconomic growth. People brought up in different societies and family conditions have different habits in consumption and decision making. People with different social status behave differently. Preference, habit, social status, and fashions and their relations to economic conditions are traditional topics in economics. Since Veblen (1899) published *The Theory of the Leisure Class*, many economists have studied economic consequences of conspicuous consumption and social status. Veblen argues that people are interested in pursuing conspicuous consumption as it signals wealth and social status. According to Duesenberry (1949), people will improve social status by imitating the consumption standard of the social or classes above them. Becker has made contributions to formally modeling human behavior about various aspects of human behavior (Becker 1976, 1992). He was fully aware of the importance to integrate microeconomics and macroeconomics. But he did not provide an analytical framework for formally modeling macroeconomic dynamics on basis of microbehavior. An early formal modeling of time preference change in neoclassical growth theory was carried out by Uzawa (1968). Lucas and Stokey (1984) and Epstein (1987) also make time preference change dependent on consumptions. There are many other studies on the implications of endogenous time preference for economic growth (Epstein and Hynes 1983; Becker and Barro 1988; Obstfeld 1990; Shin and Epstein 1993; Palivos et al. 1997; Drugeon 1996, 2000; Stern 2006; Dioikitopoulos and Kalyvitis 2010).

This chapter introduces preference change, social status, and fashions social status into the basic model. Rege (2008) argues that people are concerned with social status because it serves a signal of non-observable abilities. Rege (2008: 240) describes: "By investing in social status a person can thus improve his chance of engaging in a complementary interaction with a high ability person. The idea that status can serve as a signal of abilities is not new and has been captured in several models. It has, for example, been demonstrated that workers can signal their ability to employers

W.-B. Zhang, *The General Economic Theory*,
https://doi.org/10.1007/978-3-030-56204-5_9

by undertaking some seemingly irrelevant but costly activity interpreted as status consumption (Frank 1985) or social culture (Fang 2001) and that people can "burn-money" on fashions to signal abilities in a "datinggame" (Pesendorfer)." There are some studies on social status and growth (see also, Cole et al. 1992; Konrad 1992; Fershtman et al. 1996; Rauscher 1997). This chapter integrates some ideas on modeling social status with the basic model.

9.1 Social Status and Inequality in Wealth and Income

The economy is composed of capital goods and consumer goods sectors. The model is developed by Zhang (2017). The population is classified into multiple groups, and each group has a fixed population $\bar{N}_j (j = 1, \ldots, J)$. Let the wage rate of worker of type j and interest rate be represented by $w_j(t)$ and $r(t)$, respectively. I use $p(t)$ to denote the price of consumer goods. The total capital stock $K(t)$ is allocated between the two sectors. Subscript index i and s stand for capital good and consumer goods sectors, respectively. Let $N_m(t)$ and $K_m(t)$ and denote the labor force and capital stocks employed by sector m. The total population $\bar{N}$ and total labor supply N are:

$$\bar{N} = \sum_{j=1}^{J} \bar{N}_j, \ N = \sum_{j=1}^{J} h_j \bar{N}_j,$$

9.1.1 *The Production Sectors and Marginal Conditions*

I use $F_m(t)$ to denote the production function of sector m, $m = i, s$. The production functions are specified as follows:

$$F_m(t) = A_m K_m^{\alpha_m}(t) N_m^{\beta_m}(t), \alpha_i, \ \beta_i > 0, \ \alpha_m + \beta_m = 1.$$

The marginal conditions imply:

$$r(t) + \delta_k = \frac{\alpha_i F_i(t)}{K_i(t)} = \frac{\alpha_s p(t) F_s(t)}{K_s(t)}, \ w(t) = \frac{\beta_i F_i(t)}{N_i(t)} = \frac{\beta_s p(t) F_s(t)}{N_s(t)},$$

where $w(t)$ is the wage rate of labor input. The wage rate of group j is $w_j(t) = h_j w(t)$.

9.1.2 Disposable Incomes and Utility Functions

Let $\bar{k}_j(t)$ stand for household *j*'s wealth. I have $\bar{k}_j(t) = \bar{K}_j(t)/\bar{N}_j$, where $\bar{K}_j(t)$ is the total wealth held by group *j*. Household *j*'s disposable income is:

$$\hat{y}_j(t) = (1 + r(t))\bar{k}_j(t) + h_j w(t). \tag{9.1.1}$$

The social status is assumed to be dependent on wealth as follows:

$$\omega_j\left(\left(\bar{k}_j(t)\right)\right) = \omega_{j0} + \omega_{jL}\bar{k}_j(t), \tag{9.1.2}$$

where ω_{j0} and ω_{jL} positive parameters. This is a simplified form of possible social status functions as social status can be dependent on education, human capital, family heritage, human networks with celebrities, relative richness in the same group position, and the like.

Before continuing to model the preference change, I introduce a few typical ways of modeling social status in growth theory. Following Zou (1994, 1995), Chen and Guo (2009) introduce social status as a function of wealth as follows:

$$U = \int_0^\infty \left[\frac{c^{1-\sigma}(t) - 1}{1-\sigma} + \beta\frac{k^{1-\sigma}(t) - 1}{1-\sigma}\right] e^{\rho t} \mathrm{d}t,$$

where $c(t)$ and $k(t)$, are, respectively, the household's consumption and capital stock, ρ is the time discount rate, and β measures the degree for the spirit of capitalism. It should be noted that Kurz (1968) first uses both consumption flows and capital stocks as components of utility functions. In another study, Chen and Guo (2011) investigate effects of relative wealth-induced preferences for social status on equilibrium growth in a standard one-sector AK model. The model predicts that there is a positive output-growth effect in response to changes of the strength for social status. There are other studies on the issues (Alvarez-Cuadrado et al. 2004; Amano and Laubach 2004).

The utility is specified as follows:

$$U = \int_0^\infty \frac{\left[c(t)(k(t)/K(t))^{\beta}\right]^{1-\sigma} - 1}{1-\sigma} e^{-\rho t} dt.$$

The household is assumed to derive utilities from the wealth-based social status which is represented by its physical capital ownership $k(t)$ relative to the economy-wide level of physical capital stock $K(t)$. They interpret $\beta > 0$ as the degree of the spirit of capitalism. In another research by Corneo and Jeanne (1999), the utility function is specified as:

$$U = \int_0^\infty [u(c(t)) + v(t)]e^{\rho t} dt,$$

where $v(t)$ is a variable called an individual's social esteem or social status.

I now continue to build the model. The disposable income is distributed between saving $s_j(t)$ and consumption $c_j(t)$:

$$p(t)c_j(t) + s_j(t) = \hat{y}_j(t). \tag{9.1.3}$$

I specify the utility level $U_j(t)$ as follows:

$$U_j(t) = c_j^{\xi_{j0}(\omega_j(t))}(t)s_j^{\lambda_{j0}(\omega_j(t))}(t),\ \xi_{j0}(\omega_j(t)),\ \lambda_{j0}(\omega_j(t)) > 0,$$

where $\xi_{j0}(\omega_j(t))$ is the propensity to consume consumer good and $\lambda_{j0}(\omega_j(t))$ the propensity to save.

9.1.3 *Social Status and Propensities to Save and to Consume*

The propensities to consume and to save are assumed to be dependent on social status in the following way:

$$\xi_{j0}(\omega_j(t)) = \bar{\xi}_{j0} + \tilde{\xi}_{j0}\omega_j(t),\ \lambda_{j0}(\omega_j(t)) = \bar{\lambda}_{j0} + \tilde{\lambda}_{j0}\omega_j(t),$$

where $\bar{\xi}_{j0}$ and $\bar{\lambda}_{j0}$ are positive parameters, and $\tilde{\xi}_{j0}$ and $\tilde{\lambda}_{j0}$ are parameters which may be either positive, zero, or negative. The propensity to consume is increased by social status, for instance, through the so-called conspicuous consumption. The propensity to save is affected by social status as wealth is related to social status.

9.1.4 *Optimal Household Behavior and Wealth Accumulation*

Maximizing the utility functions subject to (9.1.3), I get the marginal conditions:

$$p(t)c_j(t) = \xi_j((\bar{k}_j(t)))\hat{y}_j(t),\ s_j(t) = \lambda_j((\bar{k}_j(t)))\hat{y}_j(t),$$

where

$$\begin{aligned}\xi_j((\bar{k}_j(t))) &\equiv \rho_j((\bar{k}_j(t)))\xi_{j0}((\bar{k}_j(t))),\ \lambda_j((\bar{k}_j(t)))\\ &\equiv \rho_j((\bar{k}_j(t)))\lambda_{j0}((\bar{k}_j(t))),\end{aligned}$$

$$\rho_j\left(\left(\bar{k}_j(t)\right)\right) \equiv \frac{1}{\xi_{j0}\left(\left(\bar{k}_j(t)\right)\right) + \lambda_{j0}\left(\left(\bar{k}_j(t)\right)\right)}.$$

The change in the household's wealth follows:

$$\dot{\bar{k}}_j(t) = s_j(t) - \bar{k}_j(t).$$

9.1.5 Market Equilibrium Conditions and Full Employment

The demand and supply equilibrium conditions for the two sectors imply:

$$\sum_{j=1}^{J} c_j(t)\bar{N}_j = F_s(t),$$

$$S(t) - K(t) + \delta_k K(t) = F_i(t),$$

in which

$$S(t) \equiv \sum_{j=1}^{J} s_j(t)\bar{N}_j, \quad K(t) = \sum_{j=1}^{J} \bar{k}_j(t)\bar{N}_j.$$

Full employment of capital and labor implies:

$$K_i(t) + K_s(t) = K(t), \ N_i(t) + N_s(t) = N.$$

I completed the model.

Lemma 9.1.1 *The motion of the economic system is determined by J differential equations with $z(t)$ and $\left\{\bar{k}_j(t)\right\}$ as the variables:*

$$\dot{z}(t) = \Lambda_1\left(z(t), \left\{\bar{k}_j(t)\right\}\right),$$

$$\dot{\bar{k}}_j(t) = \Lambda_j\left(z(t), \left\{\bar{k}_j(t)\right\}\right), \quad j = 2, \ldots, J,$$

in which $z(t) \equiv (r(t) + \delta_k)/w(t)$ and *$\Lambda_j(t)$ are unique functions of $z(t)$ and $\left\{\bar{k}_j(t)\right\}$ defined in Zhang (*2017*). The other variables are determined as unique functions of $z(t)$ and $\left\{\bar{k}_j(t)\right\}$.*

The simulation is carried out for a three-group economy. The parameter values are specified as follows:

$$A_i = 1.3, \quad A_s = 1, \quad \alpha_i = 0.34, \quad \alpha_s = 0.3, \quad \delta_k = 0.05,$$

$$\begin{pmatrix} \bar{N}_1 \\ \bar{N}_2 \\ \bar{N}_3 \end{pmatrix} = \begin{pmatrix} 10 \\ 30 \\ 60 \end{pmatrix}, \begin{pmatrix} h_1 \\ h_2 \\ h_3 \end{pmatrix} = \begin{pmatrix} 4 \\ 2 \\ 1 \end{pmatrix}, \begin{pmatrix} \omega_{10} \\ \omega_{20} \\ \omega_{30} \end{pmatrix} = \begin{pmatrix} 0.01 \\ 0.01 \\ 0.01 \end{pmatrix}, \begin{pmatrix} \omega_{1L} \\ \omega_{2L} \\ \omega_{3L} \end{pmatrix}$$
$$= \begin{pmatrix} 0.01 \\ 0.008 \\ 0.005 \end{pmatrix}, \begin{pmatrix} \bar{\lambda}_{10} \\ \bar{\lambda}_{20} \\ \vec{\lambda}_{30} \end{pmatrix} = \begin{pmatrix} 0.8 \\ 0.75 \\ 0.7 \end{pmatrix}, \begin{pmatrix} \tilde{\lambda}_{10} \\ \tilde{\lambda}_{20} \\ \tilde{\lambda}_{30} \end{pmatrix} = \begin{pmatrix} 0.1 \\ 0.1 \\ 0.1 \end{pmatrix},$$
$$\begin{pmatrix} \tilde{\xi}_{10} \\ \tilde{\xi}_{20} \\ \tilde{\xi}_{30} \end{pmatrix} = \begin{pmatrix} 0.12 \\ 0.18 \\ 0.2 \end{pmatrix}, \begin{pmatrix} \bar{\xi}_{10} \\ \bar{\xi}_{20} \\ \bar{\xi}_{30} \end{pmatrix} = \begin{pmatrix} 0.05 \\ 0.05 \\ 0.05 \end{pmatrix}.$$

The population of group 3 is largest, while the population of group 2 is the next. The choice of population sizes is not important as far as my purposes of providing some insights into mechanisms of economic dynamics and demonstrating working the model are concerned. The capital goods and consumer goods sector's total productivities are, respectively, 1.3 and 1. The parameter values related to reference changes relatively small. The initial conditions are as follows:

$$z(0) = 0.06, \quad \bar{k}_2(0) = 10, \quad \bar{k}_3(0) = 4,$$

The motion of the variables is plotted in Fig. 9.1, where $Y(t) = F_i(t) + p(t)F_s(t)$. The economy produces less and has less capital. The output level of the capital goods sector is increased. The output level of the consumer goods sector becomes lower. The price of consumer goods becomes below. The interest rate falls. The wage rates rise. Group 1's per capita wealth, per capita consumption, social status and propensity to save are all reduced. The other two groups' per capita wealth levels, per capita

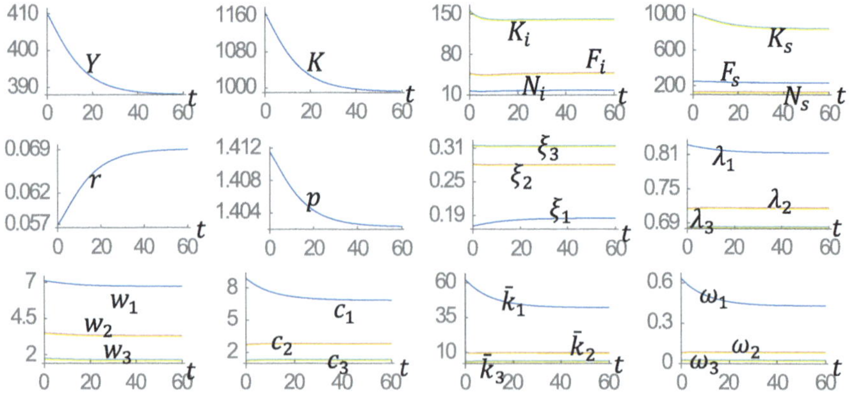

Fig. 9.1 Motion of the economy

consumption levels, social status, and propensities to save are all enhanced. The wealth inequalities between group 1 and other two groups are reduced over time.

The existence of an equilibrium point is confirmed. The equilibrium values are listed as follows:

$$Y = 388.1, \quad \bar{K}_1 = 423.6, \quad \bar{K}_2 = 312.3, \quad \bar{K}_3 = 257.9, \quad r = 0.069,$$

$$p = 1.40, \quad w_1 = 6.74, \quad w_2 = 3.37, \quad w_3 = 1.69, \quad F_i = 49.69,$$

$$F_s = 241.3, \quad N_i = 19.46, \quad N_s = 140.54, K_i = 141.8, \quad K_s = 852.1,$$

$$\omega_1 = 0.43, \quad \omega_2 = 0.09, \quad \omega_3 = 0.03, \quad \lambda_1 = 0.81, \quad \lambda_2 = 0.72,$$

$$\lambda_3 = 0.68, \quad \xi_1 = 0.19, \quad \xi_2 = 0.28, \quad \xi_3 = 0.32, \quad \bar{k}_1 = 42.36,$$

$$\bar{k}_2 = 10.41, \quad \bar{k}_3 = 4.30, \quad c_1 = 6.90, \quad c_2 = 2.92, \quad c_3 = 1.41.$$

The three eigenvalues are real and negative: $\{-0.24, -0.18, -0.09\}$. The equilibrium is locally stable.

9.2 Social Status as Spirit of Capitalism and Other Factor Are Changed

This section examines effects of changes in some parameters on the dynamic system.

9.2.1 Group 1's Spirit of Capitalism Rises

I now deal with the effects of the following change in the parameter: $\omega_{1L}: 0.01 \Rightarrow 0.012$. This change may be interpreted as that group 1's spirit of capitalism is enhanced. The simulation result is plotted in Fig. 9.2. The change has a strong impact on the national economy. Group 1's social status is enhanced. The group's propensity to save and wealth is increased. The consumption level of consumer goods becomes lower initially and higher in the long term. The other two groups' wealth and consumption levels are increased. The price of consumer goods becomes higher. The interest rate falls. The wage rates become higher. The national output and wealth are enhanced. Some of the labor force is shifted from the consumer goods sector to the capital goods sector. The output levels and capital inputs of the two sectors are increased. The inequality between group 1 and the other two groups is enlarged. If the

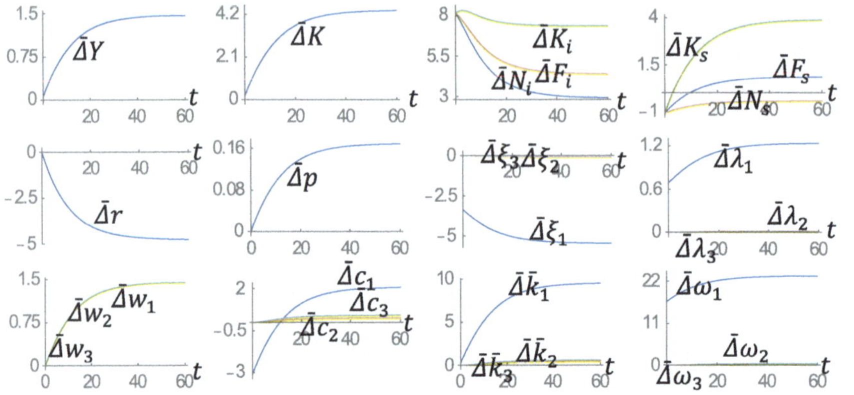

Fig. 9.2 Group 1's spirit of capitalism rises

rich strengthen its spirit of capitalism, the inequality between the rich and the poor is enlarged. By the way, if ω_{3L} is increased, then economic growth is encouraged and inequality between group 1 and group 3 is reduced.

9.2.2 The Total Factor Productivity of the Capital Goods Sector Being Enhanced

The total factor productivity of the capital goods sector is assumed to be increased as follows: A_i: $1.3 \Rightarrow 1.32$. The simulation result is plotted in Fig. 9.3. The economy produces more and has more wealth. The price of consumer goods becomes higher. The interest rate becomes higher in the short term and lower in long term. The wage

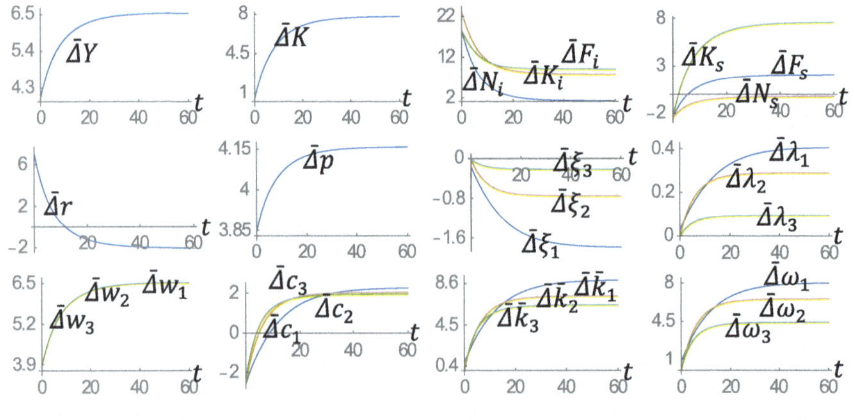

Fig. 9.3 Total factor productivity of the capital goods sector being enhanced

rates become higher. Each group's social status is enhanced. Group 1's is enhanced more than group 2's, and group 2's social status is enhanced more than group 3's social status. The change rate in wealth is in the same direction as the change rate in social status. The consumption levels of the three groups' representative households fall initially and rise in the long term. The technological change enlarges gaps in social status and wealth.

9.2.3 Group 1's Social Status More Strongly Affecting Its Propensity to Save

I now allow group 1's propensity to save to be more strongly affected by its social status as follows: $\tilde{\lambda}_{10}: 0.1 \Rightarrow 0.12$. The simulation result is plotted in Fig. 9.4. Group 1's propensity to save is increased. The other two groups' preferences are almost invariant. Group 1's social status and wealth are increased more than the other two groups' social status and wealth. Group 1's consumption falls in the short term and the other two groups' consumption levels rise slightly. Group 1's consumption level is increased more than the other two groups' in the long term. Group 1 consumes even more and has more wealth than the other two groups by weighing more social status on the propensity to save. The inequality gaps between the rich and the other two groups are enlarged. Some of the labor force is shifted from the consumer goods sector to the other sector. The economy produces more and accumulates more wealth. The price of consumer goods is enhanced. The interest rate falls, and the wage rates of all the groups are increased.

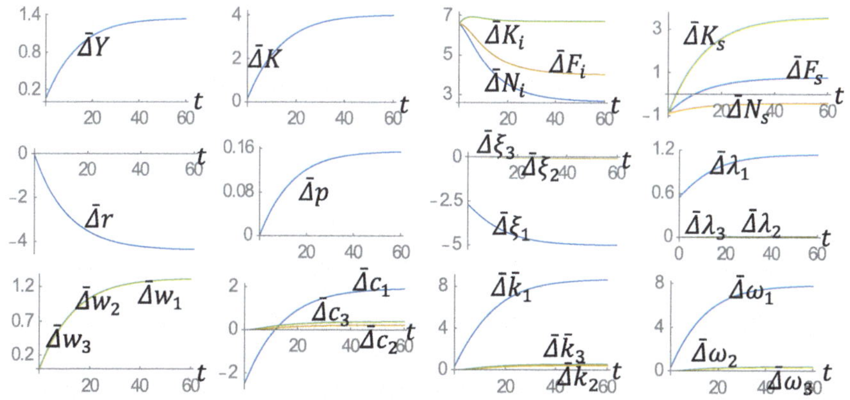

Fig. 9.4 Group 1's social status more strongly affecting its propensity to save

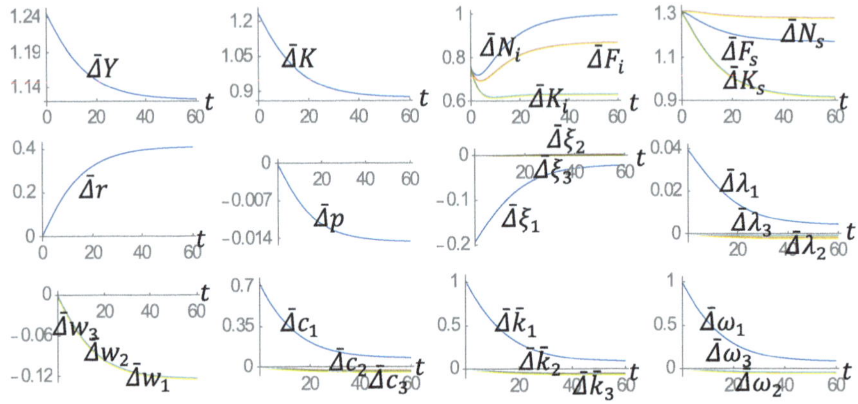

Fig. 9.5 Group 3's population being increased

9.2.4 Group 3's Population Being Increased

Group 3's population is assumed to be increased as follows: N_3: $60 \Rightarrow 62$. The simulation result is plotted in Fig. 9.5. The national output and national wealth are augmented. The two sectors produce more and employ more factor inputs. The price of consumer goods is almost invariant. The interest rate becomes higher. The wage rates fall. Group 1's social status, propensity to save, consumption level and wealth are all increased, while the other two groups' corresponding variables are all slightly reduced. Group 3's population expansion enlarges gaps in social status and wealth between group 1 and the other two groups.

9.2.5 The Depreciation Rate of Physical Capital Rises

The depreciation rate is assumed to be increased as follows: δ_k: $0.05 \Rightarrow 0.055$. The simulation result is plotted in Fig. 9.6. As physical capital depreciates faster, the economy produces less and accumulates less. The capital goods sector produces more and employs two factor inputs more. The consumer goods sector lowers output level and reduces two factor inputs. The price of consumer goods, the interest rate falls, and the wage rates of all the groups are all reduced. All the groups' social status, propensities to save, consumption levels and wealth levels are all reduced. Group 1's social status, propensities to save, consumption levels and wealth levels are reduced more than group 2's; group 2's social status, propensities to save, consumption levels and wealth levels are reduced more than group 3's. Faster capital depreciation reduces the inequalities.

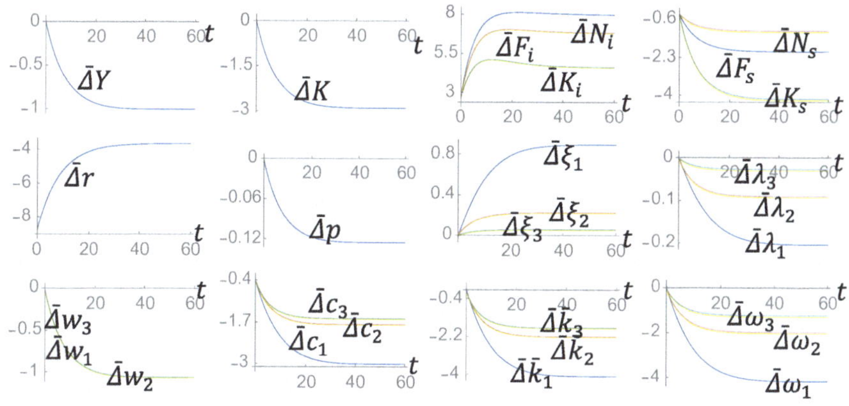

Fig. 9.6 Depreciation rate of physical capital rises

9.2.6 *Group 3's Human Capital Rises*

Group 3's human capital is assumed to be decreased as follows: h_3: $1 \Rightarrow 1.5$. The simulation result is plotted in Fig. 9.7. The economy produces more and accumulates more wealth. The two sectors enhance output levels and increase two factor inputs. The price of consumer goods is almost invariant. The interest rate becomes lower and higher in the long term. Group 3's wage becomes higher, and the other two groups' wage rates are almost invariant. Group 3's and group 1's social status, propensity to save, consumption level and wealth are all increased, while group 2's social status, propensity to save, consumption level and wealth are all slightly changed. The inequalities between group 1 and group 3 are reduced, and the inequalities between group 2 and group 1 are enlarged.

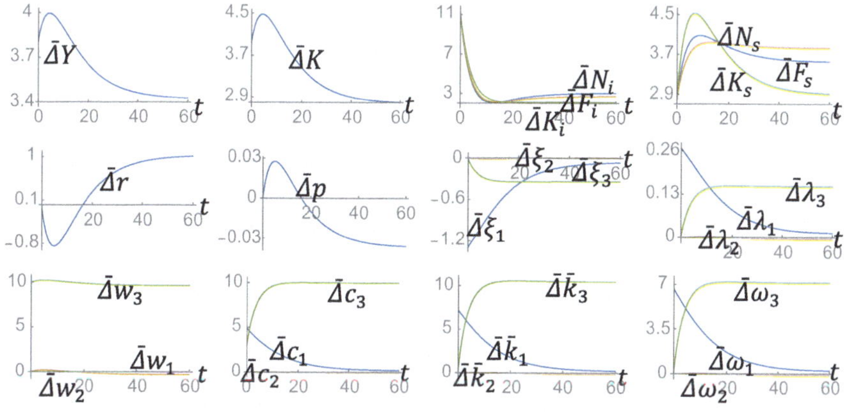

Fig. 9.7 Group 3's human capital rises

9.2.7 A rise in the Output Elasticity of Capital of the Capital Goods Sector

The output elasticity of capital of the capital goods sector is assumed to be increased as follows: $\alpha_i : 0.34 \Rightarrow 0.35$. This implies that the share of capital contribution to the output is increased. The simulation result is plotted in Fig. 9.8. The economy produces more and accumulates more wealth. The two sectors produce more and employ more capital inputs. Initially, some of the labor force is shifted from the consumer goods sector to the capital goods sector, in the long term some of the labor force is shifted from the capital goods sector to the consumer goods sector. In the long term, all the groups' social status, propensities to save, consumption levels and wealth levels are all increased. From Fig. 9.8, these variables are increased differently. In the long term, the inequalities between group 1 and the other two groups are enlarged.

9.3 Growth and Fashion with Snobs and Bandwagoners

What fashion stands for in modern life is described by Daniels (1951) as follows: "Fashion is important because it is in almost everything." According to Hemphill and Suk (2009: 1148), "It is the major output of a global business with annual U.S. sales of more than $200 billion—larger than those of books, movies, and music combined. ...It has provided economic thought with a canonical example in theorizing about consumption and conformity. Social thinkers have long treated fashion as a window upon social class and social change. Cultural theorists have focused on fashion to reflect on symbolic meaning and social ideals." Simmel (1904) points out that fashion dynamics is enforced by common people's imitation of elite. Giovinazzo and Naimzada (2015) build a model to investigate the dynamics of the fashion cycle

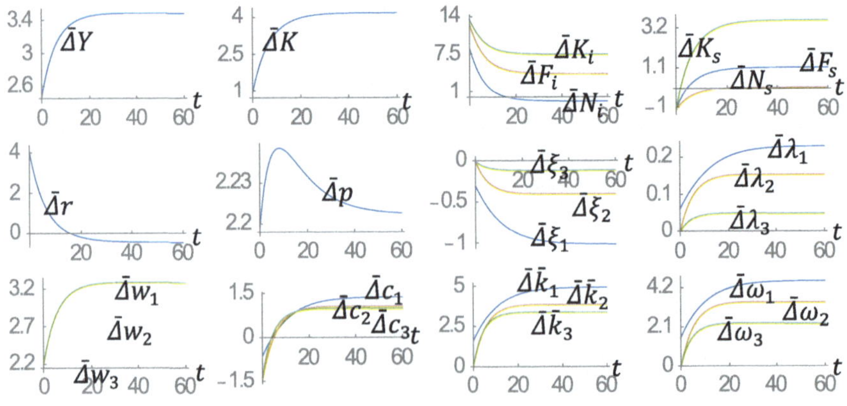

Fig. 9.8 A rise in the output elasticity of capital of the capital goods sector

described by Simmel (1904). They classify the population into the snob and the bandwagoner and consider an economy with one conspicuous good and one normal good.

This section is concerned with fashions and economic growth. It is based on Zhang (2016). The economy is composed of fashion, capital good, and consumer goods sectors. For simplicity of analysis, fashion goods are assumed to be an instantly consumed goods. It would be reasonable to further classify fashion goods as durable and instantly consumed goods. The population is classified into the snob, the bandwagoner, and common consumer. Consumers have no interest in fashion. Each group has a fixed population $\bar{N}_j$ indexed by $j = C, S, B$. All prices are measured in terms of capital good. The wage rates and interest rate are denoted, respectively, by $w_j(t)$ and $r(t)$. I use $p_C(t)$ and $p_F(t)$ to represent prices of consumer and fashion goods, respectively. The total capital stock $K(t)$ is distributed between the three sectors. Subscript index, i, s, and f are used to denote capital, consumer, and fashion goods sectors, respectively. I use $N_m(t)$ and $K_m(t)$ to stand for the labor force and capital stocks employed by sector m. The total population $\bar{N}$ and total qualified labor supply N are:

$$\bar{N} = \bar{N}_C + \bar{N}_S + \bar{N}_B, \;\; N = h_C \bar{N}_C + h_S \bar{N}_S + h_B \bar{N}_B,$$

in which h_j is the human capital of group j. Full employment of the labor force implies:

$$N_i(t) + N_s(t) + N_f(t) = N.$$

9.3.1 Technologies and Marginal Conditions

Let $F_m(t)$ denote the production function of sector m, $m = i, s, f$. The production functions and marginal conditions are:

$$F_m(t) = A_m K_m^{\alpha_m}(t) N_m^{\beta_m}(t),$$

$$\alpha_m + \beta_m = 1, \quad \alpha_m, \beta_m > 0, \quad m = i, s, f,$$

$$r(t) + \delta_k = \frac{\alpha_m p_m(t) F_m(t)}{K_m(t)}, \; w(t) = \frac{\beta_m p_m(t) F_m(t)}{N_m(t)}, \; w_j(t) = h_j w(t),$$

where $w(t)$ is the wage rate of labor input.

9.3.2 Disposable Incomes and Budgets

Household *j*'s wealth is denoted $\bar{k}_j(t)$. I have $\bar{k}_j(t) = \bar{K}_j(t)/\bar{N}_j$, where $\bar{K}_j(t)$ is the total wealth held by group *j*. Household *j*'s disposable income is:

$$\hat{y}_j(t) = (1 + r(t))\bar{k}_j(t) + w_j(t).$$

Household *j*'s disposable income is used for saving and consumption. The representative household distributes the disposable income between savings $s_j(t)$, consumer good $c_j(t)$, and fashion goods $f_j(t)$ (with $f_C(t) = 0$). The budget constraints are:

$$p_C(t)c_j(t) + s_j(t) + p_F(t)f_j(t) = \hat{y}_j(t).$$

9.3.3 Utility Functions and Optimal Decision

Utility level $U_j(t)$ is dependent on $c_j(t)$, $s_j(t)$ and $f_j(t)$ as follows

$$U_j(t) = c_j^{\xi_{j0}(t)}(t)s_j^{\lambda_{j0}(t)}(t)f_j^{\theta_{j0}(t)}(t),\ \xi_{j0}(t), \lambda_{j0}(t) > 0, \theta_{j0}(t) \geq 0,$$

where $\xi_{j0}(t)$ is the propensity to consume consumer good, $\lambda_{j0}(t)$ the propensity to save, and $\theta_{j0}(t)$ is group *j*'s propensity to consume fashion goods ($\theta_{C0}(t) = 0$). Following Giovinazzo and Naimzada (2015), I model the propensities of the snobs and the bandwagoners for consuming fashions. Maximizing the utility function subject to the budget, I get:

$$p_C(t)c_j(t) = \xi_j(t)\hat{y}_j(t),\ s_j(t) = \lambda_j(t)\hat{y}_j(t),\ p_F(t)f_j(t) = \theta_j(t)\hat{y}_j(t),$$

in which

$$\xi_j(t) \equiv \rho_j(t)\xi_{j0}(t),\ \lambda_j(t) \equiv \rho_j(t)\lambda_{j0}(t),\ \theta_j(t) \equiv \rho_j(t)\theta_{j0}(t),$$

$$\rho_j(t) \equiv \frac{1}{\xi_{j0}(t) + \lambda_{j0}(t) + \theta_{j0}(t)}. \quad (9.3.1)$$

The change in the household's wealth follows:

$$\dot{\bar{k}}_j(t) = s_j(t) - \bar{k}_j(t).$$

9.3.4 A Brief Review on Fashion Dynamics and Habit Formation

Before I specify how $\theta_{S0}(t)$ and $\theta_{B0}(t)$ change over time, I review the approach to fashion in discrete time accepted by Giovinazzo and Naimzada (2015). The model by Benhabib and Day (1981) is the seminar. The population, normalized unity, is composed of the snob and the bandwagoner, subscripted by $i = S, B$. The population shares of the bandwagoners and the snobs are respectively ω and $1-\omega$. The system has one conspicuous good and one normal good. The bandwagoner's preference is characterized by that a consumption increases in association with the rise in the social group's average consumption of the previous period. The snob's preference for a certain purchase falls with the rise of the average collective consumption of the preceding period. The utility function is specified as:

$$U(t) = x_i^{\alpha_i(t)}(t)y_i^{1-\alpha_i(t)}(t),$$

where x_i and y_i are respectively the consumption levels of conspicuous good and normal good by i. The budgets are:

$$px_i(t) + qy_i(t) = m_i(t).$$

It should be noted that price is fixed in the approach. The average conspicuous consumption of period t is:

$$\bar{x}(t) = \omega x_B(t) + (1-\omega)x_S(t).$$

The snob's preference change is given by $\alpha_S(t) = f_S(\bar{x}(t-1))$, where $f_S(\bar{x}(t-1))$ is decreasing. The bandwagoner's preference change is given by $\alpha_B(t) = f_B(\bar{x}(t-1))$, where $f_B(\bar{x}(t-1))$ is increasing. It is straightforward to conduct dynamic analysis of the model with some specified preference change functions.

9.3.5 Average Consumption of Fashion and Preference Change

As in Giovinazzo and Naimzada (2015), I introduce the average conspicuous consumption in time t as:

$$\bar{f}(t) = nf_B(t) + (1-n)f_S(t), \tag{9.3.2}$$

where $n = \bar{N}_B/(\bar{N}_B + \bar{N}_S)$. Each individual takes the average behavior of large populations $\bar{f}(t)$ as given when he makes decision. The snobs' and the bandwagoners' propensities to consume fashions are specified as:

$$\theta_j(t) = \Lambda_j\left(\bar{f}(t)\right), \ j = B, S.$$

It is assumed that $\theta_S(t)$ ($\theta_B(t)$) falls (rises) in $\bar{f}(t)$. Miller et al. (1993) summarize types of models in theory of fashion developed by the early 1990s as follows: (i) external-individual models—aesthetic perceptions and learning model; (ii) external-social models—social conflict model, art movement model, ideas of beauty model, mass market model, market infrastructure model; (iii) internal-individual models—demand model, scarcity model, conspicuous consumption model, individualism-centered model, conformity-centered model, uniqueness motivation model; (iv) internal-social models—trickle-down theory, collective behavior theory, adoption and diffusion model, symbolic communication model, subcultural leadership, model, spatial diffusion model, historical resurrection model, and historical continuity model. This section applies a highly aggregated variable called fashion good to describe fashion dynamics.

9.3.6 Demand and Supply of the Three Sectors and Full Employment of Capital

The demand and supply equilibrium conditions for the three sectors imply:

$$c_C(t)\bar{N}_C + c_S(t)\bar{N}_S + c_B(t)\bar{N}_B = F_s(t),$$

$$f_S(t)\bar{N}_S + f_B(t)\bar{N}_B = F_f(t),$$

$$S(t) - K(t) + \delta_k K(t) = F_i(t),$$

where

$$S(t) \equiv s_C(t)\bar{N}_C + s_S(t)\bar{N}_S + s_B(t)\bar{N}_B,$$

$$K(t) = \bar{k}_C(t)\bar{N}_C + \bar{k}_S(t)\bar{N}_S + \bar{k}_B(t)\bar{N}_B.$$

The total capital stock $K(t)$ is distributed between the three sectors:

$$K_i(t) + K_s(t) + K_f(t) = K(t).$$

I built the model.

Lemma 9.3.1 *The motion of the economic system follows the three differential equations with* $z(t)(\equiv (r(t)+\delta_k)/w(t))$, $\bar{k}_B(t)$, *and* $\bar{k}_S(t)$ *as the variables:*

$$\dot{z}(t) = \tilde{\Lambda}_z\left(z(t), \bar{k}_B(t), \bar{k}_S(t)\right),$$

$$\dot{\bar{k}}_B(t) = \tilde{\Lambda}_z\left(z(t), \bar{k}_B(t), \bar{k}_S(t)\right),$$

$$\dot{\bar{k}}_S(t) = \tilde{\Lambda}_z\left(z(t), \bar{k}_B(t), \bar{k}_S(t)\right),$$

in which $\tilde{\Lambda}_j(t)$ *are unique functions of* $z(t)$, $\bar{k}_B(t)$, *and* $\bar{k}_S(t)$ *defined in* Zhang (2016). *The other variables are unique functions of* $z(t)$, $\bar{k}_B(t)$, *and* $\bar{k}_S(t)$.

A computational procedure is given in Zhang (2016). The preference changes are defined as:

$$\theta_{B0}(t) = \bar{\theta}_B + \tilde{\theta}_B \bar{f}(t), \theta_{S0}(t) = \bar{\theta}_S - \tilde{\theta}_S \bar{f}(t), \tag{9.3.3}$$

where $\bar{\theta}_j$ and $\tilde{\theta}_j$ are non-negative parameters. I specify how $\xi_{j0}(t)$ and $\lambda_{j0}(t)$, $j = B, S$, are changed as follows:

$$\xi_{B0}(t) = \bar{\xi}_B - \omega_B \tilde{\theta}_B \bar{f}(t), \lambda_{B0}(t) = \bar{\lambda}_B - (1-\omega_B)\tilde{\theta}_B \bar{f}(t),$$

$$0 \le \omega_B \le 1,$$

$$\xi_{S0}(t) = \bar{\xi}_S + \omega_S \tilde{\theta}_S \bar{f}(t), \lambda_{S0}(t) = \bar{\lambda}_S + (1-\omega_S)\tilde{\theta}_S \bar{f}(t),$$

$$0 \le \omega_S \le 1, \tag{9.3.4}$$

where ω_B and ω_S are "weight" parameters. For instance, if ω_B is small, a change in the propensity to consume fashion is associated with a relatively small change in the propensity to consume consumer good and a relatively large change in the propensity to save. With (9.3.3) and (9.3.4), I get:

$$\xi_j(t) \equiv \rho_j \xi_{j0}(t), \lambda_j(t) \equiv \rho_j \lambda_{j0}(t), \theta_j(t) = \rho_j \theta_{j0}(t),$$

$$\rho_j \equiv \frac{1}{\bar{\xi}_j + \bar{\lambda}_j + \bar{\theta}_j}, j = B, S. \tag{9.3.5}$$

From (9.3.1) and (9.3.2), I get:

$$\bar{f}(t) = n\frac{\rho_B \theta_{B0}(t)\hat{y}_B(t)}{p_F(t)} + (1-n)\frac{\rho_S \theta_{S0}(t)\hat{y}_S(t)}{p_F(t)}, \tag{9.3.6}$$

Insert (9.3.3) in (9.3.6):

$$\bar{f}(t) = \frac{n\bar{\theta}_B \rho_B \hat{y}_B(t) + (1-n)\bar{\theta}_S \rho_S \hat{y}_S(t)}{p_F(t) + (1-n)\tilde{\theta}_S \rho_S \hat{y}_S(t) - n\tilde{\theta}_B \rho_B \hat{y}_B(t)}.$$

I fix the depreciation rate $\delta_k = 0.07$. The rest parameter values are specified as follows:

$$A_i = 1, A_s = 1, A_f = 1.3, \alpha_i = 0.31, \alpha_s = 0.3, \alpha_f = 0.36,$$

$$\begin{pmatrix} N_C \\ N_B \\ N_S \end{pmatrix} = \begin{pmatrix} 100 \\ 10 \\ 2 \end{pmatrix}, \begin{pmatrix} h_C \\ h_B \\ h_S \end{pmatrix} = \begin{pmatrix} 1 \\ 2 \\ 6 \end{pmatrix}, \begin{pmatrix} \lambda_{\mathrm{CO}} \\ \lambda_{\mathrm{BO}} \\ \lambda_{\mathrm{SO}} \end{pmatrix} = \begin{pmatrix} 0.8 \\ 0.9 \\ 0.95 \end{pmatrix},$$

$$\begin{pmatrix} \xi_{\mathrm{CO}} \\ \xi_{\mathrm{BO}} \\ \xi_{\mathrm{SO}} \end{pmatrix} = \begin{pmatrix} 0.15 \\ 0.11 \\ 0.1 \end{pmatrix}, \begin{pmatrix} \bar{\lambda}_{10} \\ \bar{\lambda}_{20} \\ \bar{\lambda}_{30} \end{pmatrix} = \begin{pmatrix} 0.8 \\ 0.75 \\ 0.7 \end{pmatrix}, \begin{pmatrix} \bar{\theta}_B \\ \bar{\theta}_S \end{pmatrix} = \begin{pmatrix} 0.01 \\ 0.01 \end{pmatrix},$$

$$\begin{pmatrix} \tilde{\theta}_B \\ \tilde{\theta}_S \end{pmatrix} = \begin{pmatrix} 0.001 \\ 0.001 \end{pmatrix}, \begin{pmatrix} \omega_B \\ \omega_S \end{pmatrix} = \begin{pmatrix} 0.5 \\ 0.5 \end{pmatrix}.$$

The population of the consumer is largest, while the population of the bandwagoner is the next. The capital good and consumer goods sector's total productivities are, respectively, 1.3 and 1. A change in the propensity to consume fashion is associated with the equal changes (in the opposite direction) in the propensities to consume and to save. The initial conditions are:

$$z(0) = 0.06, \bar{k}_2(0) = 10, \bar{k}_3(0) = 4.$$

The motion of the variables is plotted in Fig. 9.9, in which the national income is defined as: $Y(t) = F_i(t) + p_C(t)F_s(t) + p_F(t)F_f(t)$. Due to the fixed positions of the initial state, the national output and wealth/capital fall over time. The output level of the capital goods sector and fashion sector rise, and the output level of the consumer goods sector fall overtime. The price of consumer good falls. The interest rate rises in association with falling wage rates. The prices of consumer good and fashion goods and the propensities to consume fashion goods change slightly. Labor force is shifted from the consumer goods sector to the other two sectors. The capital input of the consumer goods sector is reduced, and the capital inputs of the two other sectors are increased. The snob consumes slightly less fashion goods and the bandwagoner more fashion goods. The average consumption level of fashion goods is increased over time. The snob consumes less consumer good and has less wealth. The bandwagoner consumes more consumer good and has more wealth. The consumer consumes less consumer good and has less wealth.

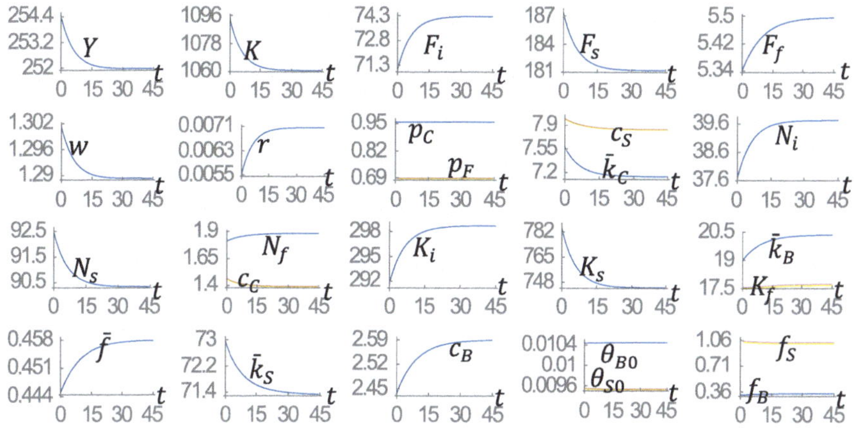

Fig. 9.9 Motion of the economy

The existence of an equilibrium point is confirmed. I list the equilibrium values as follows:

$$Y = 252,\ K = 1061.17,\ F_i = 74.28,\ F_s = 181.24,\ F_f = 5.5,$$

$$\bar{f} = 0.46,\ w_C = 1.29,\ w_B = 2.58,\ w_S = 7.74,\ r = 0.007,$$

$$p_C = 0.96,\ p_F = 0.69,\ N_i = 39.75,\ N_s = 90.37,\ N_f = 1.89,$$

$$K_i = 298.8,\ K_s = 744.64,\ K_f = 17.76,\ \bar{k}_C = 7.15,\ \bar{k}_B = 20.38,$$

$$\bar{k}_S = 71.34,\ c_C = 1.4,\ c_B = 2.59,\ c_S = 7.84,\ \theta_{B0} = 0.011,$$

$$\theta_{S0} = 0.01,\ f_B = 0.343,\ f_S = 1.306.$$

I get the three eigenvalues as follows: $\{-0.15, -0.12, -0.10\}$. The eigenvalues are real and negative. The unique equilibrium is locally stable.

9.4 Fashion and Growth with Different Exogenous Changes

This section examines effects of changes in some parameters on the economic system.

9.4.1 The Bandwagoner's Propensity to Consume Fashion is More Strongly Affected by the Average Fashion Consumption

I now examine the effects that the bandwagoner's propensity to consume fashion is more strongly affected by the average fashion consumption as follows: $\tilde{\theta}_B: 0.001 \Rightarrow 0.002$. The bandwagoner's propensity to consume fashion goods is more sensitive to change in the average consumption. This implies that, for instance, if the snob consumes more fashion goods, the bandwagoner tends to consume more fashion goods with the same disposable income. The preference change brings about lower national income and wealth. The output levels of the capital good and fashion goods sectors are increased. The level of the consumer goods sector becomes lower. The bandwagoner's propensity to consume fashion goods becomes higher. The snob's propensity to consume fashion goods becomes lower. The prices of the consumer and fashions are almost invariant. The interest rate becomes higher. The wage rates fall. The average consumption of fashion goods is augmented. The bandwagoner consumes more fashion goods and less consumer good and have less wealth. The snob consumes less fashion goods and more consumer good and have more wealth. The consumer's behavior is almost invariant (Fig. 9.10).

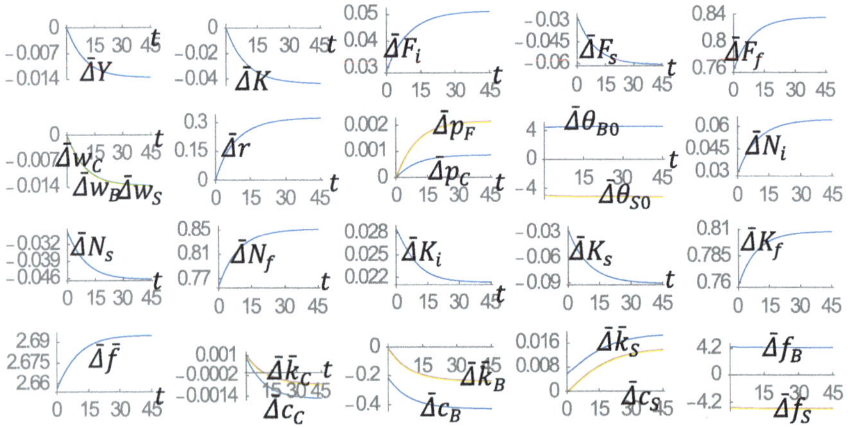

Fig. 9.10 Bandwagoner's propensity to consume fashion is more strongly affected

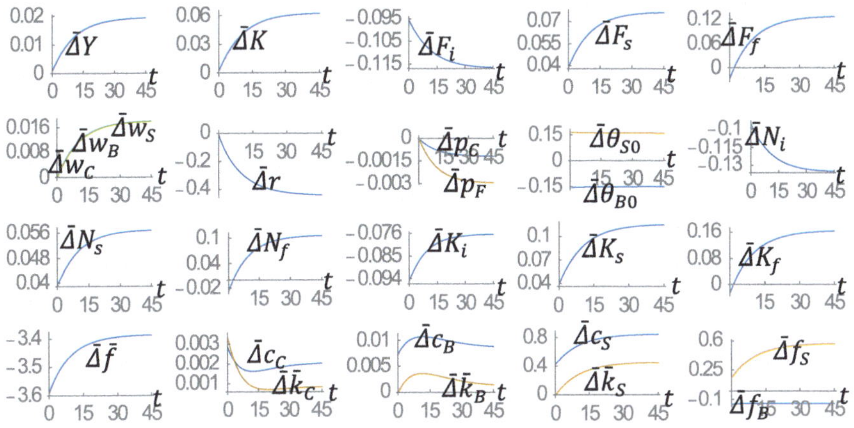

Fig. 9.11 Snob's propensity to consume fashion is more negatively affected

9.4.2 The Snob's Propensity to Consume Fashion Is More Negatively Affected by the Average Fashion Consumption

The snob's propensity to consume fashion goods is assumed to be more negatively affected by the average fashion consumption as follows: $\tilde{\theta}_S: 0.001 \Rightarrow 0.003$. The result is plotted in Fig. 9.11. The change in the parameter implies that the snob's propensity to consume fashion goods is more sensitive to change in the average consumption. The average consumption level of fashion goods becomes lower. The snob's propensity to consume fashion goods rises. The bandwagoner's propensity to consume fashion goods becomes lower. The bandwagoner consumes less fashion goods and more consumer good and have more wealth. The snob consumes more fashion goods and more consumer good and have more wealth. The consumer consumes more consumer good and have more wealth. The preference change enhances national income and wealth. The output levels of the consumer good and fashion goods sectors are enhanced. The level of the capital goods sector becomes lower. The prices of the consumer and fashions are almost invariant. The interest rate is reduced. The wage rates rise.

9.4.3 The Bandwagoner's Propensity to Consume Fashion is Increased

The intercept in the function of the bandwagoner's propensity to consume fashion goods is assumed to be increased as follows: $\overline{\theta}_B: 0.01 \Rightarrow 0.015$. The result is plotted in Fig. 9.12. If the average consumption level of fashion goods is kept constant, the

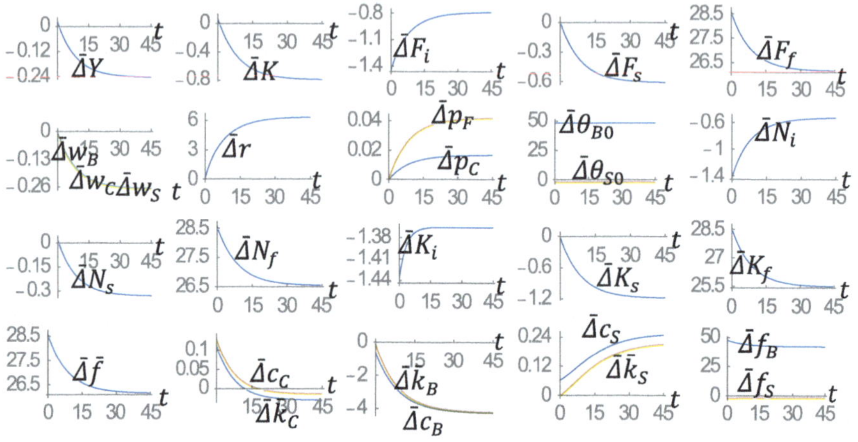

Fig. 9.12 Bandwagoner's propensity to consume fashion goods being increased

change in the parameter implies a rise in the propensity to consume fashion goods. The snob's preference is almost invariant. The economy produces more and accumulates less wealth. The output of the fashion sector is augmented. The output levels of the other two sectors become lower. Labor force is shifted to the fashion sector from the other two sectors. The capital input of the fashion sector is augmented, and the capital inputs of the other two sectors are reduced. The interest rate becomes higher. The wage rates fall. The prices of the consumer and fashions are almost invariant. The average consumption level of fashion goods is augmented. The bandwagoner consumes more fashion goods and less consumer good and has less wealth. The snob consumes less fashion goods and more consumer good and has more wealth.

9.4.4 The Bandwagoner's Human Capital is Improved

The bandwagoner's human capital is assumed to be improved as follows: $h_B: 2 \Rightarrow 2.5$. The result is plotted in Fig. 9.13. The economy has more labor force. Each sector employs more labor force. The economy accumulates more wealth and produces more. The three sectors' output levels and capital inputs are augmented. The bandwagoner's wage rate is increased, and the other two groups' wage rates are almost invariant. The interest rate and prices of the consumer and fashion goods fall. The bandwagoner's preference to consume fashion goods becomes higher. The snob's preference to consume fashion goods falls. The average consumption of fashion goods is expanded. The bandwagoner consumes more fashion and consumer good and has more wealth. The snob consumes less fashion goods. The snob consumes more consumer good and has more wealth initially and consumes less consumer good

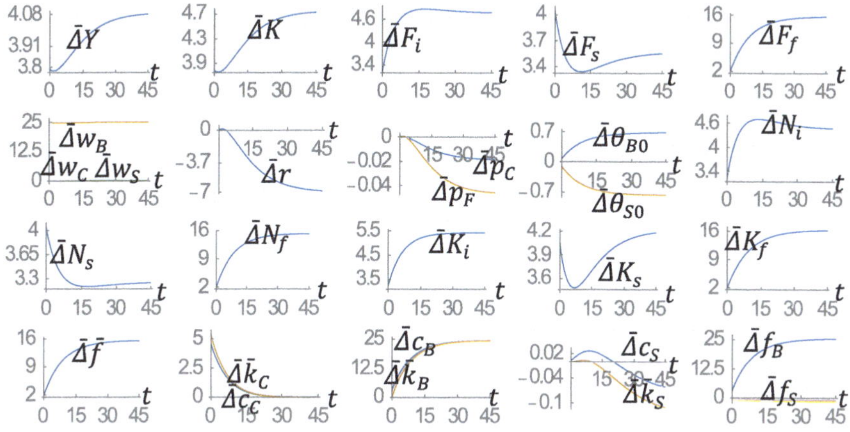

Fig. 9.13 Bandwagoner's human capital is improved

and has less wealth in the long term. The consumer's behavior is almost invariant in the long term.

9.4.5 A Rise in the Bandwagoner's Population

The bandwagoner's population is assumed to rise as follows: $N_B\colon 10 \Rightarrow 11$. The result is plotted in Fig. 9.14. The economy has more labor supply. Each sector employs more labor force. The economy accumulates more wealth and produces more. The three sectors enhance output levels and increase capital inputs. The wage rates become

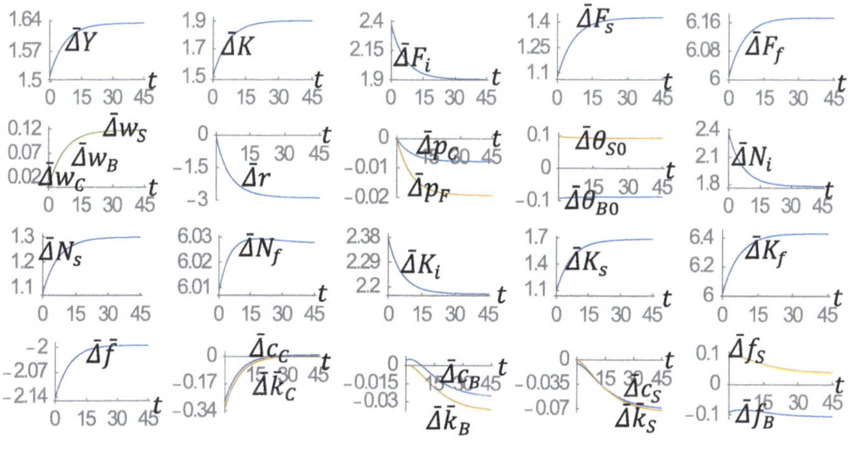

Fig. 9.14 A rise in the bandwagoner's population

higher. The interest rate and prices of the consumer and fashion goods become lower. The average consumption of fashion goods is expanded. The bandwagoner's preference to consume fashion goods is decreased, and the snob's preference to consume fashion goods is enhanced. The bandwagoner consumes more fashion and consumer good and have more wealth. The snob consumes less fashion goods. The snob consumes more consumer good and have more wealth initially and consume less consumer good and have less wealth in the long term. The consumer's behavior is slightly affected in the long term.

9.4.6 A Rise in the Snob's Propensity to Save

The intercept of the function of the snob's propensity to save is assumed to be increased as follows: $\bar{\lambda}_S: 0.95 \Rightarrow 0.97$. The result is plotted in Fig. 9.15. The economy has more wealth and higher output level. The capital goods sector produces more and employs more labor and capital inputs. The wage rates become higher. The interest rate and prices of the consumer and fashion goods become lower. The average consumption of fashion goods becomes lower initially and almost invariant in the long term. The bandwagoner's preference to consume fashion goods becomes lower initially and almost invariant in the long term. The snob's preference to consume fashion goods is enhanced initially and is almost not changed in the long term. The bandwagoner's consumption behavior and wealth are almost not affected. In the long term, the snob has more wealth and consume almost the same as before.

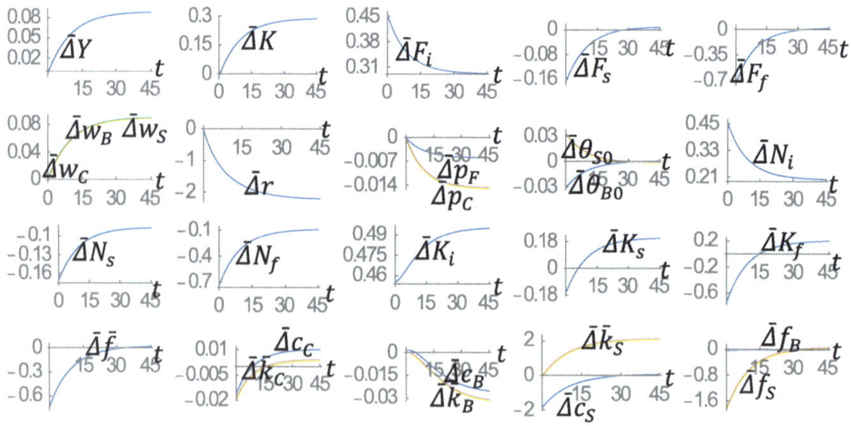

Fig. 9.15 A rise in the snob's propensity to save

9.5 Modeling Human Behavior by Integrating Psychology

This chapter shows how dynamic change in preferences interact with other aspects of economies. It shows a way to integrate microeconomics, macroeconomics, industrial economics, urban economics, international economics, and some results of psychology. Except Becker, many efforts have been made by economists to develop microeconomics on basis of psychology. Behavioral economics has become a mainstream in economics. The 2002 Nobel prize was shared by Daniel Kahneman (1934–) for integrating insights from psychological research into human behavior in economics and Vernon L. Smith (1927–) for establishing laboratory experiments as a tool in empirical economics. Kahneman's findings are related to decision making under uncertainty and applying insights from cognitive psychology to intrinsic human motivation. In 2017, the Nobel Prize was awarded to Richard H. Thaler (1945–) for his contributions to behavioral economics through integrating economics with psychology. Quite a few other economists were awarded the prize owing to their contributions to economics with the help of ideas and theories in psychology. This chapter shows an analytical direction for integrating economics and psychology. My framework also provides a possible tool for analyzing dynamics of collective psychology and economic development.

The main task of economics is not about value itself, but exchange value. Psychology is focused on individual preference. Applying psychology can enrich economists' understanding of and approach to human decisions and behavior. Economics should be enriched by other fields as well. For instance, engineering should enable economists to develop more proper descriptions of production functions with environment and technology. Political science should enable economists to properly analyze complicated decision processes and output of the political sector. History should enable economists to be aware of the validity of networking forms and parameter values. Other fields of social sciences, arts, and music should enable economists to be aware of limitations of rationality in and impossibility of predictions in human behavior.

References

Alvarez-Cuadrado F, Monteriro G, Turnovsky SJ (2004) Habit formation, catching-up with the joneses, and economic growth. J Econ Growth 9:47–80

Amano JD, Laubach T (2004) Implication of habit formation for optimal monetary policy. J Monetary Econ 51:305–325

Becker GS (1976) The economic approach to human behavior. The University of Chicago Press, Chicago

Becker GS (1992) Habits, addictions and traditions. Kyklos 45:327–345

Becker GS, Barro RJ (1988) A reformation of the economic theory of fertility. Quart J Econ 103:139–171

Benhabib J, Day R (1981) Rational choice and erratic behavior. Rev Econ Stud 48:459–471

Chen HJ, Guo JT (2009) Social status and the growth effect of money. Jpa Econ Rev 60:133–141

Chen HJ, Guo JT (2011) Money, social status and endogenous growth in a generalized cash-un-advance model. Pac Econ Rev 16:267–284
Cole HL, Mailath GJ, Postlewaite A (1992) Social norms, savings behavior, and growth. J Polit Econ 100:1092–25
Corneo G, Jeanne O (1999) Social organization in an endogenous growth model. Int Econ Rev 40:711–725
Daniels AH (1951) Fashion merchandising. Harvard Bus Rev 29:51–60
Dioikitopoulos EV, Kalyvitis S (2010) Endogenous time preference and public policy: growth and fiscal implications. Macroecon Dyn 14:243–257
Drugeon JP (1996) Impatience and long-run growth. J Econ Dyn Control 20:281–313
Drugeon JP (2000) On the roles of impatience in homothetic growth paths. Econ Theor 15:139–161
Duesenberry J (1949) Income, saving and the theory of consumer behavior. Harvard University Press, Cambridge
Epstein LG (1987) A simple dynamic general equilibrium model. J Econ Theory 41:68–95
Epstein LG, Hynes JA (1983) The rate of time preference and dynamic economic analysis. J Polit Econ 91:611–635
Fang H (2001) Social culture and economic performance. Am Econ Rev 91:924–937
Fershtman C, Murphy KM, Weiss Y (1996) Social status, education and growth. J Polit Econ 106:108–132
Frank R (1985) The demand for non-observable and other non-positional goods. Am Econ Rev 75:101–116
Giovinazzo VD, Naimzada A (2015) A model of fashion: Endogenous preferences in social interaction. Econ Model 47:12–17
Hemphill CS, Suk J (2009) The law, culture, and economics of fashion. Stanford Law Rev 61:1147–1176
Konrad K (1992) Wealth seeking reconsidered. J Econ Behav Organ 18:215–227
Kurz M (1968) Optimal economic growth and wealth effects. Int Econ Rev 9:348–357
Lucas RE Jr, Stokey NL (1984) Optimal growth with many consumers. J Econ Theor 32:139–171
Miller CM, McIntyre SH, Mantrala MK (1993) Toward formalizing fashion theory. J Mark Res 30:142–157
Obstfeld M (1990) Intertemporal dependence, impatience, and dynamics. J Monetary Econ 26:45–75
Palivos T, Wang P, Zhang J (1997) On the existence of balanced equilibrium. Int Econ Revi 38:205–224
Rauscher M (1997) Conspicuous consumption, economic growth, and taxation. J Econ 66:35–42
Rege M (2008) Why do people care about social status? J Econ Behav Organ 66:233–242
Shin S, Epstein LG (1993) Habits and time preference. Int Econ Rev 34:61–84
Simmel G (1957) [1904] Fashion. Reprinted in Am J Sociology 62:541–58
Stern ML (2006) Endogeneous time preference and optimal growth. Econ Theor 29:49–70
Uzawa H (1968) Time preference, the consumption function, and optimum asset holdings. In: Wolfe JN (ed) Value, capital and growth: papers in honor of Sir John Hicks. Aldine, Chicago, pp 485–504
Veblen T (1899) The theory of the leisure class. Modern Library, New York
Zhang WB (2016) Fashion with snobs and bandwagoners in a three-type households and three-sector neoclassical growth model. Mex J Econ Finance 11:1–19
Zhang WB (2017) Social status and inequality in an integrated Walrasian-general equilibrium and neoclassical-growth theory. J Econ Devel 42:95–118
Zou HF (1994) The spirit of capitalism and long-run growth. Eur J Polit Econ 10:279–293
Zou HF (1995) The spirit of capitalism and savings behavior. J Econ Behav Organ 28:131–143

Chapter 10
Portfolio Choice in General Dynamic Equilibrium

Households of contemporary economies are characterized by holding many kinds of assets such as housing, land, stocks, precious metals, and cashes in different currencies. The complexity of portfolio is constantly increased in globalizing economies (Uhler and Gragg 1971; Gaudecker 2015). Guiso et al. (2002) review the literature on the complexity of portfolio and conclude:

> Until recently, researchers in economics and finance paid relatively little attention to household portfolios. Reasons included the tendency of most households to hold simple portfolios, the inability of the dominant asset pricing models to account for household portfolio incompleteness, and the lack of detailed databases on household portfolios in many countries until the late 1980s or 1990s. Now, however, the analysis of household portfolios is emerging as a field of vigorous study.

The mainstreams of formal economic growth theory still pay little attention to the complexity of portfolio choice. As mentioned in Chap. 2, the Ramsey approach to household behavior is not suitable for the problem and the Solow model does not have a microeconomic foundation for rational behavior of households. Traditional dynamic economic theories fail to provide an effective microeconomic foundation for analyzing growth with portfolio choice.

This chapter shows how to introduce portfolio choice into the basic model. Dynamics of gold and other assets prices are modeled in some partial economic models (Barro 1979; Bordo and Ellson 1985; Abel 1990; Agell and Edin 1990; Dowd and Sampson 1993; Chappell and Dowd 1997). This study differs from these studies in that it examines growth with portfolio choice equilibrium with land, gold and physical capital, and human capital within a comprehensive framework.

W.-B. Zhang, *The General Economic Theory*,
https://doi.org/10.1007/978-3-030-56204-5_10

10.1 Exchange Values of Gold, Land, Physical Capital, and Human Capital

The model is based on Zhang (2016a). The economy is composed of industrial, agricultural, and education sectors. Let subscript index, i, a, and e, represent industry, agriculture, and education, respectively. The economy has a fixed and homogeneous population $\overline{N}$. I use $H(t)$ to represent for the level of human capital. The total amounts of land and gold are fixed and privately owned by households. Land and gold can be sold and bought in free markets without any friction and transaction costs. Households can own land, gold, and physical wealth. The economy has a fixed land L, which is distributed between housing and agricultural production. Let $N_j(t)$ and $K_j(t)$ represent for the labor force and capital stocks employed by sector j, $j = i, a$, and e. Variables $T(t)$ and $T_e(t)$ are used to denote, respectively, the work time and study time of a representative worker. All markets are competitive. The interest rate $r(t)$ and wage rate $w(t)$ are determined by markets. Labor force $N(t)$ is given by:

$$N(t) = T(t)H^m(t)\overline{N},$$

where m is the efficiency of applying human capital. I use $F_j(t)$ to denote the production function of sector j, $j = i, a, e$.

10.1.1 The Industrial Sector

The production function and marginal conditions of the industrial sector are:

$$F_i(t) = A_i K_i^{\alpha_i}(t) N_i^{\beta_i}(t), \quad A_i, \alpha_i, \beta_i > 0, \quad \alpha_i + \beta_i = 1,$$
$$r(t) + \delta_k = \frac{\alpha_i F_i(t)}{K_i(t)}, \quad w(t) = \frac{\beta_i F_i(t)}{N_i(t)}.$$

10.1.2 The Agricultural Sector

The production function and marginal conditions of the agricultural sector are:

$$F_a(t) = A_a K_a^{\alpha_a}(t) N_a^{\beta_a}(t) L_a^{\varsigma}(t), \ A_a, \alpha_a, \beta_a, \varsigma > 0, \alpha_a + \beta_a + \varsigma = 1,$$
$$r(t) + \delta_k = \frac{\alpha_a p_a(t) F_a(t)}{K_a(t)}, w(t) = \frac{\beta_a p_a(t) F_a(t)}{N_a(t)},$$
$$R_L(t) = \frac{\varsigma p_a(t) F_a(t)}{L_a(t)},$$

where $p_a(t)$ is the price of agricultural good and $R_L(t)$ the land rent.

10.1.3 The Education Sector and Marginal Conditions

The production function and marginal conditions of the education sector are:

$$F_e(t) = A_e K_e^{\alpha_e}(t) N_e^{\beta_e}(t),\ A_e, \alpha_e, \beta_e > 0, \alpha_e + \beta_e = 1,$$
$$r(t) + \delta_k = \frac{\alpha_e p_e(t)}{K_e(t)},\ w(t) = \frac{\beta_e p_e(t) F_e(t)}{N_e(t)}, \tag{3}$$

where $p_e(t)$ is the price of education.

10.1.4 Choice Between Physical Wealth, Gold, and Land

Let $p_L(t)$ and $p_G(t)$ stand for, respectively, the prices of land and gold. For convenience of analysis, it is assumed that gold can be "rented" through markets for decoration use. The rent of gold is denoted by $R_G(t)$. The gold owned by the representative household is assumed to be fully used either by the household for decoration or rented out to other households. Consider now a household with one unity of capital good. He can either invest in capital good thereby earning a profit equal to the net own-rate of return $r(t)$ or invest in land (gold) thereby earning a profit equal to the net own-rate of return $R_L(t)/p_L(t)$ $(R_G(t)/p_G(t))$. As I assume capital, gold, and land markets to be at competitive equilibrium at any point in time, three options yield equal returns, i.e.,

$$\frac{R_G(t)}{p_G(t)} = \frac{R_L(t)}{p_L(t)} = r(t). \tag{10.1.1}$$

10.1.5 Disposable Income, Budget, and Decision

Housing is measured by lot size. The household's utility is related to consumption levels of education, industrial good, agricultural good, gold and lot size, as well as on how much to save. I use $\bar{k}(t)$ to stand for the household's value of physical wealth, $\bar{g}(t)$ for gold owned by the household, and $\bar{l}(t)$ for the lot size. The total value of wealth owned by the household $a(t)$ is the sum of the three assets' values:

$$a(t) = \bar{k}(t) + p_L(t)\bar{l}(t) + p_G(t)\bar{g}(t).$$

The wage payment is $H^m(t)T(t)w(t)$, the gold interest income is $R_G(t)\bar{g}(t)$, and the land revenue is $R_L(t)\bar{l}(t)$. The disposable income is:

$$\hat{y}(t) = a(t) + r(t)\bar{k}(t) + H^m(t)T(t)w(t) \\ + R_L(t)\bar{l}(t) + R_G(t)\bar{g}(t). \quad (10.1.2)$$

The household distributes the disposable income between education $T_e(t)$, consumption of industrial goods $c(t)$, consumption of agricultural goods $c_a(t)$, use of gold for decoration $\hat{g}(t)$, lot size $l_h(t)$, and saving $s(t)$. The budget constraint is given by:

$$p_e(t)T_e(t) + c(t) + s(t) + p_a(t)c_a(t) + R_G(t)\hat{g}(t) + R_L(t)l_h(t) = \hat{y}(t). \quad (10.1.3)$$

The available time is distributed between education and work: $T(t) + T_e(t) = T_0$. Insert the time constraint in (10.1.3):

$$\bar{p}_e(t)T_e(t) + c(t) + s(t) + p_a(t)c_a(t) \\ + R_G(t)\hat{g}(t) + R_L(t)l_h(t) = \bar{y}(t), \quad (10.1.4)$$

where

$$\bar{p}_e(t) \equiv p_e(t) + H^m(t)w(t), \ \bar{y}(t) \equiv (1 + r(t))a(t) + H^m(t)T_0 w(t).$$

The household decides: $s(t)$, $T_e(t)$, $c(t)$, $c_a(t)$, $l_h(t)$, and $\hat{g}(t)$. The variable $\bar{p}_e(t)$ represents the opportunity cost of education. The utility function is specified as follows:

$$U(t) = T_e^{\kappa_0}(t)c^{\xi_0}(t)c_a^{\mu_0}(t)l_h^{\eta_0}(t)\hat{g}^{\gamma_0}(t)s^{\lambda_0}(t), \\ \kappa_0, \xi_0, \mu_0, \eta_0, \gamma_0, \lambda_0 > 0,$$

in which κ_0, ξ_0, η_0, γ_0, and λ_0 are the household's elasticity of utility with regard to education, industrial good, agricultural good, housing, gold decoration, and saving. Maximizing $U(t)$ subject to (10.1.4), I get the marginal conditions:

$$\bar{p}_e(t)T_e(t) = \kappa\bar{y}(t), \ \ c(t) = \xi\bar{y}(t), \ \ p_a(t)c_a(t) = \mu\bar{y}(t), \\ R_L(t)l_h(t) = \eta\bar{y}(t), R_G(t)\hat{g}(t) = \gamma\bar{y}(t), s(t) = \lambda\bar{y}(t), \quad (10.1.5)$$

where

$$\kappa \equiv \rho\kappa_0, \xi \equiv \rho\xi_0, \mu \equiv \rho\mu_0, \eta \equiv \rho\eta_0, \gamma \equiv \rho\gamma_0, \lambda \equiv \rho\lambda_0, \\ \rho \equiv \frac{1}{\kappa_0 + \xi_0 + \mu_0 + \eta_0 + \gamma_0 + \lambda_0}.$$

The change in the household's wealth follows the differential equation:

$$\dot{a}(t) = s(t) - a(t).$$

10.1.6 Dynamics of Human Capital

This section considers three sources of human capital growth: learning by doing (Arrow 1962), learning by formal education (Uzawa 1965), and the creative leisure (Zhang (2007), also Chap. 4 in this book) as follows:

$$\dot{H}(t) = \frac{\upsilon_e F_e^{a_e}(t)\left(H^m(t)T_e(t)\overline{N}\right)^{b_e}}{H^{\pi_e}(t)\overline{N}} + \frac{\upsilon_i F_i^{a_i}(t)}{H^{\pi_i}(t)\overline{N}} + \frac{\upsilon_h C^{a_h}(t)}{H^{\pi_h}(t)\overline{N}} - \delta_h H(t),$$

where $\delta_h (> 0)$ is the depreciation rate of human capital, $\upsilon_e, \upsilon_i, \upsilon_h, a_e, b_e, a_i$, and a_h are non-negative parameters. The signs of the parameters π_{je}, π_{ji}, and π_{jh} are not specified as they may be either negative or positive. The term $\upsilon_e F_e^{a_e}\left(H^m T_e \overline{N}\right)^{b_e} / H^{\pi_e}\overline{N}$ implies that the contribution to human capital improvement through education. Human capital increases in the level of education service F_e, and in the (qualified) total study time, $H^m T_e \overline{N}$. The population $\overline{N}$ in the denominator measures the contribution in terms of per capita. The term H^{π_e} indicates that as the level of human capital of the population increases, it may be more difficult (in the case of π_e being large) or easier (in the case of π_e being small) to accumulate human capital via formal education. The term $\upsilon_i F_i^{a_i} / H^{\pi_i}\overline{N}$ implies the learning by producing. The term $\upsilon_h C^{a_h} / H^{\pi_h}\overline{N}$ takes account of learning by consuming.

10.1.7 Equilibrium for Demand and Supply and Full Use of Resources

The balance between demand for education $T_e(t)\overline{N}$ and supply of education $F_e(t)$ is:

$$T_e(t)\overline{N} = F_e(t).$$

The balance condition for demand for and supply of agricultural good is:

$$C_a(t) = c_a(t)\overline{N} = F_a(t).$$

Each asset owned by the population is equal to the asset in the system:

$$\bar{l}(t)\overline{N} = L, \bar{g}(t)\overline{N} = G.$$

The amount of gold used for decoration by the population equals the total gold:

$$\hat{g}(t)\overline{N} = G.$$

I use $K(t)$ to stand for the total capital stock. Full employment of input factors implies:

$$K_i(t) + K_a(t) + K_e(t) = K(t), N_i(t) + N_a(t) + N_e(t) = N(t),$$
$$l_h(t)\overline{N} + L_a(t) = L.$$

The value of physical capital is equal to the value of physical wealth: $\bar{k}(t)\overline{N} = K(t)$. I built the model. The following lemma is proved by Zhang (2016a).

Lemma 10.1.1 *The following two differential equations with $z(t)$ and $H(t)$ as the variables describe the motion of the economic system:*

$$\dot{z}(t) = \Lambda(z(t), H(t)), \dot{H}(t) = \Omega(z(t), H(t)), z(t) \equiv \frac{r(t) + \delta_k}{w(t)},$$

where Λ and Ω are functions of $z(t)$ and $H(t)$ given in Zhang (2016a). The other variables are given as functions of $z(t)$ and $H(t)$.

The parameter values are specified as follows:

$$\overline{N} = 10, T_0 = 24, L = 100, m = 0.6, \alpha_i = 0.29, \alpha_e = 0.3,$$
$$\alpha_a = 0.1, \beta_a = 0.2, A_i = 1, A_a = 0.8, A_e = 1, \lambda_0 = 0.8,$$
$$\xi_0 = 0.07, \mu_0 = 0.04, \eta_0 = 0.07, \kappa_0 = 0.01, \gamma_0 = 0.01,$$
$$\upsilon_e = 0.8, \upsilon_i = 0.1, \upsilon_h = 0.2, a_e = 0.3, b_e = 0.5, a_i = 0.4,$$
$$a_h = 0.1, b_e = 0.5, \pi_e = 0.5, \pi_i = 0.5, \pi_h = 0.3, G = 0.5,$$
$$\delta_k = 0.05, \delta_h = 0.03.$$

The three sources of human capital accumulation exhibit decreasing return to scales. The amount of gold is $G = 0.5$. This number is not significant in the sense that a change in the amount only affects the gold price and rent and has no effects on the other variables. The following variables are invariant in time:

$$l_h = 7.14, \ L_a = 28.57, \ \bar{l} = 10, \ \bar{g} = \hat{g} = 0.05.$$

I specify the initial conditions: $z(0) = 0.25$ and $H(0) = 21$. I plot the motion of the variables in Fig. 10.1 in which the national gross product (GDP) is:

$$Y(t) = F_i(t) + p_a(t)F_a(t) + p_e(t)F_e(t) + l_h\overline{N}R(t).$$

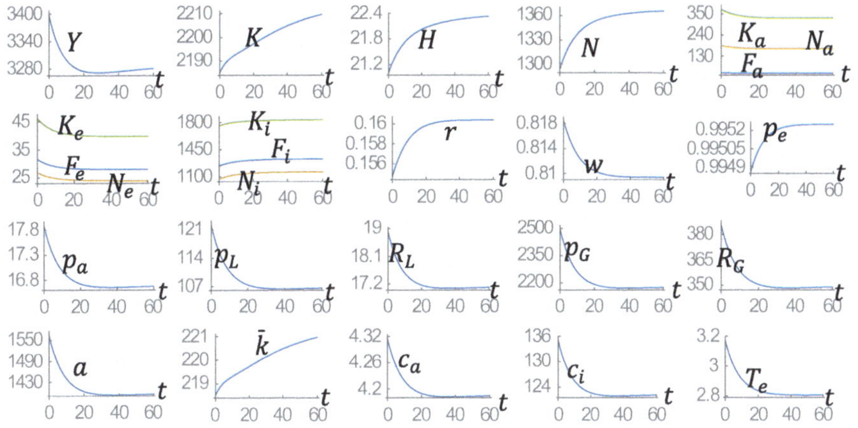

Fig. 10.1 Motion of the economic system

The GDP falls over time till it achieves at the long-term equilibrium value. The national capital stock, human capital, and total labor force are augmented. The wage rate falls, and the interest rate rises. The prices of land and gold and rents of land and gold are reduced. The price of agricultural goods falls, and the price of education rises. The output and input factors of the industrial sector are enhanced. The output levels and input factors of the other two sectors are reduced. The household works more hours and studies less. The household's physical wealth rises, and the total wealth falls. The household also consumes less agricultural goods and industrial goods.

I confirm the existence of equilibrium point as follows:

$$Y = 3291.7,\ K = 2216.1,\ H = 22.4,\ w = 0.81,\ p_L = 107.1,$$
$$R_L = 17.2,\ p_G = 2184.6,\ R_G = 350.3,\ r = 0.16,\ p_a = 16.7,$$
$$p_e = 0.995,\ F_a = 41.9,\ F_i = 1336.9,\ F_e = 28.1,\ K_a = 333.1,$$
$$K_i = 1843.1,\ K_e = 39.9,\ N_a = 173.1,\ N_i = 1172.6,\ N_e = 24.2,$$
$$\bar{k} = 221.6,\ c_a = 4.2,\ c_i = 122.6,\ a = 1401.3,\ T_e = 2.81.$$

The eigenvalues at the equilibrium point are −0.114 and −0.029. The equilibrium point is locally stable.

10.2 The Dynamics of Exchange Values with Exogenous Conditions Changes

This section examines effects of changes in some parameters on the dynamics of exchange values.

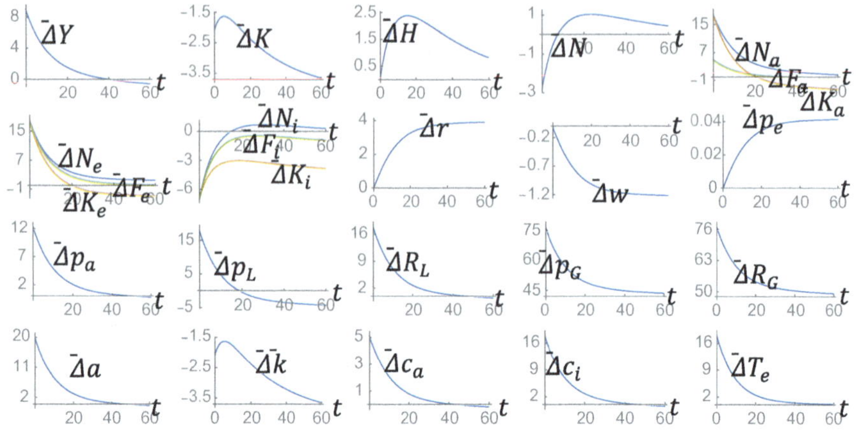

Fig. 10.2 Propensity to use gold is augmented

10.2.1 The Propensity to Use Gold is Augmented

The propensity to use gold is assumed to be enhanced as follows: $\gamma_0 : 0.01 \Rightarrow 0.015$. The lot size, agricultural land use, and gold per capita are not affected, i.e., $\overline{\Delta} l_h = \overline{\Delta} L_a = \overline{\Delta} \bar{g} = 0$. The motion of the variables is plotted in Fig. 10.2. The gold price and gold rent become higher. The total capital and physical wealth per household become lower. The human capital is increased. The total labor force and GDP become higher initially and lower in the long term. The labor inputs of all the three sectors are augmented in the long term, and the capital inputs of all the three sectors become lower in the long term. The output levels of the agricultural and education sectors are slightly changed in the long term. The output level of the industrial sector becomes lower. The interest rate falls in tandem with rise in the wage rate. The price of agricultural goods rises initially and remains almost invariant in the long term. The education fee is slightly affected. The land price is increased initially and reduced in the long term. The land rent rises initially and remains almost invariant in the long term. The consumption levels of agricultural and industrial goods and education time are augmented initially and changed slightly in the long term.

10.2.2 A Rise in the Propensity to Receive Education

I now examine what will happen to the economic system if the propensity to receive education is increased as follows: $\kappa_0 : 0.01 \Rightarrow 0.015$. The lot size, agricultural land use, and gold per capita are not affected. The effects on the other variables are plotted in Fig. 10.3. The price of education is slightly increased. The time to receive education is augmented, and the working time is reduced. The human capital is

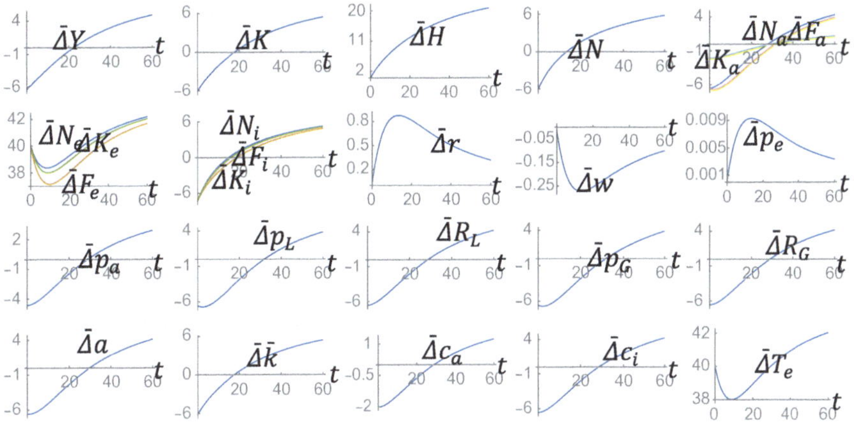

Fig. 10.3 A rise in the propensity to receive education

enhanced. The total labor supply falls initially and rises in the long term. In the short run, the time shifted to education reduces the labor supply, while the rise is human capital increases labor supply. The net effect reduces the labor supply in the short term. In the long term, the net impact increases labor supply. The inputs and output level of the education sector are enhanced. The GDP and national physical wealth fall initially and rise in the long term. The prices of agricultural goods, land and gold and rents of land fall initially and rise in the long term. The output and capital and labor inputs of the two sectors are reduced initially and augmented in the long term. The wage rate falls, and the interest rate rises. The household's physical wealth and total wealth and consumption levels of two goods are lowered initially and are enhanced in the long term. As the household increases the propensity to receive education, the household's economic conditions worsen initially and become improved in the long term.

10.2.3 The Propensity to Consume Housing is Increased

The propensity to consume housing is assumed to be increased as: $\eta_0 : 0.07 \Rightarrow 0.08$. The lot size and agricultural land use are affected as follows:

$$\overline{\Delta} l_h = 3.7, \overline{\Delta} L_a = -9.26.$$

Some land use is shifted from the agricultural use to the residential use. The interest rate becomes higher. The wage rate becomes lower. The effects on the other variables are plotted in Fig. 10.4. The price of agricultural goods becomes higher. The price of education is almost invariant. The land rent and land price become higher. The gold price becomes higher initially and lower in the long term. The gold

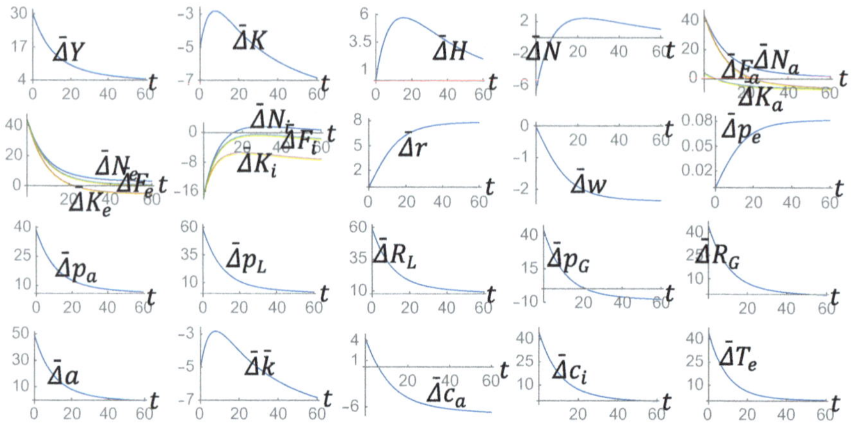

Fig. 10.4 Propensity to consume housing is increased

rent rises and is almost invariant in the long term. The household's physical wealth per capita falls. The household's total wealth rises initially and changes slightly in the long term. The consumption level of agricultural goods rises initially and falls in the long term. The household's consumption level of industrial goods rises initially and falls in the long term. The labor inputs of the education and agricultural sectors rise. The labor input of the industrial sector falls initially and rises in the long term. The capital inputs of the three sectors fall in the long term. The output level of the industrial (education) sector falls (rises). The output level of the agricultural sector rises initially and falls in the long term.

10.2.4 A Rise in the Propensity to Save

Like almost any question in economic theory, one finds opposite answers in different theories. Keynesian economic theory shows that a rise in the propensity to saving lowers national income, while neoclassical growth theory suggests the opposite effect. The propensity to save is assumed to be increased as follows: $\lambda_0 : 0.8 \Rightarrow 0.82$. The change in the propensity has no impact on the lot size, agricultural land use, and gold per capita. The rest of the simulation results are plotted in Fig. 10.5. The physical wealth rises, and the human capital falls. The national income is lowered initially and enhanced slightly in the long term. The wage rate becomes higher. The interest rate becomes lower. The price of education is reduced. The price of agricultural goods becomes lower initially and higher in the long term. The prices of land and gold fall initially and rise in the long term. The rents of land and gold fall initially and change slightly in the long term. The consumption levels of industrial goods and agricultural goods and education time fall and change slightly. The physical wealth per household is increased. The total wealth falls initially and is enhanced in the long term.

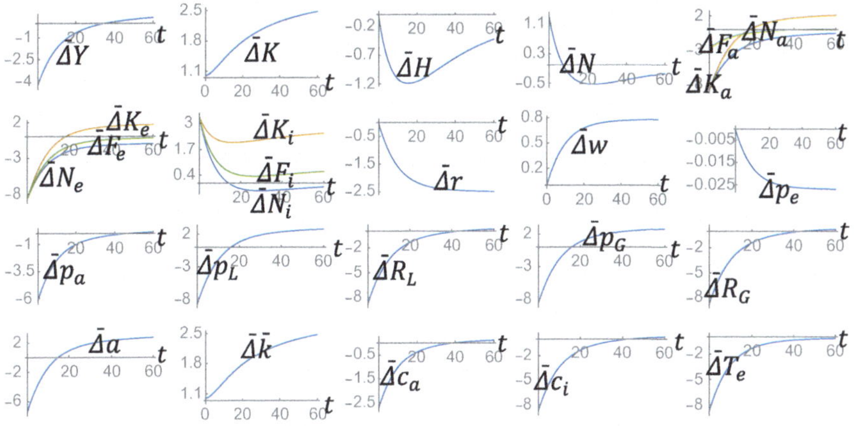

Fig. 10.5 A rise in the propensity to save

10.2.5 A Rise in the Total Factor Productivity of the Industrial Sector

I now study the effects of the following change in the total factor productivity of the industrial sector: $A_i : 1 \Rightarrow 1.1$. The effects on the time-dependent variables are plotted in Fig. 10.6. The physical wealth rises. The human capital falls. The national income falls initially and rises slightly in the long term. The wage rate and the interest rate rise. The labor force rises initially and falls in the long term. The education time falls and changes slightly. The price of education falls. The price of agricultural goods falls initially and rises in the long term. The prices and rents of land and gold

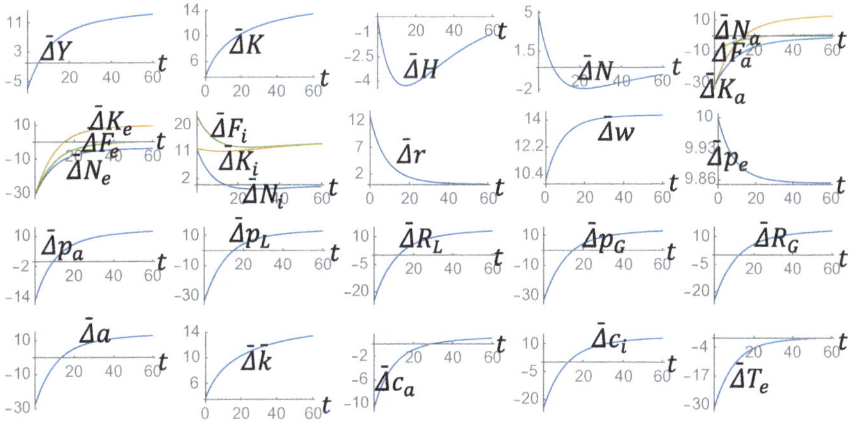

Fig. 10.6 A rise in the total factor productivity of the industrial sector

fall initially and rise in the long term. The consumption levels of industrial goods and agricultural goods fall and change slightly. The physical wealth per household is increased. The total wealth falls initially and is enhanced in the long term.

10.2.6 *The Population is Increased*

The population rises as follows: $N_0 : 10 \Rightarrow 11$. The effects on the time-invariant variables are given as follows:

$$\overline{\Delta} l_h = -9.09, \overline{\Delta} L_a = 0, \overline{\Delta} \bar{g} = -9.09.$$

The lot size and gold per capita fall. The agricultural land use is not affected. The effects on the time-dependent variables are plotted in Fig. 10.7. The interest rate falls. The wage rate rises slightly. The prices and rents of land and gold are enhanced. The output levels and inputs of the three sectors are increased. The national output, total capital, and total labor force are augmented. The human capital falls. The household initially spends more hours on education and reduces education time in the long term. The household's wealth levels and consumption levels of two goods are reduced. A larger population enhances the macroeconomic real variables and reduces the household's microeconomic real variables.

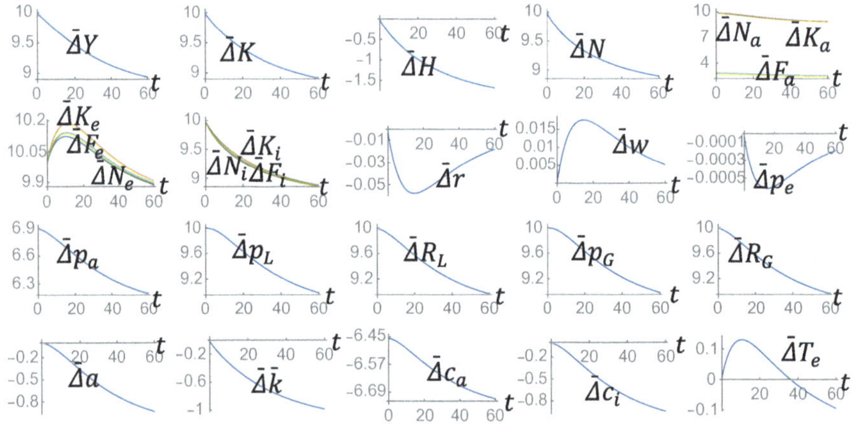

Fig. 10.7 Population is increased

10.3 A Few Remarks on Asset Prices

This chapter shows how to analyze asset prices within a dynamic general equilibrium framework. One may also simulate another case that the system has multiple equilibrium points as in Chap. 4. This chapter provides a rigorous treatment of the subject on portfolio choice in economic growth theory. The next chapter introduces money. The model can be enriched when it is integrated with monetary growth theory. It should be noted that endogenous human capital with increasing returns may lead to multiple equilibrium and monetary growth models tend be unstable. Introduction of endogenous money and endogenous human capital into the basic model tends to result in unstable dynamic systems. This makes it more difficult to predict what happen in economic systems.

Although there are a few theoretical growth models with heterogeneous assets, empirical studies on asset prices are broad and technically sophisticated. The 2013 Nobel Prize was awarded jointly to Eugen F. Fama (1939–), Lars Peter Hansen (1952–), and Robert J. Shiller (1946–) for their empirical studies of asset prices. They use empirical methods to follow prices of different assets and provide some insights into long-term trends of price changes. Although their studies are not theoretically related to growth theory, some important insights and relations among various variables they identified can be applied to enrich the theory proposed in this book.

References

Abel AB (1990) Asset prices under habit formation and catching up with the joneses. Am Econ Rev 80:38–42
Agell J, Edin PA (1990) Marginal taxes and the asset portfolios of Swedish households. Scandinavian J Econ 92:47–64
Arrow KJ (1962) The economic implications of learning by doing. Rev Econ Stud 29:155–173
Barro RJ (1979) Money and the price level under the classical gold standard. Econ J 89:13–33
Bordo MD, Ellson RW (1985) A model of the classical gold standard with depletion. J Monetary Econ 6:109–120
Chappell D, Dowd K (1997) A simple model of the gold standard. J Money Credit Bank 29:94–105
Dowd K, Sampson AA (1993) A new model of the gold standard. Can J Econ 26:380–391
Guiso L, Haliassos M, Jappelli T (2002) Household portfolios. MIT Press, Mass, Boston
Uhler RS, Gragg JG (1971) The structure of the asset portfolios of households. Rev Econ Stud 38:341–357
Uzawa H (1965) Optimal technical change in an aggregative model of economic growth. Int Econ Rev 6:18–31
von Gaudecker H (2015) How does household portfolio diversification vary with financial literacy and financial advice? J Finan 70:489–507
Zhang WB (2007) Economic growth with learning by producing, learning by education, and learning by consuming. INDECS 5:21-38
Zhang WB (2016) Exchange values of gold, land, physical capital, and human capital in a neoclassical growth model. Econ Altern 3:265–286

Chapter 11
Money and Unstable Economic Changes

Money, like blood in human body, affects and is affected by the rest of the system. Its importance is illustrated by William Rees-Mogg (Times, Dec. 1, 2003, from Wickens 2011: 350):

> If I look at the most bloody events of modern history, from the French Revolution and the Terror, the great slump, the rise of Nazis, the Second World War and the holocaust, or to the 70-year Soviet tyranny, I find the mismanagement of currencies among the main causative factors. Incompetent central bankers are more lethal than incompetent generals.

The traditionally accepted roles of money are a unit of account, a means of exchange, standard of deferred payments, and a store of value. A review on the literature of money is given by Zhang (2009). It is generally accepted that the modern monetary theory began from David Hume's essays of 1752, *Of Money and Interest*. Hume holds that the effect of changes in money should depend on the way in which the change is affected. For instance, he stresses the units-change aspect of changes in the money stock and the irrelevance of such changes to the behavior of rational people. He also observes that it would encourage industrial development by properly increasing the money supply. As the money supply is increased, prices rise till they reach a new level proportional to the new money supply. During the period in which prices rise output will be increased. As prices reach the new equilibrium level, output is back to normal. The national spirit of industry can thus be maintained by timely increasing money.

Keynes intensified debates over money after he published *General Theory* in 1936. He holds that a fully competitive economy could get trapped into a disequilibrium situation (with unemployment). Pigou (1943) does not agree with Keynes, arguing that Keynes overlooked an important class of regulating mechanisms, namely, the real balance, or wealth effects, which are interacting with nominal prices, wages, and interest rates. Friedman (1964) describes a trend in the post war period in monetary theory and policy as follows: "The post-war period has seen a dramatic change in the views of academic students of economics about monetary theory and of government

W.-B. Zhang, *The General Economic Theory*,
https://doi.org/10.1007/978-3-030-56204-5_11

officials about monetary policy. At the end of the war most professional economists and most governmental officials concerned with economic policy took it for granted that money did not matter, that it was a subject of minor importance. Since then, there has been something of a counter-revolution in both theory and policy."

It is not easy to incorporate money, especially under the form of fiat money, into general equilibrium models. As far as general equilibrium theory is concerned, Grandmont (1983: 1) pointed out a popular view of point: "A broad agreement was reached in the 1950s, known as "neoclassical synthesis": If such wealth effects were properly integrated in the analysis, the full price flexibility … was bound to remove all excess demands and supplies, both in the short run and in the long run. Keynes was theoretically mistaken, and the unemployment he talked about was entirely due to his assumption that nominal wages were rigid down." Money is a peculiar 'commodity' in that its usefulness depends on its price. As Starr (1974: 45) points out, "It would not upset the theory of value if water or diamond had a price of zero, but monetary theory depends on money having a positive value in exchange." Different authors emphasize different aspects of money with different modeling frameworks. For instance, with regards to effects of a shift to a fully anticipated, more inflationary policy on capital accumulation, economists answer quite differently. In his well-known paper on long-run effects of inflationary policies, Tobin (1965) shows that an increase in the level of the inflation rate will increase the capital stock of an economy. Sidrauski (1967a) constructs an economic model in which no real variable will be affected in the economy's inflation rate. Stockman (1981) presents another influential economic model which forecasts negative long-run impact of inflation on the real variables. Since the classical papers by Tobin and Sidrauski in the 1960s, the analysis of the effects of anticipated inflation on capital accumulation has been a central issue in monetary growth theory. In the contemporary literature of monetary economics, three approaches to incorporating money into general equilibrium models are mostly employed (Walsh 2003: 2.1): (1) assume that money yields direct utility by introducing money directly into the utility functions of the agents (Sidrauski 1967a); (2) consider transactions costs of some form that yields a demand for money, either by making asset exchanges costly (Baumol 1952; Tobin 1956), requiring that money be employed by some types of transactions (Clower 1967), or assuming that direct barter of commodities is costly (Kiyotaki and Wright 1989); or (3) use money like any other asset for transferring resources intertemporally (Samuelson 1958). The following state of macroeconomics described by Gale (1983: 1) is still valid for the current state of monetary economics: "Patinkin's great work in the fifties, for example, was a serious attempt at placing macroeconomics in a general-equilibrium framework. Likewise the work by countless authors on the theory of the consumption and investment functions was a serious attempt at grounding elements of the IS-LM framework in microeconomic principles. But these attempts, valuable though they were, were piecemeal and did not go far enough."

Orphanides and Solow (1990: 258) also point out: "The fundamental difficulty is that I do not yet have any clearly preferred way to introduce money into models of the real economy, especially those that feature durable productive assets as well. Models of a monetary economy without real capital cannot be taken seriously as vehicles for the study of money-and-growth." In a recent review on studies about relationship between economic growth and inflation, Akinsola and Odhiambo (2017) demonstrate that there are varied relations between inflation and growth in the literature.

This chapter is especially concerned with growth with money. Tobin (1965) makes a seminal contribution to the theory of monetary growth within the framework of neoclassical growth theory. He is concerned with an isolated economy in which the outside money issued by the government competes with real capital in the portfolios of agents by extending the Solow model. With regard to outside money holdings as net wealth, Tobin (1965: 676) points out: "The community's wealth … has two components: the real goods accumulated through past real investment and fiduciary or paper 'goods' manufactured by the government from thin air. Of course the non-human wealth of such a nation 'really' consists only of its tangible capital. But, as viewed by the inhabitants of the nation individually, wealth exceeds the tangible capital stock by the size of what I might term the fiduciary issue. This is an illusion, but only one of the many fallacies of composition which are basic to any economy or any society. The illusion can be maintained unimpaired so long as the society does not actually try to convert all of its paper wealth into goods."

11.1 Growth with the Money-in-Utility (MIU) Approach

This section integrates the MIU approach with the basic model defined in Chap. 2. In the MIU approach money yields some services and directly enters the utility function. The approach was applied initially by Patinkin (1965), Sidrauski (1967a, b) and Friedman (1969). See also Wang and Yip (1992) and Handa (2009). The variables, $N(=1)$, $K(t)$, $F(K(t), N)$, $y(t) = f(k(t))$, $k(t)$, $\bar{k}(t)$, δ_k are the same as in Chap. 2. Suppose that the economy contains two outside assets: fiat money and physical capital.

11.1.1 The Real Sector

The marginal conditions for the production sector are:

$$r(t) + \delta_k = f'(k(t)), \ w(t) = f(k(t)) - k(t)f'(k(t)). \tag{11.1.1}$$

11.1.2 The Money via the "Helicopter Drop"

I use $M(t)$ to stand for the quantity of money supplied, $P(t)$ the price level, $\mu(= \dot{M}(t)/M(t))$ the rate of change of money, and $\pi(t)(= \dot{P}(t)/P(t))$ the rate of change of the price level. With μ being the constant net growth rate of the per-capita money stock.

The government expenditure in real terms per capita $\tau(t)$ is given by:

$$\tau(t) = \frac{\dot{M}(t)}{P(t)} = \frac{\mu M(t)}{P(t)} = \mu m(t), \ m(t) \equiv \frac{M(t)}{P(t)}.$$

The representative household receives $\mu m(t)$ units of paper money from the government through a "helicopter drop", also considered to be independent of his money holdings.

11.1.3 The Disposable Income and Optimal Decision

The disposable income in real terms $\hat{y}(t)$ is:

$$\hat{y}(t) = r(t)k(t) + w(t) - \pi(t)m(t) + \tau(t) + a(t), \tag{11.1.2}$$

where $a(t) \equiv k(t) + m(t)$. The utility function is dependent on holding money, consuming goods, and saving as follows:

$$U(t) = m^{\varepsilon_0}(t)c^{\xi_0}(t)s^{\lambda_0}(t), \ \varepsilon_0, \xi_0, \lambda_0 > 0,$$

where ε_0 is the propensity to hold money, ξ_0 the propensity to consume, and λ_0 the propensity to own wealth. The "price" of holding money is $1 + r(t)$. The budget constraint is given by:

$$(1 + r(t))m(t) + c(t) + s(t) = \hat{y}(t).$$

Insert (11.1.2) in the above budget constraint:

$$\begin{aligned}(r(t) + \pi(t))m(t) + c(t) + s(t) &= \bar{y}(t) \\ &\equiv f(t) + \delta\bar{k}(t) + \tau(t),\end{aligned} \tag{11.1.3}$$

where I use $f(t) = r(t)k(t) + w(t) + \delta_k k(t)$ and $\delta \equiv 1 - \delta_k$. Maximizing $U(t)$ subject to (11.1.3), I have:

$$(r(t) + \pi(t))m(t) = \varepsilon\bar{y}(t), \ c(t) = \xi\bar{y}(t), \ s(t) = \lambda\bar{y}(t), \tag{11.1.4}$$

in which

$$\varepsilon \equiv \rho \varepsilon_0, \ \xi \equiv \rho \xi_0, \ \lambda \equiv \rho \lambda_0, \ \rho \equiv \frac{1}{\varepsilon_0 + \xi_0 + \lambda_0}.$$

The expenditure spent on 'consuming money' $(r + \pi)m$ is proportional to the potential disposable income $\bar{y}(t)$, and the (relative) propensity to use money. I see that $m(t)$ is negatively related to $r + \pi$. This relation is assumed in the Tobin model and the Levhari and Patinkin's monetary model as mentioned before.

The change in the value of wealth follows the following differential equation:

$$\dot{a}(t) = s(t) - a(t). \tag{11.1.5}$$

I have thus built the model. Before examining the properties of the model, I show how the demand function for money is derived in early literature. The first formal models with money as a medium of exchange that facilitate transactions were due to Baumol (1952) and Tobin (1956). As cash balances are typically non-interest bearing, it is costly for individuals to hold money. Individuals choose to hold only the cash they need and save the rest of their disposable income to earn interest. This means that the transactions demand for money should be negatively related to the interest rate. I now derive Baumol's square-root rule which relates individual's demand for real cash balances, income, and interest rate. An early formal explanation between cash holdings and interest rate is given by Baumol (1952). The discussion below about the Baumol's equation is based on Pentecost (2000: Chap. 11). See Baumol (1952) for further explanations about the economic implications of the model.

Let us consider an individual with a nominal income of y per month. He spends all the income during the month. If all his income is held as cash, then the average cash balance held over the month is $y/2$. If he withdraws half of the money from the bank at start of the month and withdraws half at the start of the third week, then the average cash balance is $(1/2)(y/2)$. If he withdraws n times over the month, then his average cash balance is given by $m = 0.5y/n$. Consider that the bank offers interest on the funds remaining in the account with a fixed interest rate, r per month. His average deposit in the bank is $y/2$ if he withdraws infinite times. When he withdraws n times, his average deposit is $y/2$ less $y/2n$. Hence, the net interest earned is $(1 - 1/n)ry/2$. There are costs in terms of time and trouble of withdrawing cash for the individual. Assume that the average cost of each withdrawal is c. The total cost of withdrawing n times equals cn. The individual's profit is thus given by

$$\Pi = r\left(\frac{y}{2} - \frac{1}{2}\frac{y}{n}\right) - cn.$$

The rational individual will choose n in such a way that Π is maximized. The optimal number is $n = \sqrt{yr/2c}$. Hence, the optimal money holding is given by $m = \sqrt{cy/2r}$.This is known as Baumol's square-root rule. An individual's demand for real cash balance is positively related to the income and cost of withdrawing and negatively related to the interest rate. The above equation describes the demand of individuals. To find out the aggregate money demand, suppose, for instance, that the consumer buys goods from a representative firm and the firm periodically converts its money-holdings into bonds. The firm's pattern of bond and money holdings would follow the pattern exactly complementary to the consumer's pattern. Hence, the firm's demand for money would also be given by $m = \sqrt{cy/2r}$. The aggregate money demand is thus equal to 2 m. Hence, the aggregate demand for real money transactions balances, M/P, is given by: $M/P = \sqrt{2cy/r}$.

In the above equation, y is the national real income. The elasticity of aggregate demand for real money balances for transactions purposes with respect to both income and the interest rate is 0.5 and -0.5 respectively. Different from Keynes' demand for transactions balances which is proportional to income, Baumol's equation shows that the demand is related both to income and the interest rate.

11.2 Equilibrium and Comparative Steady State

To analyze behavior of the model, from $\pi = \mu - \dot{m}/m$ and $(r + \pi)m = \varepsilon \bar{y}$, I obtain:

$$\dot{m}(t) = (r(t) + \mu - \varepsilon\mu)m(t) - \varepsilon f(t) - \varepsilon\delta\bar{k}(t), \tag{11.1.6}$$

where I use $\tau = \mu m$. As r and w are functions of $\bar{k}$, the right-hand side of (3.3.7) is a function of $\bar{k}$ and m.

Insert $s(t) = \lambda\bar{y}(t)$ and the definition of a and (11.1.3) in (11.1.5):

$$\dot{\bar{k}}(t) = \lambda f(t) - (1 - \lambda\delta)\bar{k}(t) - (1 - \lambda\mu)m(t) - \dot{m}(t). \tag{11.1.7}$$

I see that $\dot{\bar{k}}(t)$ is a function of $\bar{k}(t)$ and $m(t)$. The dynamics consists of two differential equations, (11.1.6) and (11.1.7), with two variables, $\bar{k}(t)$ and $m(t)$.

By (11.1.6) and (11.1.7), a steady state is given by:

$$\begin{gathered}(r + \mu - \varepsilon\mu)m - \varepsilon f - \varepsilon\delta\bar{k} = 0, \\ \lambda f - (1 - \lambda\delta)\bar{k} - (1 - \lambda\mu)m = 0.\end{gathered} \tag{11.1.8}$$

From the last equation of (11.1.8), I obtain m as follows:

$$m = \frac{\lambda f - (1 - \lambda\delta)\bar{k}}{1 - \lambda\mu}. \tag{11.1.9}$$

As $1-\lambda\delta>0$ and $1-\lambda\mu$, and $m>0$, I should require $f/\bar{k}>(1-\lambda\delta)/\lambda$. I have a unique value of $\bar{k}$, denoted as $\bar{k}^*$, such that $f\left(\bar{k}^*\right)/\bar{k}^*=(1-\lambda\delta)/\lambda$, that is, $m=0$. As $f/\bar{k}$ falls in $\bar{k}$, I should require $0<\bar{k}<\bar{k}^*$. Moreover, it is required $r+\mu>0$ at steady state, that is, $f'\left(\bar{k}\right)-\delta_k+\mu>0$. To guarantee this inequality, $\delta_k>\mu$. There is a unique value of value of $\bar{k}$, denoted as $\bar{k}^\circ$, such that:

$$f'\left(\bar{k}^\circ\right)-\delta_k+\mu=0.$$

Introduce $\bar{k^c}\equiv min\left\{\bar{k}^\circ,\bar{k}^*\right\}$. It is required $0<\bar{k}<\bar{k^c}$. Inserting (11.1.9) in (11.1.8) yields:

$$\Omega\left(\bar{k}\right)\equiv(r+\mu-\varepsilon\mu)\frac{\lambda f-(1-\lambda\delta)\bar{k}}{1-\lambda\mu}-\varepsilon f-\varepsilon\delta\bar{k}=0. \tag{11.1.10}$$

I confirm:

$$\Omega(0)>0,$$

$$\Omega\left(\bar{k^c}\right)=\begin{cases}-\varepsilon f\left(\bar{k}^*\right)-\varepsilon\delta\bar{k}^*<0, & f\left(\bar{k^c}\right)=\bar{k}^*,\\ -\varepsilon\mu\bar{k}^\circ\frac{\frac{\lambda f\left(\bar{k}^\circ\right)}{\bar{k}^\circ}-(1-\lambda\delta)}{1-\lambda\mu}-\varepsilon f\left(\bar{k}^\circ\right)-\varepsilon\delta\bar{k}^\circ<0, & f\left(\bar{k^c}\right)=\bar{k}^\circ,\end{cases} \tag{11.1.11}$$

where I use $r=f'(0)-\delta_k\to+\infty$ and require $\bar{k}f'\left(\bar{k}\right)\to 0$ and $f\left(\bar{k}\right)f'\left(\bar{k}\right)\to\infty$ as $\bar{k}\to 0$. For instance, when $f=A\bar{k}^\alpha$, if $\alpha<1/2$ the requirements are satisfied. Hence, the equation has at least one solution for $0<\bar{k}<\bar{k^c}$. I have:

$$\Omega'=mf''+(r+\mu-\varepsilon\mu)\frac{\lambda r-(1-\lambda)}{1-\lambda\mu}-\varepsilon f'-\varepsilon\delta.$$

As mf'', $-\varepsilon f'$ and $-\varepsilon\delta$ are negative, if $(r+\mu-\varepsilon\mu)(\lambda r-1+\lambda)<0$, then $\Omega'<0$. At a steady state, the two eigenvalues φ_j are determined by:

$$\varphi^2-(m_1-m_2+m_3)\varphi+(1-\lambda\mu)m_2+m_3m_1=0,$$

where

$$m_1\equiv r+\mu-\varepsilon\mu>0,\, m_2\equiv f''m-\varepsilon f'-\varepsilon\delta<0,$$
$$m_3\equiv\lambda f'-(1-\lambda\delta).$$

I confirm that irrespective of the sign of m_2, the real part of at least one eigenvalue is positive. This implies that the dynamic system has at least one steady state. If the steady state is unique, it is locally unstable. It is straightforward to check that if $f=A\bar{k}^\alpha$,, the dynamic system has a unique stead state. The steady state is locally unstable.

The rest of this section examines effects of changes in some parameters on the steady state. I get:

$$\frac{d\Omega}{d\bar{k}} = mf'' - \frac{(f - f'\bar{k})\varepsilon}{\lambda f - (1 - \lambda\delta)\bar{k}} < 0. \tag{11.1.12}$$

This is important for judging the effects of changes in the parameters.

11.2.1 The Inflationary Policy

Taking derivatives of (11.1.10) with respect to μ yields:

$$-\frac{d\Omega}{d\bar{k}}\frac{d\bar{k}}{d\mu} = \left[(1 - \varepsilon) + \frac{r + \mu - \varepsilon\mu}{(1 - \lambda\mu)}\right]m > 0.$$

A rise in μ increases the per capita physical wealth. As the capital intensity rises, the interest rate falls and per capita output level and wage rate rise. The Tobin effect prevails. I calculate:

$$\frac{dm}{d\mu} = \frac{\lambda m}{1 - \lambda\mu} + \left[\frac{\lambda f' - (1 - \lambda\delta)}{1 - \lambda\mu}\right]\frac{d\bar{k}}{d\mu},$$

$$\frac{da}{d\mu} = \frac{d\bar{k}}{d\mu} + \frac{dm}{d\mu} = \frac{\lambda m}{1 - \lambda\mu} + \left[\frac{\lambda f' + \lambda\delta - \lambda\mu}{1 - \lambda\mu}\right]\frac{d\bar{k}}{d\mu} > 0,$$

$$\frac{d\bar{y}}{d\mu} = \frac{1}{1 - \lambda\mu} + \left[f' + \frac{\lambda\mu f' + \delta - \mu}{1 - \lambda\mu}\right]\frac{d\bar{k}}{d\mu} > 0,$$

$$\frac{1}{\xi}\frac{dc}{d\mu} = \frac{1}{\lambda}\frac{ds}{d\mu} = \frac{d\bar{y}}{d\mu} > 0,$$

where I require $\delta_k + \mu < 1$ in judging the sign of a and $\bar{y}$. The impact on the real money holding is ambiguous. The total wealth and consumption level are increased. The effects of an increase in μ are all positive for the real economy.

11.2.2 The Effects of Change in the Propensity to Hold Money

Taking derivatives of (11.1.10) with respect to ε_0 yields

$$
\begin{aligned}
-\frac{d\Omega}{dk}\frac{d\bar{k}}{d\varepsilon_0} = & -\frac{(\xi_0+\lambda_0)\mu\varepsilon^2}{\varepsilon_0^2}\frac{\lambda f-(1-\lambda\delta)\bar{k}}{1-\lambda\mu} \\
& -(r+\mu-\varepsilon\mu)\frac{\left(f+\delta\bar{k}\right)\lambda^2}{(1-\lambda\mu)\lambda_0}, \\
& -\frac{\mu\lambda^2 m}{(1-\lambda\mu)\lambda_0}-\left(f+\delta\bar{k}\right)\frac{(\xi_0+\lambda_0)\varepsilon^2}{\varepsilon_0^2}<0.
\end{aligned}
$$

A rise in ε_0 reduces the per capita physical wealth. As capital intensity falls, the interest rate rises and per capita output level and wage rate rise. The following results also hold:

$$
\begin{aligned}
\frac{dm}{d\varepsilon_0} &= -\frac{\left(f+\delta\bar{k}\right)\lambda^2}{(1-\lambda\mu)\lambda_0}-\frac{\mu\lambda^2 m}{(1-\lambda\mu)\lambda_0}+\left[\frac{\lambda f'-(1-\lambda\delta)}{1-\lambda\mu}\right]\frac{d\bar{k}}{d\varepsilon_0}, \\
\frac{da}{d\varepsilon_0} &= \frac{d\bar{k}}{d\varepsilon_0}+\frac{dm}{d\varepsilon_0}=-\frac{\left(f+\delta\bar{k}\right)\lambda^2}{(1-\lambda\mu)\lambda_0}-\frac{\mu\lambda^2 m}{(1-\lambda\mu)\lambda_0} \\
&\quad +\left[\frac{\lambda f'+\lambda\delta-\lambda\mu}{1-\lambda\mu}\right]\frac{d\bar{k}}{d\varepsilon_0}<0, \\
\frac{d\bar{y}}{d\varepsilon_0} &= -\frac{\left(f+\delta\bar{k}\right)\mu\lambda^2}{(1-\lambda\mu)\lambda_0}-\frac{\mu^2\lambda^2 m}{(1-\lambda\mu)\lambda_0}+\left(\frac{f'+\delta-\mu}{1-\lambda\mu}\right)\frac{d\bar{k}}{d\varepsilon_0}<0, \\
\frac{dc}{d\varepsilon_0} &= \xi\frac{d\bar{y}}{d\varepsilon_0}-\frac{\xi^2\bar{y}}{\xi_0}<0, \quad \frac{ds}{d\varepsilon_0}=\lambda\frac{d\bar{y}}{d\varepsilon_0}-\frac{\lambda^2\bar{y}}{\lambda_0}<0.
\end{aligned}
$$

The impact on the real money holding is ambiguous. As the propensity to hold money rises, the total wealth, consumption level and savings are reduced.

11.2.3 Effects of Change in the Propensity to Own Wealth

The effects of change in the propensity to own wealth λ_0 are given as:

$$
\begin{aligned}
-\frac{d\Omega}{dk}\frac{dk}{d\lambda_0} = & \left[\varepsilon+\frac{r+\mu-\varepsilon\mu}{1-\lambda\mu}(\varepsilon_0+\xi_0)\rho\right]\rho\mu m \\
& +\left[\frac{(f+\delta k)(\varepsilon_0+\xi_0)}{\lambda f-(1-\lambda\delta)k}-\frac{1}{\rho}\right](f+\delta k)\rho^2\varepsilon.
\end{aligned}
$$

The impact of a rise in the propensity to save is ambiguous. As the impact on capital intensity is ambiguous, the effects on the interest rate, per capita output level and wage rate are also ambiguous.

11.3 A Small Open-Country Economy with the Cash-in-Advance Approach

Clower (1967) proposes a model to incorporate the role of money as a medium of exchange through the so-called cash-in-advance constraint. The role of money is to carry out transactions by introducing transaction technology. In this approach goods cannot be exchanged for goods and only money can buy goods. Stockman (1981) develops a growth model through CIA constraints. The model predicts that there is long-term superneutrality if only consumption expenditures are subject to a CIA constraint. If investment is also subject to a CIA constraint then steady state capital will fall when the growth rate of money rises. It is worthwhile mentioning that Feenstra (1986) proves that under certain conditions, the maximization problem with money under a CIA constraint may be equivalent to a maximization problem with the MIU approach (see also, Chang 2002).

Most aspects of the model are the same as the basic model. The representative household's financial wealth is divided between domestic fiat money and internationally traded bonds denominated in foreign currency. The economy is small and open. It has influence neither on the foreign currency price of the consumption good nor on the world bond rate. The exchange rate floats freely. It is assumed that foreigners do not hold domestic money. The exchange rate adjusts to maintain equality between the real money supply and domestic real money demand. Perfect foresight is assumed. The foreign price of traded goods is given in the world market. The domestic residents may hold two assets, domestic money and a traded world bond. I neglect transport cost, customs, or any other possible impediments to trade. I have perfect mobility of goods. For each good the law of one price holds. The absolute purchasing power parity (PPP) holds, which means that measured in the same currency, the same basket of goods costs the same at home and abroad. Thus $P(t) = E(t)\widetilde{P}(t)$, where $P(t)$ is the domestic price level, $\widetilde{P}(t)(= 1)$ is the foreign price level measured in foreign currency, and $E(t)$ is the exchange rate. The assumption of the PPP implies:

$$\pi(t) = \tilde{\pi} + e(t), \tag{11.3.1}$$

where $\pi(t)$ and $\tilde{\pi}\,(= 0)$ are the rates of inflation of the good, respectively, in domestic currency and foreign currency, and $e(t) \equiv \dot{E}(t)/E(t)$ is the rate of exchange depreciation of domestic currency. Assume that $\tilde{\pi}$ is fixed in the world market. Under free trade the rate of inflation in the domestic economy is equal to the world rate of inflation plus the rate of depreciation of domestic currency. There is a traded world bond with uncovered interest parity (UIP) holding at any point of time:

$$i(t) = \tilde{i} + e(t), \tag{11.3.2}$$

where $i(t)$ and $\tilde{i}$ are respectively domestic and (fixed) foreign nominal interest rates. Generally, $i(t) = \tilde{i}(t) + \varepsilon(t)$, where $\varepsilon(t)$ is expected rate of exchange depreciation. Under the assumption of perfect foresight, the expected rate of exchange depreciation is equal to the actual rate of exchange depreciation rate $e(t)$.

The household allocates its disposable income between current expenditure and saving. Real output f is taken to be exogenous and fixed. The government's inflation tax, $e(t)m(t)$, is spent upon unproductive public services. The real disposable income is given by:

$$\hat{y}(t) = f + a(t) + (i(t) - \pi(t))b(t) - \pi(t)m(t), \tag{11.3.3.}$$

where

$$a(t) \equiv m(t) + b(t), \ m(t) \equiv \frac{M(t)}{P(t)}, \ b(t) \equiv \frac{E(t)B(t)}{P(t)} = \frac{B(t)}{\tilde{P}(t)}.$$

The budget constraint implies $c(t) + s(t) = \hat{y}(t)$. When deciding the composition of the portfolios, the household knows that a certain fraction of consumption needs to be financed by payment in cash. Assume that cash has to be held in advance of purchasing goods. The liquidity constraint of the household is formed as $m(t) = \chi c(t)$, where χ is a positive parameter. I require $0 < \chi < 1$. Inserting $m(t) = \chi c(t)$ in the definition of $\hat{y}(t)$ and then substituting the resulted equation into $c(t) + s(t) = \hat{y}(t)$, I have:

$$\hat{y}(t) = f + a(t) + (i - \pi(t))b(t) - \chi\pi(t)c(t). \tag{11.3.4}$$

The utility function is specified as follows: $U(t) = c^{\xi_0}(t)s^{\lambda_0}(t)$. Maximizing $U(t)$ subject to the budget constraint, I get:

$$(1 + \chi\pi(t))c(t) = \xi\bar{y}(t), s(t) = \lambda\bar{y}(t), \tag{11.3.5}$$

where

$$\bar{y}(t) = f + a(t) + (i - \pi(t))b(t), \ \xi \equiv \rho\xi_0, \ \lambda \equiv \rho\lambda_0, \ \rho \equiv \frac{1}{\xi_0 + \lambda_0}.$$

The real wealth changes as follows:

$$\dot{a}(t) = s(t) - a(t). \tag{11.3.6}$$

11.4 Dynamics and Equilibrium

Substituting $i(t) - \pi(t) = i_0 \equiv \tilde{i} - \tilde{\pi}$ into the definition of $\bar{y}$ yields:

$$\bar{y}(t) = f + m(t) + (1 + i_0)b(t). \tag{11.4.1}$$

Insert $s = \lambda \bar{y}$ and (11.4.1) in (11.3.6)

$$\dot{b}(t) = \lambda f + (\lambda i_0 - \xi)b(t) - \xi m(t) - \dot{m}(t). \tag{11.4.2}$$

Insert $\pi = -\dot{m}/m$ in $(1 + \chi\pi)c = \xi\bar{y}$

$$\dot{m}(t) = \frac{(\chi - \xi)m(t) - \xi f + (1 + i_0)\xi b(t)}{\chi}, \tag{11.4.3}$$

where I use $m(t) = \chi c(t)$ and (11.4.1).

I conclude that the two linear differential Eqs. (11.4.2) and (12.4.3) have two variables, $b(t)$ and $m(t)$. With proper initial conditions, the motion of the two variables can be determined. The other variables are determined as functions of the two variables. At steady state I have

$$\lambda f + (\lambda i_0 - \xi)b - \xi m = 0,$$
$$(\chi - \xi)m - \xi f + (1 + i_0)\xi b = 0. \tag{11.4.4}$$

I solve (11.4.4):

$$m = \frac{\lambda f}{\xi} + \frac{(\lambda i_0 - \xi)\xi f}{(\chi - \xi)(\lambda f + \lambda i_0 - \xi) + (1 + i_0)\xi^2},$$
$$b = \frac{\xi^2 f}{(\chi - \xi)(\lambda f + \lambda i_0 - \xi) + (1 + i_0)\xi^2}. \tag{11.4.5}$$

The two eigenvalues $\varphi_{1,2}$ are given by:

$$\varphi_{1,2} = \frac{-a_1 \pm \sqrt{a_1^2 - 4a_0}}{2}, \tag{11.1.5}$$

where

$$a_1 \equiv \frac{(2 + i_0)\xi}{\chi} - \lambda i_0 - \lambda, \quad a_0 \equiv \frac{(1 + i_0)\xi^2 + (\xi - \lambda i_0)(\xi - \chi)}{\chi}.$$

For convenience of discussion, I assume that $\chi = 1$ and i_0 is small. As $\xi = 1 - \lambda$, I have:

$$a_1 = \xi + (\xi - \lambda)(1 + i_0),\ a_0 = (\xi - \lambda)(\xi + i_0).$$

If $\xi > \lambda$, I have $a_1 > 0$ and $a_0 > 0$. The steady state is stable. If $\xi = \lambda$, I have $a_1 > 0$ and $a_0 = 0$. One eigenvalue is negative and the other one is equal to zero. If $\xi < \lambda$, I have $a_0 < 0$. The steady state is unstable.

As I explicitly solved the steady state, it is straightforward to analyze how change in a parameter affects the steady state. First, I examine effects of change in the foreign nominal interest rate, i_0. In the rest of the section I require $\chi = 1$. I have:

$$\frac{dm}{di_0} = \frac{(\lambda^3 f + \xi^2)\xi f}{\left[(\lambda f + \lambda i_0 - \xi)\lambda + (1 + i_0)\xi^2\right]^2} > 0,$$
$$\frac{db}{di_0} = -\frac{(\lambda^2 + \xi^2)\xi^2 f}{\left[(\lambda f + \lambda i_0 - \xi)\lambda + (1 + i_0)\xi^2\right]^2} < 0.$$

As the foreign nominal interest rate rises, the real money balance rises, and real bonds is reduced. It should be noted that this result depends on the assumptions that the output is fixed, and no capital accumulation is allowed. As $Pm = M$, I have:

$$\frac{dP}{di_0} = -\frac{P}{m}\frac{dm}{di_0} < 0.$$

The price of goods fall. From the above equations, I get:

$$\frac{dB}{di_0} = P\frac{db}{di_0} + b\frac{dP}{di_0} < 0.$$

From $a = m + b$, I get:

$$\frac{da}{di_0} = \frac{\lambda^2 f + (\xi - \lambda)\xi}{\left[(\lambda f + \lambda i_0 - \xi)\lambda + (1 + i_0)\xi^2\right]^2}\lambda \xi f.$$

I see that the sign of da/di_0 is the same as that of $\lambda^2 f + (\xi - \lambda)\xi$. From $m = \chi c$, the consumption level is increased.

11.5 An Integration of the Taylor Rule and the Solow-Tobin Model

The Taylor rule is referred to how central banks should determine nominal interests as economic conditions are changed. The rule was first suggested by Taylor (1993) and Henderson and McKibbin (1993) for price stabilization. It has helped central banks in practice. Taylor proposes that the nominal interest rate should be related to the divergences of actual inflation from the targeted inflation rate and actual GDP from the potential GDP. It proposes that the Federal Reserve should enhance interest rates when inflation is high or when employment is higher than full employment levels; on the other hand, the Federal Reserve should reduce interest rates when inflation and employment levels are low. Economists have extensively applied the rule or its generalized forms in theoretical studies on relations between money and economic growth (Leeper 1991; Backus and Smith 1993; Benhabib et al. 2001, 2014; Dupor 2001; Meng and Yip 2004; Schmitt-Grohe and Uribe 2009). This chapter is based on Zhang (2019), applying the Taylor rules to the Solow-Tobin model with the MIU approach and endogenous labor supply.

The economy is basically framed as the Tobin monetary growth model (Tobin 1965; Nagatani 1970), except the determination of money demand and money supply. Money enters the utility function. The economy has three assets, money, bond issued by the government, and capital. There is a fixed number of homogeneous households $\overline{N}$.. The household can hold three assets. The nominal bonds pay the (positive) nominal interest rate $R(t)$, which will be determined by the government by the Taylor rule. Let $P(t)$ represent the nominal price and $\pi(t)$ the inflation rate. I have: $\pi(t) = \dot{P}(t)/P(t)$. I use $T(t)$ to represent the work time of a representative household and $N(t)$ for the labor force. I have: $N(t) = T(t)\overline{N}$.

11.5.1 The Sector Behavior and Marginal Conditions

The sector has the Cobb-Douglas technology as:

$$F(t) = AK^{\alpha}(t)N^{\beta}(t), \ \alpha, \beta > 0, \ \alpha + \beta = 1.$$

The marginal conditions imply:

$$r(t) + \delta_k = \frac{\alpha F(t)}{K(t)}, \ w(t) = \frac{\beta F(t)}{N(t)},$$

where δ_k is the fixed depreciation rate of physical capital and $r(t) \equiv R(t) - \pi(t)$.

11.5.2 Household Behavior

The household holds nominal government bonds, denoted by $B(t)$, that pay the nominal interest rate. The household holds money $M(t)$. I use $\overline{\tau}$ to stand for the (fixed) real lump-sum taxes. I use the variable $a(t)$ to denote the total value of wealth of the household. The household disposable income is given by:

$$\hat{y}(t) = a(t) + r(t)\big(\bar{k}(t) + b(t)\big) + T(t)w(t)$$
$$- \frac{\dot{B}(t)}{P(t)} - \frac{\dot{M}(t)}{P(t)} - \pi(t)m(t) - \bar{\tau},$$

where

$$m(t) \equiv \frac{M(t)}{P(t)}, \; b(t) \equiv \frac{B(t)}{P(t)}, \; a(t) \equiv \bar{k}(t) + b(t) + m(t).$$

The time constraint is expressed by: $T(t) + \overline{T}(t) = T_0$. From this equation and concept of the disposable income, I have:

$$\hat{y}(t) = \bar{y}(t) + m(t) - \overline{T}(t)w(t) - \pi(t)m(t), \tag{11.5.1}$$

where

$$\bar{y}(t) \equiv (1 + r(t))\big(\bar{k}(t) + b(t)\big) + T_0 w(t) - \frac{\dot{B}(t)}{P(t)} - \frac{\dot{M}(t)}{P(t)} - \bar{\tau}.$$

The utility function is taken on:

$$U(t) = \overline{T}^{\sigma_0}(t)m^{\varepsilon_0}(t)c^{\xi_0}(t)s^{\lambda_0}(t), \; \sigma_0, \varepsilon_0, \xi_0, \lambda_0 > 0,$$

where σ_0 is the propensity to enjoy leisure time, ε_0 is propensity to hold money, ξ_0 the propensity to consume, and λ_0 the propensity to own wealth. The disposable income is spent on holding money, consumption of the good, and saving:

$$(1 + R(t))m(t) + c(t) + s(t) = \hat{y}(t).$$

Inserting (11.5.1) in the above budget yields:

$$w(t)\overline{T}(t) + \overline{\pi}(t)m(t) + c(t) + s(t) = \bar{y}(t), \tag{11.5.2}$$

where $\overline{\pi}(t) \equiv \pi(t) + R(t)$. Maximizing $U(t)$ subject to (11.5.2), I get:

$$w(t)\overline{T}(t) = \sigma\bar{y}(t), \; \overline{\pi}(t)m(t) = \varepsilon\bar{y}(t), \; c(t) = \xi\bar{y}(t),$$
$$s(t) = \lambda\bar{y}(t), \tag{11.5.3}$$

where

$$\sigma \equiv \rho\sigma_0, \varepsilon \equiv \rho\varepsilon_0, \; \xi \equiv \rho\xi_0, \; \lambda \equiv \rho\lambda_0, \; \rho \equiv \frac{1}{\varepsilon_0 + \xi_0 + \lambda_0 + \sigma_0}.$$

The change in wealth is saving minus dissaving:

$$\dot{a}(t) = s(t) - a(t).$$

11.5.3 Monetary and Fiscal Policy

The rule suggested by Taylor (1993) is as follows:

$$R(t) = \pi(t) + r^*(t) + 0.5\big(\pi(t) - \pi^*(t)\big) + 0.5\big(y(t) - y^*(t)\big),$$

where is $r^*(t)$ the assumed equilibrium real interest rate, $\pi^*(t)$ is the desired rate of inflation, $y(t)$ is the logarithm of real GDP, and $y^*(t)$ is the logarithm of potential real GDP. The rule implies that if inflation is above its target or output is above its full-employment level, the central bank should enhance the interest rate to reduce inflationary pressure. This section assumes that the monetary authority follows an interest rate feedback rule as follows: $R(t) = R(\pi(t)) \geq 0$.The monetary policy is called active (passive) at an inflation rate π if $R'(\pi) > (<)1$. Instead of the original Taylor rule, I follow Benhabib et al. (2001) in assuming that the monetary authority sets the nominal interest as follows:

$$R(t) = q_0 e^{q(\pi(t) - \pi^*)}, \quad q_0, q, \pi^* > 0, \tag{11.5.4}$$

where q_0, q and π^* are parameters.

11.5.4 The Government's Budget Constraint

The government prints money $M(t)$ and issues nominal bonds $B(t)$. The government pays the nominal interest rate to its bonds and consumes nothing. The government has the budget constraint as:

$$\dot{B}(t) = R(t)B(t) - \dot{M}(t) - P(t)\overline{\tau}. \tag{11.5.5}$$

11.5.5 Capital Change

The change in capital stock is equal to the net of output, consumption and depreciation as follows:

$$\dot{K}(t) = F(t) - \overline{N}c(t) - \delta_k K(t).$$

I built the dynamic model. The dynamics is given by the following lemma.

Lemma The motion of the economic system follows the two differential equations with $\bar{k}(t)$ and $\pi(t)$ as the variables:

$$\dot{\bar{k}}(t) = \varphi_k\left(\bar{k}(t), \pi(t)\right), \ \dot{\pi}(t) = \varphi_\pi\left(\bar{k}(t), \pi(t)\right),$$

where φ_k and φ_π are functions of $\bar{k}(t)$ and $\pi(t)$ defined Zhang (2019). The rest variables are given as functions of $\bar{k}(t)$ and $\pi(t)$ by a given computational procedure

I specify the parameter values as follows:

$$\overline{N} = 50, \quad T_0 = 24, \quad \alpha = 0.33, \quad A = 1.5, \quad \pi^* = 0.01, \quad \overline{\tau} = 1,$$
$$\lambda_0 = 0.6, \quad \xi_0 = 0.1, \sigma_0 = 0.18, \quad \varepsilon_0 = 0.005, \quad q_0 = 0.01, \quad q = 150,$$
$$\delta_k = 0.03.$$

The population is 50. The total available time is 24. The target inflation rate is 1%. The propensity to save is 0.6. The propensities to consume goods and use leisure time are respectively 0.1 and 0.18. The propensity to hold money is 0.005. The system has a unique equilibrium point as follows:

$$F = 846.1, \quad N = 362, \quad K = 3897.5, \quad R = 0.201, \quad r = 0.171,$$
$$\pi = 0.03, \quad w = 1.57, \quad m = 3.16, \quad b = 6.4, \quad \bar{k} = 78, \quad a = 87.5,$$
$$c = 14.6, \quad T = 7.24.$$

The long-run inflation rate is 3%. The two eigenvalues are: {0.349, −0.234}. The equilibrium point is a saddle point. The system starts from the initial conditions:

$$\bar{k}(0) = 77, \ \pi(0) = 0.029.$$

The changes of the variables over time are plotted in Fig. 11.1. The national output rises over time from the initial state. Similarly, the other real variable variables fall. The household works more hours. The nominal rate falls in association with falls in the inflation rate. The real money holding rises. The real bond falls.

11.6 Comparative Dynamic Analysis

11.6.1 The Targeted Inflation Rate Is Enhanced

The targeted inflation rate is assumed to be enhanced as follows: $\pi_0 = 0.01 \Rightarrow 0.0102$. The deviations of the variables from Fig. 11.1 are plotted in Fig. 11.2. The nominal interest rate is reduced. The actual Inflation rate is reduced. The real wage is increased.

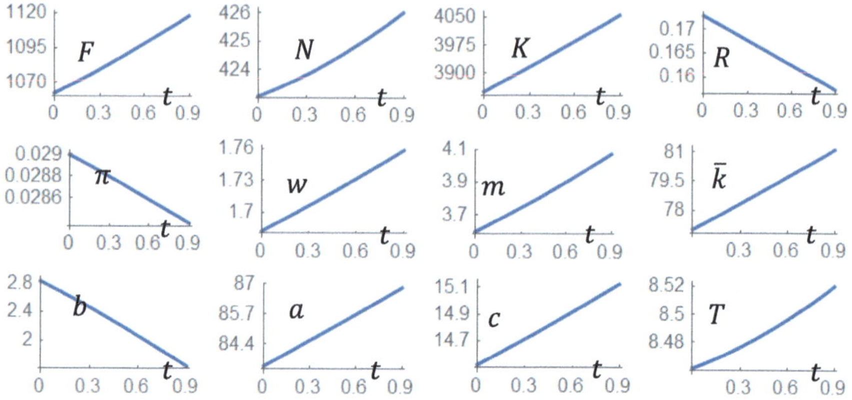

Fig. 11.1 The motion of the system with wealth and money

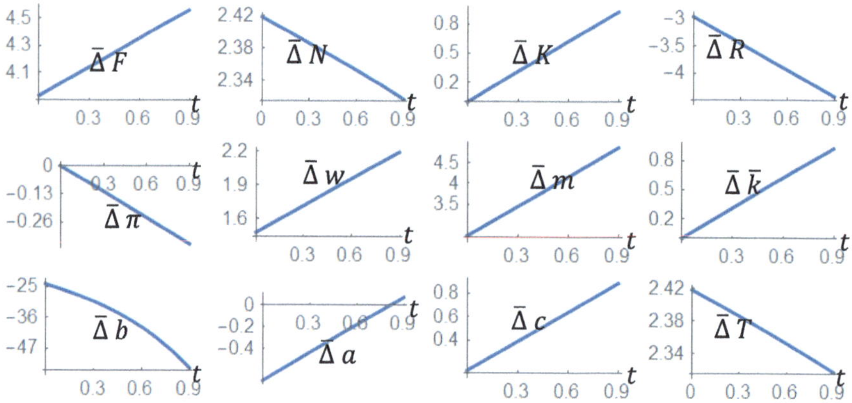

Fig. 11.2 The targeted inflation rate is enhanced

The money holding is increased. The household works more hours and the labor supply rises. The wealth per household is increased. The physical wealth is increased. The bond is reduced. The output is increased.

11.6.2 The Total Factor Productivity Is Enhanced

I now examine what will happen if the technological improvement occurs as follows: $A = 1.5 - 1.55$. The deviations of the variables from Fig. 11.1 are plotted in Fig. 11.3. The nominal interest rate is reduced. The actual Inflation rate is reduced. The real wage is increased. The money holding is increased. The household works more hours and the labor supply rises. The wealth per household is reduced initially but is

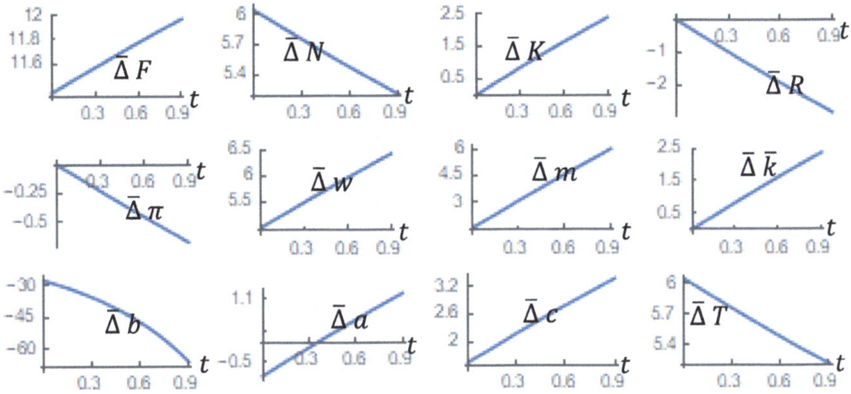

Fig. 11.3 The total factor productivity is enhanced

increased in the long term. The physical wealth is increased. The bond is reduced. The output is enhanced.

11.6.3 The Propensity to Hold Money Is Enhanced

The propensity to hold money is assumed to be increased as follows: $\epsilon_0 = 0.005 - 0.006$. The deviations of the variables from Fig. 11.1 are plotted in Fig. 11.4. The household has more money. The nominal interest rate becomes lower. The actual Inflation rate is decreased. The real wage becomes higher. The household works more hours and the labor supply rises. The wealth per household is decreased. The physical

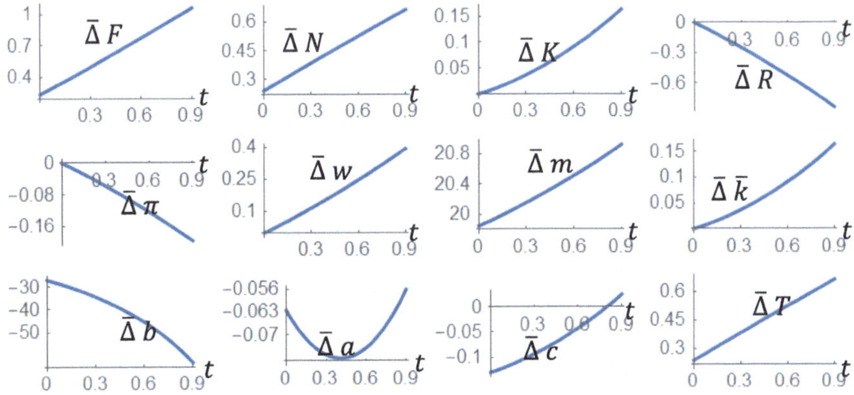

Fig. 11.4 The propensity to hold money is enhanced

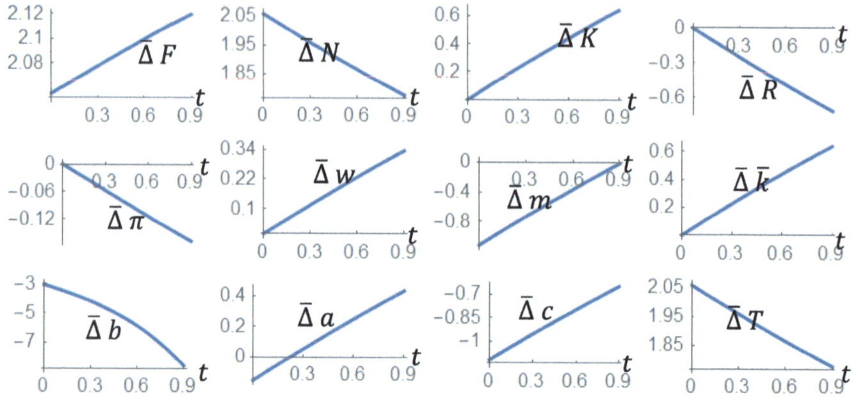

Fig. 11.5 An increase in the propensity to save

wealth is increased. The bond is reduced. The output is enhanced. The household consumes less initially but more in the long term.

11.6.4 An Increase in the Propensity to Save

The propensity to save is assumed to be increased as follows: $\lambda_0 = 0.6{-}0.61$. The deviations of the variables from Fig. 11.1 are plotted in Fig. 11.5. The household has less wealth initially but more in the long term. The bond is reduced. The household has more physical wealth. The household holds more money. The nominal interest rate and inflation rate become lower. The real wage becomes higher. The household works more hours and the labor supply rises. The physical wealth is increased. The output is enhanced. The household consumes less.

11.6.5 The Tax is Increased

The tax is assumed to be increased: $\bar{\tau} = 1{-}1.1$. The deviations of the variables from Fig. 11.1 are plotted in Fig. 11.6. The nominal interest rate and inflation rate become lower. The household works more hours. The total labor supply is increased. The national output rises. The national physical stock rises. The bond rises initially but falls in the long term. The household has more wealth. The physical wealth becomes lower. The household holds less money. The nominal interest rate and inflation rate become higher. The real wage is increased. The household consumes more.

The comparative analysis provided some insights into relations between growth and inflation over the whole dynamic process rather than only with regards to steady states as in most of the theoretical literature of monetary growth. For instance, after

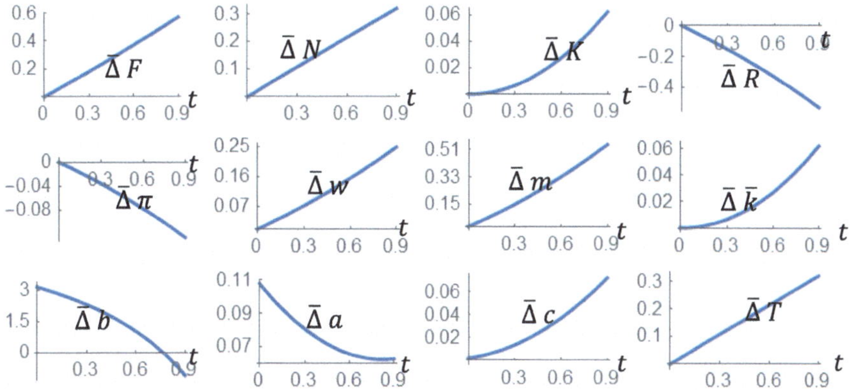

Fig. 11.6 The tax is increased

comprehensively and extensively reviewing the literature of both empirical and theoretical researches on growth and inflation, Akinsola and Odhiambo (2017) show that there is an "overwhelming support in favour of a negative relationship between inflation and growth, especially in developed economies." From the figures of the comparative dynamic analysis the change rate in the national output is opposite to that in the inflation rate. The Taylor rule has different formations in the contemporary literature on money, inflation, and growth. I may generalize my model with other forms of production or utility functions.

11.7 Comments on Further Extensions

The 1981 Nobel prize was awarded to James Tobin for research on the financial system and its effects on inflation and employment. He makes important contributions in different fields, such as economic growth and modern portfolio selection theory. His selection theory studies households' and firms' decisions to have various real and financial assets. He shows how these decisions are made with weighing risk and expected rate of return. Different from most of his contemporary economists in the field, he is concerned not only money, but the entire range of assets and debts. The model in Chap. 3 shows possible inclusions of multiple assets. Tobin tries to develop his portfolio selection theory into a general equilibrium theory for financial and real assets. He analyzes the interaction between financial and real markets. His important ideas should be integrated into a rigorously modelling framework with endogenous growth mechanisms. Chapter 3 and this chapter imply that my approach can be applied to analyze other issues related to financial and real assets addressed by Tobin and other researchers in an integrated manner.

References

Akinsola FA, Odhiambo NM (2017) Inflation and economic growth: a review of the international literature. Comp Econ Res 20:41–56
Backus DK, Smith GW (1993) Consumption and real exchange rates in dynamic economies with non-traded goods. J Int Econ 35:297–316
Baumol WJ (1952) The transactions demand for cash: An inventory theoretic approach. Quart J Econ 66:545–556
Benhabib J, Schmitt-Grohe S, Uribe M (2001) The perils of Taylor rules. J Econ Theory 96:40–69
Benhabib J, Evans GW, Honkapohja S (2014) Liquidity traps and expectation dynamics: fiscal stimulus or fiscal austerity. J Econ Dyn Control 45:220–238
Chang WY (2002) Examining the long-run effect of money on economic growth: an alternative view. J Macroecon 24:81–102
Clower RW (1967) A reconsideration of the microfoundations of monetary theory. W Econ J 6:1–9
Dupor B (2001) Investment and interest rate policy. J Econ Theory 98:85–115
Feenstra RC (1986) Functional equivalence between liquidity costs and the utility of money. J Monetary Econ 17:271–292
Friedman M (1964) Post-war trends in monetary theory and practice. National Banking Review 2: reprinted in The optimum quantity of money and other essays. Aldine, Chicago
Friedman M (1969) The optimum quantity of money. In: Friedman M (ed) The optimum quality of money and other essays. Aldine, Chicago
Gale D (1983) Competitive models with Keynesian features. Econ J 93:17–33
Grandmont JM (1983) Money and value. Cambridge University Press, Cambridge
Handa J (2009) Monetary economics. Routledge, London
Henderson DW, McKibbin W (1993) A comparison of some basic monetary policy regimes for open economies: implications of different degrees of instrument adjustment and wage persistence. Carnegie-Rochester Conf Ser Pub Policy 39:221–318
Kiyotaki N, Wright R (1989) On money as a medium of exchange. J Polit Econ 97:927–954
Leeper E (1991) Equilibrium under 'active' and 'passive' monetary and fiscal policies. J Monetary Econ 27:129–147
Meng QL, Yip CY (2004) Investment, interest rate rules, and equilibrium determinacy. Econ Theor 23:863–878
Nagatani K (1970) A note on Professor Tobin's "Money and Economic Growth". Econometrica 38:171–175
Orphanides A, Solow R (1990) Money, inflation and growth. In: Friedman B, Hahn F (eds) Handbook of monetary economics. North-Holland, Amsterdam
Patinkin D (1965) Money, interest, and prices: An integration of monetary and value theory, 2nd edn. Harper & Row, New York
Pentecost E (2000) Macroeconomics—an open economy approach. St. Martin's Press, New York
Pigou AC (1943) The classical stationary state. Econ J 53:343–351
Samuelson PA (1958) An exact consumption loan model of interest with or without the social contrivance of money. J Polit Econ 66:467–482
Schmitt-Grohe S, Uribe M (2009) Liquidity traps with global Taylor rules. Int J Econ Theory 5:85–106
Sidrauski M (1967a) Rational choice and patterns of growth in a monetary economy. Am Econ Rev 57:534–544
Sidrauski M (1967b) Inflation and economic growth. J Polit Econ 75:789–810
Starr RM (1974) The price of money in a pure exchange monetary economy with taxation. Econometrica 42:45–54
Stockman AC (1981) Anticipated inflation and the capital stock in a cash-in-advance economy. J Monetary Econ 8:387–393
Taylor JB (1993) Discretion versus policy rules in practice. Carnegie-Rochester Conf Ser Public Policy 39:195–214

Tobin J (1956) The interest elasticity of the transactions demand for cash. Rev Econ Stat 38:241–247
Tobin J (1965) Money and economic growth. Econometrica 33:671–684
Walsh CE (2003) Monetary theory and policy. The MIT Press, Mass., Cambridge
Wang P, Yip CK (1992) Examining the long-run effect on economic growth. J Macroecon 14:359–369
Wickens M (2011) Macroeconomic theory: a dynamic general equilibrium approach, 2nd edn. Princeton University Press, Princeton
Zhang WB (2009) Monetary growth theory: Money, interest, prices, capital, knowledge, and economic structure over time and space. Routledge, London
Zhang WB (2019) Economic growth and the Taylor rule in the Solow-Tobin model. Asian Bus Rev 9:49–56

Chapter 12
Growth Theory Enriched with Monopoly, Monopsony, and Game Theories

I have studied dynamics of economies with perfectly competitive markets and government intervention. Various markets coexist in a modern economy. In modern microeconomic textbooks, students study perfect competition, imperfect competition, oligopoly, monopoly, and various games in the same course in microeconomics. But when students study macroeconomics, heterogeneous markets are seldom introduced in an integrated framework. Most of studies on imperfect competitive markets are not fully integrated with macroeconomics. Partial economic theories are proposed to examine demand and supply equilibrium, efficiencies, issues related to welfare and profit distribution of different market structures under varied rules and institutions. These markets are examined in microeconomics, industrial economics, and organization theory (Nikaido 1975; Mas-Colell et al. 1995; Brakman and Heijdra 2004; Wang 2012; Behrens and Murata 2007, 2017; and Parenti et al. 2017).

This chapter and the next chapter introduce a few of my models to demonstrate how to integrate monopoly, monopsony, monopolistic competition, and games with the basic model. The approach opens a path to further integrate microeconomics and macroeconomics in a unified manner.

12.1 Monopolies and Perfect Competition in Solow–Uzawa's General Equilibrium Growth Model

I am first concerned with the role of monopoly in economic growth. Although monopoly is well studied when macroeconomic environment is given, the following model is seminal on issues related to dynamic interdependence between growth and monopoly. This section is based on Zhang (2019). The economy produces three goods and services—final goods and two monopoly products. The final good sector

W.-B. Zhang, *The General Economic Theory*,
https://doi.org/10.1007/978-3-030-56204-5_12

produces capital good as in the basic model. All input factors are competitive. There are two monopolies, each producing a single homogenous product solely consumed by consumers. The two monopolies produce different products. Capital and labor are used as inputs in producing final goods and monopoly products. Monopolies may have positive profits. It is assumed that profits are equally shared among the homogenous households. The final good is chosen as numeraire.

12.1.1 The Production of Final Product

Output of the final good sector $F_i(t)$, capital input $K_i(t)$ and labor input $N_i(t)$ are related as follows:

$$F_i(t) = A_i K_i^{\alpha_i}(t) N_i^{\beta_i}(t), 0 < \alpha_i, \beta_i, \alpha_i + \beta_i = 1, \tag{12.1.1}$$

where A_i, α_i and β_i are parameters. Let $w(t)$ and $r(t)$ denote the wage rate and the interest rate. The marginal conditions for the sector are:

$$r_\delta(t) = \frac{\alpha_i F_i(t)}{K_i(t)}, \ w(t) = \frac{\beta_i F_i(t)}{N_i(t)}, \tag{12.1.2}$$

where $r_\delta(t) \equiv r(t) + \delta_k$.

12.1.2 Consumer Behaviors and Wealth Dynamics

Let $\bar{k}(t)$ stand for per household's wealth, $\bar{k}(t) = K(t)/\bar{N}$, where $K(t)$ is the total capital. I use $\pi_j(t)$ to stand for monopoly $j's$ profit. The disposable income of the representative household is:

$$\hat{y}(t) = R(t)\bar{k}(t) + hw(t) + \frac{\pi_1(t) + \pi_2(t)}{\bar{N}}, \tag{12.1.3}$$

where R$(t) \equiv 1 + r(t)$ and h is human capital. The representative household distributes the disposable income between consumption of monopoly product $c_j(t)$, consumption of final goods $c_i(t)$, and savings $s(t)$. I have the budget constraint as:

$$p_1(t)c_1(t) + p_2(t)c_2(t) + c_i(t) + s(t) = \hat{y}(t), \tag{12.1.4}$$

where $p_j(t)$ is the price of monopoly product j. Utility level $U(t)$ is dependent on $c_j(t)$, $c_i(t)$, and $s(t)$ as follows:

$$U(t) = \left(\xi_1 c_1^{\xi_0}(t) + \xi_2 c_2^{\xi_0}(t) + \xi_i c_i^{\xi_0}(t)\right)^{\frac{1}{\xi_0}} s^{\lambda_0}(t),$$
$$\xi_j, \xi_i, \xi_0, \lambda_0 > 0, \tag{12.1.5}$$

where λ_0 is called the propensity to save. The optimal problem is solved as follows (Zhang 2019):

$$s(t) = \frac{\lambda_0 \tilde{P}(t)\hat{y}(t)}{\bar{P}(t)+\lambda_0 \tilde{P}(t)}, \ c_i(t) = \frac{\hat{y}(t)}{\bar{P}(t)+\lambda_0 \tilde{P}(t)},$$
$$c_j(t) = \frac{P_j(t)\hat{y}(t)}{\bar{P}(t)+\lambda_0 \tilde{P}(t)}, \tag{12.1.6}$$

in which

$$\bar{P}(t) \equiv p_1(t)P_1(t) + p_2(t)P_2(t) + 1,$$
$$\tilde{P}(t) \equiv \bar{\xi}_1 P_1^{\xi_0}(t) + \bar{\xi}_2 P_2^{\xi_0}(t) + 1,$$
$$P_j(t) \equiv \bar{\xi}_j^{-\xi_4} p_j^{\xi_4}(t), \ \bar{\xi}_j \equiv \frac{\xi_j}{\xi_i}, \ \xi_4 \equiv \frac{1}{\xi_0 - 1}.$$

The behavior of the household is determined once $p_j(t)$ and $\hat{y}(t)$ are determined.

12.1.3 Wealth Accumulation

The change in the household's wealth follows:

$$\dot{\bar{k}}(t) = s(t) - \bar{k}(t) = \frac{\lambda_0 \tilde{P}(t)\hat{y}(t)}{\bar{P}(t) + \lambda_0 \tilde{P}(t)} - \bar{k}(t). \tag{12.1.7}$$

12.1.4 Equilibrium for Monopoly Product

I use $F_j(t)$ to stand for the output of monopoly j. I have:

$$c_j(t)\bar{N} = F_j(t), \ j = 1, 2. \tag{12.1.8}$$

12.1.5 The Behavior of the Monopolies

The monopoly power implies that the price is determined by the single player, monopoly, in the market. I use $F_j(t)$, $K_j(t)$ and $N_j(t)$ to represent, respectively, the output of monopoly j, its capital input and labor input. I specify:

$$F_j(t) = A_j K_j^{\alpha_j}(t) N_j^{\beta_j}(t), 0 < \alpha_j, \beta_j < 1. \tag{12.1.9}$$

The profit of monopoly j is:

$$\pi_j(t) = p_j(t) F_j(t) - r_\delta(t) K_j(t) - w(t) N_j(t). \tag{12.1.10}$$

From (12.1.8) and (12.1.6), I have:

$$F_j(t) = c_j(t)\bar{N} = \frac{P_j(t)\hat{y}(t)\bar{N}}{\bar{P}(t) + \lambda_0 \tilde{P}(t)}. \tag{12.1.11}$$

From (12.1.3) and (12.1.10), I have:

$$\hat{y}(t) = \tilde{y}(t) + \frac{p_1(t)F_1(t) + p_2(t)F_2(t)}{\bar{N}}, \tag{12.1.12}$$

where

$$\tilde{y}(t) = R(t)\bar{k}(t) + hw(t) - \frac{r_\delta(t)(K_1(t)+K_2(t)) + w(t)(N_1(t)+N_2(t))}{\bar{N}}.$$

From (12.1.11) and (12.1.12), I have:

$$F_j(t) = \frac{P_j(t)\big(\tilde{y}(t)\bar{N} + p_1(t)F_1(t) + p_2(t)F_2(t)\big)}{\bar{P}(t) + \lambda_0 \tilde{P}(t)}. \tag{12.1.13}$$

From (12.1.13), I have:

$$\frac{F_1(t)}{F_2(t)} = \frac{P_1(t)}{P_2(t)}.$$

That is

$$\frac{p_1(t)}{p_2(t)} = f(F_1(t), F_2(t)) \equiv \xi \left(\frac{F_1(t)}{F_2(t)}\right)^{\frac{1}{\xi_4}}, \xi \equiv \frac{\xi_1}{\xi_2}. \tag{12.1.14}$$

From (12.1.13) and (12.1.14), I solve variables $p_j(t)$ as functions of $F_j(t)$ and $\tilde{y}(t)$. Suppose that these solutions are expressed as: $p_j = G_j(F_1, F_2, \tilde{y})$. The profit is given by:

$$\pi_j(t) = G_j(F_1(t), F_2(t), \tilde{y}(t)) F_j(t) - r_\delta(t) K_j(t) - w(t) N_j(t). \tag{12.1.15}$$

Monopoly j Maximizes the profit with capital and labor as the choice variables. I have the marginal conditions:

$$\frac{\partial \pi_j}{\partial K_j} = \left(F_j \frac{\partial G_j}{\partial F_j} + G_j\right)\frac{\alpha_j F_j}{K_j} - \left(1 + \frac{F_j}{\bar{N}}\frac{\partial G_j}{\partial \tilde{y}}\right) r_\delta = 0,$$
$$\frac{\partial \pi_j}{\partial N_j} = \left(F_j \frac{\partial G_j}{\partial F_j} + G_j\right)\frac{\beta_j F_j}{N_j} - \left(1 + \frac{F_j}{\bar{N}}\frac{\partial G_j}{\partial \tilde{y}}\right) w = 0, \quad (12.1.16)$$

in which I omit time in the expressions. By these equations, each monopoly determines the labor and capital inputs as functions of the wage rate, the interest rate and wealth. The price and output and of monopoly product are then determined separately by (12.1.9) and (12.1.16). The monopoly's profit is given by (12.1.15).

12.1.6 Demand and Supply and Full Employment

$$\dot{K}(t) = F_i(t) - c_i(t)\bar{N} - \delta_k K(t),$$
$$N_i(t) + N_1(t) + N_2(t) = h\bar{N},$$
$$K_i(t) + K_1(t) + K_2(t) = \bar{k}(t)\bar{N}. \quad (12.1.17)$$

I thus completed the model. The following lemma is proved in Zhang (2019).

Lemma 12.1.1 *The dynamics of the economic system is given by following differential equation*:

$$\dot{z}(t) = \bar{\varphi}(z(t)),$$

where $z(t) \equiv (r(t) + \delta_k)/w(t)$ and $\bar{\varphi}(z(t))$ is a function of $z(t)$. All the other variables are explicitly given as functions of $z(t)$.

The parameter values are specified as follows:

$$\bar{N} = 50, \xi_0 = 0.5, h = 4, A_i = 1, A_1 = 1.5, A_2 = 1.3, \alpha_i = 0.33,$$
$$\alpha_1 = 0.36, \alpha_2 = 0.35, \lambda_0 = 1, \xi_0 = 0.5, \xi_i = 0.6, \xi_1 = 0.2,$$
$$\xi_2 = 0.2, \delta_k = 0.03. \quad (12.1.18)$$

The simulation identifies an equilibrium point as follows:

$$Y = 219, K = 211.6, F_i = 189.6, F_1 = 12.5, F_2 = 8.98,$$
$$N_i = 186.6, N_1 = 8.19, N_2 = 6.79, K_i = 195.9, K_1 = 8.59,$$
$$K_2 = 7.13, \pi_1 = 7.59, \pi_2 = 6.58, r = 0.29, w = 0.69,$$
$$p_1 = 1.27, p_2 = 1.5, \hat{y} = 8.46, \bar{k} = 4.23, c_i = 4.63,$$
$$c_1 = 0.25, c_2 = 0.18, U = 7.49, \quad (12.1.19)$$

where the national income is $Y \equiv F_i + p_1 F_1 + p_2 F_2$. The final good sector has zero profit due to perfect competition, and the monopolies have positive profits.

12.2 Long-Term Growth with Changes in Monopoly Productivity and Preference

This section conducts comparative statics analysis with regards to some parameters.

12.2.1 A Monopoly's Total Factor Productivity Is Enhanced

Monopoly 1's total factor productivity is assumed to be enhanced as follows: $A_1 = 1.5$–1.6 The effects on the variables are listed in (12.2.1). The output of monopoly product 1 is increased. Monopoly 1 employs more capital and labor force. Monopoly 2's output is reduced. Monopoly 2 employs less labor force bur more capital. Monopoly 1 earns more profits, while monopoly 2 earns less profit. The final good sector produces less. It employs less work force but more capital. The economy has more income and physical capital. The wage rate becomes higher. The interest rate becomes lower. The consumer consumes more monopoly product 1, but less final goods and monopoly product 2. The prices of monopoly products become lower. The household has more wealth and disposable income. The utility is enhanced.

$$\begin{aligned}
&\bar{\Delta} Y = 0.34,\ \bar{\Delta} K = 0.32,\ \bar{\Delta} F_i = -0.12,\ \bar{\Delta} F_1 = 13,\ \bar{\Delta} F_2 = -0.14,\\
&\bar{\Delta} N_i = -0.22,\ \bar{\Delta} N_1 = 5.85,\ \bar{\Delta} N_2 = -0.24,\ \bar{\Delta} K_i = 0.08,\\
&\bar{\Delta} K_1 = 6.2,\ \bar{\Delta} K_2 = 0.05,\ \bar{\Delta} \pi_1 = 6.5,\ \bar{\Delta} \pi_2 = -0.15,\ \bar{\Delta} r = -0.22,\\
&\bar{\Delta} w = 0.1,\ \bar{\Delta} p_1 = -6,\ \bar{\Delta} p_2 = -0.01,\ \bar{\Delta} \hat{y} = 0.32,\ \bar{\Delta} \bar{k} = 0.32,\\
&\bar{\Delta} c_i = -0.16,\ \bar{\Delta} c_1 = 13,\ \bar{\Delta} c_2 = -0.14,\ \bar{\Delta} U = 1.13.
\end{aligned} \tag{12.2.1}$$

12.2.2 The Share Parameter of a Monopoly Product Is Increased

The share of monopoly product 1 is assumed to be enhanced as follows: $\xi_1 = 0.2 - 0.22$. The effects on the variables are listed in (12.2.2). Monopoly 1 produces more and employs more capital and labor force. Monopoly 2 produces less. It employs less labor force but more capital. Monopoly 1 earn more profits, while monopoly 2 earns less profit. The final good sector produces less. It employs less work force but more capital. The economy has higher income and more physical capital. The wage rate becomes higher. The interest rate becomes lower. The consumer consumes more monopoly product 1, but less final goods and monopoly product 1. The price of monopoly product 1 is increased, while the price of monopoly product 2 is reduced. The utility is enhanced. The household has more wealth and disposable income. As far as the directions of change are concerned, the rise in the share parameter has similar effects on the economic system as the rise in the total productivity factor, except the effects on the price.

$$\begin{aligned}
&\bar{\Delta} Y = 1.1,\ \bar{\Delta} K = 1,\ \bar{\Delta} F_i = -0.37,\ \bar{\Delta} F_1 = 18.5,\ \bar{\Delta} F_2 = -0.4,\\
&\bar{\Delta} N_i = -0.7,\ \bar{\Delta} N_1 = 18.1,\ \bar{\Delta} N_2 = -0.75,\ \bar{\Delta} K_i = 0.24,\\
&\bar{\Delta} K_1 = 19.2,\ \bar{\Delta} K_2 = 0.17,\ \bar{\Delta} \pi_1 = 20.5,\ \bar{\Delta} \pi_2 = -0.47,\ \bar{\Delta} r = -0.7,\\
&\bar{\Delta} w = 0.3,\ \bar{\Delta} p_1 = 0.8,\ \bar{\Delta} p_2 = -0.03,\ \bar{\Delta} \hat{y} = 1,\ \bar{\Delta} \bar{k} = 1,\\
&\bar{\Delta} c_i = -0.5,\ \bar{\Delta} c_1 = 18.5,\ \bar{\Delta} c_2 = -0.43,\ \bar{\Delta} U = 3.6. \qquad (12.2.2)
\end{aligned}$$

12.2.3 The Share Parameter of Final Goods Is Increased

I now examine what happen to the economic system if the share of final goods is increased in the following way:$\xi_i = 0.6 - 0.61$. The effects on the variables are listed in (12.2.3). The final good sector produces more and employs more capital and labor force. The two monopolies produce more. They employ less capital and labor force. They earn less profits. The economy has less income and less physical capital. The wage rate becomes lower. The interest rate is enhanced. The consumer consumes less monopoly products and more final goods. The prices of monopoly products are decreased. The household has less wealth and disposable income. The utility is enhanced.

$$\begin{aligned}
&\bar{\Delta} Y = -0.31,\ \bar{\Delta} K = -0.29,\ \bar{\Delta} F_i = 0.11,\ \bar{\Delta} F_1 = -2.88,\\
&\bar{\Delta} F_2 = -2.9,\ \bar{\Delta} N_i = 0.2,\ \bar{\Delta} N_1 = -2.8,\ \bar{\Delta} N_2 = -2.8,\ \bar{\Delta} K_i = -0.1,\\
&\bar{\Delta} K_1 = -3.1,\ \bar{\Delta} K_2 = -3.1,\ \bar{\Delta} \pi_1 = -3.1,\ \bar{\Delta} \pi_2 = -3.1,\ \bar{\Delta} r = 0.2,\\
&\bar{\Delta} w = -0.1,\ \bar{\Delta} p_1 = -0.12,\ \bar{\Delta} p_2 = -0.1,\ \bar{\Delta} \hat{y} = -0.29,\ \bar{\Delta} \bar{k} = -0.29,\\
&\bar{\Delta} c_i = 0.14,\ \bar{\Delta} c_1 = -2.9,\ \bar{\Delta} c_2 = -2.9,\ \bar{\Delta} U = 2.3. \qquad (12.2.3)
\end{aligned}$$

12.2.4 A Monopoly's Output Elasticity of Labor Is Enhanced

Monopoly 1's product elasticities of capital and labor are assumed to be changed, respectively, as follows $\alpha_1 = 0.37 - 0.36$ and $\beta_1 = 0.63$ to 0.64. The effects on the variables are listed in (12.2.4). Monopoly 1 produces more and employs more capital and labor force. Monopoly 2 produces less and employs less labor force and capital. Monopoly 1 earns more profits, while monopoly 2 earns less profit. The final good sector produces less. It employs less work force and capital. The economy has more income and physical capital. The wage rate becomes lower. The interest rate becomes higher. The consumer consumes more monopoly product 1, but less final goods and monopoly product 2. The prices of monopoly products are reduced. The household has more wealth and disposable income. The utility is enhanced.

$$\begin{aligned}
&\bar{\Delta} Y = 0.16,\ \bar{\Delta} K = 0.07,\ \bar{\Delta} F_i = -0.2,\ \bar{\Delta} F_1 = 9.7,\ \bar{\Delta} F_2 = -0.3,\\
&\bar{\Delta} N_i = -0.2,\ \bar{\Delta} N_1 = 7.3,\ \bar{\Delta} N_2 = -0.3,\ \bar{\Delta} K_i = -0.23,\\
&\bar{\Delta} K_1 = 7.2,\ \bar{\Delta} K_2 = -0.34,\ \bar{\Delta} \pi_1 = 1.6,\ \bar{\Delta} \pi_2 = -0.3,\ \bar{\Delta} r = 0.05,\\
&\bar{\Delta} w = -0.02,\ \bar{\Delta} p_1 = -4.7,\ \bar{\Delta} p_2 = -0.002,\ \bar{\Delta} \hat{y} = 0.07,\\
&\bar{\Delta} \bar{k} = 0.07,\ \bar{\Delta} c_i = -0.3,\ \bar{\Delta} c_1 = 9.7,\ \bar{\Delta} c_2 = -0.3,\ \bar{\Delta} U = 0.5. \qquad (12.2.4)
\end{aligned}$$

I analyze the effects of some other parameters (Zhang 2019).

12.3 Growth with Monopsony Against Woman in Labor Market

The previous section introduced monopoly into the basic model. This section is concerned with introducing monopsony into the basic model. Monopsony implies a market in which there is a single purchaser. Labor market monopsony exists when firms can exercise powers over their suppliers of labor. Explanation of gender discrimination against woman with monopsony was initiated by Joan Robinson in *The Economics of Imperfect Competition* published in 1933 (Robinson 1933). Monopsony theory is applied to different issues in different markets. As far as I am aware, the model to be introduced is the first application of monopsony theory to discrimination against woman in neoclassical growth theory with capital accumulation and gender division of labor. This section is based on (Zhang 2019a), which contributes to growth theory by studying interdependence between economic growth and market structure with gender division of labor. It makes a unique contribution to modeling mechanisms of economic growth by integrating neoclassical growth theory and monopsony theory within a comprehensive analytical framework. I attempt to integrate theory of discrimination against woman due to monopsony in labor market with neoclassical growth theory within a general equilibrium framework.

The population is classified into man and woman. Family is composed of husband and wife. Each gender has population $\bar{N}$. An aggregated utility function for family is applied to describe household behavior. Woman is subject to discrimination in labor market due to monopsony. Labor market for man is perfectly competitive, while for woman is monopsony. Let subscript $j = 1$ and $j = 2$ denote, respectively, man and woman. Assets of the economy are owned by the families. Saving is done solely by the families. Input factors are fully employed. The wage rate of worker of gender j and interest rate are represented by $w_j(t)$ and $r(t)$, respectively. The total capital stock of the economy is $K(t)$. The sum of the labor supply of man and woman population is the total labor supply $N(t)$:

$$N(t) = h_1 T_1(t)\bar{N} + h_2 T_2(t)\bar{N}, \tag{12.3.1}$$

where $T_j(t)$ stands for the work time of gender j and h_j stands for the fixed human capital of gender j.

12.3.1 Utility, Disposable Income, Budget, and Optimal Behavior

Let $\bar{k}(t)$ stand for the wealth owned by the family, $\bar{k}(t) = K(t)/\bar{N}$. The total profit of the production sector $\pi(t)$ is distributed equally between the families. Each family's share of the profit is $\pi(t)/\bar{N}$. The family's current income is the sum of the interest payment $r(t)\bar{k}(t)$, the profit share $\pi(t)/\bar{N}$, and the wage incomes $h_j T_j(t) w_j(t)$ as:

$$\hat{y}(t) = \bar{k}(t) + r(t)\bar{k}(t) + h_1 T_1(t) w_1(t) + h_2 T_2(t) w_2(t) + \frac{\pi(t)}{\bar{N}}. \tag{12.3.2}$$

The budget constraint is:

$$\begin{aligned} c(t) + s(t) &= \hat{y}(t) \\ &= (1 + r(t))\bar{k}(t) + h_1 T_1(t) w_1(t) + h_2 T_2(t) w_2(t) + \frac{\pi(t)}{\bar{N}}, \end{aligned} \tag{12.3.3}$$

where $s(t)$ is saving and $c(t)$ is consumption, and I use (12.3.2). Let T_0 stand for the total available time of each person and $\bar{T}_j(t)$ for the leisure time of gender j. I have:

$$T_j(t) + \bar{T}_j(t) = T_0. \tag{12.3.4}$$

Inserting (12.3.3) in (12.3.4), I have:

$$\begin{aligned} h_1 \bar{T}_1(t) w_1(t) + h_2 \bar{T}_2(t) w_2(t) + c(t) + s(t) &= \bar{y}(t) \\ \equiv R(t) + \tfrac{\pi(t)}{\bar{N}} + h_2 T_0 w_2(t), \end{aligned} \tag{12.3.5}$$

in which

$$R(t) \equiv (1 + r(t))\bar{k}(t) + h_1 T_0 w_1(t).$$

The family's utility function $U(t)$ is related to the members' leisure hours $\bar{T}_j(t)$, the family's consumption of goods $c(t)$, and the family's saving $s(t)$ as follows:

$$U(t) = \bar{T}_1^{\sigma_{10}}(t)\bar{T}_2^{\sigma_{20}}(t)c^{\xi_0}(t)s^{\lambda_0}(t), \sigma_{j0}, \xi_0, \lambda_0 > 0,$$

where σ_{j0} is gender j's propensity to use leisure time, ξ_0 is the family's propensity to consume goods, and λ_0 is the family's propensity to save. Maximizing the utility subject to (12.3.5) yields the marginal conditions:

$$h_j\bar{T}_j(t)w_j(t) = \sigma_j\bar{y}(t), c(t) = \xi\bar{y}(t), s(t) = \lambda\bar{y}(t), \tag{12.3.6}$$

where

$$\sigma_j \equiv \sigma_{j0}\rho, \xi \equiv \xi_0\rho, \lambda \equiv \lambda_0\rho, \rho \equiv \frac{1}{\sigma_{10} + \sigma_{20} + \xi_0 + \lambda_0}.$$

12.3.2 Wealth Accumulation

The change in the family's wealth follows:

$$\dot{\bar{k}}(t) = s(t) - \bar{k}(t). \tag{12.3.7}$$

12.3.3 Production Sector

The production function $F(t)$ is:

$$F(t) = AK^{\alpha}(t)N^{\beta}(t), \alpha, \beta > 0, \alpha + \beta = 1. \tag{12.3.8}$$

Perfect competition in labor market for man implies that $w_1(t)$ is given for each firm in the industry. Each firm takes man's wage as given and decides woman's wage rate. From (12.3.6) and (12.3.5), I have:

$$w_2(t) = \frac{\sigma_2\big(R(t) + \pi(t)/\bar{N}\big)}{(\tilde{\sigma} - T_2(t))h_2}, \tag{12.3.9}$$

where $\tilde{\sigma} \equiv (1 - \sigma_2)T_0$. The profit is:

$$\begin{aligned}\pi(t) = F(t) - R_\delta(t)K(t) - w_1(t)h_1T_1(t)\bar{N} \\ -w_2(t)h_2T_2(t)\bar{N},\end{aligned} \tag{12.3.10}$$

where $R_\delta(t) \equiv r(t) + \delta_k$. It is straightforward to give the profit:

$$\pi(t) = \left(F(t) - R_\delta(t)K(t) - w_1(t)h_1T_1(t)\bar{N}\right)\hat{T}(t) - \frac{\bar{\sigma}T_2(t)R(t)}{T_0 - T_2(t)}, \tag{12.3.11}$$

where

$$\bar{\sigma} \equiv \frac{\sigma_2\bar{N}}{1-\sigma_2}, \ \hat{T}(t) \equiv \frac{\tilde{\sigma} - T_2(t)}{(T_0 - T_2(t))(1-\sigma_2)}.$$

I express the first-order conditions for maximizing the profit as follows:

$$\begin{gathered} \frac{\partial\pi(t)}{\partial K(t)} = \frac{\alpha F(t)}{K(t)} - R_\delta(t) = 0, \\ \frac{\partial\pi(t)}{\partial T_1(t)} = \frac{\beta h_1\bar{N}F(t)\hat{T}(t)}{N(t)} - w_1(t)h_1\bar{N}\hat{T}(t) = 0, \\ \frac{\partial\pi(t)}{\partial T_2(t)} = \frac{\beta h_2\bar{N}F(t)\hat{T}(t)}{N(t)} - \frac{\bar{\sigma}T_0R(t)}{(T_0-T_2(t))^2} - \\ \frac{\left(F(t)-R_\delta(t)K(t)-w_1(t)h_1T_1(t)\bar{N}\right)\sigma_2T_0}{(1-\sigma_2)(T_0-T_2(t))^2} = 0. \end{gathered} \tag{12.3.12}$$

It can be shown that the profit satisfying the first-order conditions is positive:

$$\pi(t) = w_1(t)h_2T_2(t)\bar{N}\hat{T}(t) - \frac{\bar{\sigma}T_2(t)R(t)}{T_0 - T_2(t)} > 0. \tag{12.3.13}$$

12.3.4 Demand and Supply Balance

$$c(t)\bar{N} + s(t)\bar{N} - K(t) + \delta_k K(t) = F(t), \ K(t) = \bar{k}(t)\bar{N}.$$

12.3.5 Equilibrium and Comparative Statics Analysis

Because of analytical difficulty, this section is concerned with equilibrium as given in Zhang (2019). To simulate the model, the parameters are taken on the following values:

$$\begin{gathered} A = 1.3, \alpha = 0.34, \bar{N} = 50, h_1 = 1.4, h_2 = 1.3, T_0 = 24, \\ \delta_k = 0.05, \lambda_0 = 0.8, \xi_0 = 0.12, \sigma_{10} = 0.2, \sigma_{20} = 0.21. \end{gathered} \tag{12.3.14}$$

Under (12.3.14), the system has an equilibrium point given as follows:

$$F = 2152.4, K = 10761.8, N = 631.3, r = 0.018, \pi = 36.9,$$
$$w_1 = 2.25, w_2 = 2, W_1 = 21.8, W_2 = 5.87, \bar{k} = 215.2, \quad (12.3.15)$$
$$c = 32.3, T_1 = 6.92, T_2 = 2.26,$$

in which $W_j \equiv w_j h_j T_j$ is gender j's total wage income brought to the family. The profit is positive due to monopsony. Woman's wage rate is lower than man's wage rate. The monopsony in female labor market reduces woman's wage rate.

12.4 Long-Term Equilibrium with Woman's Characters

This section examines effects of changes in some parameters on the long-term equilibrium point in the economy with monopsony against woman.

12.4.1 Woman's Human Capital Is Enhanced

Woman's human capital is assumed to be enhanced as follows: h_2: $1.3 \Rightarrow 1.35$. The effects on the variables are listed in (12.4.1). The change rates are with regards to the equilibrium values in (12.3.15). The wife spends more hours in labor market and brings more wage income to the family. The profit of the sector is augmented. The husband spends more time at home and earns less income. The family has more wealth and consumes more. The interest rate is not affected. The national income, national capital, and national labor supply are increased. I conclude that a rise in an improvement of woman's human capital increases firms' profits and enables men to spend more time at home when woman labor market is characterized of monopsony.

$$\bar{\Delta} F = 1.23, \bar{\Delta} K = 1.23, \bar{\Delta} N = 1.23, \bar{\Delta} r = 0, \bar{\Delta} \pi = 28,$$
$$\bar{\Delta} w_1 = 0, \bar{\Delta} w_2 = -1.39, \bar{\Delta} W_1 = -3.04, \bar{\Delta} W_2 = 13.7, \quad (12.4.1)$$
$$\bar{\Delta} \bar{k} = 1.23, \bar{\Delta} c = 1.23, \bar{\Delta} T_1 = -3, \bar{\Delta} T_2 = 11.$$

12.4.2 Woman's Propensity to Use Leisure Time Is Increased

I now study what happen to the economic system when woman's propensity to stay at home is enhanced as follows: σ_{20}: $0.21 \Rightarrow 0.22$. The effects on the variables are listed in (12.4.2). The wife spends more hours on leisure at home and brings less wage income to the family. The husband works more hours and brings more wage income to home. The profit of the industry is reduced. The family has less wealth and consumes less. The interest rate is not affected. The national income, national capital, and national labor supply are decreased. A rise in woman's propensity to stay at home reduces firms' profits and makes men to work more hours in labor market.

$$\begin{gathered}\bar{\Delta}F = \bar{\Delta}K = \bar{\Delta}N = -1.2,\ \bar{\Delta}r = 0,\ \bar{\Delta}\pi = -27.8,\ \bar{\Delta}w_1 = 0,\\ \bar{\Delta}w_2 = 1.85,\ \bar{\Delta}W_1 = 3.04,\ \bar{\Delta}W_2 = -13.8,\ \bar{\Delta}\bar{k} = \bar{\Delta}c = -1.23,\\ \bar{\Delta}T_1 = 3.04,\ \bar{\Delta}T_2 = -15.3.\end{gathered} \quad (12.4.2)$$

I also analyzed the effects of changes in other parameters, h_1, A, λ_0, σ_{10}, and $\bar{N}$ (Zhang 2019a). As the profit is not equal to zero, the comparative statics analyses give results different results from the case of perfect competition in all markets.

12.5 Monopsony Against Woman Harms National Economic Performances

This section compares the long-term economic equilibrium in the model with monopsony and the model with perfect competition. When the system is perfectly competitive, firms take price as given and equilibrium condition of demand supply determine price. In this case, woman's wage rate is determined by perfectly competition. Each firm takes woman's wage rate as given. A main difference is that profit is zero in perfect competition. I provide a computational program is for calculating equilibrium values of the competitive model. I compare the economic performances of the two market structures under the same technology, human capital, and preferences as given in (12.3.14). I have the comparative results with regards to (12.3.15) as follows:

$$\begin{gathered}\tilde{\Delta}F = \tilde{\Delta}K = \tilde{\Delta}N = -5.1,\ \tilde{\Delta}r = \tilde{\Delta}w_1 = 0,\ \tilde{\Delta}w_2 = -12.6,\\ \tilde{\Delta}W_1 = 12.6,\ \tilde{\Delta}W_2 = -84.4,\ \tilde{\Delta}\bar{k} = \tilde{\Delta}c = -5.1,\ \tilde{\Delta}T_1 = 12.6,\\ \tilde{\Delta}T_2 = -63.8,\ \tilde{\Delta}U = -4.3,\end{gathered}$$

in which

$$\tilde{\Delta}x \equiv \frac{\text{the value of} \times \text{in monopsony} - \text{the value of } \times \text{in perfect competion}}{\text{the value of} \times \text{in monopsony}}.$$

In the case of perfect competition, the profit is zero. It is concluded that the national output, national capital (and thus family's wealth), and national labor supply are lower in the economy with monopsony than in the economy with perfect competition. This implies that monopsony reduces macroeconomic performances. The interest rate and man's wage rate are the same in the two systems. Woman's wage rate is lower in the economy with monopsony. As they have monopsony in labor market for woman, firms can set woman's wage rate to maximize profit without constraints of perfect competition. On the other hand, as shown in Eq. (12.3.9), firms are faced with an upward-sloping labor supply curve (rather than an infinitely elastic labor supply curve as in the case perfect competition). From standard monopsony theory, I also know that the marginal cost is higher than the current wage rate in labor market for woman. This occurs as all women receive the same wage rate and an extra worker makes firms to raise the wage paid to all the workers already employed. As my simulation demonstrated, woman's wage rate in monopsony is lower than woman's wage rate in perfect competition. If the market for woman was perfectly competitive, a firm would enter the market and pay a lower wage rate than one in monopsony but higher than or equal to the wage rate in perfect competition so that the firm would get positive profit. Free entry in perfect competition leads to the wage rate where no firm gets positive profit. Monopoly guarantees that the firms can set the wage rate at a level lower than would be in a perfectly competitive market.

I see that man brings more wage income and woman brings less wage income in the economy with monopsony than in the economy with perfect competition. Man works more hours and woman works fewer hours in the economy with monopsony than with perfect competition. The monopsony reduces the family's wealth and consumption. The family has lower utility level in the economy with monopsony than with perfect competition. I see that monopsony harms the microeconomic performances. It should be noted that Stotsky (2006) identifies a number of phenomena related to gender differences and economic behavior: (1) gender-based differences can influence macroeconomic variables, such as aggregate consumption, savings; (2) women tend to devote a larger share of household resources to the households' basic needs; (3) women tend to have a higher propensity to save; (5) women's lack of education and other economic and social opportunities, both absolutely and relative to men, inhibits economic growth. The comparison of the two systems in this section provides some insights into economic mechanisms of the empirical results.

12.6 Cournot-Nash Family Decision in an Extended Solowian Model

A kiss is a lovely trick designed by nature to stop speech when words become superfluous.

Ingrid Bergman

In his AEA Presidential Address, Becker (1988) addressed the significance of family economics for macroeconomics. Since then, there is a sizeable amount of publications on the topic. Many important decisions, for instance, on consumption, labor supply, savings, number of children, and education, are made within families. These decisions are essential determinants of the creation and allocation of human as well as physical capital, labor force, and economic structure. Becker (1965) published his seminal work on economic rationality in the allocation of time and gender issues in a formal and rigorous theory. Since then, there are many studies on various issues of family and gender (Chiappori 1992; Gomme et al. 2001; Campbell and Ludvigson 2001; and Vendrik 2003). On the other hand, most of these studies are concentrated on microeconomics. As emphasized by Doepke and Tertilt (2016: 1791), "typical macroeconomic models ignore the family and instead build on representative agent modelling that abstracts from the presence of multiple family members, who may have conflicting interests, who might make separate decisions, and may split up and form new households."

This section is based on Zhang (2020). It deals with behavior of a two-person family in a non-cooperative or Cournot-Nash framework (Chen and Woolley 2001). Cournot game is a mathematically well-examined in game theory and economically widely applied in microeconomics. Cournot (1801–1877) developed Cournot competition theory in his 1838 volume *Recherches sur less Principles Mathematiques de la Theorie des Richesses* when he studied the competition with a market dominated a duopoly. The best response function is defined for each firm for given exogenous output level of the other firm. An equilibrium point is determined at intersection point of the best response functions. This equilibrium is now called a Nash equilibrium in game theory.

The economy is composed of two homogenous populations, man and woman, with the same number $\bar{N}$. Man and woman form a family. All the markets are perfectly competitive. I use subscript $j = 1$ and $j = 2$ to describe, man and woman, respectively. Most aspects of the model are the same as the basic model in this book. The wage rate of spouse j $w_j(t)$ and interest rate $r(t)$ are determined by free markets. I use h_j to stand for a constant level of gender j's human capital. As there is no discrimination, I have $w_j(t) = h_j w(t)$, where $w(t)$ is the wage rate. The total labor supply N is given by:

$$N = h_1 \bar{N} + h_2 \bar{N}.$$

12.6.1 The Disposable Income and Optimal Behavior

I consider that man and woman live together and form a family. Each maximizes his or her utility. As a member of the union, they will care each other. They have a family (public) goods, their own consumption goods and wealth. They make decisions interdependently. Each spouse's utility is dependent not only his/her own consumption and wealth, but also the partner's and utility. Cournot-Nash approach implies that each player maximizes his/her utility with the other's behavior as given. I use $\bar{k}_j(t)$ to stand for the wealth held by spouse j. The family members have the following disposable incomes:

$$\hat{y}_j(t) = R(t)\bar{k}_j(t) + h_j w(t),\ j = 1, 2, \tag{12.6.1}$$

where $r(t)\bar{k}_j(t)$ and $h_j w(t)$ are spouse j's incomes from interest payment and wage, and where $R(t) \equiv 1 + r(t)$.

12.6.2 Utility Functions and Budgets

Gender j's well-being is given by an egocentric utility function $U_j(t)$ which is dependent on gender j's private consumption $c_j(t)$, contribution to the family saving $s_j(t)$, and family good $\bar{c}(t)$ as follows:

$$U_j(t) = c_j^{\xi_{j0}}(t)\bar{c}^{\gamma_{j0}}(t)s_j^{\lambda_{j0}}(t), \xi_{j0}, \gamma_{j0}, \lambda_{j0} > 0,$$

where ξ_{j0} is gender j's propensity to consume private goods, γ_{j0} is propensity to consume family goods, and λ_{0j} is propensity to make contribution to the family's savings. Household good is characterized by being non-rival. Husband and wife's egocentric utility functions are different. Suppose that each spouse cares the other's well-being. Spouse j's utility function is specified by:

$$\tilde{U}_j(t) = U_j(t)U_i^{\varepsilon_j}(t), \ \varepsilon_j \ge 0, i \ne j, \tag{12.6.2}$$

where ε_j is a parameter measuring how strongly spouse j cares about the other. When each spouse cares the other's utility rather than consumption levels, the preference is termed caring preferences.

Family goods is bought by the couple:

$$\bar{c}(t) = \bar{c}_1(t) + \bar{c}_2(t). \tag{12.6.3}$$

where $\bar{c}_j(t)$ is spouse j's contribution to family goods. Spouse j spends the disposable income on consuming private goods, paying family goods, and making savings. The budget is formed as:

$$c_j(t) + \bar{c}_j(t) + s_j(t) = \hat{y}_j(t). \tag{12.6.4}$$

Spouse j maximizes the utility function under (12.6.4). As shown in Zhang (2020), the optimal problem is as follows:

$$\bar{c} = \bar{\gamma}\hat{y}, c_j = \frac{\xi_{j0}\bar{\gamma}\hat{y}}{\bar{\gamma}_j}, s_j = \frac{\lambda_{j0}\bar{\gamma}\hat{y}}{\bar{\gamma}_j}, \bar{c}_j = \hat{y}_j - \left(\xi_{j0} + \lambda_{j0}\right)\frac{\bar{\gamma}\hat{y}}{\bar{\gamma}_j}, \tag{12.6.5}$$

where I omit time index and

$$\hat{y}(t) = \hat{y}_1(t) + \hat{y}_2(t),$$
$$\bar{\gamma}_j \equiv \gamma_{j0} + \varepsilon_j\gamma_{i0}, i \ne j, \bar{\gamma} \equiv \left(\frac{\xi_{10}+\lambda_{10}}{\bar{\gamma}_1} + \frac{\xi_{20}+\lambda_{20}}{\bar{\gamma}_2} + 1\right)^{-1}.$$

From (12.6.5) and (12.6.1), for $\bar{c}_1(t)$ and $\bar{c}_2(t)$ to be positive, the following requirements should be satisfied:

$$\left(\frac{\xi_{10}+\lambda_{10}}{\bar{\gamma}_1}+1\right)\left(\frac{\xi_{20}+\lambda_{20}}{\bar{\gamma}_2}\right)^{-1} > \frac{\hat{y}_1(t)}{\hat{y}_2(t)}$$
$$> \left(\frac{\xi_{10}+\lambda_{10}}{\bar{\gamma}_1}\right)\left(\frac{\xi_{20}+\lambda_{20}}{\bar{\gamma}_2}+1\right)^{-1}.$$

This implies that if the disposable income gap between the couple is too large, one spouse will not spend his/her disposable income on family goods.

The change in spouse j's wealth follows:

$$\dot{\bar{k}}_j(t) = s_j(t) - \bar{k}_j(t).$$

12.6.3 The Production Sector

The production function $F(t)$ is as follows:

$$F(t) = AK^{\alpha}(t)N^{\beta}, \alpha, \beta > 0, \alpha + \beta = 1.$$

The marginal conditions are:

$$r(t) + \delta_k = \frac{\alpha F(t)}{K(t)}, w(t) = \frac{\beta F(t)}{N}.$$

12.6.4 Equilibrium Conditions

The equilibrium condition that the output of the production sector is equal to the depreciation of capital stock and the net savings is expressed as:

$$C(t) + S(t) - K(t) + \delta_k K(t) = F(t),$$

in which

$$S(t) = s_1(t)\bar{N} + s_2(t)\bar{N}, C(t) = c_1(t)\bar{N} + c_2(t)\bar{N}.$$

The total family wealth is equal to national wealth:

$$K(t) = \bar{k}_1(t)\bar{N} + \bar{k}_2(t)\bar{N}.$$

The model is completed. As shown in Zhang (2020), the movement of the economic system is given by two differential equations:

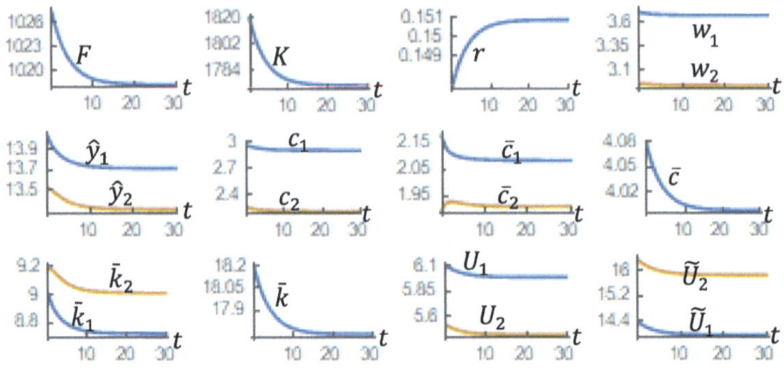

Fig. 12.1 Movement of the family-based economy

$$\dot{\bar{k}}_j(t) = s_j\left(\bar{k}_j(t)\right) - \bar{k}_j(t),\ j = 1, 2. \tag{12.6.6}$$

Once (12.6.6) is solved, all the other variables are given as unique functions of the solution. The parameter values are specified as follows:

$$A = 1.4, \alpha = 0.35, \bar{N} = 100, h_1 = 2.5, h_2 = 2, \delta_k = 0.05,$$
$$\lambda_{10} = 0.6, \gamma_{10} = 0.2, \xi_{10} = 0.2, \lambda_{20} = 0.62, \gamma_{20} = 0.15,$$
$$\xi_{20} = 0.15.$$

The initial conditions are chosen as:

$$k_1(0) = 9, k_2(0) = 9.2.$$

The movement of the economy is plotted in Fig. 12.1.

The system has an equilibrium point given as follows:

$$F = 1018.3, K = 1774, r = 0.151, w_1 = 3.68, w_2 = 2.94,$$
$$\hat{y}_1 = 13.7, \hat{y}_2 = 13.3, c_1 = 2.91, c_2 = 2.22, \bar{c}_1 = 2.09,$$
$$\bar{c}_2 = 1.91, \bar{c} = 4, \bar{k}_1 = 8.73, \bar{k}_2 = 9.02, \bar{k} = 17.74, U_1 = 5.99,$$
$$U_2 = 5.43, \tilde{U}_1 = 14, \tilde{U}_2 = 15.9.$$

At equilibrium, the husband has higher income than the wife; he consumes more consumption goods than she. The husband makes more contribution to family goods than the wife. The wife has more wealth than the husband. The husband has higher egocentric utility than the wife; but the wife has higher well-being than the husband as she derives much more pleasure from her husband than he from his wife. The two eigenvalues are -1 and -0.245. The equilibrium point is stable.

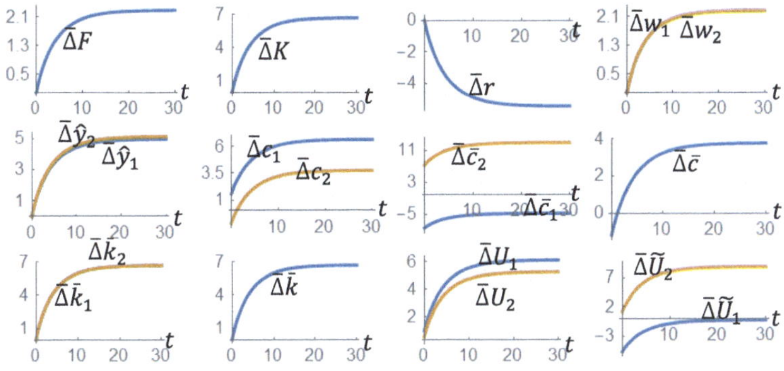

Fig. 12.2 Man derives less well-being from his wife's well-being

12.7 Dynamics of Cournot-Nash Family Decision with Exogenous Changes

This section conducts comparative dynamic analysis in some parameters.

12.7.1 The Husband Derives Less Well-Being from His Wife's Well-Being

The husband is assumed to derive less well-being from his wife's well-bring in the following way: $\varepsilon_1 : 0.5 \Rightarrow 0.45$. Figure 12.2 provides the simulation result. He spends less on family goods. The wife spends more on family goods. The family holds less family goods initially but has more in the long term. Each spouse has more wealth. The national output and capital are enhanced. The interest rate becomes lower. The wage incomes become higher. Each spouse has more disposable income and consumes more goods. Each spouse has higher egocentric utility level. The wife has higher utility, while the husband has lower utility.

12.7.2 The Wife's Human Capital Is Enhanced

The wife's human capital is assumed to be enhanced in the following way: h_2: $2 \Rightarrow 2.1$. Figure 12.3 provides the simulation result. The wife's wage is enhanced, while the husband's wage income is almost invariant. The wife spends more on family goods, while the husband spends less on family goods. The total consumption of family goods is enhanced. The interest rate rises initially and changes slightly in the

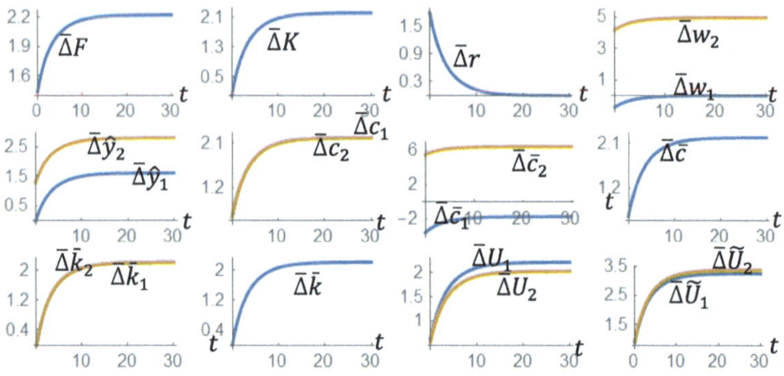

Fig. 12.3 Wife's human capital is enhanced

long term. The national output and national capital are increased. Each spouse spends on consumption goods and has more wealth. All the utility levels are enhanced.

12.7.3 The Wife Increases Her Propensity to Save

The wife's human capital is assumed to be enhanced in the following way: λ_{20}: $0.62 \Rightarrow 0.64$. Figure 12.4 provides the simulation result. The wife has more wealth. The husband owns less wealth initially but more in the long term. The interest rate falls. The wife spends less on family goods initially but more in the long term. The husband spends more on family goods initially but less in the long term. The total consumption of family goods falls initially but rises in the long term. The utility levels are enhanced.

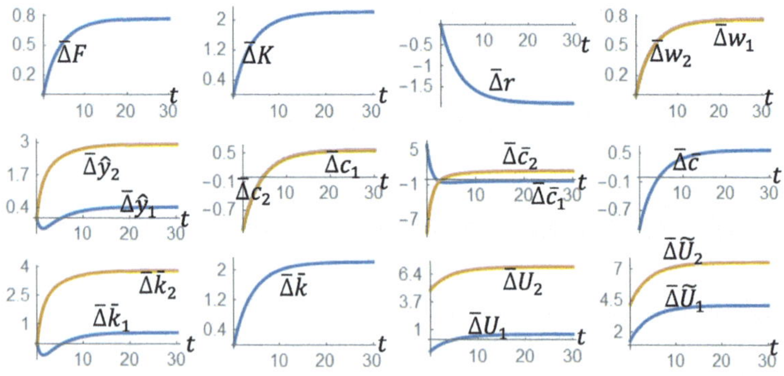

Fig. 12.4 Wife increases her propensity to save

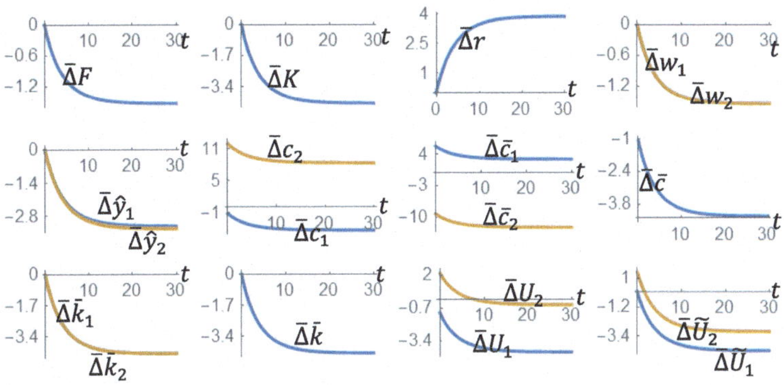

Fig. 12.5 Wife increases her propensity to consume consumption goods

12.7.4 *The Wife Increases Her Propensity to Consume Consumption Goods*

The wife is assumed to increase her propensity to consume consumption goods in the following way: ξ_{20}: $0.15 \Rightarrow 0.17$. Figure 12.5 provides the simulation result. The wife spends more on consumption goods and less on family goods. Her disposable income and wealth fall. The husband spends less on consumption goods and more on family goods. His disposable income and wealth fall. The economy produces less and has less capital stock. In the long term, all the utility levels are reduced.

12.7.5 *The Wife Increases Her Propensity to Consume Family Goods*

The wife is assumed to increase her propensity to consume family goods in the following way: γ_{20}: $0.15 \Rightarrow 0.17$. Figure 12.6 provides the simulation result. The wife purchases more family goods, while the husband purchases less. The total consumption of family goods is augmented. The wife spends less consumption goods initially but slightly increases in the long term. The husband spends more on consumption goods. The economy has more wealth and capital stock. The interest rate becomes lower. The wage incomes are increased. The wealth levels of spouses are enhanced. All the utility levels are reduced.

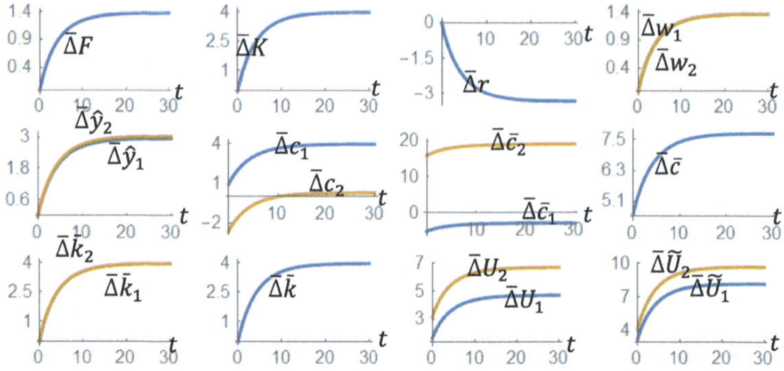

Fig. 12.6 Wife increases her propensity to consume family goods

12.7.6 The Total Factor Productivity Is Enhanced

The total factor productivity is assumed to be enhanced in the following way: A: $1.4 \Rightarrow 1.42$. Figure 12.7 provides the simulation result. The economy produces more and has more capital stocks. The couple's wage incomes become higher. The interest rate rises initially and remains almost invariant in the long term. Each spouse has more wealth, more disposable income, spends more on consumption goods and family goods. All the utility levels are enhanced.

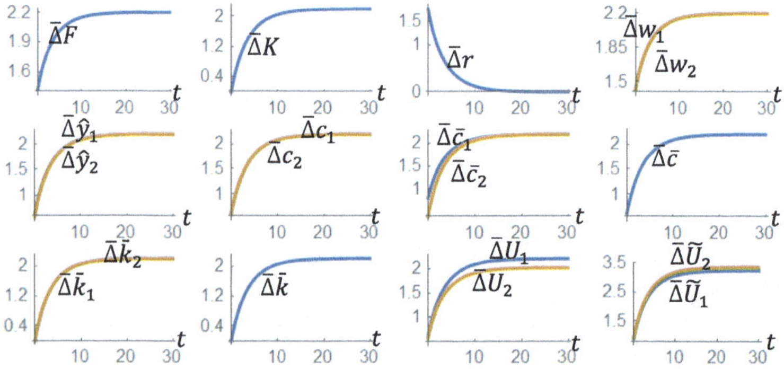

Fig. 12.7 Total factor productivity is enhanced

12.8 On Contract Theory, Agent-Based Economics, and the General Theory

The models in this chapter can be integrated into a single model in which various market structures and different games are taken into account. Many models for different issues of families provide basic ideas for further research within the framework proposed in this chapter. For instance, the family is a driving force for institutional change. There are issues related to modeling interregional resource transmission (Becker et al. 2018). Marriage and divorce are interdependent with growth, preference, and education (Chiappori et al. 2018). Marriage is a social contract, someone loyal to it and someone cheating it for additional benefits out of regulated life. Breaking this contract with low social and economic costs might be a significant determinant of falling birth rates in different societies and other problems in association with high rates of divorces and falling population in the long term.

In 2016, the Nobel Prize was awarded jointly to Oliver Hart (1948-) and Bengt Holmstrom (1949-) for their researches on contract theory. Contract theory and validity of contracts (a part of social trust) are not only important for understanding daily real-life contracts like marriage and firms and potential pitfalls of contract design, but also essential for understanding cultural and spatial differences in short-run and long-run economic performances. The model in Sector 12.5 opens a way for introducing contract theory to marriage dynamics and economic growth. An interesting question is whether low social and economic costs of divorces have contributed positively to modern Western economic growth.

Another interesting approach which may be applied to enrich the theory proposed in this book is agent-based economics. Agent-based economics, like my synergetic economics, is based on complexity theory. It treats the economy as a complex system of interacting agents. These agents are heterogeneous, have limited information, and characterized by bounded rationality. The approach in this book can be enriched by some ideas in agent-based economics. My approach in this book focuses on applying the basic model to construct a general economic theory in which different economic theories and ideas can be examined within an integrated framework. It is limited to rational behavior and should be extended to include bounded rationality in human behavior.

References

Becker GS (1965) A theory of the allocation of time. Econ J 75:493–517

Becker GS (1988) Family economics and macro behavior. Am Econ Rev 78:1–13

Becker GS, Kominers SD, Murphy KM, Spenkuch JL (2018) A theory of intergenerational mobility. J Polit Econ 126:7–25

Behrens K, Murata Y (2007) General equilibrium models of monopolistic competition: a new approach. J Econ Theory 136:776–787

Behrens K, Murata Y (2017) City size and the Henry George theorem under monopolistic competition. J Urban Econ 65:228–235

Brakman S, Heijdra BJ (2004) The monopolistic competition revolution in retrospect. Cambridge University Press, Cambridge

Campbell JY, Ludvigson S (2001) Elasticities of substitution in real business cycle models with home production. J Money Credit Bank 33:847–875

Chen ZQ, Woolley F (2001) A cournot-nash model of family decision making. Econ J 111:722–748

Chiappori PA (1992) Introducing household production in collective models of labor supply. J Polit Econ 105:191–209

Chiappori PA, Dias MC, Meghir C (2018) The marriage market, labor supply, and education choice. J Polit Econ 126:26–72

Doepke M, Tertilt M (2016) Families in macroeconomics. In: Taylor JB, Uhlig H (eds) Handbook of macroeconomics, vol 2B. Elsevier, Amsterdam, pp 1789–1891

Gomme P, Kydland FE, Rupert P (2001) Home production meets time to build. J Polit Econ 109:1115–31

Mas-Colell A, Whinston MD, Green JR (1995) Microeconomic theory. Oxford University Press, Oxford

Nikaido H (1975) Monopolistic competition and effective demand. Princeton University Press, Princeton, New Jersey

Parenti M, Ushchev P, Thisse JF (2017) Toward a theory of monopolistic competition. J Econ Theory 167:86–115

Robinson J (1933) The economics of imperfect competition. MacMillan, London

Stotsky JG (2006) Gender and its relevance to macroeconomic policy: a survey. IMF Working Paper, WP/06/233

Vendrik MCM (2003) Dynamics of a household norm in female labour supply. J Econ Dyn Control 27:823–841

Wang WW (2012) Monopolistic competition and product diversity: Review and extension. J Econ Surv 26:879–910

Zhang WB (2019) Monopolies and perfect competition in Solow-Uzawa's general equilibrium growth model. Russ J Ind Econ

Zhang WB (2019b) Monopsony and discrimination against woman in labor market in an extended Solowian model. Res Econ Bus: CentL East Eur 11:1–15

Zhang WB (2020) Cournot-Nash family decision and economic growth in an extended Solowian model. Acad Int Sci J 21:101–114

Chapter 13
Growth with Perfect and Monopolistic Competition

Monopolistic competition is an important form of markets in modern economies. Monopolistic competition is characterized by many producers who produce differentiated products. Products are differentiated from each other and are not perfect substitutes. Each firm takes the prices charged by other firms as given and maximizes its profit. Each firm has some degree of market power, which is measured by controlling power over the terms and conditions of demand and supply equilibrium. Theory of monopolistic competition is formed initially by Chamberlin (1933). It has been applied to different issues of economics related to economic structures, growth, economic geography, international trade, and innovation and technological diffusion (Dixit and Stiglitz 1977; Krugman 1979, 1980; Lancaster 1980; Waterson 1984; Grossman and Helpman 1990; Benassy 1996; Behrens and Murata 2007; Bertoletti and Etro 2015; Nocco et al. 2017; Parenti et al. 2017). This chapter contributes to the literature by integrating neoclassical growth theory and Walrasian general equilibrium theory with monopolistic competition (more generally, new growth theory).

13.1 The Dixit–Stiglitz Monopolistic Competition

The Dixit–Stiglitz monopolistic competition model is essential for understanding recent development in macroeconomics and economic geography (Dixit and Stiglitz 1977). The model has a significant influence on recent developments of macroeconomics, trade theory, and economic geography. Like the Solow model in neoclassical growth theory, it is the core model for modeling monopolistic competition. We now describe the model.

There are one good, labeled as 0, and a potential range of related products, labeled 1, 2, 3, ... Good 0 is chosen as numeraire. The economy's endowment is normalized

W.-B. Zhang, *The General Economic Theory*,
https://doi.org/10.1007/978-3-030-56204-5_13

at unity. Writing the amounts of various commodities as x_0 and $x = (x_1, x_2, x_3, \ldots)$. The utility is specified as follows:

$$U\left(x_0, \left\{\sum_i x_i^\rho\right\}^{1/\rho}\right),$$

where $0 < \rho < 1$ and U is homothetic in its arguments. The budget constraint is given by

$$x_0 + \sum_{i=1}^{n} p_i x_i = I,$$

where p_i are prices of the goods being produced and I is income in terms of the numeraire, i.e., the endowment which has been set at 1 plus the profits of firms distributed to the consumers.

Dual quantity and price indices are defined as follows:

$$y = \left\{\sum_{i=1}^{n} x_i^\rho\right\}^{1/\rho}, q = \left\{\sum_{i=1}^{n} p_i^{-1/\beta}\right\}^{-\beta}, \tag{13.1.1}$$

where $\beta \equiv (1-\rho)/\rho > 0$. The problem is solved in two stages. In the first stage,

$$y = I\frac{s(q)}{q}, x_0 = I(1 - s(q)), \tag{13.1.2}$$

where s is a function dependent on the form of U. In the second stage, each x_i is solved as follows:

$$x_i = y\left[\frac{q}{p_i}\right]^{1/(1-\rho)}. \tag{13.1.3}$$

I also have

$$\frac{x_i}{x_j} = \left(\frac{p_j}{p_i}\right)^{1/(1-\rho)}.$$

From (13.1.3), I have

$$\frac{\partial \log q}{\partial \log p_i} = \left(\frac{q}{p_i}\right)^{1/\beta}.$$

It is assumed that n is reasonably large so that the direct effect of p_i on q is negligible. The indirect effects on x_i are also negligible. The elasticity of the dd curve is

$$\frac{\partial log\, x_i}{\partial log\, p_i} = \frac{-1}{1-\rho} = \frac{-(1+\beta)}{\beta}.$$

For large n, $\partial log\, x_i / \partial log\, p_i \approx 0$ for $i \neq j$.

To model scale economies, assume that each potential commodity involves some fixed setup cost and has a constant marginal cost. It can be shown that each commodity is produced by one firm. Each firm attempts to maximize its profit, and entry occurs until the marginal firm can only just break even. Let c stand for the common marginal cost, and note that the elasticity of demand for each firm is $(1+\beta)/\beta$. For each active firm, equality of the marginal revenue and marginal cost is expressed as

$$p_i\left(1 - \frac{\beta}{1+\beta}\right) = c.$$

The common equilibrium price for each variety being produced is thus

$$p = c(1+\beta) = \frac{c}{\rho}.$$

It can be shown that under certain conditions, the equilibrium output for each active firm is $x = a/\beta c$, where a is the fixed cost. Dixit and Stiglitz also examined other cases when the utility functions or varieties of commodities take on other forms.

The model of monopolistic competition and product is constructed for the large group case. The examination of the model requires an approximation neglecting the own and cross-elasticities in terms of order $1/n$, where n is the number of firms. As pointed by Yang and Heijdra (1993), this is a very strict assumption and not easy to relax even for analytical tractability. With regards to the Dixit–Stiglitz model, Brakman et al. (2001: 69) observe: "The big step forward was to make some heroic assumptions concerning the symmetry of raw varieties and the structural form. This allowed for an elegant and consistent way to model production at the firm level benefiting from internal economies of scale in conjunction with a market structure of monopolistic competition, without getting bogged down in a taxonomy of oligopoly models."

13.2 Integrating the Basic Model and Dixit–Stiglitz Model

This section is based on Zhang (2018). It integrates neoclassical growth theory and economic equilibrium with monopolistic completion. Coexistence of perfect competition and monopolistic competition in macroeconomic dynamics with wealth accumulation is introduced by, for instance, Romer (1990). I am concerned with basic model and Dixit–Stiglitz's equilibrium model with monopolistic competition. The final good sector is based on the basic model. I apply the modeling strategy in the previous section. I especially follow Grossman and Helpman (1990) in that intermediate goods are used as inputs of the final good sector rather than consumer good in the Dixit–Stiglitz model. I differ from the Grossman–Helpman model in that the profits of intermediate inputs sectors are distributed among the homogeneous population rather than are used for innovation. The supply side consists of two kinds of activities: the production of a final good and the production of a variety of differentiated middle products (i.e., intermediate inputs). Capital is used as inputs in the production of final product. Labor is distributed between production of final goods and intermediate inputs.

13.2.1 The Final Good Sector

I use $F_i(t)$, $K(t)$ and $N_i(t)$ to represent, respectively, output of the final good sector, capital input, and labor input. I use $X_i(t)$ to stand for the (aggregate) input of intermediate inputs of the sector as follows:

$$X_i(t) = \sum_{\varepsilon=1}^{n} x_\varepsilon^\theta(t), 0 < \theta < 1, \tag{13.2.1}$$

in which $x_\varepsilon(t)$ stands for the input of middle product ε, n is the number of varieties of middle products available, and θ is a parameter. Following Grossman and Helpman (1990), I specify the production function of final goods as follows:

$$\begin{gathered} F_i(t) = A_i K^{\alpha_i}(t) N_i^{\beta_i}(t) X_i^{\gamma_i}(t), \\ 0 < \alpha_i, \beta_i, \ \alpha_i + \beta_i < 1, \ \gamma_i = \frac{1-\alpha_i-\beta_i}{\theta} < 1, \end{gathered} \tag{13.2.2}$$

where A_i, α_i, and β_i are parameters. The production function exhibits constant returns to scale for given n, but exhibits an increase in n. This function shows that an increasing degree of specialization enhances technical efficiency as a rise in n. Developing new middle products implies increasing the degree of specialization. This implies that there exist scale economies at the industry level that are exogenous to the individual firms in the final good sector.

The final good serves as numeraire. Variables $w(t)$, $r(t)$, and $p_\varepsilon(t)$, are used to denote the wage rate, the interest rate, and the price of middle good ε. The profit of the final good sector is

$$\pi_i(t) = F_i(t) - (r(t) + \delta_k)K(t) - w(t)N_i(t) - \sum_{\varepsilon=1}^{n} p_\varepsilon(t)x_\varepsilon(t).$$

I have the marginal conditions

$$r(t) + \delta_k = \frac{\alpha_i F_i(t)}{K(t)}, \; w(t) = \frac{\beta_i F_i(t)}{N_i(t)},$$
$$p_\varepsilon(t) = \frac{\gamma_i \theta x_\varepsilon^{\theta-1}(t) F_i(t)}{X_i(t)}. \tag{13.2.3}$$

The share of factor X_i equals $\gamma_i F_i$. From (13.2.3), I get

$$K(t) = \Lambda(t) X_i(t), \; N_i(t) = \left(\frac{w(t)}{\beta_i A_i K^{\alpha_i}(t) X_i^{\gamma_i}(t)}\right)^{1/(\beta_i - 1)}, \tag{13.2.4}$$

where

$$\Lambda(r, w, t) \equiv \left[\left(\frac{r_\delta(t)}{\alpha_i A_i}\right)^{\beta_i - 1} \left(\frac{\beta_i A_i}{w(t)}\right)^{\beta_i}\right]^{\frac{1}{\gamma_i}}, \; r_\delta(t) \equiv r(t) + \delta_k.$$

The function $\Lambda(t)$ is independent of variety. From (13.2.3), I have

$$p_\varepsilon(t) = \frac{\gamma_i \theta_i r_\delta(t) x_\varepsilon^{\theta-1}(t) K(t)}{\alpha_i X_i(t)}. \tag{13.2.5}$$

Insert (13.2.4) in (13.2.6)

$$x_\varepsilon(t) = \tilde{\Lambda}(t) p_\varepsilon^{-\overline{\theta}}(t), \tag{13.2.6}$$

where

$$\tilde{\Lambda}(t) \equiv \left(\frac{\gamma_i \theta_i r_\delta(t) \Lambda(t)}{\alpha_i}\right)^{\overline{\theta}}, \; \overline{\theta} \equiv \frac{1}{1-\theta}.$$

Function $\tilde{\Lambda}(t)$ is independent of variety. The share of variety ε in terms of the total value of intermediate inputs is

$$\varphi_\varepsilon(t) \equiv \frac{x_\varepsilon(t) p_\varepsilon(t)}{\sum_{m=1}^{n} x_m(t) p_m(t)}. \tag{13.2.7}$$

Insert (13.2.7) in (13.2.8)

$$\varphi_\varepsilon(t) = \frac{p_\varepsilon^{1-\overline{\theta}}(t)}{\sum_{m=1}^{n} p_m^{1-\overline{\theta}}(t)}. \tag{13.2.8}$$

13.2.2 The Middle Good Sector

The producer of variety ε earns the following profit:

$$\pi_\varepsilon(t) = [p_\varepsilon(t) - a_N w(t)] \frac{\varphi_\varepsilon(t) \gamma_i F_i(t)}{p_\varepsilon(t)},$$

where a_N is the unit labor requirement for the production of intermediates. Insert (13.2.8) in the profit function:

$$\pi_\varepsilon(t) = [p_\varepsilon(t) - a_N w(t)] \frac{\gamma_i F_i(t) p_\varepsilon^{-\overline{\theta}}(t)}{\sum_{m=1}^{n} p_m^{1-\overline{\theta}}(t)}. \tag{13.2.9}$$

From (13.2.3) and (13.2.1), I get

$$F_i(t) = \frac{p_\varepsilon(t)}{\gamma_i \theta x_\varepsilon^{\theta-1}(t)} \sum_{\varepsilon=1}^{n} x_\varepsilon^{\theta}(t). \tag{13.2.10}$$

Insert (13.2.10) in (13.2.13)

$$\frac{F_i(t)}{\sum_{m=1}^{n} p_m^{1-\overline{\theta}}(t)} = \frac{\widetilde{\Lambda}(t)}{\gamma_i \theta}. \tag{13.2.11}$$

From (13.2.9) and (13.2.11), the profit is given by

$$\pi_\varepsilon(t) = [p_\varepsilon(t) - a_N w(t)] \frac{\gamma_i \widetilde{\Lambda}(t) p_\varepsilon^{-\overline{\theta}}(t)}{\gamma_i \theta}.$$

The firm chooses $p_\varepsilon(t)$ to maximize its profit. The first-order condition (i.e., $\partial \pi_\varepsilon / \partial p_\varepsilon = 0$) of the above implies the following fixed-markup pricing rule:

$$\theta p_\varepsilon(t) = a_N w(t). \tag{13.2.12}$$

The price is independent of variety. With (13.2.9) and (13.2.12), I have the profit per firm as follows:

$$\pi(t) = \frac{(1-\theta)\gamma_i F_i(t)}{n}, \tag{13.2.13}$$

which is independent of ε. From (5), I also conclude that $x_\varepsilon(t)$ is independent of ε, denoted by $x(t)$. From (13.2.14), I get

$$X_i(t) = nx^{\theta_i}(t). \tag{13.2.14}$$

The total profit is

$$\overline{\pi}(t) = n\pi(t). \tag{13.2.15}$$

13.2.3 Consumer Behaviors and Wealth Dynamics

Let $\bar{k}(t)$ stand for the value of wealth held by the representative household. I have $\bar{k}(t) = K(t)/\overline{N}$, where $K(t)$ is the total capital. I assume that the profit is equally shared among households. The work time $T(t)$ and leisure time $\overline{T}(t)$ satisfy

$$T(t) + \overline{T}(t) = T_0. \tag{13.2.16}$$

I use h to stand for human capital. The disposable income of the representative household is

$$\hat{y}(t) = \overline{y}(t) - hw(t)\overline{T}(t), \tag{13.2.17}$$

where

$$\bar{y}(t) = (1 + r(t))\bar{k}(t) + hw(t)T_0 + \frac{\overline{\pi}(t)}{\overline{N}}.$$

The household distributes the disposable income on savings $s(t)$ and consuming goods $c(t)$:

$$c(t) + s(t) = \hat{y}(t). \tag{13.2.18}$$

From (13.2.17) and (13.2.18), I get

$$h\, w(t)\overline{T}(t) + c(t) + s(t) = \bar{y}(t). \tag{13.2.19}$$

Specify utility function $U(t)$ as function of $\overline{T}(t)$, $c(t)$, and $s(t)$ as follows:

$$U(t) = \overline{T}^{\sigma_0}(t)c^{\xi_0}(t)s^{\lambda_0}(t), \ \ \sigma_0, \xi_0, \lambda_0 > 0,$$

where σ_0 is the propensity to use leisure time, ξ_0 is the propensity to consume goods, and λ_0 is the propensity to save. Maximizing U to (13.2.20) yields

$$w(t)\overline{T}(t) = \sigma \bar{y}(t),\ c(t) = \xi \bar{y}(t),\ s(t) = \lambda \bar{y}(t), \tag{13.2.20}$$

where

$$\sigma \equiv \frac{\rho \sigma_0}{h},\ \xi \equiv \rho \xi_0,\ \lambda \equiv \rho \lambda_0,\ \rho \equiv \frac{1}{\sigma_0 + \xi_0 + \lambda_0}.$$

The change in the household's wealth follows

$$\dot{\bar{k}}(t) = s(t) - \bar{k}(t) = \lambda \bar{y}(t) - \bar{k}(t). \tag{13.2.21}$$

13.2.4 Demand and Supply of Final Goods and Full Employment

$$\dot{K}(t) = F_i(t) - c(t)\overline{N} - \delta_k K(t),$$
$$N_i(t) + a_N x(t) n = hT(t)\overline{N}.$$

Lemma 13.2.1 *The dynamics of the economic system follows the differential equation:*

$$\dot{x}(t) = \left(\frac{dv(x(t))}{dx}\right)^{-1} f(x(t)),$$

where functions $v(x(t))$ **and** $f(x(t))$ *are defined in* Zhang (2018). *All the other variables are explicitly given as functions of* $x(t)$.

I simulate the model to illustrate behavior of the system. The parameters and initial condition are as follows:

$$\overline{N} = 10,\ T_0 = 24,\ h = 1.5,\ \alpha_i = 0.3,\ \alpha_i = 0.3,\ \beta_i = 0.4,\ \theta = 0.6,$$
$$A_i = 1,\ n = 20,\ a_N = 0.2,\ \lambda_0 = 0.9,\ \xi_0 = 0.2,\ \sigma_0 = 0.4,$$
$$\delta_k = 0.03,\ x(0) = 6.4.$$

The simulation result is plotted in Fig. 13.1, in which $nN_x(t) = N(t) - N_i(t)$. The output of the final good sector is enhanced. The growth rate is positive initially and becomes zero in the long term. The labor force and labor inputs of the final good sector and intermediate good sector are augmented. The net input of intermediate good sector becomes higher. The output of each variety is augmented. The price becomes lower. The representative intermediate good sector gets more profit. The wage rate becomes lower. The household works more hours. The household has less wealth, lower consumption, and lower utility level over time.

The system has the following equilibrium point:

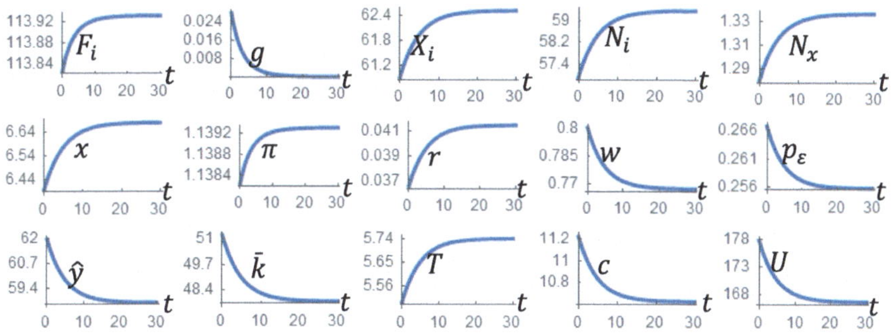

Fig. 13.1 Motion of the economy

$$F_i = 113.9,\ X_i = 62.5,\ N_i = 59.4,\ N_x = 1.34,\ x = 6.68,$$
$$\pi = 1.14,\ r = 0.042,\ w = 0.77,\ p_\varepsilon = 0.26,\ \hat{y} = 58.7,$$
$$\bar{k} = 47.8,\ T = 5.54,\ c = 10.6,\ U = 166.5.$$

The eigenvalue is -0.21. The equilibrium point is locally stable.

13.3 Comparative Dynamic Analysis in the Solow–Dixit–Stiglitz Model

This section analyzes the effects of changes in some parameters on the economy developed in the previous section.

13.3.1 A Rise in the Degree of Specialization

The degree of specialization is assumed to be increased as follows: $n = 20 \Rightarrow 21$. The simulation result is plotted in Fig. 13.2. The output of per intermediate input is reduced. The total inputs of intermediate inputs are augmented. The household spends more hours on work initially and does not change the work time in the long term. The labor input to the final good sector is augmented initially and remains invariant in the long term. The labor input to each intermediate input sector is decreased. The growth rate becomes lower during the transitory process. The output of the final good sector is augmented. The profit falls for each intermediate input sector. The interest rate rises initially and changes slightly in the long term. The wage rate and price of each intermediate input fall initially but rise in the long term. The household's disposable income, wealth, consumption, and utility level all become lower initially but higher in the long term. I conclude that the enhanced degree of specialization benefits the

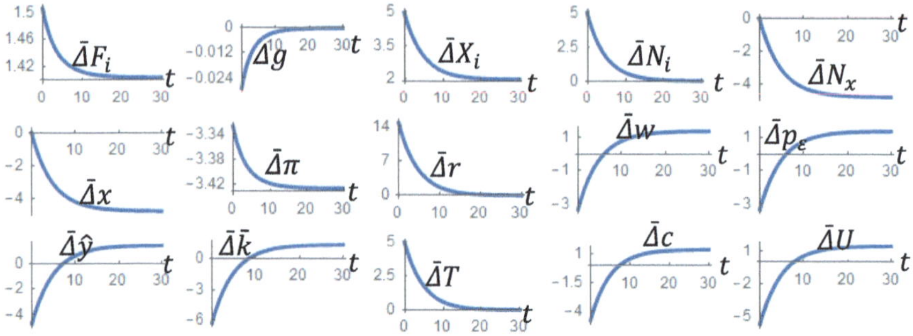

Fig. 13.2 Rise in the degree of specialization

national economic growth and household's welfare in the long term, even though the national final goods output rises but the household is worse off in the short term.

13.3.2 A Rise in Output Elasticity of Intermediate Inputs

The efficiency of intermediate inputs is assumed to be enhanced as follows: $\theta = 0.6 \Rightarrow 0.65$. The simulation result is plotted in Fig. 13.3. The output of per intermediate input and the total input of intermediate inputs are enhanced. The household works fewer hours initially and works more hours in the long term. The labor input to the final good sector is reduced initially and is almost invariant in the long term. The labor input to each intermediate input sector is increased. The growth rate rises during the transitory process. The output of the final good sector is enhanced. The profit falls for each intermediate input sector. The interest rate falls initially and rises slightly in the long term. The wage rate rises. The price of each intermediate input rises initially but changes slightly in the long term. The household's disposable income, wealth, consumption, and utility level are enhanced.

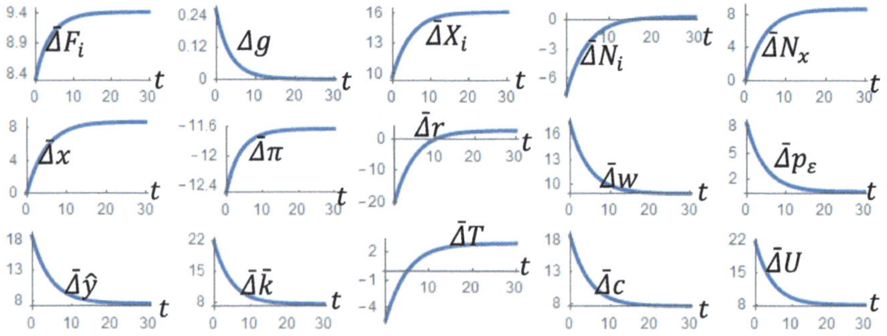

Fig. 13.3 Rise in output elasticity of intermediate inputs

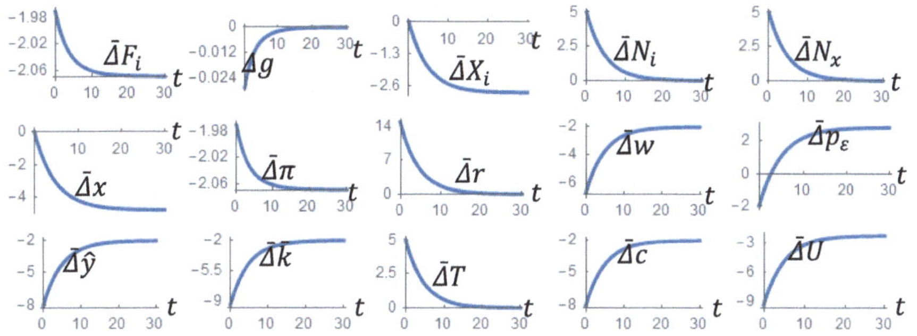

Fig. 13.4 Unit labor requirement for the production of intermediates rises

13.3.3 The Unit Labor Requirement for the Production of Intermediates Rises

The efficiency of intermediate inputs is now assumed to be increased: $a_N = 0.2 \Rightarrow 0.31$. The simulation result is plotted in Fig. 13.4. The household spends more hours on work initially and almost the same time in the long term. The labor inputs of all the sectors are increased initially and remain almost invariant in the long term. The output of per intermediate input and the total input of intermediate inputs are reduced. The growth rate falls during the transitory process. The output of the final good sector is decreased. The profit falls for each intermediate input sector. The interest rate becomes higher. The wage rate becomes lower. The price of each intermediate input falls initially but rises in the long term. The household's disposable income, wealth, consumption, and utility level are enhanced.

13.3.4 The Propensity to Use Leisure Time Rises

The propensity to use leisure is assumed to become higher in the following way: $\sigma_0 = 0.4 \Rightarrow 0.42$. The simulation result is plotted in Fig. 13.5. The household spends fewer hours on work. The labor inputs to all the sectors are reduced. The output of per intermediate input and the total input of intermediate inputs are reduced. The growth rate falls during the transitory process. The output of the final good sector is decreased. The profit falls for each intermediate input sector. The interest rate rises initially and changes slightly in the long term. The wage rate falls initially and rises in the long term. The price of each intermediate input falls initially but rises in the long term. The household's disposable income, wealth, and consumption are reduced. In the long term, the utility level is enhanced.

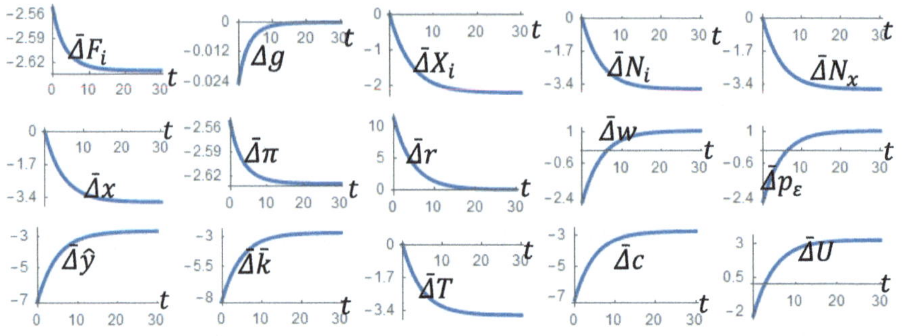

Fig. 13.5 Propensity to use leisure time rises

13.3.5 The Propensity to Save Rises

The propensity to save is assumed to be increased as follows:$\lambda_0 = 0.9 \Rightarrow 0.91$. The simulation result is plotted in Fig. 13.6. The output of per intermediate input and the total input of intermediate inputs rise. The household works a little more hour. The output of the final good sector is increased. The profit rises for each intermediate input sector. The interest rate falls. The wage rate and price of each intermediate input rise. The labor input to the final good sector is augmented. The labor input to each intermediate input sector is increased. The growth rate rises during the transitory process. The household's disposable income, wealth, consumption, and utility level all rise.

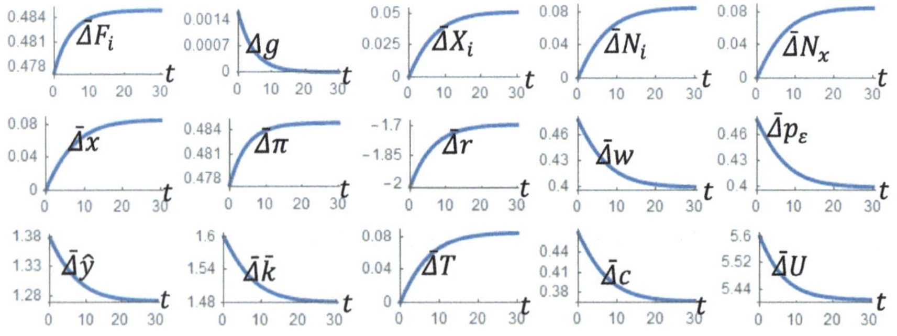

Fig. 13.6 Propensity to save rises

13.3.6 A Rise in Human Capital

I now deal with the impact that the following rise in human capital has on the economic system: $h = 1.5 \Rightarrow 1.6$. The simulation result is plotted in Fig. 13.7. The household works fewer hours. The labor input to the final good sector is augmented. The labor input to each sector is increased. The output of per intermediate input and the total input of intermediate inputs fall. The growth rate rises during the transitory process. The output of the final good sector is reduced. The profit rises for each intermediate input sector. The interest rate falls. The wage rate and price of each intermediate input rise. The household's disposable income, wealth, consumption, and utility level all rise.

13.4 An Integration of Neoclassical Growth, Dixit–Stiglitz Monopolistic Competition, and Walrasian General Equilibrium Theories

This section is based on Zhang (2019). The economy is composed of two sectors. The final good sector is characterized by perfect competition and produces a single homogenous capital good with identical firms. The middle good sector is characterized by monopolistic competition. It produces a variety of different goods with different firms. The population is classified into J groups according to human capital and preference. I use subscripts j to denote group j, $j = 1, \ldots, J$. I use $\overline{N}_j$, $T_j(t)$, and h_j to denote, respectively, the population, work time, and level of human capital of group j. This section follows Dixit and Stiglitz (1977) in that middle goods are consumed by households.

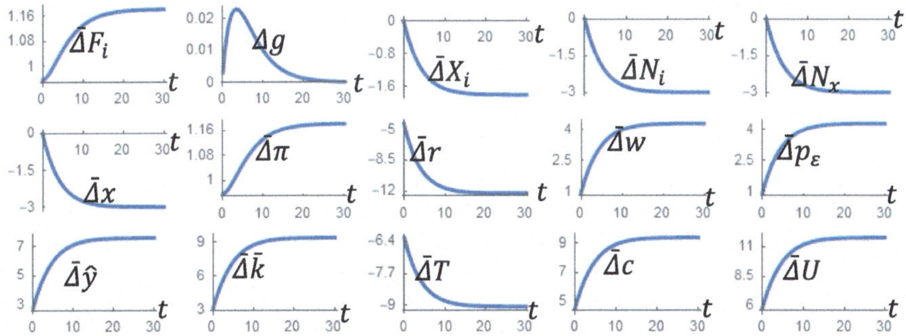

Fig. 13.7 Rise in human capital

13.4.1 The Total Labor Force

The total labor supply $N(t)$ is

$$N(t) = \sum_{j=1}^{J} h_j T_j(t) \overline{N}_j. \tag{13.4.1}$$

13.4.2 The Final Good Sector

Let $F(t)$, $K(t)$ and $\widetilde{N}(t)$ stand for, respectively, output of the final good sector, capital input, and labor input. The production function is taken on

$$F(t) = AK^{\alpha}(t)\widetilde{N}^{\beta}(t),\ 0 < \alpha, \beta < 1,\ \alpha + \beta = 1. \tag{13.4.2}$$

The marginal conditions imply

$$R(t) = \frac{\alpha F(t)}{K(t)},\ w(t) = \frac{\beta F(t)}{\widetilde{N}(t)},\ w_j(t) = h_j w(t), \tag{13.4.3}$$

where $R_{\delta}(t) \equiv r(t) + \delta_k$.

13.4.3 Disposable Income and Budgets

The total profit of all the firms of the middle good sector is shared among the households. I use $\pi_j(t)$ to stand for the profit shared by the representative household in group j. The household disposable income $\hat{y}_j(t)$ is given by

$$\hat{y}_j(t) = (1 + r(t))\bar{k}_j(t) + h_j T_j(t) w(t) + \pi_j(t). \tag{13.4.4}$$

The representative household spends the disposable income on saving $s_j(t)$, on consuming final goods $d_j(t)$, and on consuming middle goods $\tilde{c}_j(\varepsilon, t)$. Here, $\tilde{c}_j(\varepsilon, t)$ stands for the amount of variety ε that is consumed by group j's representative household. Let variety ε distribute within the range from 0 to n, $\varepsilon \in [0, n]$. The composite good for each group is introduced as follows:

$$c_j(t) = \left(\int_0^n \tilde{c}_j^{\overline{\theta}}(\varepsilon, t) d\varepsilon \right)^{1/\overline{\theta}},\ 1 > \overline{\theta}_j > 0, \tag{13.4.5}$$

where $\overline{\theta}$ is positive. I use $\tilde{p}(\varepsilon, t)$ to denote the price of $\tilde{c}_j(\varepsilon, t)$. The budget constraint is given as follows:

$$d_j(t) + \int_0^n \tilde{p}(\varepsilon, t)\tilde{c}_j(\varepsilon, t)d\varepsilon + s_j(t) = \hat{y}_j(t). \tag{13.4.6}$$

Insert time constraint $T_j(t) + \overline{T}_j(t) = T_0$ in (13.4.4)

$$\hat{y}_j(t) = R(t)\bar{k}_j(t) - h_j\overline{T}_j(t)w(t) + W_j(t), \tag{13.4.7}$$

in which

$$R(t) \equiv 1 + r(t), \ \ W_j(t) \equiv h_j T_0 w(t) + \pi_j(t).$$

Substituting (13.4.7) into (13.4.6), I get

$$h_j\overline{T}_j(t)w(t) + d_j(t) + \int_0^n \tilde{p}(\varepsilon, t)\tilde{c}_j(\varepsilon, t)d\varepsilon + s_j(t) = \bar{y}_j(t), \tag{13.4.8}$$

in which

$$\bar{y}_j(t) \equiv R(t)\bar{k}_j(t) + W_j(t).$$

13.4.4 Utility Functions and Optimal Behavior

I assume that utility level $U_j(t)$ is dependent on $\overline{T}_j(t)$, $d_j(t)$, $c_j(t)$, and $s_j(t)$ as follows:

$$U_j(t) = \overline{T}_j^{\sigma_{0j}}(t)c_j^{\chi_{0j}}(t)d_j^{\xi_{0j}}(t)s_j^{\lambda_{0j}}(t), \ \sigma_{0j}, \xi_{0j}, \lambda_{0j}, \chi_{0j} > 0, \tag{13.4.9}$$

where σ_{0j} is the propensity to use leisure time, ξ_{0j} is the propensity to consume final good, χ_{0j} is the propensity to consume intermediates, and λ_{0j} is the propensity to save. The problem is to maximize utility (13.4.9) subject to (13.4.8). I apply the two-stage method to solve the optimization problem. In the first stage, I imagine that there is a price $p(t)$ for $c_j(t)$. The budget for the question is

$$h_j w(t)\overline{T}_j(t) + d_j(t) + p(t)c_j(t) + s_j(t) = \bar{y}_j(t). \tag{13.4.10}$$

The first-order conditions imply

$$h_j w(t)\overline{T}_j(t) = \sigma_j \bar{y}_j(t),\ d_j(t) = \xi_j \bar{y}_j(t),\ p(t)c_j(t) = \chi_j \bar{y}_j(t),\\ s_j(t) = \lambda_j \bar{y}_j(t), \tag{13.4.11}$$

in which

$$\sigma_j \equiv \rho_j \sigma_{0j},\ \xi_j \equiv \rho_j \xi_{0j},\ \chi_j \equiv \rho_j \chi_{0j},\ \lambda_j \equiv \rho_j \lambda_{0j},\\ \rho_j \equiv \frac{1}{\sigma_{0j} + \xi_{0j} + \chi_{0j} + \lambda_{0j}}.$$

The second-stage maximization is defined by: maximize $c_j(t)$ by choosing $\tilde{c}_j(\epsilon, t)$ subject to

$$\int_0^n \tilde{p}(\varepsilon, t)\tilde{c}_j(\varepsilon, t)d\varepsilon = p(t)c_j(t). \tag{13.4.12}$$

Introduce the following Langrangian function:

$$\mathcal{L}_j(t) \equiv \left(\int_0^n \tilde{c}_j^{\overline{\theta}}(\varepsilon, t)d\varepsilon\right)^{\frac{1}{\overline{\theta}}}\\ +\hbar_j(t)\left\{p(t)c_j(t) - \int_0^n \tilde{p}(\varepsilon, t)\tilde{c}_j(\varepsilon, t)d\varepsilon\right\}, \tag{13.4.13}$$

where $\hbar_j(t)$ is the Lagrangian multiplier. From (13.4.11), the first-order conditions are given as follows:

$$\frac{\partial \mathcal{L}_j(t)}{\partial \tilde{c}_j(\varepsilon, t)} = c_j^{1-\overline{\theta}}(t)\tilde{c}_j^{\overline{\theta}-1}(\varepsilon, t) - \hbar_j(t)\tilde{p}(\varepsilon, t) = 0,\\ \frac{\partial \mathcal{L}_j(t)}{\partial \hbar_j(t)} = p(t)c_j(t) - \int_0^n \tilde{p}(\varepsilon, t)\tilde{c}_j(\varepsilon, t)d\varepsilon = 0. \tag{13.4.14}$$

From the first equations in (13.4.14), I get

$$c_j^{1-\overline{\theta}}(t)\tilde{c}_j^{\overline{\theta}-1}(\varepsilon, t) = \hbar_j(t)\tilde{p}(\varepsilon, t). \tag{13.4.15}$$

From (13.4.15), I get

$$\frac{\tilde{c}_j(\varepsilon, t)}{\tilde{c}_j(\mu, t)} = \left(\frac{\tilde{p}(\varepsilon, t)}{\tilde{p}(\mu, t)}\right)^{\frac{1}{\overline{\theta}-1}} = \left(\frac{\tilde{p}(\varepsilon, t)}{\tilde{p}(\mu, t)}\right)^{-\omega},\\ \overline{\theta} = 1 - \frac{1}{\omega}, \tag{13.4.16}$$

where ω_j is the elasticity of substitution between any two varieties:

$$\frac{(\tilde{p}(\varepsilon, t)/\tilde{p}(\mu, t))}{(\tilde{c}_j(\varepsilon, t)/\tilde{c}_j(\mu, t))} \frac{d(\tilde{c}_j(\varepsilon, t)/\tilde{c}_j(\mu, t))}{d(\tilde{p}(\varepsilon, t)/\tilde{p}(\mu, t))} = \omega.$$

From (13.4.14), I obtain

$$\tilde{c}_j(\varepsilon,t)\tilde{p}(\varepsilon,t) = \left(\frac{\tilde{p}(\varepsilon,t)}{\tilde{p}(\mu,t)}\right)^{\gamma} \tilde{p}(\varepsilon,t)\tilde{c}_j(\mu,t),$$

in which $\gamma \equiv 1/(\overline{\theta} - 1)$. From the above equations, I get

$$\begin{aligned} p(t)c_j(t) &= \chi_j \bar{y}_j(t) = \int_0^n \tilde{p}(\varepsilon,t)\tilde{c}_j(\varepsilon,t)d\varepsilon \\ &= \frac{\tilde{c}_j(\gamma,t)}{\tilde{p}^{\gamma}(\gamma,t)} \int_0^n \tilde{p}^{\overline{\theta}\gamma}(\varepsilon,t)d\varepsilon = \frac{\tilde{c}_j(\gamma,t)P_j(t)}{\tilde{p}^{\gamma}(\gamma,t)}, \end{aligned} \tag{13.4.17}$$

where

$$P_j(t) \equiv \int_0^n \tilde{p}^{\overline{\theta}\gamma}(\varepsilon,t)d\varepsilon.$$

Hence, I have

$$\tilde{c}_j(\varepsilon,t) = \chi_j \bar{y}_j(t)\tilde{p}^{\gamma}(\varepsilon,t)P_j^{-1}(t). \tag{13.4.18}$$

From (13.4.18), I obtain

$$\begin{aligned} p(t) &= \frac{\chi_j \bar{y}_j(t)}{c_j(t)} \\ &= \left(\int_0^n \tilde{c}_j^{\overline{\theta}}(\varepsilon,t)d\varepsilon\right)^{-\frac{1}{\overline{\theta}}} \chi_j \bar{y}_j(t) = P_j(t)^{\frac{1}{\overline{\theta}\gamma}}. \end{aligned} \tag{13.4.19}$$

The value share of variety ε in the total value of intermediates for consumption is

$$\varphi(\varepsilon,t) = \frac{\tilde{p}(\varepsilon,t)\tilde{c}(\varepsilon,t)}{\bar{y}(t)}, \tag{13.4.20}$$

where

$$\bar{y}(t) \equiv \sum_{j=1}^{J} \overline{N}_j \int_0^n \tilde{p}(\varepsilon,t)\tilde{c}_j(\varepsilon,t)d\,\varepsilon,\ \ \tilde{c}(\varepsilon,t) \equiv \sum_{j=1}^{J} \tilde{c}_j(\varepsilon,t)\overline{N}_j.$$

The change in the household's wealth follows:

$$\dot{k}_j(t) = s_j(t) - \bar{k}_j(t). \tag{13.4.21}$$

13.4.5 The Middle Good Sector

Markets of middle goods are characterized of monopolistic competition. Firms act atomistically in that no firm takes account of possible impacts of its decisions on any other firm. Let $x(\varepsilon, t)$ represent for the output level of the producer of variety ε. Demand equals supply

$$\sum_{j=1}^{J} \tilde{c}_j(\varepsilon, t)\overline{N}_j = x(\varepsilon, t). \tag{13.4.22}$$

All middle goods are assumed to be produced with the same cost function. The labor force used in producing each good is linearly related to output as follows:

$$l(\varepsilon, t) = \widetilde{\alpha} + \widetilde{\beta} x(\varepsilon, t), \tag{13.4.23}$$

where $l(\varepsilon, t)$ is labor force used in producing good ε, $\widetilde{\alpha}$ is a fixed cost, and $\widetilde{\beta}$ is a positive coefficient. The total labor force $N_x(t)$ used by the middle good sector is the sum of labor force used by all the firms:

$$N_x(t) = \int_0^n l(\varepsilon, t) d\varepsilon. \tag{13.4.24}$$

The profit of the producer of variety ε is

$$\overline{\pi}(\varepsilon, t) = \tilde{p}(\varepsilon, t)x(\varepsilon, t) - \left(\widetilde{\alpha} + \widetilde{\beta} x(\varepsilon, t)\right)w(t). \tag{13.4.25}$$

The symmetry of the problem means that all immediate firms will produce the same quantity at the same price. Introduce the shorthand notations

$$x(t) = x_j(\varepsilon, t), \;\; \pi(t) = \overline{\pi}(\varepsilon, t), \;\; \tilde{p}(t) = \tilde{p}(\varepsilon, t), \quad \text{for all } \varepsilon.$$

From (13.4.26), I get

$$\overline{\pi}(t) = \left(\tilde{p}(t) - \widetilde{\beta} w(t)\right) \sum_{j=1}^{J} \tilde{c}_j(\varepsilon, t)\overline{N}_j - \widetilde{\alpha} w(t). \tag{13.4.26}$$

Insert (13.4.18) in (13.4.26)

$$\overline{\pi}(t) = \left(\tilde{p}(t) - \widetilde{\beta} w(t)\right)\tilde{p}^{\gamma}(t)M(t) - \widetilde{\alpha} w(t), \tag{13.4.27}$$

where

$$M(t) \equiv P_j^{-1}(t) \sum_{j=1}^{J} \chi_j \bar{y}_j(t) \overline{N}_j.$$

From the first-order condition (i.e., $\partial \overline{\pi} / \partial \tilde{p} = 0$), I get the fixed-markup pricing rule

$$\tilde{p}(t) = \frac{\widetilde{\beta} w(t)}{\overline{\theta}}. \tag{13.4.28}$$

Insert (13.4.25) in (13.4.24)

$$\overline{\pi}(t) = \vartheta w^{1+\gamma}(t) M(t) - \widetilde{\alpha} w(t), \tag{13.4.29}$$

where

$$\vartheta \equiv \left(\frac{1}{\overline{\theta}} - 1 \right) \widetilde{\beta} \left(\frac{\widetilde{\beta}}{\overline{\theta}} \right)^{\gamma}.$$

By the definitions, I have the profit share of the representative household

$$\pi_j(t) = \frac{\mu_j n \overline{\pi}(t)}{\overline{N}_j}, \tag{13.4.30}$$

where $n\overline{\pi}(t)$ is the total profit of the middle good sector. The share distribution of the total profit is specified as follows:

$$\sum_{j=1}^{J} \mu_j = 1, \ \ \mu_j \ge 0.$$

The specification may be relaxed in different ways. For instance, as in Krugman (1980), $\overline{\pi}(t) = 0$ is assumed as an equilibrium condition of free entry and exit. It is also reasonable to assume that $\overline{\pi}(t)$ is positive and is invested as R&D activities so that the number of firms becomes endogenous. Another condition is that the profit is shared between households and firms.

13.4.6 Balances in Final Good Market, Labor Market, and National Wealth

$$\dot{K}(t) = F(t) - d(t)\overline{N} - \delta_k K(t),$$
$$\widetilde{N}(t) + N_x(t) = \mathrm{N}(t),$$
$$\overline{K}(t) = \sum_{j=1}^{J} \bar{k}_j(t) \overline{N}_j,$$

where $N_x(t) = nl(t)$ is the labor force employed by the middle good sector and $\overline{K}(t)$ is the national wealth. Full employment of capital stock implies $\overline{K}(t) = K(t)$. I built the model. The following lemma is shown in Zhang (2019).

Lemma 13.4.1 *The motion of the economic system follows the following differential equations:*

$$\dot{z}(t) = \Phi_1\left(z(t), \left\{\bar{k}_j(t)\right\}\right),$$
$$\dot{\bar{k}}_j(t) = \Phi_j\left(z(t), \left\{\bar{k}_j(t)\right\}\right), \ j = 2, \ldots, J,$$

where

$$z(t) \equiv \frac{r(t) + \delta_k}{w(t)}, \ \left\{\bar{k}_j(t)\right\} \equiv \left(\bar{k}_2(t), \ldots, \bar{k}_J(t)\right),$$

and $\Phi_j(t)$ are functions of $z(t)$ and $\left\{\bar{k}_j(t)\right\}$. All the variables are expressed as functions of $z(t)$ and $\left\{\bar{k}_j(t)\right\}$.

As the expressions are complicated, I show dynamic behavior of the system by simulation for an economy with three groups. The parameter values are specified as follows:

$$T_0 = 24, \ \overline{\theta} = 0.4, \ \delta_k = 0.05, \ A = 1.4, \ n = 200, \ \alpha = 0.35,$$
$$\widetilde{\alpha} = 0.01, \ \widetilde{\beta} = 0.05, \ \overline{N}_1 = 10, \ \overline{N}_2 = 40, \ \overline{N}_3 = 100, \ h_1 = 4,$$
$$h_2 = 1.5, \ h_3 = 1, \ \mu_1 = 0.3, \ \mu_2 = 0.3, \ \mu_3 = 0.4, \ \lambda_{01} = 0.7,$$
$$\chi_{01} = 0.1, \ \xi_{01} = 0.2, \ \sigma_{01} = 0.2, \ \lambda_{02} = 0.65, \ \chi_{02} = 0.1,$$
$$\xi_{02} = 0.2, \ \sigma_{02} = 0.25, \ \lambda_{03} = 0.6, \ \chi_{03} = 0.15, \ \xi_{03} = 0.25.$$

We specify the initial conditions as follows:

$$\sigma_{03} = 0.3, \ z_1(0) = 0.07, \ \bar{k}_2(0) = 90, \ \bar{k}_2(0) = 46.$$

The simulation result is plotted in Fig. 13.8. From the initial state, the national wealth and final good sector's output fall. The national labor supply rises over time. The middle good sector employs less labor force, while the final good sector employs more. Each firm of the middle goods produces less and employs less. The changes in the other variables over time are given in the figure.

The system has the following equilibrium point:

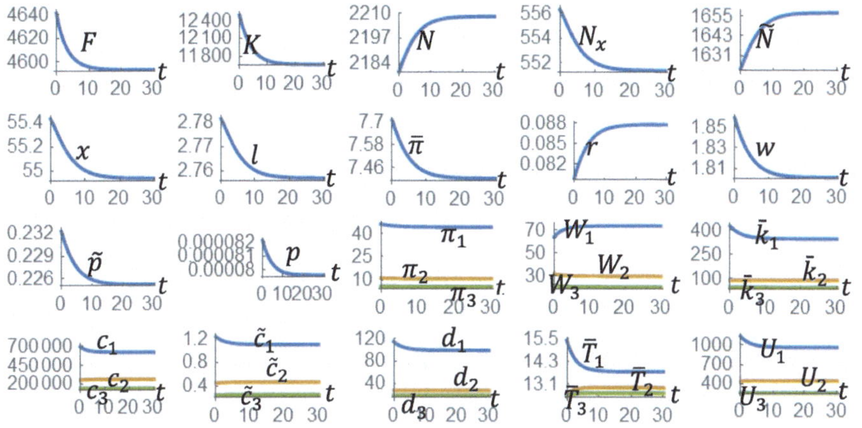

Fig. 13.8 Movement of the economy

$$F = 4593, K = 11,666, N = 2208, N_x = 551, \tilde{N} = 1657, x = 55,$$
$$l = 2.76, \bar{\pi} = 7.41, r = 0.088, w = 1.8, \tilde{p} = 0.23,$$
$$p = 0.00008, \pi_1 = 44.44, \pi_2 = 11.1, \pi_3 = 5.93, W_1 = 73.8,$$
$$W_2 = 29.9, W_3 = 20.5, \bar{k}_1 = 347, \bar{k}_2 = 90.96, \bar{k}_3 = 45.6,$$
$$c_1 = 622,588, c_2 = 263598, c_3 = 143082, \tilde{c}_1 = 1.1, \tilde{c}_2 = 0.47,$$
$$\tilde{c}_3 = 0.25, d_1 = 99, d_2 = 28, d_3 = 19, \overline{T}_1 = 13.9, \overline{T}_2 = 12.9,$$
$$\overline{T}_3 = 12.6, U_1 = 965, U_2 = 450, U_3 = 262.$$

The eigenvalues at the equilibrium point are

$$-0.468, -0.395, -0.265.$$

The equilibrium point is locally stable. This guarantees the validity of the dynamic comparative analysis.

13.5 Comparative Dynamic Analysis in Preferences and Market Characters

This section conducts comparative dynamic analysis in some parameters.

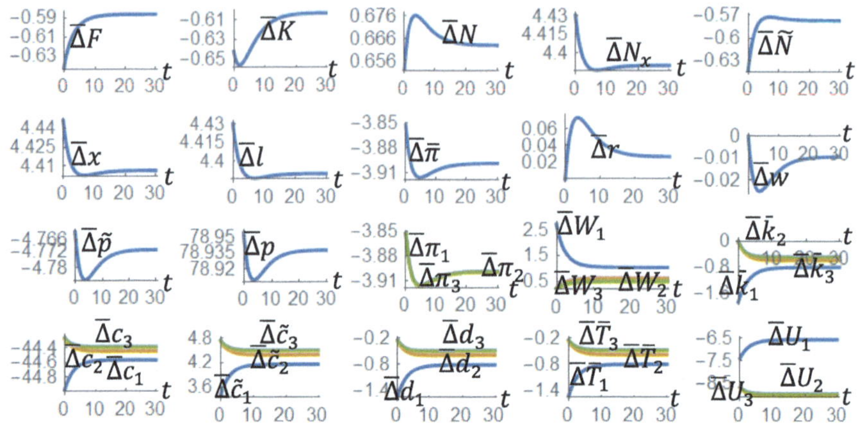

Fig. 13.9 Elasticity of substitution between two varieties rises

13.5.1 The Elasticity of Substitution Between Two Varieties Rises

The elasticity of substitution between two varieties is assumed to be increased as follows: $\overline{\theta} = 0.4 \Rightarrow 0.42$. The simulation result is plotted in Fig. 13.9. A rise in $\overline{\theta}$ implies a fall in the price of middle goods and rise in the output of each firm in the middle good sector. The profit of each firm and profit shared by each household fall. All the households work more hours. The total labor supply is augmented. The labor forces employed by the middle good sector and by each firm rise. The labor force employed by the final good sector is augmented. The output of the final good sector and national wealth are decreased. The interest rate becomes higher. The wage rate becomes lower. The aggregated good price rises. The consumption levels by the three groups are reduced. The wage incomes of the three groups are enhanced. The utility levels of the three groups are all reduced.

13.5.2 Fixed Labor Cost of the Middle Goods Firm Is Increased

The fixed labor cost of the middle goods firm is assumed to be increased as follows: $\tilde{\alpha} : 0.01 \Rightarrow 0.02$. The simulation result is plotted in Fig. 13.10. Each firm in the middle good sectors produces less. The price of middle goods becomes lower. The profit of each firm and profit shared by each household are reduced. All the households increase work hours, and the total labor supply is increased. The labor force employed by the middle good sector is increased. The labor force by each firm is increased. The labor force employed by the final good sector falls. The output of the final good sector

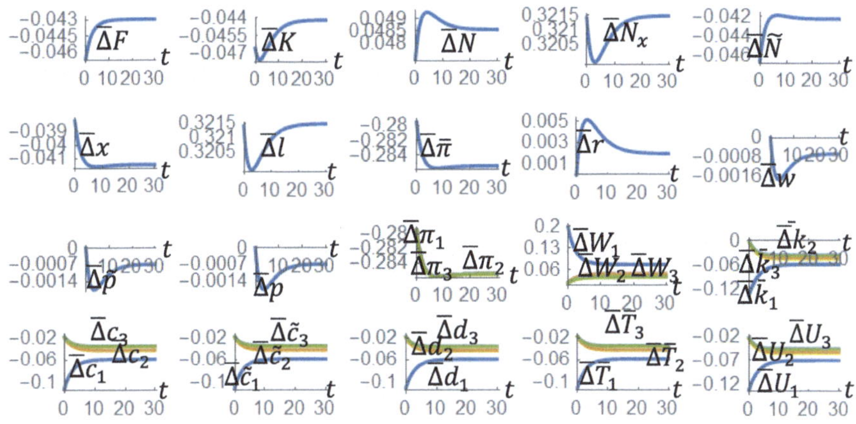

Fig. 13.10 Fixed labor cost of the middle goods firm is increased

and national wealth are reduced. The interest rate becomes higher. The wage rate becomes lower. The aggregated good price is enhanced. The consumption levels by the three groups are enhanced. The wage incomes of the three groups are increased. The household has lower level of wealth and consumes less final goods. The utility levels of the three groups are all reduced.

13.5.3 A Rise in Variety of Middle Goods

The variety of middle goods is assumed to be increased as follows: n: 200 $\Rightarrow$ 210. The simulation result is plotted in Fig. 13.11. Macroeconomic variables are almost not affected. The consumption levels of each firm's product and each firm's production activities are affected. The household utility levels are enhanced by the love of variety.

13.5.4 Group 1's Propensity to Consume Middle Goods is Enhanced

Group 1's propensity to consume middle goods is assumed to be increased as follows: $\chi_{01} = 0.1 \Rightarrow 0.12$. The simulation result is plotted in Fig. 13.12. The economy has lower wealth and output level of final good sector. Group 1's leisure time is reduced, while the other two groups' leisure hours are increased. The national labor force is increased. The middle good sector employs more labor force, while the final good sector employs less labor force. Each firm's profit is enhanced. Each household receives more profit. The interest rate becomes higher. The wage rate is reduced. Group 1's wage income becomes higher, while the other two groups' wage incomes

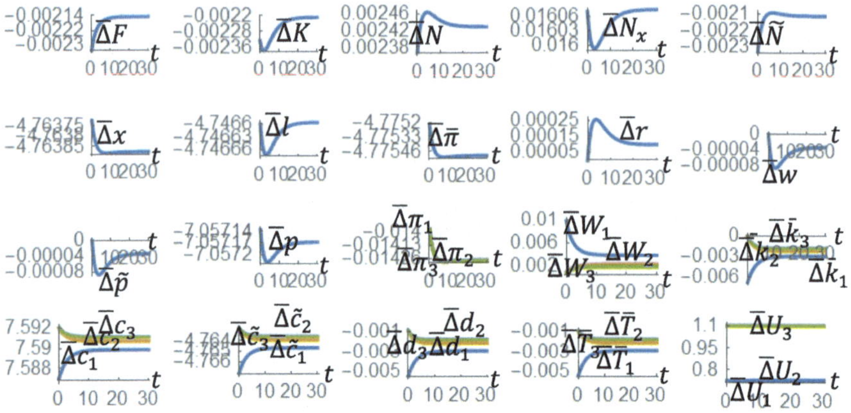

Fig. 13.11 Rise in variety of middle goods

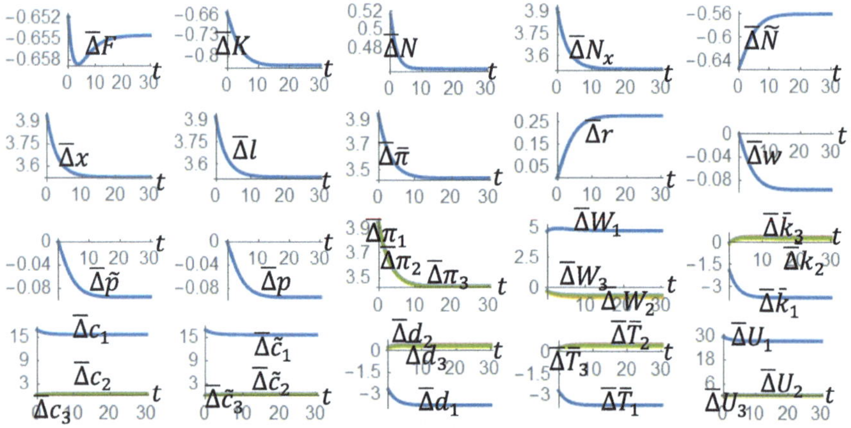

Fig. 13.12 Group 1's propensity to consume middle goods is enhanced

become lower. Household 1 has less wealth, while the households in the other two groups get more. Each firm produces more and employs more labor force. The prices of middle goods are reduced. Household 1 consumes more middle goods and less final goods, while the households in the other groups slightly change their consumption levels.

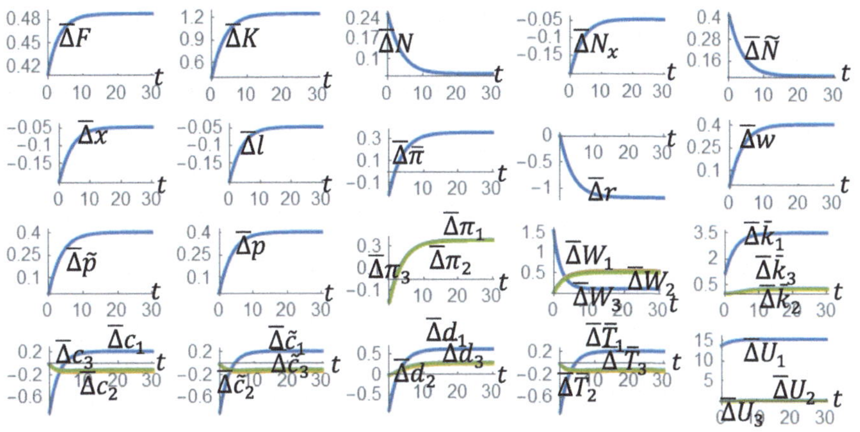

Fig. 13.13 Group 1's propensity to save is enhanced

13.5.5 Group 1's Propensity to Save Is Enhanced

Group 1's propensity to save is assumed to be increased as follows: $\lambda_{01} = 0.7 \Rightarrow 0.72$. The simulation result is plotted in Fig. 13.13. The economy has more capital. The interest rate falls. The wage rate rises. The households receive more wage incomes. Household 1 works more hours initially and less in the long term. The households from the other two groups have less leisure hours. The firm gets less profits initially but more in the long term. Each household shares less profits initially but more in the long term. The prices of middle goods are augmented. The household of group 1 has higher utility levels, while the households from the other groups have almost the same levels.

13.5.6 Group 3 Enhances Human Capital

Group 1's human capital is on the economy: $h_3 = 1 \Rightarrow 1.2$. The simulation result is plotted in Fig. 13.14. The national labor force is augmented. The national capital and output of the final good sector are augmented. The final goods and middle good sectors employ more labor force. Each firm has more profits, employs more labor force, and produces more. The interest rate falls initially and rises in the long term. The wage rate rises initially and falls in the long term. The household gets more wage income. In the long term, the households of the other two groups get almost the same wage incomes. In long term, the household from group 3 consumes more and has higher utility level.

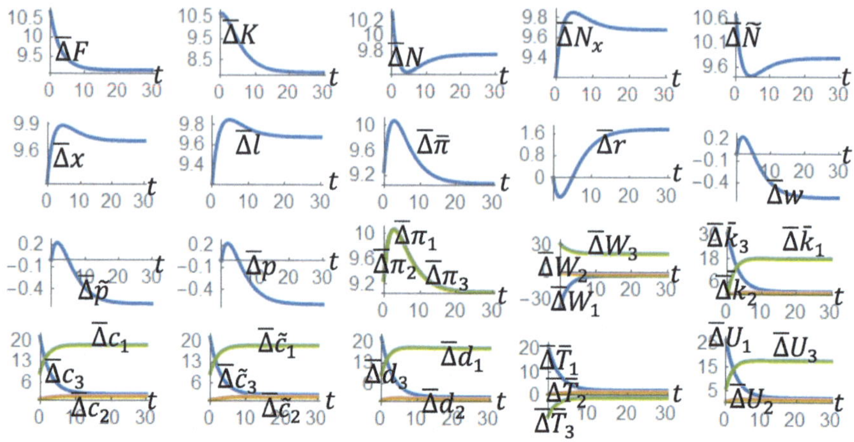

Fig. 13.14 Group 3 enhances human capital

13.5.7 Group 3's Population Is Increased

Group 3's population is assumed to be increased as follows: $\overline{N}_3 = 100 \Rightarrow 110$. The simulation result is plotted in Fig. 13.15. The national capital and output of the final good sector are increased. The interest rate falls. The wage rate rises. The households receive more wage incomes. Household 3 has less leisure hours. The households from the other two groups have more leisure hours. The firm gets more profits. Each household of group 2 shares less profit. Each household of the other two groups shares more profit. The prices of middle goods become higher. Household 3 consumes less goods and has less wealth, while the households from the other groups

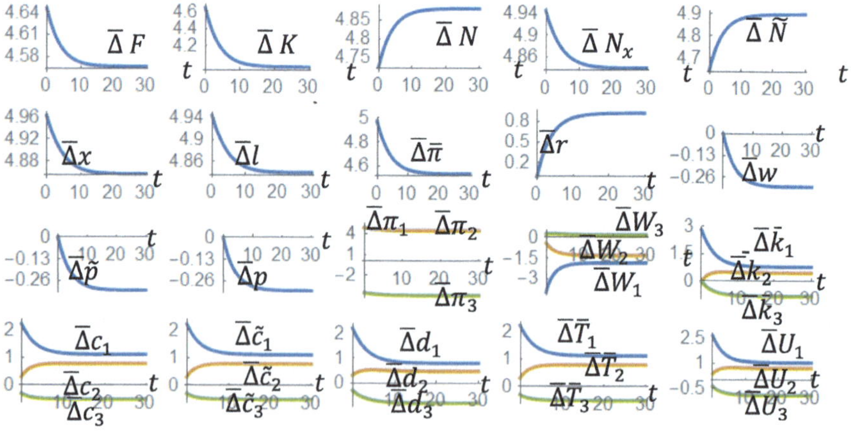

Fig. 13.15 Group 3's population is increased

consume more goods and have more wealth. The household of group 3 has lower utility level, while the households from the other groups have higher utility levels. A population expansion of a poor group enlarges the national economy, benefits the individuals of the other groups, and deteriorates the poor household's living conditions.

13.5.8 The Profit Distribution Is Shifted

The profit distribution is assumed to be shifted as follows:

$$\mu 1 = 0.3 \Rightarrow 0.32; \;\; \mu 2 = 0.3 \Rightarrow 0.29; \;\; \mu 3 = 0.4 \Rightarrow 0.39.$$

Group 1's profit share is increased, while the other two groups' share is reduced. The simulation result is plotted in Fig. 13.16. The economy has more capital and output of the final good sector. The interest rate becomes lower. The wage rate becomes higher. Household 1's leisure time is increased; while the other two households' leisure times are reduced. The household from group 1 has less wage income, while the households of the other groups receive more wage income. The firm's profit remains almost invariant. Household 1 shares more profit, while each of the other two households receives less profit. The prices of middle goods are slightly augmented. Household 1 consumes more goods and has more wealth, while the other two households consume less goods and have less wealth. Group 1 has higher utility level, while the households from the other groups have lower utility levels.

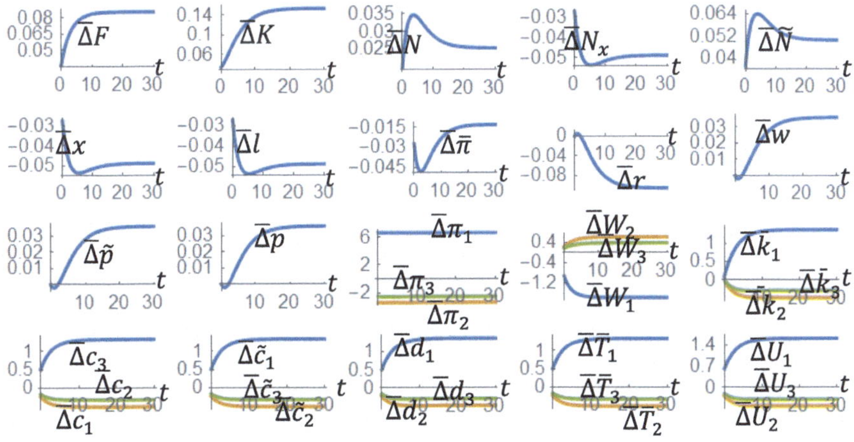

Fig. 13.16 Profit distribution is shifted

13.6 On Growth with Contracts, Games, and Market Powers

This and previous chapters introduced imperfect markets to Walrasian and neoclassical growth theories. Market structures and regulations are important for explaining macroeconomic performances across cultures and nations. The two chapters also show a way to introduce imperfect competition and games to the basic model. Other economic theories can be integrated with the basic model in similar manner.

One important theory for enriching the general theory is mechanism design theory. The 2007 Nobel Prize was shared by Leonid Hurwicz (1917–2008), Eric S. Maskin (1950–), and Roger B. Myerson (1951–) for their fundamental contributions to mechanism design theory. When an economic system is characterized by imperfect competition, asymmetry information or lack of any relevant information, positive or negative externalities, games between individuals and firms, Smith's metaphor is not proper for analyzing economic mechanisms. Mechanism design theory examines various economic phenomena under different institutions. The theory explores the properties of optimal allocation mechanisms of, for instance, trading, regulation schemes, and voting procedures.

The 2012 Nobel Prize was awarded to Alvin E Roth (1951–) and Lloyd S. Shapley (1923–) for their contributions to the theory of stable allocations and the practice of market design. Marching of different agents is essential for understanding free markets. Marching activities are related to economic conditions as well. Shapley applied cooperative game theory to analyze different matching methods. Roth applied empirical methods to deal with the stability of different matchings, such as new doctors with hospitals or students with schools. The 2014 Nobel Prize was awarded to Jean Tirole (1953–) for his contributions to analyzing market power and regulation. He examined monopolistic industries. Further generalization of my theory is possible by applying more broadly game theory to industries, agents, and households.

References

Behrens K, Murata Y (2007) General equilibrium models of monopolistic competition: a new approach. J Econ Theory 136:776–787

Benassy JP (1996) Taste for variety and optimum production patterns in monopolistic competition. Econ Lett 52:41–47

Bertoletti P, Etro F (2015) Monopolistic competition when income matters. Econ J 127:1217–1243

Brakman S, Garretsen H, van Marrewijk C (2001) An introduction to geographical economics: trade, location and growth. Cambridge University Press, Cambridge

Chamberlin E (1933) The theory of monopolistic competition. Harvard University Press, Cambridge

Dixit A, Stiglitz JE (1977) Monopolistic competition and optimum product diversity. Am Econ Rev 67:297–308

Grossman GM, Helpman E (1990) Comparative advantage and long-run growth. Am Econ Rev 80:796–815

Krugman PR (1979) A model of innovation, technology transfer, and the world distribution of income. J Polit Econ 87:253–266

Krugman PR (1980) Scale economies, product differentiation, and the pattern of trade. Am Econ Rev 70:950–959

Lancaster K (1980) Intra-industry trade under perfect monopolistic competition. J Int Econ 10:151–175

Nocco A, Ottaviano GLP, Salto M (2017) Monopolistic competition and optimum product selection: why and how heterogeneity matters. Res Econ 71:704–717

Parenti M, Ushchev P, Thisse JF (2017) Toward a theory of monopolistic competition. J Econ Theory 167:86–115

Romer PM (1990) Endogenous technological change. J Polit Econ 98:S71–S102

Waterson M (1984) Economic theory of the industry. Cambridge University Press, Cambridge

Yang XK, Heijdra BJ (1993) Monopolistic competition and optimum product diversity: comment. Am Econ Rev 83:295–301

Zhang WB (2018) An integration of Solow's growth and Dixit-Stiglitz's monopolistic competition models. SPOUDAI J Econ Bus 64:3–19

Zhang WB (2019) A simple growth model based on neoclassical growth, monopolistic competition, and Walrasian general equilibrium theories. Int J Acad Res Bus Soc Sci 9:1005–1027

Chapter 14
Trade Pattern, Tourism, and Global Development

National economies are closely interrelated to each other. Most of the previous chapters in this book neglect the role of trade on national and international economic growth. This chapter deals with interdependence between international trade, global economic growth, and income and wealth distribution between countries. I give an extensive treatment of international trade theory in Zhang (2008). I am now focused on the Heckscher–Ohlin (H–O) model. It is a core model in neoclassical trade theory. The standard H-O model is built for a two-country global economy. Each country has access to the same technology for producing two goods using two fixed factors (labor and capital) under conditions of perfect competition and constant returns to scale. Factors of production are mobile between sectors within a country, but immobile internationally. No international borrowing and lending are allowed. The 1977 Nobel Prize was awarded jointly to Berlin Ohlin (1899–1979) and James Meade (1907–1995) for their contributions to the theory of international trade and international capital movements. Ohlin was considered as founder of the modern theory of international trade. His trade theory deals with the determinants of trade pattern, international division of labor, and effects of trade on the allocation of resources, price relations, and income distribution. Meade studied the effects of economic policy on international trade and many other issues related to open economies. Their works open theoretical examinations of international trade, international price fluctuations, international allocation of economic activities as well as international payment systems. Chen (1992: 923–4) points a main problem of the H–O model in explaining global growth due to differences in saving behavior: "Yet explaining trade in terms of differences in preferences is no longer in the spirit of the Heckscher–Ohlin model in which trade arises because of differences in relative factor proportions." This chapter overcomes some essential problems in the H–O model by extending the basic model to a multi-country and multi-sector economy.

W.-B. Zhang, *The General Economic Theory*,
https://doi.org/10.1007/978-3-030-56204-5_14

14.1 Integrating Heckscher–Ohlin and Oniki–Uzawa Trade Models

This section is based on Zhang (2015). The model is neoclassical and Ricardian since it postulates cross-country differences in technology and labor productivity. The trade is modeled on basis of the Oniki–Uzawa model. The world economy is composed of two national economies, indexed by $j = 1, 2$. Extending the two goods assumption in the standard H–O model, I assume that each national economy produces three goods. Both countries produce a homogeneous capital good which can be used as capital and consumer good. The sectors in the two countries are called industrial sector as in the model by Ikeda and Ono (1992). Capital good is freely mobile between sectors and countries. Each country provides services and country-specified goods which are not internationally tradable and can be consumed only by domestic households. Each country specifies in producing a good called global commodity which is internationally tradable and consumed by both countries. Global commodities are pure consumption goods. The industrial sector, global commodity sectors, and service sectors are indexed by i, j, s. Production sectors use capital and labor. Exchanges take place in perfectly competitive markets. Factors are fully utilized at every moment. Labor is internationally immobile. Saving is undertaken only by households. Let prices be measured in terms of capital good. I use $p_j(t)$ to represent the price of country j's services. The price of global commodity supplied by country j is denoted by $p_{jj}(t)$. I denote the wage rate in the jth country and globally equal interest rate by $w_j(t)$ and $r(t)$, respectively. Capital is depreciated at a constant rate δ_{jk}. Depreciation rates may vary between countries. I use $N_{jq}(t)$ and $K_{jq}(t)$ to stand for the labor force and capital stocks employed by sector q in country j. Let $F_{jq}(t)$ stand for the output level of sector q in country j.

14.1.1 Production Functions and Marginal Conditions

The production function of section q in country j is specified as:

$$F_{jq}(t) = A_{jq} K_{jq}^{\alpha_{jq}}(t) N_{jq}^{\beta_{jq}}(t),$$
$$A_{jq}, \alpha_{jq}, \beta_{jq} > 0, \alpha_{jq} + \beta_{jq} = 1, \tag{14.1.1}$$

where A_{jq}, α_{jq}, and β_{jq} are positive parameters. Different from the Ricardian trade theory which assumes technological differences between countries, the H–O model assumes variations in capital and labor endowments with the identical technology between countries. This study follows the Ricardian assumption. The marginal conditions imply

$$r(t) + \delta_{jk} = \frac{\alpha_{ji} F_{ji}(t)}{K_{ji}(t)}, \ w_j(t) = \frac{\beta_{ji} F_{ji}(t)}{N_{ji}(t)}, \ j = 1, 2,$$

$$r(t)+\delta_{jk}=\frac{\alpha_{jj}p_{jj}(t)F_{jj}(t)}{K_{jj}(t)},\ w_j(t)=\frac{\beta_{jj}p_j(t)F_{jj}(t)}{N_{jj}(t)},\ j=1,2.$$
$$r(t)+\delta_{jk}=\frac{\alpha_{js}p_{js}(t)F_{js}(t)}{K_{js}(t)},\ w_j(t)=\frac{\beta_{js}p_{js}(t)F_{js}(t)}{N_{js}(t)},\ j=1,2. \tag{14.1.2}$$

14.1.2 Household Behavior

The disposable income is given by:

$$\hat{y}_j(t)=(1+r(t))\bar{k}_j(t)+w_j(t). \tag{14.1.3}$$

Let $c_{jq}(t)$ stand for consumption level of consumer good q in country j. Variable $s_j(t)$ denotes the saving made at the current time by the representative household in country j. I have the budget constraint for household j:

$$c_{ji}(t)+p_1(t)c_{j1}(t)+p_2(t)c_{j2}(t)+p_{js}(t)c_{js}(t)+s_j(t)=\hat{y}_j(t). \tag{14.1.4}$$

Household j's utility function is

$$U_j(t)=c_{ji}^{\xi_{ji0}}(t)c_{j1}^{\xi_{j10}}(t)c_{j2}^{\xi_{j20}}(t)c_{js}^{\gamma_{js0}}(t)s_j^{\lambda_{j0}}(t),$$
$$\xi_{ji0},\xi_{j10},\xi_{j20},\xi_{js0},\lambda_{j0}>0,$$

where ξ_{ji0} is the propensity to consume industrial goods, ξ_{jj0} the propensity to consume global commodity j, and λ_{j0} the propensity to own wealth. Maximizing the utility subject to (14.1.4), I have

$$c_{ji}(t)=\xi_{ji}\hat{y}_j(t),\ p_1(t)c_{j1}(t)=\xi_{j1}\hat{y}_j(t),\ p_2(t)c_{j2}(t)$$
$$=\xi_{j2}\hat{y}_j(t),\ p_{js}(t)c_{js}(t)=\xi_{js}\hat{y}_j(t),\ s_j(t)=\lambda_j\hat{y}_j(t), \tag{14.1.5}$$

where

$$\xi_{ji}\equiv\rho_j\xi_{ji0},\ \xi_{j1}\equiv\rho_j\xi_{j10},\ \xi_{j2}\equiv\rho_j\xi_{j20},\ \xi_{js}\equiv\rho_j\xi_{js0},\ \lambda_j\equiv\rho_j\lambda_{j0},$$
$$\rho_j\equiv\frac{1}{\xi_{ji0}+\xi_{j10}+\xi_{j20}+\xi_{js0}+\lambda_{j0}}.$$

The change in wealth of the household in country j follows

$$\dot{\hat{k}}_j(t)=s_j(t)-\bar{k}_j(t). \tag{14.1.6}$$

14.1.3 Factor Markets and Demand and Supply

Let $K_j(t)$—denote the capital stocks employed by country j. Full employment of capital stock by the three sectors implies

$$K_{ji}(t) + K_{jj}(t) + K_{js}(t) = K_j(t), \; j = 1, 2.$$

Full employment of the labor force by the three sectors implies

$$N_{ji}(t) + N_{jj}(t) + N_{js}(t) = N_j, \; j = 1, 2.$$

Equilibrium between demand and supply of services implies

$$c_{js}(t)N_j = F_{js}(t), \; j = 1, 2.$$

Equilibrium between demand and supply of tradable goods implies

$$c_{1q}(t)N_1 + c_{2q}(t)N_2 = F_{qq}(t), q = 1, 2.$$

The global capital production equals the global net savings:

$$\sum_{j=1}^{2}\left(s_j(t)N_j - \bar{k}_j(t)N_j + \delta_{kj}K_j(t)\right) = \sum_{j=1}^{2} F_{ji}(t).$$

The wealth owned by the global population equals the total global wealth:

$$\bar{k}_1(t)N_1 + \bar{k}_2(t)N_2 = K_1(t) + K_2(t) = K(t), \; j = 1, 2.$$

I completed the dynamic model.

Lemma 14.1.1 *The motion of the two variables $z_1(t)$ and $\bar{k}_2(t)$ follows two differential equations:*

$$\dot{z}_1(t) = \tilde{\Lambda}_1\left(z_1(t), \bar{k}_2(t)\right), \dot{\bar{k}}_2(t) = \tilde{\Lambda}_2\left(z_1(t), \bar{k}_2(t)\right),$$
$$z_1(t) \equiv \frac{r(t) + \delta_{1k}}{w_1(t)}.$$

where $\tilde{\Lambda}_1(t)$ and $\tilde{\Lambda}_2(t)$ are functions of *$z_1(t)$ and $\bar{k}_2(t)$, defined in* Zhang (2015). *The values of the other variables are given as functions of $z_1(t)$ and $\bar{k}_2(t)$.*

The parameter values are specified as follows:

$$N_1 = 10, N_2 = 20, \delta_{jk} = 0.05, A_{1i} = 1.2, A_{2i} = 1.3, A_{11} = 1.3,$$

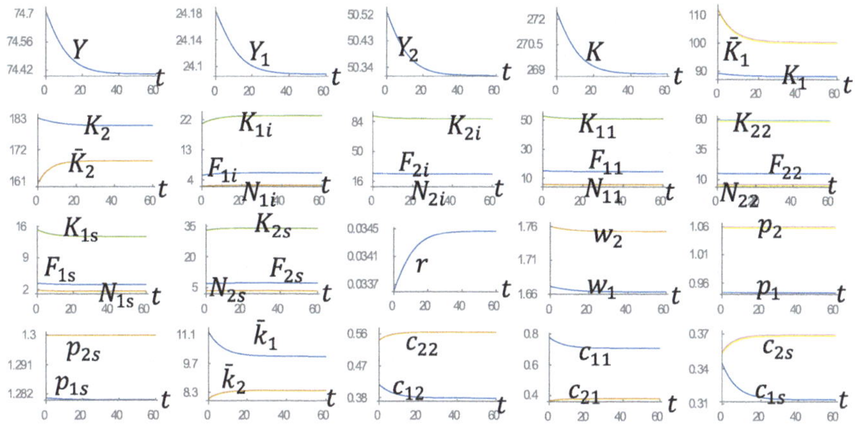

Fig. 14.1 Motion of the global economy

$$A_{22} = 1.2, A_{1s} = 1, A_{2s} = 1, \alpha_{1i} = 0.32, \alpha_{2i} = 0.3, \alpha_{11} = 0.31,$$
$$\alpha_{22} = 0.31, \alpha_{1s} = 0.29, \alpha_{2s} = 0.3, \xi_{1i0} = 0.04, \xi_{110} = 0.05,$$
$$\xi_{120} = 0.03, \xi_{1s0} = 0.03, \lambda_{1s0} = 0.75, \xi_{2i0} = 0.05, \xi_{210} = 0.03,$$
$$\xi_{220} = 0.05, \xi_{2s0} = 0.04, \lambda_{2s0} = 0.7.$$

Country 1 has a larger population. The depreciation rates are equal. The total factor productivity of country 1's industrial sector is higher than that of country 2's. The propensity to save country 1's household is higher than that of country 2's. I specify the initial conditions as follows: $z_1(0) = 0.05$and $\bar{k}_2(0) = 8$. The motion of the system is given in Fig. 14.1. The national incomes and the global income are defined as follows:

$$Y_j \equiv F_{ji} + p_{js}F_{js} + p_jF_{jj}, Y \equiv Y_1 + Y_2.$$

The global income and wealth fall in association with rising interest rate and falling wage rates. The national and global incomes fall over time. Country 1's value of wealth is more than the capital stock employed by the national economy, implying that the country is in trade surplus. Country 2's value of wealth is less than the capital stock employed by the national economy, implying that the country is in trade deficit. Country 1's wealth and the capital employed fall over time. Country 2's wealth rises, and the capital employed falls. Each sector also experiences changes over time as illustrated in Fig. 14.1. The prices of two commodities and services are slightly changed. The consumption levels of commodities and services and wealth of country 1's (2's) representative household fall (rise) over time.

The system has an equilibrium point as follows:

$$Y = 74.4, Y_1 = 241, Y_2 = 50.3, K = 268.77, K_1 = 88.18,$$

$$\bar{K}_1 = 100.53, K_2 = 180.59, \bar{K}_2 = 168.24, r = 0.035, w_1 = 1.66,$$
$$w_2 = 1.75, p_1 = 0.94, p_2 = 1.06, p_{1s} = 1.28, p_{2s} = 1.3,$$
$$c_{1i} = 0.54, c_{2i} = 0.6, c_{11} = 0.71, c_{21} = 0.38, c_{12} = 0.38,$$
$$c_{22} = 0.57, c_{1s} = 0.31, c_{2s} = 0.37, \bar{k}_1 = 10.05, \bar{k}_2 = 8.41,$$

$$\begin{pmatrix} F_{1i} \\ N_{1i} \\ K_{1i} \end{pmatrix} = \begin{pmatrix} 6.16 \\ 2.52 \\ 23.32 \end{pmatrix}, \begin{pmatrix} F_{2i} \\ N_{2i} \\ K_{2i} \end{pmatrix} = \begin{pmatrix} 24.66 \\ 9.85 \\ 87.58 \end{pmatrix}, \begin{pmatrix} F_{11} \\ N_{11} \\ K_{11} \end{pmatrix} = \begin{pmatrix} 14.74 \\ 5.77 \\ 51.06 \end{pmatrix},$$
$$\begin{pmatrix} F_{22} \\ N_{22} \\ K_{22} \end{pmatrix} = \begin{pmatrix} 15.14 \\ 6.13 \\ 59.86 \end{pmatrix}, \begin{pmatrix} F_{1s} \\ N_{1s} \\ K_{1s} \end{pmatrix} = \begin{pmatrix} 3.14 \\ 17.2 \\ 13.81 \end{pmatrix}, \begin{pmatrix} F_{2s} \\ N_{2s} \\ K_{2s} \end{pmatrix} = \begin{pmatrix} 7.4 \\ 3.84 \\ 34.14 \end{pmatrix}.$$

It is straightforward to calculate the two eigenvalues: $\{-0.17, -0.14\}$.

14.2 Global Growth and Capital Flows with Various Exogenous Changes

This section shows how changes in some parameters affect global growth, trade pattern, and economic structures.

14.2.1 A Rise in the Total Factor Productivity of Country 1's Industrial Sector

The total factor productivity is assumed to be changed as follows $A_{1i} : 1.2 \Rightarrow 1.25$. The simulation result is plotted in Fig. 14.2 which shows how the system deviates from the variables in Fig. 14.1. Country 1's industrial sector is expanded. More output is produced, and more labor and capital inputs are employed. Country 2's industrial sector produces less and employs labor and capital inputs. The global and country 1's total incomes are enhanced. Country 2's total income initially falls and rises in the long term. The global wealth is reduced initially and increased in the long term. Country 1's wealth and capital employed are reduced initially and increased in the long term. Country 2's capital employed is almost invariant. Its wealth falls initially and is almost invariant in the long term. The wage rate in country 1 becomes higher. The wage rate in country 2 varies slightly in the long term. The prices of country 1's services and global commodity are increased. The prices of country 2's services and global commodity are almost invariant. Country 1's household initially reduces the wealth and consumption levels of all goods and services and augments these variables in the long term. Country 2's household reduces consumption of country 1's global

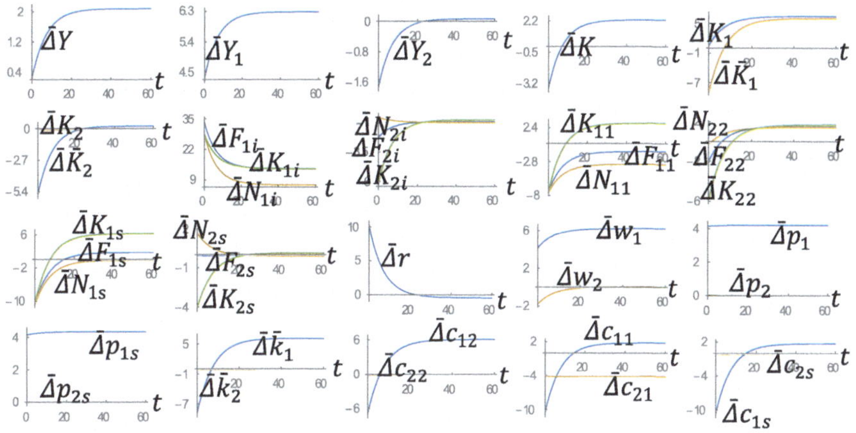

Fig. 14.2 Rise in the total factor productivity of country 1's industrial sector

commodity and keeps the wealth and consumption levels of its own country's global commodity and services almost invariant. The technological change has almost no impact on the other country's service sector, and though it changes the other country's industrial and global commodity sectors.

14.2.2 A fall in the Output Elasticity of Country 1's Industrial Sector

The output elasticity of country 1's industrial sector is assumed to fall as follows α_{1i} : 0.32 $\Rightarrow$ 0.31. The simulation result is plotted in Fig. 14.3. The output level and capital and labor inputs of country 1's industrial sector are reduced. The output level and capital and labor inputs of country 2's industrial sector are increased. The change in the parameter reduces the global and country 1's total incomes. Country 2's total income initially rises and changes slightly in the long term. The global wealth rises initially and falls in the long term. Country 1's wealth and capital employed fall in the long term. Country 2's wealth is almost invariant. The capital employed by country 2 is increased. The wage rate in country 1 becomes lower. The wage rate in country 2 is almost invariant. The interest rate is reduced. The prices of country 1's services and global commodity are reduced, and the prices of country 2's services and global commodity are slightly affected. Country 1's household initially increases the wealth and consumption levels of all goods and services and reduces these variables in the long term. Country 2's household increases consumption of country 1's global commodity and keeps the wealth and consumption levels of its own country's global commodity and services almost invariant. There are also some changes in the industrial structures. Country 1's global commodity sector produces more and employs more labor force, and the sector initially employs more capital

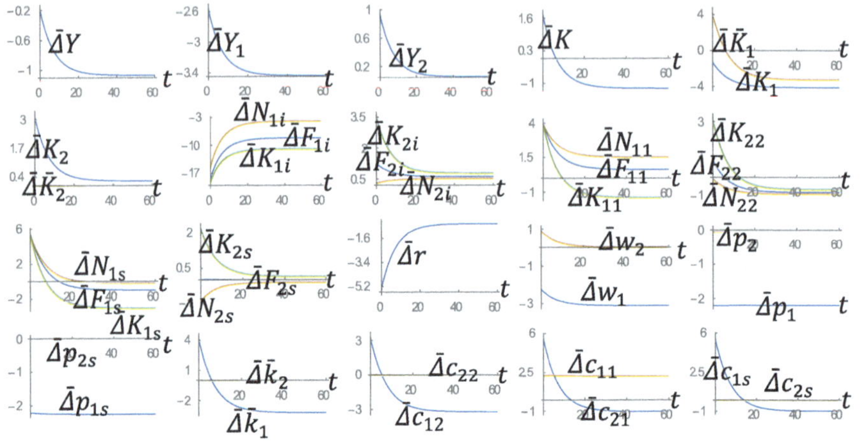

Fig. 14.3 Fall in the output elasticity of country 1's industrial sector

input. Country 2's global commodity sector produces less and employs less the two input factors in the long term.

14.2.3 *Country 1's Population is Increased*

Chen (1992) observed: "There have been few attempts in the literature to explain long-run comparative advantage in terms of differences in initial factor endowment ratios among countries." As economists failed to analytically solve or simulate their dynamic models, it is difficult to explain transitory as well as long-run effects of initial factor endowments. As my model follows the dynamics of the global system with any conditions, I can completely illustrate the effects of differences in any factor endowments. Country 1's population is assumed to rise as follows $N_1 : 10 \Rightarrow 20$. The simulation result is plotted in Fig. 14.4. The world has more income and wealth. The two countries' total incomes are increased. The wage rates of the two economies become higher. The interest rate falls. The prices in the two economies remain almost invariant. The wealth and consumption levels of all the goods and services of country 1's representative household are reduced in the short term and are almost not affected in the long term. The wealth and consumption levels of all the goods and services of country 1's representative household are almost not changed. Country 1 expands the scales of the three sectors. Country 2 reduces the scale of its industrial sector. The output level of services sector is almost not affected. Country 2 expands the scale of its global commodity sector.

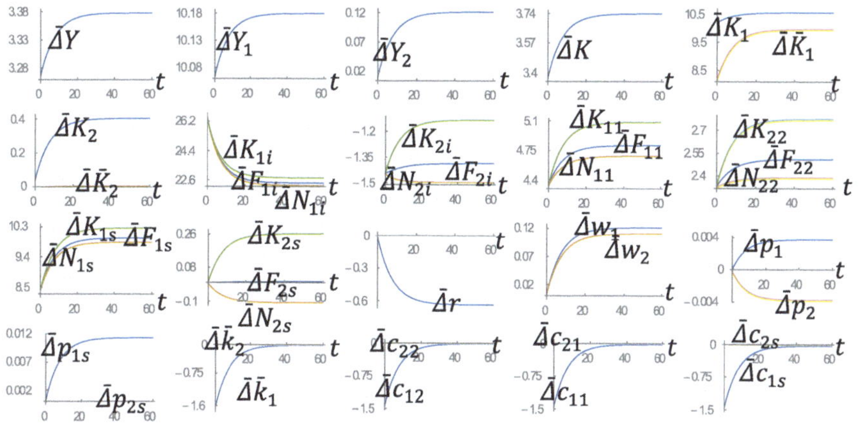

Fig. 14.4 Consequences of country 1's population expansion

14.2.4 Country 1 Increases Its Propensity to Consume the Domestic Commodity

Country 1's propensity to consume the country's global commodity is increased as follows: ξ_{110}:0.05 $\Rightarrow$ 0.06. The simulation result is plotted in Fig. 14.5. Household 1 consumes more country 1's global commodity. The household has less wealth and consumes less the other global commodity and domestic services. Household's wealth level and consumption levels of two commodities and services remain invariant. Country 1's global commodity sector expands its output. The sector employs more capital and labor force. Country 2's global commodity sector raises its output. It employs more capital and labor force. A higher propensity to consume

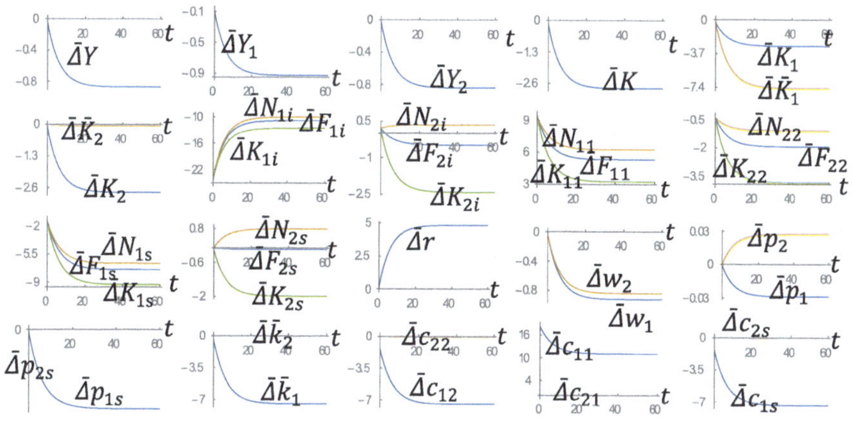

Fig. 14.5 Country 1 increases its propensity to consume the domestic commodity

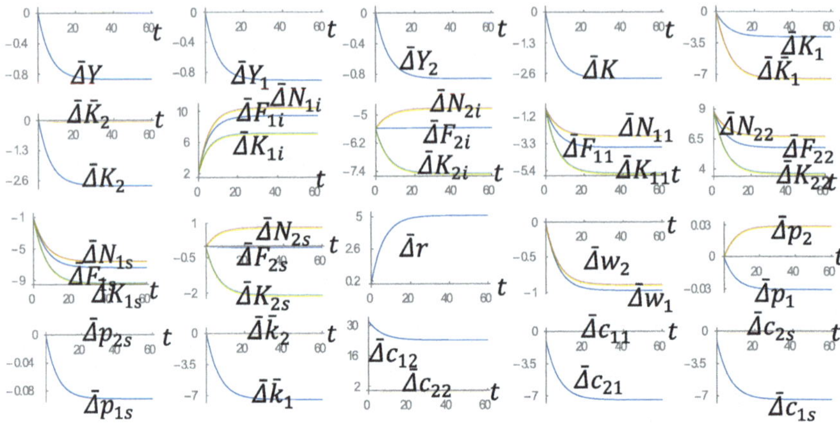

Fig. 14.6 Country 1 increases its propensity to consume country 2's global commodity

consumer good reduces the global total income and wealth, and two countries' total incomes. Country 1 has less wealth and employs less capital stocks. Country 2 has almost same level wealth and employs less capital stocks. The increased propensity to consume goods reduces the wage rates and augments the interest rate. The prices are almost invariant.

14.2.5 Country 1 Increases Its Propensity to Consume Country 2's Global Commodity

Country 1's propensity to consume country 2's global commodity is increased as follows: ξ_{110} : 0.03 $\Rightarrow$ 0.04. The simulation result is plotted in Fig. 14.6. Country 1's household consumes more country 2's global commodity. The household has less wealth and consumes less the domestic global commodity and services. Household's wealth level and consumption levels of two commodities and services remain invariant. The rest effects are similar with the previous case when country 1's propensity to consume country 2's global commodity is increased.

14.2.6 Country 1 Increases Its Propensity to Consume Services

Country 1's propensity to consume services is assumed to rise as follows: ξ_{1s0}:0.03 $\Rightarrow$ 0.04. The simulation result is plotted in Fig. 14.7.

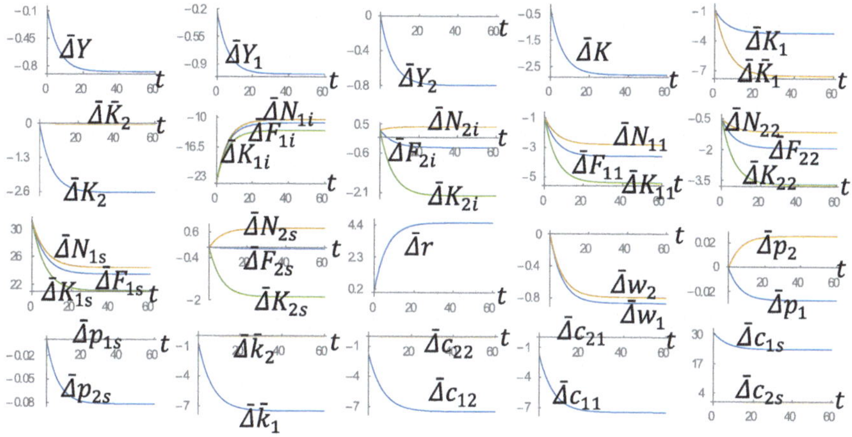

Fig. 14.7 Country 1 increases its propensity to consume services

14.2.7 *Country 1 Augments Its Propensity to Save*

Country 1's propensity to save is assumed to be increased as follows: λ_{10}:0.75 $\Rightarrow$ 0.77. The simulation result is plotted in Fig. 14.8. The world has total income and wealth. The two countries have more incomes. Household 1 has more wealth. The household initially reduces the consumption levels of two goods and services and raises these variables in the long term. Household 1's behavior is slightly affected. The wage rates become higher. The interest rate falls. The prices of services become higher. The price of global commodity 1 is slightly increased, and the price of global commodity 2 is slightly decreased. The output levels and two inputs of the industrial sectors are increased.

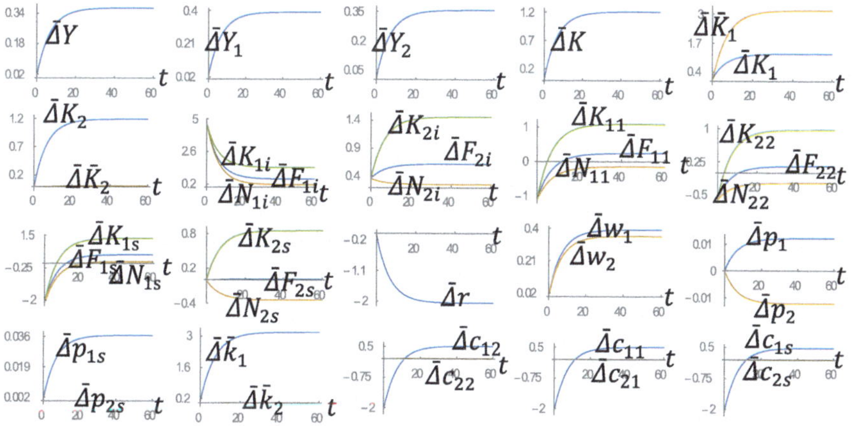

Fig. 14.8 Country 1 augments its propensity to save

14.3 Habit Formation and Preference Change with Free Trade

In *The Theory of Moral Sentiments*, Adam Smith illustrates how people change their preferences as living conditions : "The man who lives within his income is naturally contented with his situation, which, by continual, though small accumulations, is growing better and better every day. He is enabled gradually to relax, both in the rigour of his parsimony and in the severity of his application; and he feels with double satisfaction this gradual increase of ease and enjoyment, from having felt before the hardship which attended the want of them." Fisher (1930: 72) emphasizes the influence of wealth and income on preference difference: "Poverty bears down heavily on all portions of a man's expected life. But it increases the want for immediate income even more than it increases the want for future income."

This sector is to develop a neoclassical global economic growth model with any (finite) number of countries with preference change. The model is developed by Zhang (2017a). I show that changes in one country's preference affect not only the domestic consumption, but also global trade pattern and growth. The global economy consists of J countries, indexed by $j = 1, \ldots, J$; each with a fixed population, N_j, $j = 1, \ldots, J$. The global economy produces a single commodity which is traded without any barriers. There is no international migration. All prices are measured in terms of the commodity. Let $w_j(t)$ and $r_j(t)$ represent the wage rate in country j and global interest rate.

14.3.1 The Production Sector and Marginal Conditions

Country j employs capital $K_j(t)$ and labor N_j to produce:

$$F_j(t) = A_j K_j^{\alpha_j}(t) N_j^{\beta_j}, \alpha_j, \beta_j \geq 0, \alpha_j + \beta_j = 1, j = 1, \ldots J.$$

The marginal conditions imply

$$r(t) = \frac{\alpha_j F_j(t)}{K_j(t)} - \delta_{kj}, w_j(t) = \frac{\beta_j F_j(t)}{N_j},$$

in which δ_{kj} is the depreciation rate of physical capital in country j.

14.3.2 Households Behavior

The disposable income is

$$\hat{y}_j(t) = (1 + r(t))\bar{k}_j(t) + w_j(t),\ j = 1, \cdots, J. \tag{14.3.1}$$

The representative household uses the disposable income for saving $s_j(t)$ and consuming $c_j(t)$ subject to the following budget constraint:

$$c_j(t) + s_j(t) = \hat{y}_j(t). \tag{14.3.2}$$

I specify household j's utility:

$$U_j(t) = \theta_j c_j^{\xi_{0j}(t)}(t) s_j^{\lambda_{0j}(0)}(t),\ \xi_{0j}(t),\ \lambda_{0j}(t) > 0,$$

in which $\xi_{0j}(t)$, and $\lambda_{0j}(t)$ are, respectively, the household's utility elasticities of commodity and savings. I call $\xi_{0j}(t)$, and $\lambda_{0j}(t)$ propensities to consume the commodity and to save. Maximizing $U_j(t)$ subject to (14.3.2), I have

$$c_j(t) = \xi_j(t)\hat{y}_j(t),\ s_j(t) = \lambda_j(t)\hat{y}_j(t), \tag{14.3.3}$$

where

$$\xi_j(t) \equiv \rho_j(t)\xi_{0j}(t),\ \lambda_j(t) \equiv \rho_j(t)\lambda_{0j}(t),\ \rho_j(t) = \frac{1}{\xi_{0j}(t) + \lambda_{0j}(t)}.$$

Variables $\xi_j(t)$ and $\lambda_j(t)$ are, respectively, called the relative propensities to consume and to save. It is not the propensities but the relative propensities that matter in allocating the disposable income. In my approach, I do not assume identical preference of the households across the countries.

The change in household j's wealth follows

$$\bar{k}_j(t) = s_j(t) - \bar{k}_j(t).$$

The total capital stocks employed by all the sectors in the global economy $K(t)$ equals the world wealth:

$$K(t) = \sum_{j=1}^{J} K_j(t) = \sum_{j=1}^{J} \bar{k}_j(t) = \sum_{j=1}^{J} \bar{k}_j(t) N_j,$$

where $\bar{K}_j(t)$ is the capital stock owned by country j. I define $B_j(t)$ as the value of country j's net foreign assets at t. The income from the net foreign assets $E_j(t)$ is $r(t)B_j(t)$. I have

$$\bar{K}_j(t) = K_j(t) + B_j(t).$$

If $E_j(t) > (=, <)0$, country j's trade is said to be in surplus (balance, deficit) where

$$E_j(t) \equiv \left(\bar{K}_j(t) - K_j(t)\right) r(t).$$

14.3.3 The Time Preference and Habit Formation

Following Chapter 9, I specify the dynamics of the propensity to save as follows:

$$\lambda_{0j}(t) = \bar{\lambda}_j + \lambda_{wj} w_j(t) + \lambda_{kj} k_j(t), \tag{14.3.4}$$

where $\bar{\lambda} > 0$, λ_w, and λ_k are parameters. When $\lambda_{wj} = \lambda_{kj} = 0$, the propensity to hold wealth is constant.

Let habit stock be denoted by $\hbar_j(t)$. The habit formation is modeled as

$$\dot{\hbar}_j(t) = \hbar_{j0}\left[c_j(t) - \hbar_j(t)\right]. \tag{14.3.5}$$

The propensity to consume is assumed a function of the habit stock in the following way:

$$\xi_{0j}(t) = \bar{\xi}_j + \xi_{wj} w(t) + \xi_{hj} \hbar_j(t), \tag{14.3.6}$$

where $\bar{\xi}_j > 0$, ξ_{wj} and $\xi_{hj} \geq 0$ are parameters. If $\xi_{wj} = 0$ and $\xi_{hj} = 0$, the propensity is constant. The term $\xi_{wj} w_j(t)$ implies that the propensity to consume is affected by the wage. If $\xi_{wj} > (<)0$, then a rise in the wage rate raises (reduces) the propensity to consume. It is reasonable to assume $\xi_{wj} \geq 0$. The term $\xi_{wj} \hbar_j(t)$ implies that a rise in the habit stock causes the propensity to consume to rise, and vice versa.

I built the multi-country growth model with habit formation and preference change.

Lemma 14.3.1 *The motion of the global economy is given by the following 2J autonomous differential equations with* $K_1(t)$, $\{\bar{k}_j(t)\}$, and $\left(\hbar_j(t)\right)$ *as the variables*:

$$\dot{K}_1(t) = \Phi_1\left(K_1(t), \{\bar{k}_j(t)\}, \left(\hbar_j(t)\right)\right),$$
$$\dot{\bar{k}}_j(t) = \Phi_j\left(K_1(t), \{\bar{k}_j(t)\}, \left(\hbar_j(t)\right)\right),\ j = 2, \ldots, J,$$
$$\dot{\hbar}_j(t) = \Lambda_j\left(K_1(t), \{\bar{k}_j(t)\}, \left(\hbar_j(t)\right)\right),\ j = 1, \ldots, J,$$

in which Φ_j and Λ_j are functions of $K_1(t)$, $\{\bar{k}_j(t)\}$, and $\left(\hbar_j(t)\right)$ defined in Zhang (2019a). The other variables are calculated as functions of $K_1(t)$, $\{\bar{k}_j(t)\}$, and $\left(\hbar_j(t)\right)$ by a computational program.

The lemma is checked in Zhang (2017a). Consider that the world is composed of three economies. The parameter values are specified

$$\alpha_{ij} = 0.3, \lambda_{wj} = -0.1, \lambda_k = 0.02, \hbar_{j0} = 0.1, \xi_{wj} = 0.01, \xi_{hj} = 0.04,$$

$$\begin{pmatrix} N_1 \\ N_2 \\ N_3 \end{pmatrix} = \begin{pmatrix} 2 \\ 3 \\ 6 \end{pmatrix}, \begin{pmatrix} A_1 \\ A_2 \\ A_3 \end{pmatrix} = \begin{pmatrix} 1.3 \\ 0.9 \\ 0.7 \end{pmatrix}, \begin{pmatrix} \bar{\lambda}_1 \\ \bar{\lambda}_2 \\ \bar{\lambda}_3 \end{pmatrix} = \begin{pmatrix} 0.7 \\ 0.62 \\ 0.65 \end{pmatrix},$$

$$\begin{pmatrix} \bar{\xi}_1 \\ \bar{\xi}_2 \\ \bar{\xi}_3 \end{pmatrix} = \begin{pmatrix} 0.09 \\ 0.1 \\ 0.12 \end{pmatrix}, \begin{pmatrix} \delta_{k1} \\ \delta_{k2} \\ \delta_{k3} \end{pmatrix} = \begin{pmatrix} 0.04 \\ 0.05 \\ 0.05 \end{pmatrix}.$$

$$K_1(0) = 23, \bar{k}_2(0) = 5, \bar{k}_3(0) = 3, \hbar_1(0) = 2,$$
$$\hbar_2(0) = 1.1, \hbar_3(0) = 0.8.$$

Figure 14.9 plots the simulation result. All the three countries' habit stocks of consumption fall, even though country 1's consumption level lowers, while the other two countries' consumption levels rise. Country 1's propensity to consume initially rises and subsequently falls, while the other two countries' propensities to consume rise slightly. Country 1's propensity to save falls, while the other two countries' propensities to save rise slightly. It should be noted that the change patterns in the relative propensities are different from these of the propensities. For instance, the change in the propensity to save is monotonic, while the relative propensity to save is of waveform. This occurs because the relative strengths affecting a country's two propensities change over time. As the propensity to save lowers in the long term (to compare, respectively, with their initial conditions) and the propensity to consume becomes higher, each country's wealth is lessened. Consequently, the global wealth and output are diminished. The capital stock and output level of each country are lowered. Although country 1's per capita wealth falls, the per capita levels in the other two countries are augmented. This occurs as country 1's relative propensity falls more than the other two countries' corresponding variables. As the global wealth is lessened, the interest rate is increased. The wage rates are slightly affected. Country 1's trade balance is deteriorated, while the other two countries' trade balances are improved.

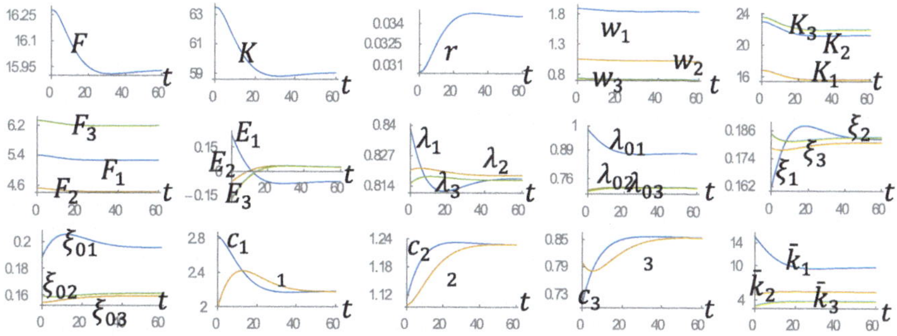

Fig. 14.9 Motion of the global economy

The global economy has an equilibrium point. The equilibrium values of the variables are given as:

$$F = 15.93,\ K = 59.08,\ r = 0.035,$$

$$\begin{pmatrix} F_1 \\ F_2 \\ F_3 \end{pmatrix} = \begin{pmatrix} 5.29 \\ 4.44 \\ 6.20 \end{pmatrix},\ \begin{pmatrix} K_1 \\ K_2 \\ K_3 \end{pmatrix} = \begin{pmatrix} 21.28 \\ 15.77 \\ 22.03 \end{pmatrix},\ \begin{pmatrix} E_1 \\ E_2 \\ E_3 \end{pmatrix} = \begin{pmatrix} -0.06 \\ 0.03 \\ 0.03 \end{pmatrix},$$

$$\begin{pmatrix} \lambda_1 \\ \lambda_2 \\ \lambda_3 \end{pmatrix} = \begin{pmatrix} 0.817 \\ 0.819 \\ 0.817 \end{pmatrix},\ \begin{pmatrix} \xi_1 \\ \xi_2 \\ \xi_3 \end{pmatrix} = \begin{pmatrix} 0.183 \\ 0.181 \\ 0.184 \end{pmatrix},\ \begin{pmatrix} \lambda_{01} \\ \lambda_{02} \\ \lambda_{03} \end{pmatrix} = \begin{pmatrix} 0.88 \\ 0.72 \\ 0.72 \end{pmatrix},$$

$$\begin{pmatrix} \xi_{01} \\ \xi_{02} \\ \xi_{03} \end{pmatrix} = \begin{pmatrix} 0.20 \\ 0.16 \\ 0.16 \end{pmatrix},\ \begin{pmatrix} w_1 \\ w_2 \\ w_3 \end{pmatrix} = \begin{pmatrix} 1.85 \\ 1.04 \\ 0.72 \end{pmatrix},\ \begin{pmatrix} c_1 \\ c_2 \\ c_3 \end{pmatrix} = \begin{pmatrix} \hbar_1 \\ \hbar_2 \\ \hbar_3 \end{pmatrix}$$

$$= \begin{pmatrix} 2.19 \\ 1.23 \\ 0.86 \end{pmatrix},\ \begin{pmatrix} \bar{k}_1 \\ \bar{k}_2 \\ \bar{k}_3 \end{pmatrix} = \begin{pmatrix} 9.79 \\ 5.55 \\ 3.81 \end{pmatrix}.$$

The six eigenvalues are

$$\{-0.11 \pm 0.05i,\ -0.10 \pm 0.06i,\ -0.09 \pm 0.07i\}.$$

14.4 Global Growth and Trade Pattern with Exogenous Changes

This section studies how global growth and trade pattern are affected by various exogenous changes in different countries.

14.4.1 Country 1's Household Giving Lower Weights to More Distant Values of Consumption

It is assumed that country 1's household gives lower weights to more distant values of the levels of consumption as follows: $\hbar_{01}$:0.1 $\Rightarrow$ 0.3. Figure 14.10 plots the simulation result. As demonstrated in the figure, the change in the weight distribution has no impact on the equilibrium of the global economy, even though the transitional paths of the variables vary as the adjustment speed is changed. As the household in country 1 has lower weights of more distant values of consumption, initially country 1's habit stock deviates from the original path as plotted in Fig. 14.1

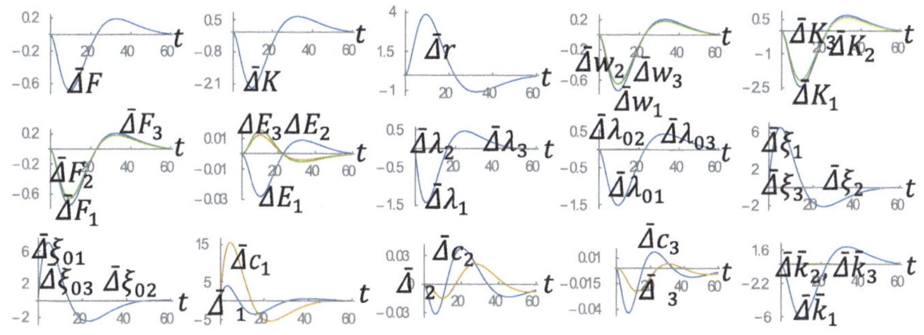

Fig. 14.10 Lower weights given to more distant values of consumption

and moves upwards. The rise in the habit stock draws the country's consumption level up. This change is association the falling in the propensity to save and the rising in the relative propensity to consume in country 1. As country 1's consumption level is increased, the country saves less, and world's capital is decreased. As the global capital is reduced, the interest rate is enhanced, and the output levels of the three national economies are reduced. The propensities and relative propensities of the other two countries remain almost invariant by the parameter change. Country 1's trade balance is almost invariant. The other two countries' trade balances are improved. The subsequent development reverses the change directions of these variables. As the output levels and global wealth are reduced, country 1's habit stock begins to fall, which is associated with falling in the country's consumption. As the consumption level lowers, more savings are made, and the global wealth starts to increase. The capital stocks employed by and the output levels of the three economies all begin to increase. The variables oscillate around the original paths before they come back to their original equilibrium values.

14.4.2 Country 1's Wealth Effect on the Propensity to Save Becoming Stronger

Country 1's wealth effect on the propensity is increased as follows: $\lambda_{1k}:0.02 \Rightarrow 0.03$. Figure 14.11 plots the simulation result. The initial effect of the exogenous disturbance enhances country 1's propensity and relative propensity to save and lowers the relative propensity to consume. The world has more output and wealth. The interest rate falls. The three economies employ more capital inputs, increase their wage rates, and enhance the output levels. Countries 1's and 3's propensities are almost invariant. As its propensity to consume falls initially, household 1's consumption level becomes lower, which is associated with lessening in the habit stock. The both consumption level and habit stock of consumption are enhanced in association with rise in per capita wealth. Different from the monotonically increasing pattern in the consumption level after its initial falling, country 1's habit stock exhibits a waveform.

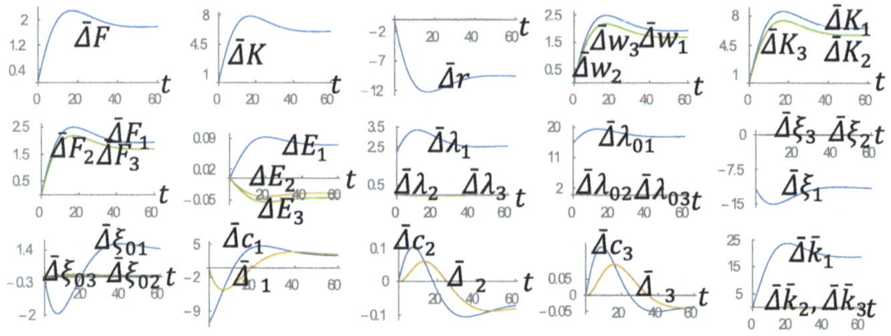

Fig. 14.11 Stronger wealth effect on the propensity to save

Country 1's trade balance is improved, while the other two countries' trade balances are deteriorated.

14.4.3 Country 1's Propensity to Consume Being More Strongly Affected by Habits

Country 1's propensity to consume is assumed to be influenced by habits of consumption: ξ_{h1}:0.04 $\Rightarrow$ 0.05. The simulation result is summarized as follows. The relative propensity to consume is enhanced, and the relative propensity to save is lowered. The propensities and relative propensities of the other two countries remain almost invariant. As country 1 saves less from its disposable income, the wealth owned by the country is reduced. The other two countries' wealth levels are slightly changed. The interest rate becomes higher. The wage rates become lower. The global wealth and output level are reduced. The capital inputs and output levels of each national economy are decreased. Country $1's$ trade balance is almost invariant. The other two countries' trade balances are slightly improved. Country $1's$ consumption and habit stock become higher initially and lower in the long term. Country 1's output level is reduced. Country $2's$ and country $3's$ per capita wealth and consumption levels are almost invariant. It is concluded that country $1's$ preference change lowers its own living standards but has little impacts on the other countries' wealth and consumption.

14.5 Trade in Goods and Tourism with Infrastructure and Externalities

An important phenomenon in modern economies is that tourism has been domestically and internationally rapidly expanded. This section studies economic theory with trade goods and tourism. It is based on Zhang (2015b). I deal with dynamic interactions between economic growth, economic change, tourism, and trade with externalities and endogenous infrastructures. Tourism needs special attention in studying international trade because tourism is different from what is called tradable goods in traditional trade theory. Tourist goods such as monuments of national heritage, historical sites, beaches, and hot springs are non-tradable in the traditional trade theory as one has to travel to the location in order to consume them. Tourism converts non-traded goods into tradable ones. Tourism affects local economies in different ways. Tourism uses national resources such as labor, capital, and housing and thus may make these resources less available for other sectors of the economy. Tourism also generates income which may be used to develop other economic activities. Tourism has been analyzed by economists from different aspects within different theoretical frameworks (Copeland 1991; Chao et al. 2009; Zeng and Zhu 2011).

This study is to introduce infrastructure (public goods), externalities, and congestion into a growth model with tourism. The government's income is spent only on supplying infrastructure. The public sector gets the government's income and supplies public goods. As in Chapter 11, I accept an analytical framework for small open economies. The open economy can import goods and borrow resources from the rest of the world or exports goods and lend resources abroad. The economy produces two goods: an internationally traded good (called industrial good) and a non-traded good (called services). Domestic households consume both goods. Foreign tourists consume only services. The rate of interest, r^*, is fixed in international market. Capital depreciates at rate δ_k. The households hold wealth and land and receive income from wages, land rent, and interest payments of wealth. Land is only for residential and service use. Technologies of the production sectors are described by the Cobb–Douglas production functions. All markets are perfectly competitive. Capital and labor are completely mobile between the three sectors. Capital is perfectly mobile in international market, and I neglect possibility of emigration or/and immigration. Labor is homogeneous and is fixed. Let $\bar{N}$ stand for the population and $T(t)$ for the work time of the representative household. The labor force $N(t)$ is given by: $N(t) = hT(t)\bar{N}$, where h is the fixed level of human capital. Subscript index, i, s, and p, denote, respectively, the industrial, service, and public sectors. Let $K_j(t)$ and $N_j(t)$ stand for the capital stock and labor force employed by sector j, $j = i, s, p$, at time t. I introduce

$$k_j(t) \equiv \frac{K_j(t)}{N_j(t)}, r_\delta \equiv r^* + \delta_k, \bar{\tau}_j \equiv 1 - \tau_j, j = i, s, e,$$

where τ_j is the fixed tax rate on sector j, $0 < \tau_j < 1$, $j = i, s$.

14.5.1 Industrial Sector

The production function is dependent on private inputs, public goods, externalities, and congestion. Infrastructure introduces a positive externality in production so that the complete production is one of overall increasing returns to scale in the productive factors. Basing on Eicher and Turnovsky (2000), the production function of the industrial sector $F_i(t)$ is taken on the following form:

$$F_i(t) = \Omega_i(t) K_i^{\alpha_i}(t) N_i^{\beta_i}(t), \alpha_i, \beta_i > 0, \alpha_i + \beta_i = 1, \tag{14.5.1}$$

where $\Omega_i(t)$ is a function of externalities, public service, and congestion, specified as:

$$\Omega_i(t) = A_i G^{\theta_p}(t) K_i^{\theta_e}(t) \left(\frac{K_p(t)}{K_i(t) + K_p(t)} \right)^{\theta_c}, \theta_p, \theta_e, \theta_c \geq 0,$$

where $G^{\theta_p}(t)$ measures the effect of public service on productivity, $K_i^{\theta_e}(t)$ the effect of externalities, and $\left(K_p(t)/\left(K_i(t) + K_p(t)\right)\right)^{\theta_c}$ the effect of congestion of public goods. Like Eicher and Turnovsky (2000), I interpret that when $\theta_c + \theta_e = 0$, there is no congestion and no externality. The non-rival and non-excludable infrastructure is available equally to each agent, independent of the usage of others. The congestion effect term implies that for a fixed level of infrastructure, a rise in the private capital tends to reduce the efficiency of public services. There are different ways of describing congestion (see, Gómez 2008a). It should be noted that $G(t)$ is often interpreted to be generated by learning-by-doing or human capital spill-over effects. I now interpret the variables as public goods such as physical and institutional infrastructures. The marginal conditions are

$$r_\delta = \alpha_i \bar{\tau}_i \Omega_i(t) k_i^{-\beta_i}(t), w(t) = \beta_i \bar{\tau}_i \Omega_i(t) k_i^{\alpha_i}(t). \tag{14.5.2}$$

14.5.2 Service Sector

The service sector uses three inputs, capital $K_s(t)$, labor force $N_s(t)$, and land $L_s(t)$, to supply services with the following technology:

$$F_s(t) = A_s K_s^{\alpha_s}(t) N_s^{\beta_s}(t) L_s^{\gamma_s}(t),$$
$$\alpha_s, \beta_s, \gamma_s > 0, \alpha_s + \beta_s + \gamma_s = 1, \tag{14.5.3}$$

where A_s, α_s, β_s, and γ_s are parameters. Let $p(t)$ and $R(t)$ stand, respectively, for the price of the service and the land rent. The marginal conditions for the service sector are

$$r_\delta = \alpha_s \bar{\tau}_s A_s p(t) k_s^{\alpha_s - 1}(t) l_s^{\gamma_s}(t), \; w(t) = \beta_s \bar{\tau}_s A_s p(t) k_s^{\alpha_s}(t) l_s^{\gamma_s}(t),$$
$$R(t) = \gamma_s \bar{\tau}_s A_s p(t) k_s^{\alpha_s}(t) l_s^{\gamma_s - 1}(t), \tag{14.5.4}$$

where $l_s(t) \equiv L_s(t)/N_s(t)$.

14.5.3 Full Employment of Capital and Labor

The total capital stocks employed by the country $K(t)$, is used by the three sectors. The full employment of capital and labor force implies

$$K_i(t) + K_s(t) + K_p(t) = K(t),$$
$$N_i(t) + N_s(t) + N_p(t) = N(t). \tag{14.5.5}$$

14.5.4 Behavior of Domestic Households

Let L denote the total land available for residential and service use. The household's current income is from the land ownership, wealth, and wage. It is assumed the land equally owned by the population. Each household gets the land income: $\bar{r}(t) = LR(t)/\bar{N}$. The current income is

$$y(t) = \hat{\tau}_k r^* \bar{k}(t) + \hat{\tau}_w h T(t) w(t) + \hat{\tau}_L \bar{r}(t),$$

where $r^* k(t)$ is the interest payment, $hT(t)w(t)$ the total wage income and

$$\hat{\tau}_m \equiv 1 - \hat{\tau}_m, \; m = k, w, L,$$

where $\hat{\tau}_k$, $\hat{\tau}_w$, and $\hat{\tau}_L$ are, respectively, the fixed tax rates on the wealth (excluding land) income, wage, and land income. The disposable income at any point in time is $\hat{y}(t) = y(t) + \bar{k}(t)$. The household's budget constraint is

$$(1 + \tilde{\tau}_R) R(t) l(t) + (1 + \bar{\tau}_s) p(t) c_s(t)$$
$$+ (1 + \tilde{\tau}_i) c_i(t) + s(t) = \hat{y}(t), \tag{14.5.6}$$

where $\tilde{\tau}_R$, $\tilde{\tau}_R$, and $\tilde{\tau}_R$ are, respectively, the consumer tax rates on housing, consumption of services, and consumption of goods. Let $\bar{T}(t)$ stand for the leisure time at time. The time constraint is $T(t) + \bar{T}(t) = T_0$, where T_0 is the total time available for work and leisure. Substituting the time constraint into (14.5.6) yields

$$\hat{\tau}_w h \bar{T}(t) w(t) + (1 + \tilde{\tau}_R) R(t) l(t) + (1 + \bar{\tau}_s) p(t) c_s(t)$$

$$+ (1 + \tilde{\tau}_i) c_i(t) + s(t) = \bar{y}(t), \tag{14.5.7}$$

where

$$\bar{y}(t) = \left(1 + \hat{\tau}_k r^*\right) \bar{k}(t) + \hat{\tau}_w h T_0 w(t) + \hat{\tau}_L \bar{r}(t).$$

The utility function $U(t)$ is dependent on $\bar{T}(t)$, $l(t)$, $c_s(t)$, $c_i(t)$, and $s(t)$ as follows:

$$U(t) = \theta(G(t)) \bar{T}^{\sigma_0}(t) l^{\eta_0}(t) c_s^{\gamma_0}(t) c_i^{\xi_0}(t) s^{\lambda_0}(t), \sigma_0, \eta_0, \gamma_0, \xi_0, \lambda_0 > 0,$$

in which σ_0, η_0, γ_0, ξ_0, and λ_0 are the representative household's elasticity of utility with regard to leisure time, lot size, services, industrial goods, and saving, and $\theta(G(t))$ is the amenity which is related to the level of public good. I call σ_0, η_0, γ_0, ξ_0, and λ_0 propensities to consume the leisure time, to use the lot size, to consume services, to consume industrial goods, and to hold wealth, respectively. Maximizing $U(t)$ subject to the budget constraint yields

$$\bar{T}(t) = \frac{\sigma \bar{y}(t)}{w(t)}, l(t) = \frac{\eta \bar{y}(t)}{R(t)}, c_s(t) = \frac{\gamma \bar{y}(t)}{p(t)},$$
$$c_i(t) = \xi \bar{y}(t), s(t) = \lambda \bar{y}(t), \tag{14.5.8}$$

where

$$\sigma \equiv \frac{\rho \sigma_0}{\tilde{\tau}_w h}, \eta \equiv \frac{\rho \eta_0}{1 + \tilde{\tau}_R}, \gamma \equiv \frac{\rho \gamma_0}{1 + \tilde{\tau}_s}, \xi \equiv \frac{\rho \xi_0}{1 + \tilde{\tau}_i}, \lambda \equiv \rho \lambda_0,$$
$$\rho \equiv \frac{1}{\sigma_0 + \eta_0 + \gamma_0 + \xi_0 + \lambda_0}.$$

The wealth change follows

$$\dot{\bar{k}}(t) = s(t) - \bar{k}(t). \tag{14.5.9}$$

14.5.5 Demand Function of Foreign Tourists

Let $y_f(t)$ stand for the disposable income of foreign countries. Like Schubert and Brida (2009), I specify the following iso-elastic tourism demand function:

$$D_T(t) = a(t) y_f^{\varphi}(t) \left[(1 + \tilde{\tau}_s) p(t)\right]^{-\varepsilon}, \tag{14.5.10}$$

where φ and ε are, respectively, the income and price elasticities of tourism demand. The variable, $a(t)$, is dependent on many conditions, such as infrastructures (airports and transportation systems) and social environment (like criminal rates and traffic congestions), and cultural capital. Tourists pay the same price in consumption as domestic people.

14.5.6 Full use of Land

The available land is fully used for housing and service production:

$$l(t)\bar{N} + L_s(t) = L.$$

14.5.7 Demand and Supply for Services

The equilibrium condition for services is

$$c_s(t)\bar{N} + D_T(t) = F_s(t).$$

14.5.8 Behavior of the Government

The capital stocks and workers employed by the public sector are paid at the same rates that the private sectors pay the services of these factors. The government's income is given by:

$$Y_p(t) = \tau_i F_i(t) + \tau_s p(t) F_s(t) + I_h(t)\bar{N} + \tilde{\tau}_T p(t) D_T(t),$$

where the tax income from the household is

$$I_h(t) = \tilde{\tau}_R R(t) l(t) + \tilde{\tau}_i c_i(t) + \tilde{\tau}_s p(t) c_s(t) + \tilde{\tau}_k r^* \bar{k}(t)$$
$$+ \tilde{\tau}_L \bar{r}(t) + \tilde{\tau}_w h w(t) T(t).$$

The public sector supplies public goods by utilizing capital $K_p(t)$ and labor force $N_p(t)$ as follows:

$$G(t) = A_p K_p^{\alpha_p}(t) N_p^{\beta_p}(t),\ A_p, \alpha_p, \beta_p > 0, \alpha_p + \beta_p = 1,$$

The public sector's budget constraint is

$$w(t)N_p(t) + r_\delta K_p(t) = Y_p(t).$$

Maximizing the public services under the budget constraint yields

$$w(t)N_p(t) = \alpha Y_p(t),\, r_\delta K_p(t) = \beta Y_p(t),$$

where

$$\alpha \equiv \frac{\alpha_p}{\alpha_p + \beta_p},\, \beta \equiv \frac{\beta_p}{\alpha_p + \beta_p}.$$

We thus built the dynamic model with endogenous wealth, infrastructure, and tourism.

Lemma 15.4.1 *The motion of the land rent and wage is determined by the following two differential equations*:

$$\dot{R}(t) = \Omega_1(R(t), w(t)),\, \dot{w}(t) = \Omega_2(R(t), w(t)), \tag{14.5.11}$$

where Ω_1 *and* Ω_2 *are functions of* $R(t)$ *and* $w(t)$ *determined in* Zhang (2015b). *Once* $R(t)$ *and* $w(t)$ *are determined by* (14.5.11), *I solve all the other variables.*

To simulate the model, I specify parameter values as follows:

$$r^* = 0.04,\, \delta_k = 0.05,\, \bar{N} = 20,\, h = 2,\, T_0 = 24,\, L = 8,$$
$$A_i = 1.1,\, A_s = 1.4,\, A_p = 0.5,\, \alpha_i = 0.33,\, \alpha_s = 0.25,\, \beta_s = 0.65,$$
$$\alpha_p = 0.3,\, \beta_p = 0.7,\, \lambda_0 = 0.7,\, \xi_0 = 0.15,\, \gamma_0 = 0.06,\, \eta_0 = 0.06,$$
$$\sigma_0 = 0.2,\, a = 1,\, y_f = 4,\, \varphi = 1.5,\, \varepsilon = 1.6,\, \theta_p = 0.1,$$

$$r^* = 0.04,\, \delta_k = 0.05,\, \bar{N} = 20,\, h = 2,\, T_0 = 24,\, L = 8,$$
$$A_i = 1.1,\, A_s = 1.4,\, A_p = 0.5,\, \alpha_i = 0.33,\, \alpha_s = 0.25,\, \beta_s = 0.65,$$
$$\alpha_p = 0.3,\, \beta_p = 0.7,\, \lambda_0 = 0.7,\, \xi_0 = 0.15,\, \gamma_0 = 0.06,\, \eta_0 = 0.06,$$
$$\sigma_0 = 0.2,\, a = 1,\, y_f = 4,\, \varphi = 1.5,\, \varepsilon = 1.6,\, \theta_p = 0.1,$$
$$\theta_e = \theta_c = 0.05,\, \tau_i = \tau_s = \tau_c = \tau_k = \tau_w = 0.01,\, \bar{\tau}_k = \bar{\tau}_w$$
$$= \bar{\tau}_L = 0.01,\, \bar{\tau}_R = \bar{\tau}_s = \bar{\tau}_i = 0.01,$$
$$\theta_i = 0.1,\, \theta_s = 0.05,\, \tau_i = \tau_s = \tau_c = \tau_k = \tau_w = 0.01,$$
$$\bar{\tau}_k = \bar{\tau}_w = \bar{\tau}_L = \bar{\tau}_R = \bar{\tau}_s = \bar{\tau}_i = 0.01,\, \tilde{\theta}_i = 0.05,\, \tilde{\theta}_s = 0.01,$$
$$\tilde{\theta}_T = 0.05,\, \theta_0 = 0.05,\, b_i = b_s = 0.15,\, b_e = 0.1,\, b_0 = 0.05.$$

The rate of interest is fixed at 3%, and the population is 20. Many empirical studies use the value of the parameter, α, in the Cobb–Douglas production functions approximately 0.3. Some empirical studies show that income elasticity of tourism demand is well above unity (Syriopoulos 1995; Lanza et al. 2003). According to Lanza et al. (2003), the price elasticity is in the range between 1.03 and 1.82, and income elasticities are in the range between 1.75 and 7.36. Refer to, for instance, Gaŕin-Mũnos (2007) for other studies on elasticities of tourism. Tax rates are fixed at 1 or 0.5 percent. I assume relatively weak effects of public goods, externalities, and congestions. I specify the initial conditions as follows:

$$R(0) = 30, w(0) = 1.9.$$

I plot the motion of the dynamic system in Fig. 14.12. As their initial values are fixed lower than their long-term equilibrium values, the land rent and wage rise over time. In tandem with rising land rent, the price of services is enhanced. Rising price reduces tourist demand. In association with rising wage rate and wealth, the leisure time is increased. The total labor supply falls. The GDP falls slightly. The government gets more money and spends more on supplying public goods. The public produces more and employs more capital and labor inputs. The output level of the industrial sector is reduced and that of the service sector is increased. The labor and capital inputs of the service sectors are increased, and the labor and capital inputs are reduced. The national wealth rises over time, and the capital stocks employed by the country fall. The household consumes more industrial goods and services, owns more wealth, and has larger lot size.

Figure 14.12 shows the motion of the variables over time. From figure I observe that all the variables of the economic system tend to become stationary in the long term. This implies that the system approaches an equilibrium point:

$$w = 1.744,\ p = 1.911,\ R = 35.9,\ Y = 1426.8,\ Y_p = 27.65,$$
$$N = 451.4,\ K = 4090.1,\ \bar{K} = 3073.8,\ DT = 2.79,\ N_i = 342.1,$$
$$N_s = 98.2,\ N_p = 11.1,\ K_i = 3265.9,\ K_s = 732,\ K_p = 92.2,$$

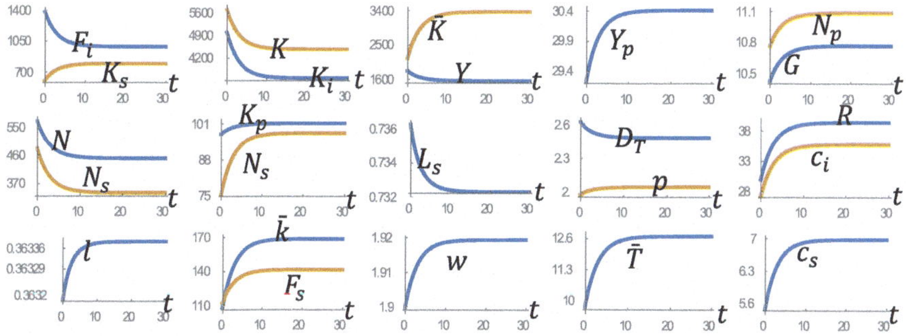

Fig. 14.12 Motion of the national economy

$$L_s = 0.73,\ F_i = 899.7,\ F_s = 139.2,\ G = 10.47,\ \bar{T} = 12.7,$$
$$c_i = 32.6,\ c_s = 6.82,\ l = 0.36,\ \bar{k} = 153.7.$$

The eigenvalues are $\{-0.332, 0\}$.

14.6 Impact of Various Shocks on the Tourist Economy

I now study how changes in some parameters affect the national economy over time.

14.6.1 A Rise in the Rate of Interest in the Global Market

First, I study the effects of changes in the rate of interest r^* on the national economy. The rate of interest is changed as follows: $r^* = 0.04 \Rightarrow 0.05$. It should be remarked that as I have explicitly given the procedure to follow the motion of the economy system, I can also carry out comparative dynamic analysis by assuming that the rate of interest varies in time, $r^*(t)$. This is true also for other parameters. The effects are plotted in Fig. 14.13. In the rest of the paper, a solid (dashed) line in a plot demonstrates the value before (after) a parameter is changed. As the cost of capital is increased, the wage rate is increased. The economy employs less capital, and the GDP is slightly reduced. The household's and national wealth are increased. Although the public sector gets more money, the public sector's output falls due to the rising costs of the two input factors. The two inputs of the public sector are decreased. The rise in the cost of capital causes the two sectors to use less capital. The output level and labor input of the industrial sector are reduced. The service sector's output is reduced, and its labor input is increased. Less foreign tourists visit the country in tandem with rising price of services. The land rent is increased. The service sector uses less land, and the lot size is expanded. The leisure time rises in association with rising wage

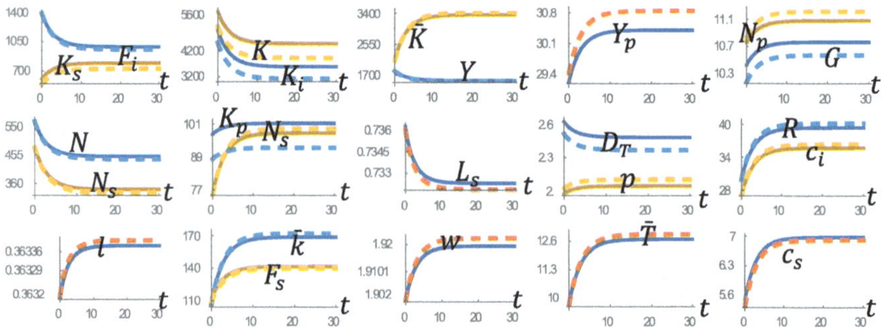

Fig. 14.13 Rise in the rate of interest

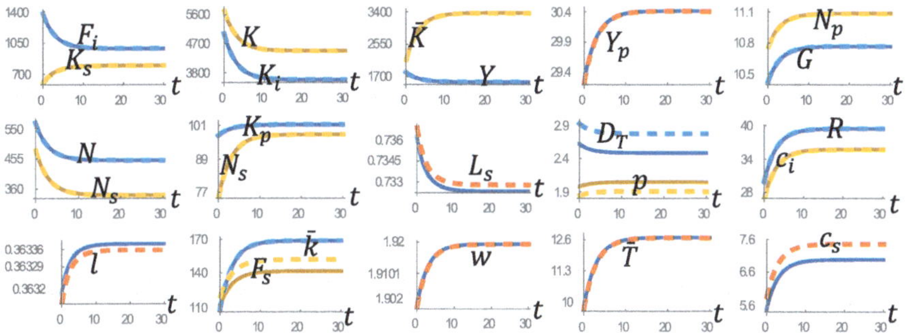

Fig. 14.14 Rise in the total productivity of the service sector

rate (i.e., opportunity cost of leisure). The household consumes less services and more industrial goods.

14.6.2 A Rise in the Total Productivity of the Service Sector

We now examine the impact of the following change in the total productivity of the service sector: $A_s = 1.4 \Rightarrow 1.5$. I plot the effects on the variables in Fig. 14.14. The increased productivity of the service sector raises the output of services and lowers the price of services. More foreign tourists are attracted to the country. The leisure time, total labor supply, the total capital, the national wealth, the GDP, the public sector, and the output of the industrial sector are slightly affected. The land use is redistributed, the lot size being reduced. The household's consumption of services is increased in association with falling price of services. I see that changes in the service sector's productivity mainly affect services-related activities and have weak effects on the nationally aggregated real variables.

14.6.3 Raising Tax Rate on the Service Sector

We now study the effects of raising the tax rate on the service sector in the following way: $\tau_s = 0.01 \Rightarrow 0.02$. The effects are plotted in Fig. 14.15. As the tax rate is increased, the government gets more income. The public sector employs more capital and labor inputs and supplies more public goods. The labor input of the service sector is reduced, and the labor input of the industrial sector is slightly affected. The household's wealth and national wealth are slightly augmented. The national economy employs more capital. Less foreign tourists visit the country in tandem with rising price of services. The wage rate, leisure time, and total labor supply are slightly affected. The industrial sector produces more and employs more capital. The land rent is increased. The service sector uses less land, and the lot size

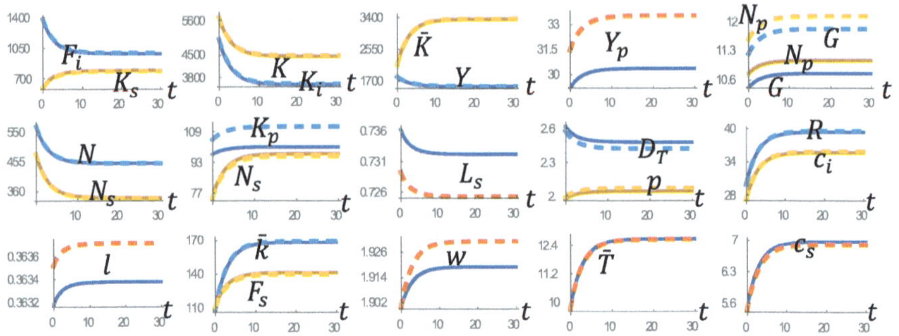

Fig. 14.15 Raising tax rate on the service sector

is expanded. The household consumes less services and more industrial goods. The GDP is slightly reduced.

14.6.4 Raising Tax Rate on Consumption of Services

We now study the effects of raising the tax rate on consumption of services in the following way: $\tilde{\tau}_s = 0.01 \Rightarrow 0.02$. The effects are plotted in Fig. 14.16. Rather than raising taxes on producers, the government gets more income from consumers. Nevertheless, by comparing Figs. 14.15 and 14.16, I see that the effects on the economy are almost the same by two different tax policies.

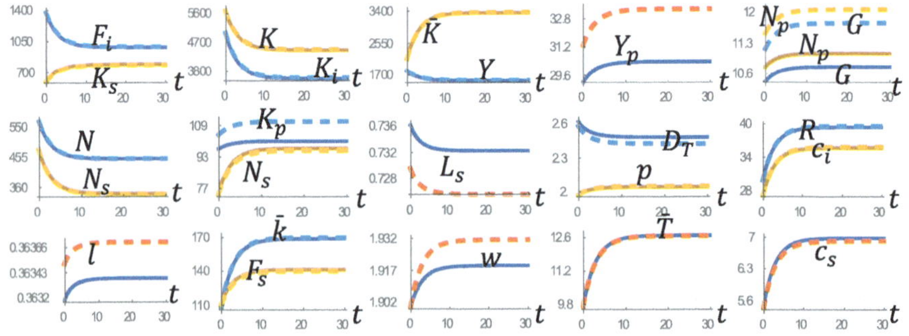

Fig. 14.16 Raising tax rate on consumption of services

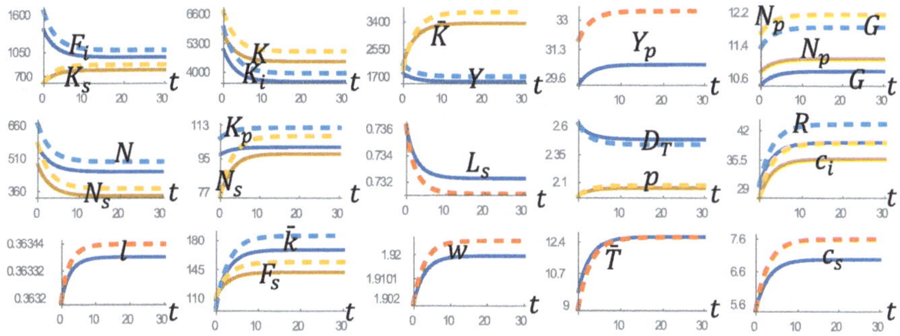

Fig. 14.17 Improvement in human capital

14.6.5 An Improvement in Human Capital

We now examine what will happen to the national economy when human capital is improved as follows: $h = 2 \Rightarrow 2.2$. The changes in the variables are plotted in Fig. 14.17. The leisure time is slightly affected, and the total labor supply is increased in tandem with rising wage rate. The GDP and the total capital employed by the economy are increased. The household's wealth and national wealth are augmented. The price of services and the land rent are increased. The increased price reduces foreign tourists. The lot size is increased. The land use of the service sector is reduced. The household consumes more goods and services and owns more wealth. Each sector increases their inputs and output level. The government gets more money for supplying public goods. The government sector's output and its two inputs are augmented.

14.6.6 A Rise in the Household's Propensity to Consume Services

We now examine what will happen to the national economy when the household's propensity to consume services is augmented as follow: $\gamma_0 = 0.06 \Rightarrow 0.08$. The changes in the variables are plotted in Fig. 14.18. The consumption level of services by the domestic households is increased. The price and tourism are slight affected. The consumption level of industrial goods falls in association with rising consumption level of the household. The leisure time is increased, and the total labor supply is increased in tandem with rising wage rate. The GDP and the total capital employed by the economy are increased. The household's wealth and national wealth are lowered. The land rent is reduced. The lot size is decreased. The land use of the service sector is augmented. The service sector increases the two inputs and output level. The industrial sector decreases the two inputs and output level. The government gets

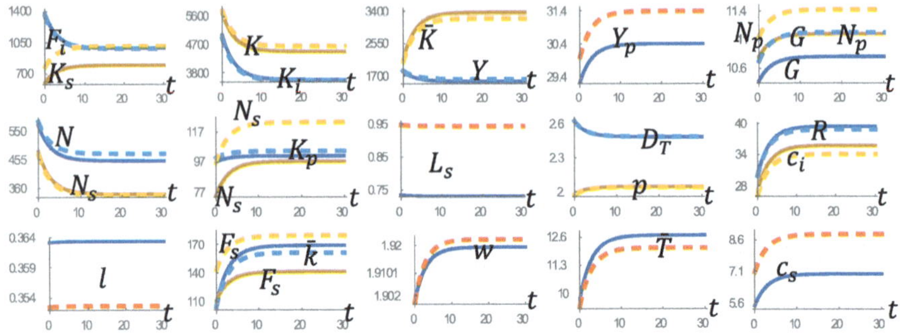

Fig. 14.18 Rise in the household's propensity to consume services

more money for supplying public goods. The government sector's output and its two inputs are augmented.

14.6.7 Public Services More Strongly Affecting the Productivity of the Industrial Sector

We now allow public services to more strongly affect the productivity of the industrial sector in the following way: $\theta_p = 0.1 \Rightarrow 0.2$. The changes in the variables are plotted in Fig. 14.19. The wage rate and output level of the industrial sector are increased. The industrial sector also employs more capital input. The leisure time, total labor supply, labor inputs of the industrial and service sectors are slightly affected. The GDP and the capital employed by the economy are augmented. The price is increased, and tourism is reduced. The land rent is enhanced, and the lot size is expanded. The government gets more money for supplying public goods. The government sector's output and its two inputs are augmented.

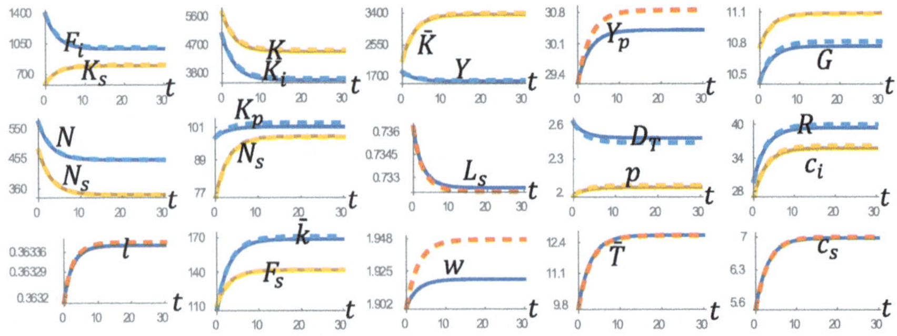

Fig. 14.19 Public services more strongly affecting the productivity

This paper built a growth model of a small open economy. Various issues of growth with regional interdependence and international interdependence are modeled by me in other papers.

14.7 On Nominal Exchange Rates and Capital Flows

This chapter is focused on generalizing the O–H model. The contents of the previous chapters also imply important issues not properly addressed even one looks at the complexity of national economies in this book. A comprehensive review on the literature of trade and trade pattern is provided by Zhang (2008). Ethier (1974) shows that the traditional trade theory has four core proportions. They are, respectively: (1) factor-price equalization theorem by Lerner (1952) and Samuelson (1948, 1949), which says that free trade in final goods alone brings about complete international equalization of factor prices; (2) Stolper–Samuelson theory by Stolper and Samuelson (1941) shows that that an increase in the relative price of one commodity enhances the real return of the factor used intensively in producing that commodity and lowers the real return of the other factor; (3) Rybczynski theorem by Rybczynski (1955) states that if commodity prices are held fixed, an increase in the endowment of one factor causes a more than proportionate increase in the output of the commodity which uses that factor relatively intensively and an absolute decline in the output of the other commodity; and (4) Heckscher–Ohlin theorem by Heckscher (1919) and Ohlin (1933 see also Heckscher and Ohlin 1991) states that a country tends to have a bias toward producing and exporting the commodity which uses intensively the factor with which it is relatively well-endowed. As shown in Zhang (2008), it is not difficult to have all the core proportions in one general equilibrium model.

This chapter does not address another significant issue for understanding current world. Issues related to nominal and real exchange rates in global markets. Dynamic interactions between monetary and real variables are increasingly more complicated in a globalizing world. I will address some issues on exchange rates in Chap. 11. There are many studies on exchange rates (Zhang 2009). Some seminal works are carried out by Mindell. The 1999 Nobel Prize was awarded to Robert A. Mundell (1932)—for his contribution to analysis of monetary and fiscal policy under different exchange rate regimes and his research in optimum currency. From this chapter and Chap. 11, it is not difficult to show that the main models by Mundell can be easily integrated with the approach in this book and we should be able to get more proper insights into the dynamics of international interdependence between real and monetary variables.

References

Chen Z (1992) Long-run equilibria in a dynamic Heckscher-Ohlin model. Can J Econ 25:923–943

Copeland BR (1991) Tourism, welfare and de-industrialization in a small open economy. Economica 58:515–529

Eicher T, Turnovsky S (2000) Scale, congestion and growth. Economica 67:325–346
Ethier WJ (1974) Some of the theorems of international trade with many goods and factors. J Int Econ 4:199–206
Fisher I (1930) The theory of interest. Macmillan, New York
Gafin-Mũnos T (2007) German demand for tourism in Spain. Tour Manag 28:12–22
Gómez MA (2008) Fiscal policy, congestion, and endogenous growth. J Public Econ Theory 10:595–622
Heckscher E (1919) The effect of foreign trade on the distribution of income. Ekonomisk Tidskrift 1919:497–512
Heckscher E, Ohlin B (1991) Heckscher-Ohlin trade theory. In: Flam H, Flanders J (eds) The MIT Press, Mass, Cambridge
Ikeda S, Ono Y (1992) Macroeconomic dynamics in a multi-country economy—a dynamic optimization approach. Int Econ Rev 33:629–644
Lanza A, Temple P, Urga G (2003) The implications of tourism specialisation in the long run: an econometric analysis for 13 OECD economies. Tour Manag 24:315–321
Lerner AP (1952) Factor prices and international trade. Economica 19:1–15
Ohlin B (1933) Interregional and international trade. Harvard University Press, Cambridge
Rybczynski TM (1955) Factor endowments and relative commodity prices. Economica 22:336–341
Samuelson PA (1948) International trade and equalisation of factor prices. Econ J 58:163–184
Samuelson PA (1949) International factor-price equalisation once again. Econ J 59:181–197
Schubert SF, Brida JG (2009) A dynamic model of economic growth in a small tourism driven economy. Munich Personal RePEc Archive
Stolper W, Samuelson PA (1941) Protection and real wages. Rev Econ Stud 9:58–73
Syriopoulos TC (1995) A dynamic model of demand for Mediterranean tourism. Int Rev Appl Econ 9:318–336
Zeng DZ, Zhu XW (2011) Tourism and industrial agglomeration. Jpn Econ Rev 62:537–561
Zhang WB (2008) International trade theory: Capital, knowledge, economic structure, money and prices over time and space. Springer, Berlin
Zhang WB (2009) Monetary growth theory: money, interest, prices, capital, knowledge, and economic structure over time and space. Routledge, London
Zhang WB (2015a) A synthesis of the Heckscher-Ohlin and Oniki-Uzawa trade models with heterogeneous tastes, different technologies, and endogenous wealth. Scientific Annals of the "Alexandru Ioan Cuza" University of Iasi. Econ Sci 62:391–410
Zhang WB (2015b) Tourism, trade, externalities, and public goods in a three-sector growth model. UTMS J Econ 6:1–19
Zhang WB (2017) Implications of habit formation and preference change for free trade patterns and global economic growth. Int J Econ Manage 11:107–126
Zhang WB (2019) Monopsony and discrimination against woman in labor market in an extended Solowian model. Res Econ Bus Central Eastern Europe 11:1–15

Chapter 15
Alonso Urban and Solow Growth Models Integrated

Social and economic activities take place in space, even though computer has changing the role of space. Genuine dynamic spatial economics is required to understand mechanisms and processes of location as time and space are the elementary variables for spatial location over time. Mainstreams of analytical economics omitted space mainly because a genuine spatial analysis results in analytically intractable problems. Two well-known experts on theoretical spatial economics Fujita and Thisse (2002: 389) spell out the deadlock as follow: "Clearly, space and time are intrinsically mixed in the process of economic development. However, the study of their interaction is a formidable task. Because either agglomeration or growth is a complex phenomenon by itself, one should expect any integrated analysis to face many conceptual and analytical hurdles. Not surprisingly, therefore, the field is still in its infancy, and relevant contributions have been few." Fujita and Thisse extensively contributed the literature of modern spatial economics. But they did not analyze the role of physical capital in spatial growth properly. Arnott (1980: 53) describes the state of urban economics by the 1980s as follows: "In the last decade the static theory of residential urban location and land use has been extensively developed. The theory has generated many useful insights, but because it ignores growth and durability of housing and urban infrastructure there are many urban phenomena it cannot explain." The situation still lingers on among the mainstreams of spatial economic theory. According to Baldwin and Martin (2004: 2675–6): "Many of the most popular economic geography models focus on labor. … These are unsuited to the study of growth. The key to all sustained growth is the accumulation of human capital, physical capital and/or knowledge capital—with the accumulation of knowledge capital, i.e., technological progress having a privileged position. We thus need a model in which capital exists and its stock is endogenous."

This chapter provides a rigorous spatial model to show how to integrate urban economics with growth theories. Rigorous spatial economic theory has focused on the role of space on location. Economic theories with endogenous physical capital

W.-B. Zhang, *The General Economic Theory*,
https://doi.org/10.1007/978-3-030-56204-5_15

neglect the role of space. I provide a model to show how to synthesize the Solow growth model, the Alonso urban model, and the Muth housing model.

Numerous contributions to urban economics have followed the equilibrium theory of urban land market pioneered by Alonso (1964). This approach has been extended in many directions. Most of the models concentrate on the residential location and urban structure and neglect production aspects of urban dynamics. On the other hand, urban growth theory is another important theoretical approach to explain spatial phenomena. There are many studies of urban growth and dynamics (Richardson; and Henderson 1985). Urban economics studies economic geography and urban growth theory concentrates on growth factors without space. I integrated the two separated approaches in a unified framework over years. This chapter also introduces housing market and prices of land into the basic model. Housing is the largest component of non-human wealth for households and housing services are a fundamental component of the household consumption. Endogenous determination of prices of land and housing is seldom addressed in formal economic models.

15.1 Land Value, Residential Structure, and Growth

I am concerned with a small open economy which has free trade with the rest world. The model is based on Zhang (2018). Dynamic interdependence between economic growth and residential density change over space is the main concern. The model is a synthesis of the basic features of the basic model and the Alonso residential model. The modeling of the residential land use follows the Alonso model (which, like almost all formal urban models, has no microeconomic mechanism of determining land price). The economic system is an open urban economy built on a flat featureless plain. All workers reside over the city and work in the central business district (CBD). People travel only between dwelling sites and the CBD. An individual resides only at one location. The only spatial characteristic that directly matters is the distance from the residential site to the CBD. The economy consists of a finite strip of land extending from a fixed central business district with constant unit width. The system is geographically linear and consists of two parts—the CBD and the residential area. I use L to stand for the fixed (territory) length of the state. I assume that all economic activities are concentrated in the CBD. I use ω to represent the distance from the CBD to a point in the residential area. Let $R(t, \omega)$ and $p(t, \omega)$ stand for the land rent and land price at location ω at time t. The households occupy the residential area. The industrial product can be either invested or consumed. Housing is measured by lot size. The total labor force is fully employed by the industrial sector. I select industrial good to serve as numeraire. As I assume that the transportation cost of workers to the city is dependent on the travel distance, land rent for housing should be spatially different. I use $K(t)$ to stand for the total capital stock employed by the urban economy.

15.1.1 The Total Labor Input and Production Sector

I use $n(t, \omega)$ to denote the residential density at ω. All the workers work the same time, irrespective of where they live. The width of the urban area is assumed to be unity. The population $\bar{N}$ is homogenous and constant. I thus have

$$\bar{N} = \int_0^L n(t, \omega) d\omega. \tag{15.1.1}$$

The interest rate r^* and wage rate $w(t)$ are determined by markets. As in the literature of growth theory for a small open, it is assumed that r^* is constant and determined by international markets. The production function and marginal conditions are

$$F(t) = AK^{\alpha}(t)N^{\beta}, \quad \alpha, \beta > 0, \ \alpha + \beta = 1,$$

$$r^* + \delta_k = \frac{\alpha F(t)}{K(t)}, \ w(t) = \frac{\beta F(t)}{N(t)}. \tag{15.1.2}$$

From (15.1.2), I solve

$$K\left(r^*\right) = \left(\frac{\alpha A}{r^* + \delta_k}\right)^{1/\beta} N, \quad w\left(r^*\right) = \frac{\beta A K^{\alpha}}{N^{\alpha}}. \tag{15.1.3}$$

15.1.2 The Relation Between the Lot Size and Residential Density

I use $l(t, \omega)$ to denote the lot size of the household at ω. According to the definitions of l and n, I have

$$n(t, \omega) = \frac{1}{l(t, \omega)}, \quad 0 \le \omega \le L. \tag{15.1.4}$$

15.1.3 Choice Between Physical Wealth and Land

As in Chap. 10, the two options are assumed to yield equal returns, i.e.,

$$\frac{R(t,\omega)}{p(t,\omega)} = r^*. \tag{15.1.5}$$

15.1.4 Travel Time and Cost to the CBD

A resident decides the time distribution between leisure time and travel time. Let T_0 and $\Gamma(\omega)$, respectively, stand for the total available time and the time spent on traveling between the residence and CBD. I have $\bar{T}(\omega)+\Gamma(\omega)=T_0$, where $\bar{T}(\omega)$ is the leisure time at ω. This study assumes that the travel cost $c_T(\omega,t)$ from location ω to the CBD is dependent on the distance as follows

$$c_T(t,\omega) = \bar{c}(t) + c_0(\omega). \tag{15.1.6}$$

15.1.5 Land Ownership, Disposable Income, and Budget

Let $\bar{k}(\omega,t)$ stand for the representative household's physical wealth, and $a(\omega,t)$ for the value of land owned by the household at location ω. The total value of land owned by the household at ω is the sum of all the value of land the household owns in the economy. I have

$$a(t,\omega) = \int_0^L p(t,\tilde{\omega})\bar{l}(t,\omega,\tilde{\omega})d\tilde{\omega},$$

where $\bar{l}(t,\omega,\tilde{\omega})$ is the land that the household at ω owns at $\tilde{\omega}$. The total value of wealth $v(t,\omega)$ owned by the household at ω is the sum of the two assets' values:

$$v(t,\omega) = \bar{k}(t,\omega) + a(t,\omega).$$

The household at ω collects the following rent from the land that the household owns:

$$\bar{r}(t,\omega) = \int_0^L R(t,\tilde{\omega})\bar{l}(t,\omega,\tilde{\omega})d\tilde{\omega}, \quad 0 \le \omega \le L.$$

The total land rent of the economy is equal to the land rent that the population owns:

$$\int_0^L \bar{r}(t,\omega)d\omega = \int_0^L R(t,\omega)d\omega, \quad 0 \le \omega \le L.$$

The household at ω has the following disposable income:

$$\hat{y}(t,\omega) = v(t,\omega) + r^*\bar{k}(t,\omega) + w + \bar{r}(t,\omega), \quad 0 \le \omega \le L. \tag{15.1.7}$$

The household at location ω distributes the disposable income between housing $l(t,\omega)$, saving $s(t,\omega)$, consumption of industrial goods $c(t,\omega)$, and traveling, $c_T(\omega)$:

$$R(t,\omega)l(t,\omega) + c(t,\omega) + s(t,\omega) + c_T(t,\omega) = \hat{y}(t,\omega), \quad 0 \le \omega \le L. \tag{15.1.8}$$

Insert $\bar{T}(\omega) + \Gamma(\omega) = T_0$ and (15.1.7) in (15.1.8):

$$R(t,\omega)l(t,\omega) + c(t,\omega) + s(t,\omega) = \bar{y}(t,\omega), \tag{15.1.9}$$

where

$$\bar{y}(t,\omega) \equiv \left(1 + r^*\right)\bar{k}(t,\omega) + w + \bar{r}(t,\omega) + a(t,\omega) - c_T(t,\omega).$$

15.1.6 Utility, Amenity, and Optimal Solution

Utility level $U(t,\omega)$ at ω is dependent on $T(\omega)$, $l(t,\omega)$, $s(t,\omega)$, and $c(t,\omega)$ as follows:

$$U(t,\omega) = \theta(t,\omega)T^{\sigma_0}(\omega)c^{\xi_0}(t,\omega)l^{\eta_0}(t,\omega)s^{\lambda_0}(t,\omega), \quad \sigma_0, \xi_0, \eta_0, \lambda_0 > 0,$$

in which σ_0, ξ_0, η_0, and λ_0 are a typical person's elasticity of utility with regard to leisure time, industrial goods, housing, and saving. I call σ_0, ξ_0, η_0, and λ_0 propensities to use leisure time, to consume goods, to consume housing, and to hold wealth, respectively. The amenity $\theta(\omega, t)$ at ω is as follows:

$$\theta(t,\omega) = \theta_1 n^{\mu}(t,\omega), \quad \theta_1 > 0.$$

The amenity is related to the residential density at the location. Maximizing $U(t,\omega)$ subject to (15.1.9) yields

$$l(t,\omega) = \frac{\eta\bar{y}(t,\omega)}{R(t,\omega)}, c(t,\omega) = \xi\bar{y}(t,\omega), s(t,\omega) = \lambda\bar{y}(t,\omega), \tag{15.1.10}$$

where

$$\eta \equiv \rho \eta_0, \xi = \rho \xi_0, \lambda \equiv \rho \lambda_0, \rho \equiv \frac{1}{\eta_0 + \xi_0 + \lambda_0}.$$

15.1.7 Equal Utility Level, Wealth Accumulation and Market Equilibria

The assumption households get the same level of utility is represented by:

$$U(t, \omega_1) = U(t, \omega_2), \quad 0 \le \omega_1, \omega_2 \le L.$$

The wealth change of the household at location ω is given by:

$$\dot{v}(t, \omega) = s(t, \omega) - v(t, \omega), \quad 0 \le \omega \le L.$$

The total value of the national land $V(t)$ is

$$V(t) = \int_0^L p(t, \omega) d\omega.$$

The total value of land owned by the population is given by:

$$V^*(t) = \int_0^L n(t, \omega) a(t, \omega) d\omega.$$

As the land is privately owned, the two values should equal

$$\int_0^L n(t, \omega) a(t, \omega) d\omega = \int_0^L p(t, \omega) d\omega.$$

The total consumption $C(t)$ is given by

$$C(t) = \int_0^L n(t, \omega) c(t, \omega) d\omega.$$

The model is completed.

15.2 Spatial Growth with Land Value Change

This section simulates the spatial dynamics developed in the previous section.

Lemma 15.2.1 Assume $c_T = \bar{c}w(t)$, where $\bar{c}$ is a constant. The dynamics of wealth per household $v(t)$ is described by a differential equation:

$$\dot{v}(t) = \Omega(v(t)),$$

in which Ω is a function of $v(t)$ defined in Zhang (2018). For given $v(t)$, all the other variables are given as a function of $v(t)$ by a computational program.

The national wealth $\tilde{v}(t)$ is defined by:

$$\tilde{v}(t) = \int_0^L n(t, \omega)v(t, \omega)d\omega.$$

The parameter values are specified as follows:

$$r^* = 0.07, \alpha = 0.45, A = 0.8, \bar{N} = 50, L = 1, T_0 = 1,$$

$$\delta_k = 0.03, \lambda_0 = 0.8, \sigma_0 = 0.2, \xi_0 = 0.1, \eta_0 = 0.02, \bar{c} = 0.01,$$

$$\theta_1 = 1, \mu = -0.05.$$

I specify the initial conditions as: $v(0) = 15$. I get

$$K = 513.5, \ w = 1.26, \ F = 114.1.$$

The variables over time and space are plotted in Fig. 15.1.

15.3 Growth and Land Value with Exogenous Changes

This section carries out comparative dynamic analysis with regards to a few parameters.

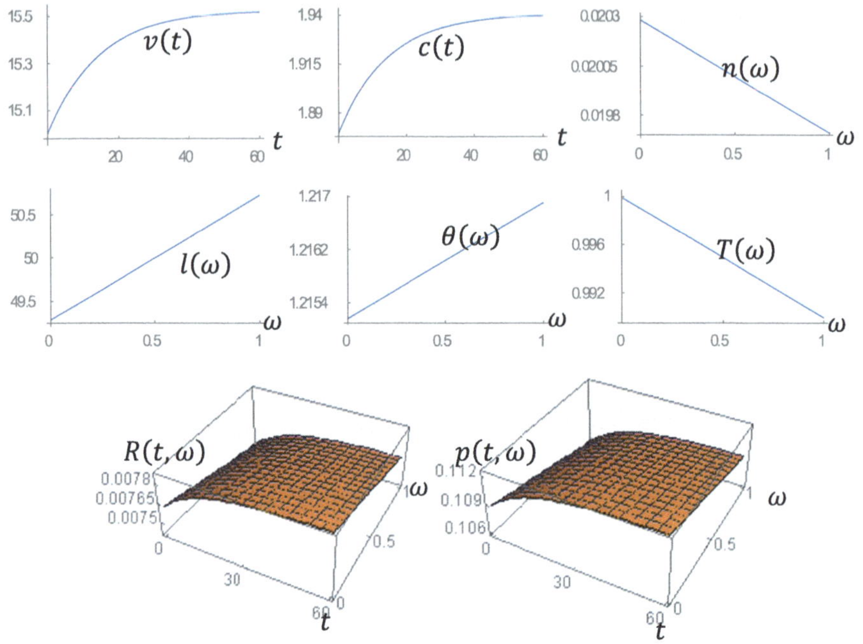

Fig. 15.1 Motion of the economy over space

15.3.1 *An Increase in the Interest Rate*

The interest rate is assumed to be increased as follows: $r^*: 0.07 \Rightarrow 0.075$. The change causes the total capital, wage rate, and national output as follows:

$$\bar{\Delta} K = -0.09, \ \bar{\Delta} w = -0.04, \ \bar{\Delta} F = -0.04.$$

The changes in the other variables are plotted in Fig. 15.2. The total wealth per capita and consumption level per capita are increased. The lot size, amenity, and leisure time are not affected. The land rent is enhanced. The land price becomes lower.

15.3.2 *The Total Factor Productivity Being Enhanced*

The total factor productivity is assumed to be enhanced as follows: $A : 0.8 \Rightarrow 0.81$. The change has no impact on the residential density, the lot size, the amenity, and leisure time. The total capital employed by the economy, the wage rate, and the national output are augmented:

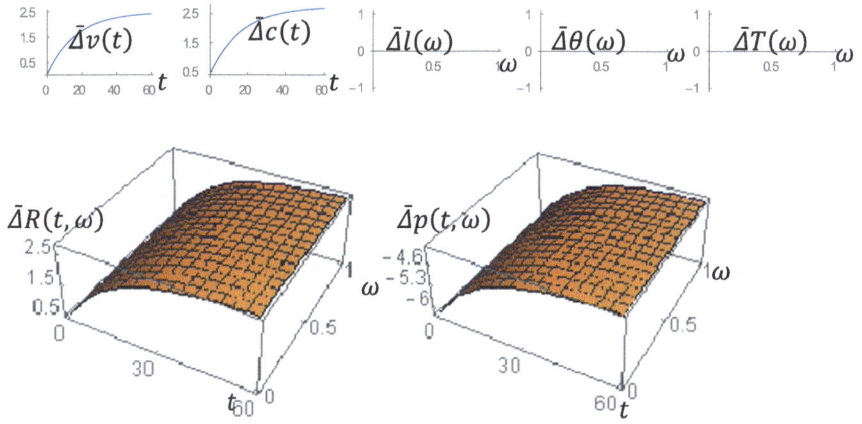

Fig. 15.2 Rise in the interest rate

$$\bar{\Delta}K = \bar{\Delta}w = \bar{\Delta}F = 0.023.$$

The simulation results on the other variables are plotted in Fig. 15.3. The total wealth and consumption level per capita are enhanced. The land value and rent are increased over time and space.

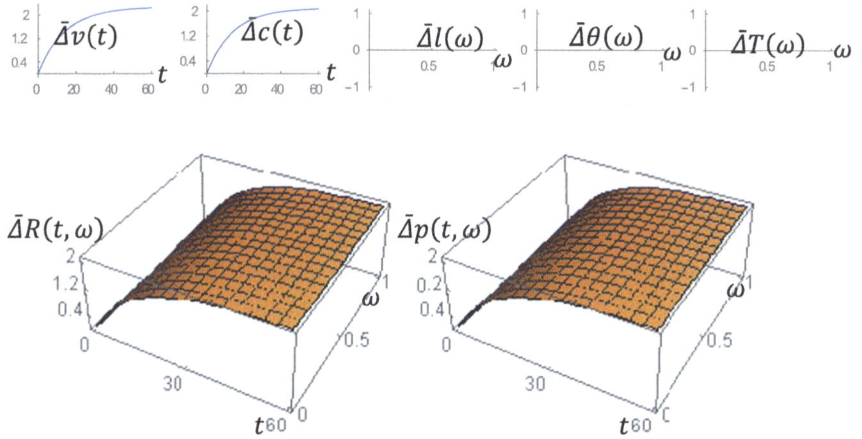

Fig. 15.3 Total factor productivity being enhanced

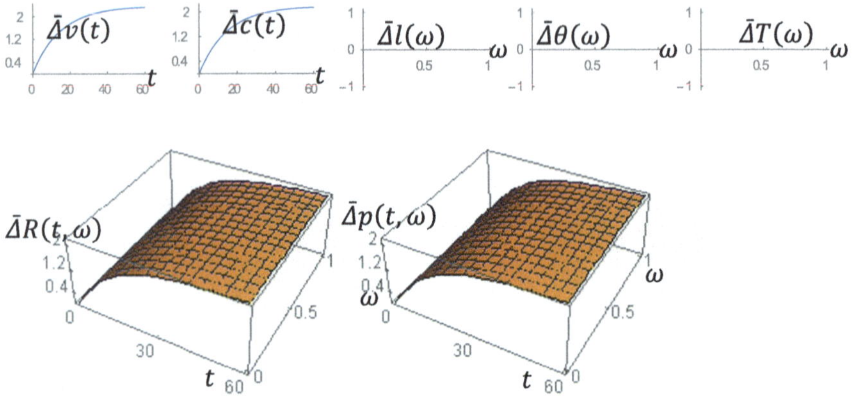

Fig. 15.4 Propensity to save being increased

15.3.3 The Propensity to Save Being Increased

The propensity to save is assumed to be changed as follows: $\lambda_0 : 0.8 \Rightarrow 0.81$. There are no changes in the residential density, the lot size, the amenity, leisure time, and K, w, and F. The simulation results on the other variables are plotted in Fig. 15.4. The total wealth and consumption level per capita are enhanced. The land value and rent are increased over time and space.

15.4 A Few Comments on Generalizing the Spatial Model

My approach to integrating various macroeconomic models and spatial economics is further demonstrated in Zhang (2002, 2003) and recent papers in https://ideas.repec.org/e/pzh151.html. Another important direction for extending my approach is to integrate my models with new economic growth model. Paul Krugman (1953–) was awarded the Nobel Prize in 2008 for his research on trade patterns and location of economic activity. He applied the Dixit–Stiglitz model to regional and international issues. He integrated two disparate research fields of trade and economic geography. He explains economic mechanisms of international trade not only in different products, but also in similar products. Applying monopolistic competition, he explains specification and large-scale production due to returns to scale and transport costs. Concentration of people in metropolitans can be explained by economies of scale with reduced transport costs. But his works do not include endogenous capital accumulation and lacks genuine dynamic analysis. I have recently integrated his models with the basic model. How to integrate Krugman's models with my basic model can be seen by how I integrated the Dixit–Stiglitz model as in Chap. 13.

References

Alonso W (1964) Location and land use. Harvard University Press, Cambridge
Arnott RJ (1980) A simple urban growth model with durable housing. Reg Sci Urban Econ 10:53–76
Baldwin RE, Martin P (2004) Agglomeration and regional growth. In: Hendersson JV, Thisse JF (eds) Handbook of regional and urban economics, vol 4. Elsevier, Amsterdam
Fujita M, Thisse JF (2002) Does geographical agglomeration foster economic growth? And who gains and loses from It? Jpn Econ Rev 54:121–145
Zhang WB (2002) An economic theory of cities—Spatial models with capital, knowledge, and structures. Springer, Berlin
Zhang WB (2003) A theory of interregional dynamics—spatial models with capital, knowledge, and structures. Springer, Berlin
Zhang WB (2018) Growth, residential distribution and endogenous land value in an integrated Solow's growth and Alonso's residential model. Asian Themes Soc Sci Res 2:23–31

Chapter 16
Miscellaneous Issues and Conclusion

When it is obvious that the goals cannot be reached, do not adjust the goals, adjust the action steps.
It does not matter how slowly you go as long as you do not stop.
Confucius.

This book applied my concepts of current and disposable incomes and utility function to develop a general economic theory. I deviated from the Ramsey approach to household behavior in theoretical economics. The necessity of abolishing the Ramsey approach to household behavior is pointed out by, except the economists mentioned in Chap. 2, (Stiglitz 2018), who was awarded the Nobel Prize for analyzing markets with asymmetric information in 2001, as follows:

> This paper provides a critique of the DSGE models that have come to dominate macroeconomics during the past quarter-century. It argues that at the heart of the failure were the wrong microfoundations, which failed to incorporate key aspects of economic behavior, e.g., incorporating insights from information economics and behavioral economics. Inadequate modelling of the financial sector meant they were ill-suited for predicting or responding to a financial crisis; and a reliance on representative agent models meant they were ill-suited for analyzing either the role of distribution in fluctuations and crises of the consequences of fluctuations on inequality.

I was aware of the contents of his critique 30 years ago and proposed the alternative approach. The previous chapters demonstrated how I solved many issues mentioned by Stiglitz with my approach. The reader can find more applications of my approach at https://ideas.repec.org/e/pzh151.html. I have made efforts in demonstrating that my approach is a far more effective tool for solving various economic problems than the Ramsey approach.

The book has integrated various ideas and theories in economics within an integrated framework. I have shown how to develop Walrasian general economic theory and neoclassical growth theory by taking account of additional relevant variables, relations, and market structures. All the models in this book can be integrated in a single model. As it involves so many ideas and theories within one framework, the reader might reasonably find it too time consuming to follow exactly what happen within the inextricable maze of symbols and equations among the models. The

W.-B. Zhang, *The General Economic Theory*,
https://doi.org/10.1007/978-3-030-56204-5_16

contents of each chapter from Chap. 3 till Chap. 15 should be explored by one book of the same size as this book.

Economics is still a collection of different ideas and theories. Economists traditionally rely on verbal descriptions or linearized equations with few variables. Traditional methods have limited capacities in describing changes of variables connected by complicated nonlinear relations. Dynamic phenomena due to complicated nonlinear relations were beyond economists' ability to examine even a few decades ago. An economic theory like the one proposed in this book should appear, even a few decades ago, only conceptual as there was no computer available to visualize movement of complicated dynamic systems. The recent development of mathematics, sciences, and computer and accesses to individuals as well as government data imply that the theory is not only operational and insightful but also can be tested, extended, and generalized.

There are more issues which can be analyzed by my analytical framework. I have focused on the main forces and simplified structures of the traditional theories. Each traditional theory referred in this book has a large amount of the literature. My theory is general with regards to connecting various main economic forces of different theories. From the beginning of constructing the theory, I have had kept in mind that each of my models should be constructed in such a way that it can be integrated with the rest of models without changing its basic assumptions. Moreover, each parameter in any model can be made exogenously or endogenously changeable. It is an "open" general economic theory in the sense that it allows to be further generalized with inputs of new knowledge in sciences, engineering, economics, psychology, political science, social sciences, and studies in history. In this sense, the work is only a step toward the grand theory. It is intended to build an economic theory like the *Yi Jing*.

It is straightforward to develop each model in the book by generalizing some of its functional forms or connections. For instance, the reader can take on more general forms of utility and functions. One can directly apply advanced mathematics to generalize some results in this book. Various ideas about markets, organization and individual decisions, in game theory can be applied to enrich the theory. Issues related to information and expectations are worthwhile to explore. Many of mathematical tools can be applied to improve the models in this book (Zhang 2009, 2010). I have also integrated many other ideas and theories, for instance by Marshall, into the basic model through my other publications.

There are different opinions about speed of adaptions, expectations, and information in demand and supply of labor, capital, money, human capital, preferences, and so on. For instance, one of the basic questions in economic theory is why modern economies do not employ fully and efficiently their available resources. Unemployment of labor force has attracted a great attention of researchers. I proposed some models with endogenous unemployment within the framework of the basic model (Zhang 2005). Since Adam Smith, there has been a long-traditional belief in economics that freely competitive market can supply the most efficient coordination mechanism in optimal allocation of resources. The Walrasian economics assumes instantaneous adaptation of labor market to its equilibrium. This book mainly follows this tradition. Friction exists everywhere; non-frictional motion is rarely observed.

Many jobs involve long-term attachments and considerable firm-specific skills on the part of workers. For instance, lifetime employment practice in Japanese companies means that market mechanism will not work smoothly in the Japanese labor market. Workers would stay in their current jobs even when they are offered some better work opportunities somewhere else. There are different reasons suggested for unemployment in the literature of unemployment. "Fixed wages" like in the Keynesian economics, "a generous social welfare policy" for unemployed people by the government, a mere "survival wage" rate like in the Marxian economics, or "friction" of structural adaptations in changeable knowledge-oriented economies, not to mention mis-matching or lack of proper information, can lead to unemployment. As far as economic efficiency is concerned, "unemployment" should not be limited to labor input. Other factors, such as land, machines, and housing, may also be "unemployed." A proper treatment of any of these factors will cause great efforts to reconstruct theories as (Hahn 2000: 65) points out: "... any study of liquidity soon leads to the conclusion that if it is an important element in an economy's analysis, then many of theories of the economy are in need of change. For instance, the recognition of the importance of transaction costs leads us to conclude that agents will maximize, subject to a number of, rather than a single, budget constraints."

Modern analytical and computational capacities allow economists to construct general theories by making more realistic assumptions and applying more reliable and proper data. This book is only one step on the way. I aspire to achieve what Einstein's appraisal about a new theory: "There could be no fairer destiny for any physical theory than that it should point the way to a more comprehensive theory in which it lives on as a limiting case."

I finalize this book by quoting my own words finalizing *Knowledge and Value* which laid the ground for this book (Zhang 1996: 342–3):

> Indeed, an imaginary reader who learns about the different schools in economics, masters the framework proposed in this study, and understands synergetics, may become aware that the historical time has come to develop a much more general political economic theory which treats all of the partial social and economic theories (which are obviously meaningful only in certain time scales in certain cultural environment) as special cases. I visualize that such a grand theory in the form of a high dimensional partial differential equations system can be developed on the basis of knowledge store of social and economic sciences, synergetic ideas, nonlinear dynamic theory and the modern computer. The direction is intellectually clear, so general talk is easy.

References

Hahn FH (2000) Liquidity. In: Friedman BM, Hahn F (eds) Handbook of monetary economics, vol I. Elsevier, Amsterdam

Stiglitz JE (2018) Where modern macroeconomics went wrong. Oxf Rev Econ Policy 34:70–106

Zhang WB (1996) Knowledge and value—Economic structures with time and space. Umeå Economic Studies, Umeå

Zhang WB (2005) Economic growth theory. Ashgate, Hampshire

Zhang WB (ed) (2009) Mathematical models in economics. In: Series of encyclopedia of mathematical sciences, vol 1. EOLSS Publishers Co Lt, Paris
Zhang WB (ed) (2010) Mathematical models in economics. In: Series of encyclopedia of mathematical sciences, vol 2. EOLSS Publishers Co Lt, Paris

Uncited References

Azariadis C (1993) Intertemporal macroeconomics. Blackwell, Oxford
Barkai H (1966) Ricardo's second thoughts on rent as a relative share. South Econ J 32:285–293
Brian AW (1988) Self-reinforcing mechanisms in economics. In: Anderson PW et al (eds) The economy as an evolving complex system. Addison Wesley, Redwood City, pp 9–32
Brian AW (1989) Competing technologies, increasing returns, and lock-in by historical events. Econ J 99:116–131
Chao CC, Hazari BR, Laffargue YP, Yu ESH (2006) Tourism, Dutch disease and welfare in an open dynamic economy. Jpn Econ Rev 57:501–515
Fukuyama F (1992) The end of history and the last man. Free Press, New York
Henderson JV (1985) Economic theories and cities, 2nd edn. Academic Press, New York
Kozicki C, Tinsley P (2002) Dynamic specifications in optimizing trend-deviation macro models. J Econ Dyn Control 26:1586–1611
Richardson HW (1977) Regional growth theory. Macmillan, London
Samuelson PA (1990) The collected scientific papers of Paul A Samuelson, vol 6. Cambridge, MA
Simmel G (1957) [1904] Fashion, Reprinted. Am J Sociol 62:541–558
Stiglitz JE (1967) A two sector two class model of economic growth. Rev Econ Stud 34:227–238
Tassel EV (2004) Household bargaining and microfinance. J Dev Econ 74:449–468
Tirole J (1988) The theory of industrial organization. MIT Press, Cambridge
Zhang WB (1986) Conservation laws in the housing market—a new approach for behavior of developers in the housing market by Lie group theory. Thesis for Graduate Degree presented to Department of Civil Engineering, Kyoto University
Zhang WB (1993) Woman's labor participation and economic growth—creativity, knowledge utilization and family preference. Econ Lett 42:105–110
Zhang WB (1994) The foreword to the Japanese version of synergetic economics. In: Asada T, Aruka Y, Inaba T, Hirosi W (trans). The Chuo University Press, Toyoko
Zhang WB (2006) Discrete dynamical systems, bifurcations and chaos in economics. Elsevier, Amsterdam
Zhang WB (2011) Economic growth with space and fiscal policies with housing and public goods. J Econ Stud 38:452–482
Zhang WB (2012) Economic growth with heterogeneous households, gender division of labor, and elastic labor supply. J Income Distrib 21:15–37
Zhang WB (2015) Tourism, trade, externalities, and public goods in a three-sector growth model. UTMS J Econ 6:1–19
Zhang WB (2016) Values of land, gold, renewable resources, and capital in a growth model with agricultural and industrial sectors. Sci J Natl Univ Life Environ Sci Ukraine. Ser Econ 247:8–32
Zhang WB (2017) Implications of habit formation and preference change for free trade patterns and global economic growth. Int J Econ Manag 11:107–126
Zhang WB (2019) Endogenous population in a neoclassical growth model with wealth and time values. Noble Int J Econ Financ Res 45:47–63

The manufacturer's authorised representative in the EU is Springer Nature Customer Service Centre GmbH, Europaplatz 3, 69115 Heidelberg, Germany. If you have any concerns regarding our products, please contact ProductSafety@springernature.com

Printed and bound by CPI Group (UK) Ltd, Croydon, CR0 4YY
30/09/2026
02225697-0011